QUEER METHODS AND METHODOLOGIES

For Donna and Katie

Queer Methods and Methodologies

Intersecting Queer Theories and Social Science Research

Edited by

KATH BROWNE
University of Brighton, UK

CATHERINE J. NASH
Brock University, Canada

Routledge
Taylor & Francis Group

LONDON AND NEW YORK

First published 2010 by Ashgate Publishing

Published 2016 by Routledge
2 Park Square, Milton Park, Abingdon, Oxfordshire OX14 4RN
711 Third Avenue, New York, NY 10017, USA

First issued in paperback 2016

Routledge is an imprint of the Taylor & Francis Group, an informa business

British Library Cataloguing in Publication Data
Queer methods and methodologies : intersecting queer
    theories and social science research.
    1. Queer theory. 2. Social sciences--Research. 3. Gay and
    lesbian studies.
    I. Browne, Kath. II. Nash, Catherine.
    306.7'66'072-dc22

Library of Congress Cataloging-in-Publication Data
Browne, Kath.
    Queer methods and methodologies : intersecting queer theories and social science
research / by Kath Browne and Catherine J. Nash.
        p. cm.
    Includes bibliographical references and index.
    ISBN 978-0-7546-7843-4 -- ISBN 978-0-7546-9663-6 (ebk)
    1. Queer theory. 2. Social sciences--Research--Methodology. I. Nash, Catherine
J. II. Title.
    HQ76.25.B78 2010
    306.7601--dc22

                                                                    2010008468

ISBN 13: 978-1-138-24566-2 (pbk)
ISBN 13: 978-0-7546-7843-4 (hbk)

Contents

Notes on Contributors

Tony E. Adams (Ph.D., University of South Florida) is an Assistant Professor in the Department of Communication, Media and Theatre at Northeastern Illinois University. His research interests include autoethnography and life writing, the discourse of nature at zoos and aquaria, and the ways in which identities such as sex, gender, and sexuality affect human interaction. His work has appeared in journals such as *Qualitative Inquiry*, *Soundings*, and *The Review of Communication*, and books such as *The Handbook of Critical and Interpretive Methodologies* and the *Encyclopedia of Identity*.

Tom Boellstorff is a Professor in the Department of Anthropology at the University of California, Irvine, and Editor-in-Chief of *American Anthropologist*, the flagship journal of the American Anthropological Association. His research projects have focused on questions of virtual worlds, sexuality, globalization, nationalism, language and HIV/AIDS. He is the author of *The Gay Archipelago: Sexuality and Nation in Indonesia* (2005), *A Coincidence of Desires: Anthropology, Queer Studies, Indonesia* (2007) and *Coming of Age in Second Life: An Anthropologist Explores the Virtually Human* (2008). He is also co-editor of *Speaking in Queer Tongues: Globalization and Gay Language* (2004), and the author of a number journal publications. At Irvine, he is a Core Faculty member for the Culture and Theory Ph.D. program, as well as a Program Faculty member for the Arts, Computation, and Engineering graduate program. He sits on the advisory boards of two community-based HIV/AIDS organisations in Indonesia.

Kath Browne is a Senior Lecturer in the University of Brighton. She is the co-author of *Queer Spiritual Spaces* and co-editor of *Geographies of Sexualities: Theory, Practices and Politics*. Her work spans and intersects the areas of geographies, sexualities, genders, methodologies and social engagements. In 2007 Kath was awarded the Gill Memorial Award from the Royal Geographical Society/Institute of British Geographers recognising young researchers who have shown great potential. Kath has written over 40 publications across a range of disciplines using diverse formats, and is completing the Community-University Research project *Count Me In Too*. Kath sat on the (UK) National Statistics Office Expert Research Group advising on the development of questions regarding sexual identity in 2006–2009.

Michael Connors Jackman is a Ph.D. candidate in Social Anthropology at York University. His doctoral research focuses on affective experience, queer publics, and activism in Canada in connection with *The Body Politic*, a Toronto-based gay liberation magazine published by Pink Triangle Press from 1971–1987. His Master's thesis at Memorial University of Newfoundland, 'Get Out of the Garden: AIDS, Art, Politics and the Queerness of Identity', is the product of the field experiences described in his contribution to this volume.

Ann Cronin is a Lecturer in Sociology at the University of Surrey where she teaches courses in social theory, qualitative methods and gender and sexuality studies. Her research interests include the interaction between gender, sexuality and ageing, narrative analysis and the sociology of storytelling, integration methodologies and sociological theory. Building on earlier research, which explored the social networks of older lesbian women, she has recently completed, with Andrew King, a study examining the social and health care needs of older LGBT adults living in an inner city borough. She is lead coordinator of the European Sociological Association Sexuality Research Network.

Ulrika Dahl is Senior Lecturer and Chair of Gender Studies at Södertörn University in Stockholm. She is the author (with Del LaGrace Volcano) of *Femmes of Power: Exploding Queer Femininities* (2008) and *Skamgrepp*, (forthcoming) her collection of essays on feminism, queer community politics and femininity is forthcoming from Atlas förlag. Currently Ulrika is completing a project about place making and canon formation in Nordic gender studies and a monograph about feminist theory and the politics of femininity. With a Ph.D. in Cultural Anthropology from UC Santa Cruz, her earlier work addressed the gendered politics of European integration and regional 'development' in rural northern Sweden and on heteronormativity and Swedish gender equality. A committed feminist activist at heart, Ulrika remains passionate about (queer) methodologies for both research and social change.

Mathias Detamore is a doctoral candidate in the Department of Geography at the University of Kentucky. He studies the spatial impacts of gender on social geographies, the relationship of the body to governmentality and power, rurality and the production of rural identity and the biopolitics of sexuality as they are deployed toward the production of sexual citizenship and its exclusions. His dissertation research focuses on how queer space is produced in rural Central Appalachia. Specifically, this research seeks to uncover how/if sexual identity is claimed in these rural places, how are social networks formed by these sexual minorities, do these networks constitute community, if so how/are these communities/networks maintained and negotiated across rural places. He is very happy that this is his first serious academic publication.

Andrew Gorman-Murray is a Research Fellow in Human Geography at the University of Wollongong. His key research areas are geographies of sexuality, gender and home, with further interests across urban and rural geographies. He has published widely on gay and lesbian experiences of urban, rural and domestic spaces in Australia, and is currently undertaking a project about men's changing attachments to home in twenty-first century Sydney. With Gordon Waitt and Lynda Johnston he co-edited a special issue of *Australian Geographer* on 'Geographies of sexuality and gender Down Under' (2008, vol. 39, no. 3). His first book, *Geographies of Sexualities Down Under: Gay and Lesbian Spatialities in Australia*, will be published by Ashgate in 2010.

Mark Graham is Associate Professor at the Department of Social Anthropology, Stockholm University. His research interests and publications cover refugee studies, immigration, gender and sexuality, diversity and the European Union, material culture and, most recently, the community and gender dimensions of urban sustainability. He is Editor-in-Chief of the journal *Ethnos*.

Jamie Heckert currently lives in the south of England where he listens, gardens and invites the impossible. Following on from his Ph.D. at the University of Edinburgh, his research has focused largely on the intersections of anarchism and sexuality while drifting into questions around ecological and emotional sustainability. All in all, he's interested in how we relate to ourselves, each other and the rest of the natural world. He is the editor of a special issue of *Sexualities* on anarchism and sexuality and co-editor, with Richard Cleminson, of the collection *Anarchism & Sexuality: Ethics, Relationships and Power*. His other writings are published in a number of books including *Changing Anarchism: Anarchist Theory and Practice in a Global Age, Understanding Non-Monogamies, The Postanarchism Reader, Anarchism and Moral Philosophy*, and *Anarchism: A Documentary History Of Libertarian Ideas* as well as activist magazines such as *Green Pepper* and *Fifth Estate*. He has also helped organise Pride events, helped subvert them, taught sex education, studied permaculture and co-facilitated activist/academic gatherings.

Stacy Holman Jones is an Associate Professor in the Department of Communication at the University of South Florida. She is the author of *Torch Singing: Performing Resistance and Desire from Billie Holiday to Edith Piaf* (2007) and *Kaleidoscope Notes: Writing Women's Music and Organizational Culture* (1998). She has also published work on the intersections of feminism, writing, performance, and cultural production in publications including *Text and Performance Quarterly, Qualitative Inquiry*, and *Cultural Studies↔Critical Methodologies*.

Andrew King is a Lecturer in Sociology at Kingston University, London. His research interests and publications have explored the intersection of age, sexuality and identity, drawing upon a range of theoretical and methodological traditions. He is particularly interested in combining queer theory with ethnomethodology and conversation analysis. He has recently completed, with Ann Cronin, a study of the experiences of older LGBT adults in an inner city borough. He is supporting coordinator of the European Sociological Association Sexuality Research Network.

Lorena Muñoz is an Assistant Professor in Geography and Ethnic and Gender Studies at Westfield State College in Massachusetts. Her research interests focus on the production of gendered immigrant street-vending landscapes in developed economies. Specifically, Lorena is interested in how Latina immigrant vendors negotiate and navigate 'queer' and gendered identities across trans-border spaces. Her research is partially funded by the Ford Foundation: Low wage, Gender and Migration group, the National Science Foundation and the National Institute of Health.

Catherine J. Nash is an Associate Professor at Brock University in St. Catharine's, Ontario. Catherine teaches both undergraduate and graduate courses in Human Geography, theories of landscape and power, social justice, gender and geography and queer geographies. Her major areas of interest include the geographies of gender and sexuality, trans geographies as well as feminist and queer pedagogy and research methodologies and practices. Currently, her research focus is on the changing queer geographies of the city of Toronto, particularly with respect to trans and lesbian communities.

Alison Rooke is a Visual Sociologist based at Goldsmiths College, London, UK. Her research interests are focused around class, gender and sexualities in urban contexts. She has published work on issues relating to cosmopolitanism, visibility, embodiment and belonging in classed and queer cultures. Alison's Ph.D. research *Lesbian Landscapes and Portraits: The Sexual Geographies of Everyday Life* was a visual ethnography exploring the interconnections of spatiality and subjectivity for working class lesbian and bisexual women. In addition, Alison has developed expertise in participative action research and evaluation with a specific focus on the social, economic and cultural impact of creativity and arts based research methodologies.

Yvette Taylor is a Senior Lecturer in Sociology, Newcastle University and held the Lillian Robinson Research Fellowship at Concordia University, Canada in 2009. Her interests are in the interconnections between class, gender and sexuality, manifest in two recent books: *Working-Class Lesbian Life: Classed Outsiders* (2007) and, based on British Academy funded research, *Lesbian and Gay Parents: Social and Educational Capitals* (2009). Yvette is currently editing a Special Issue of *Sexualities* (Sexuality and Class) as well as co-editing a book project on

Theorizing Intersectionality and Sexuality (forthcoming, Palgrave Macmillan). She recently completed ESRC funded research on the intersections of class and gender in women's lives in the North East of England (2007–09) which will be published in a forthcoming monograph: *Fitting into Place? Transitions and Intersections of Gender, Class and Identity* (Ashgate, 2011).

Gordon Waitt is Associate Professor of Human Geography at the University of Wollongong. He has an international research focus on the geographies of gender and sexuality, as well as geographies of tourism, festivals, urban revitalisation and rural change. His publications include *Understanding Gay Tourism: Culture and Context* (2006), co-authored with Kevin Markwell, and *Introducing Human Geography: Globalisation, Difference and Inequality* (2000), co-authored with Kate Hartig, Pauline McGuirk, Kevin Dunn and Ian Burnley.

Acknowledgements

We would like to thank all the contributors to the book for their perseverance and dedication in producing any number of drafts of their chapters while seriously considering our comments and suggestions. The strength of this collection is a testament to their commitment.

We would like to thank Gavin Brown for his insights and support in getting this project off the ground and Neil Jordan for his encouragement throughout the review stage and editing.

Thanks go to those at the Feminist Conference in Stockholm for inviting Kath to open the Queer Methodologies session, which led to some of the chapters in this book. It also was instrumental in shaping the introduction. Thanks to those who presented and participated in the sessions.

Kath would like to thank the University of Brighton for the sabbatical leave to pursue this project and the financial support in the final stages. Catherine thanks Brock University and the Social Sciences and Humanities Research Council for their financial support and Nancy Cook for her insightful comments on early drafts of the Introduction

We would like to express our appreciation to Olu Jenzen for her work in bringing this volume together. Her positioning as an English scholar was invaluable and her work impeccable.

Kath: I want to thank Donna Imrie for all her love, support and encouragement. Catherine has been tolerant, patient and understanding throughout this project and although she has yet to master mind-reading(!), I have enjoyed working with her and learned a lot. I am indebted to my family, particularly mum and dad, for their unfailing love and enquiries about this book. My friends as ever have supported and cared for me. Thanks to all of you.

Catherine: I want to express my sincere appreciation to Kath for drawing me into this project and for her patience and commitment to the book and its contributors. It is only through engaged debate and sometimes muddled and obtuse conversations that inspiration strikes – we certainly had all of those and more. A special thanks to Cindy Berry, whose tolerance for my flights of fancy, and steadfast support of all that I do, keeps me grounded and sane. And finally, to Katie, who takes me for walks, makes sure I am fed and reminds me that chasing toys is just as important as writing books.

Copyright Information

Queer Methods and Methodologies: An Introduction

Kath Browne and Catherine J. Nash

Introduction: What we thought this book would be about

When we first envisaged this book, we anticipated that those reflecting on queer methods and methodologies might experience similar possibilities, tensions and anxieties to those we encountered in our own work. A major impetus for producing this book was our own awareness of how often we ignored or skimmed over thinking about how some methodologies and methods might not neatly fit the 'queer' conceptual frames we use in our research. Queer researchers are in good company with other scholars drawing on poststructuralist and postmodernist approaches such as some feminist, anti-racist and postcolonial scholars, in consciously seeking to articulate their ontologies and epistemologies but who are seemingly less inclined to consider the implications of these approaches to methodologies and methods (or at least in print). Many scholars who use queer theorisations can use undefined notions of what they mean by 'queer research' and rarely undertake a sustained consideration of how queer approaches might sit with (particularly social scientific) methodological choices. In research deemed 'queer', the methods we use often let us speak to or interact with people, usually on the basis of sexual/gender identities and within anti-normative frameworks – again, a focus shared with many scholars including feminist, gay/lesbian, anti-racist and postcolonial. If, as queer thinking argues, subjects and subjectivities are fluid, unstable and perpetually becoming, how can we gather 'data' from those tenuous and fleeting subjects using the standard methods of data collection such as interviews or questionnaires? What meanings can we draw from, and what use can we make of, such data when it is only momentarily fixed and certain? And what does this mean for our thinking about ourselves as researchers? How does this perpetual destabilising position us as researchers and what can we make of this destabilisation? We found it disconcerting that we often do not apply our queer re-theorising, re-considering and re-conceptualising to our social science methodologies and choice of methods. As queer approaches to research proliferate across the social sciences, we argue there is a certain 'sweeping under the carpet' of how we actually 'do' research as 'social scientists' given our attractions, and attachments, to queer theory. We believe it is timely to grapple more formally with these concerns.

Just as we were putting this collection together, the *Graduate Journal of Social Science* (*GJSS*) published two special editions entitled 'Queer studies: methodological approaches', focusing on the meanings and functions of the word 'queer' (Liinason and Kulpa 2008, Kulpa and Liinason 2009). Understanding queer as a contested and locationally contingent term, the articles in these special issues offered intriguing insights into queer thinking in relation to a number of important and ongoing debates in the Social Sciences. However, whilst 'queer as method' held pride of place in the *GJSS* articles, there was little sustained consideration about methodologies themselves. Rather, the implicit understanding seemed to be that queer can be a method or perhaps a mode of theoretical or conceptual engagement. While this is, of course, an important endeavour, we are convinced we also need to engage overtly with questions that intersect these workings of 'queer' together with (social science) methodologies, that is, those sets of logical organising principles that link our ontological and epistemological perspectives with the actual methods we use to gather data. As Tom Boellstorff argues (this volume): theory, data and method cannot be understood in isolation from each other and the 'relationship between theory and data is a methodological problem' (210). When we think of this intersection, persistent and unresolved questions emerge: What impact, if any, could (or should) queer conceptualisations have on our methodological choices and in what ways? Can social science methods be 'queered' or even made 'queer enough'? How can social science methodologies feed into and question queer epistemological paradigms? How are social science methodologies, and the knowledges created by them, addressed in queer theories? If methodologies are meant to coherently link ontological and epistemological positions to our choice of methods, are methodologies automatically queer if queer conceptualisations are used? Can we have queer knowledges if our methodologies are not queer? Is there such a thing as queer method/methodology/research? These sorts of questions often overlooked in the excitement of new revelations and insights gained by queer interventions into empirical data are the types of questions we hoped might be addressed in a volume such as this, and work that emerges from it. We want to promote overt consideration of the implications underlying the use of queer approaches in research design and/or its execution, as well as on the research and writing process. This book offers a range of critical engagements with these largely unaddressed concerns lurking at the intersections between the range of queer ontological and epistemological approaches and the methodological choices made in social science research. Many of the chapters here explicitly acknowledge the parallels between this work and that of other scholars, and the debt owed to feminist scholars in particular, who have also turned their attention to these issues. One of the main objectives of this book is to have those engaged in queer research wrestle with how and in what way 'queer' might operate in concert with social science methodologies and methods.[1] Neither 'queer' nor 'social science' is left

---

1   More general discussions about methods and methodologies can be found in both social science and textual/humanities research texts. Although this book necessarily focuses

untouched in this engagement – not only is social science research queried (as in 'made strange' or prodded for guiding and exclusionary normativities), but so are the limitations and possibilities of 'queer' approaches in social science research.

As queer has come to be central in much theorising regarding sexual and gendered lives, we begin by considering the emergence of 'queer' as a scholarly conceptual or theoretical approach, a political perspective and a form of self-identification or assemblage of practices of the self. While some might argue that 'queer' has its historical roots in forms of political activism linked to the North American AIDS epidemic in 1980s and 1990s, in this text, the focus is on how queer conceptualisations gained admittance as a form of scholarly research and, most importantly, how queer might be related to methodologies and methods. We sketch out recently emerging questions about the place of conventional research techniques in examinations of messy and unstable subjectivities and social lives and consider the place of queer approaches in these debates. We conclude with a discussion of the contributions made in this book and the rationale for its overall structure.

In organising this collection, we initially envisioned writing a more traditional concluding chapter; one committed to drawing out the common themes, approaches and ideas emerging from the collection and proposing productive possibilities for further queer and/or social science research. It became clear in the editing process that the search for or creation of such 'common themes, approaches and ideas' would undoubtedly be a rather forced and artificial affair highlighted by the constructed 'finding' of arbitrary coherences and illogical 'logical' connections. Given the diversity of arguments, perspectives and approaches, we had to admit it was impossible to push and prod different chapters into some sort of categorical relationship with each other. Likewise, we also determined we were not comfortable offering a pronouncement of 'ways forward' in a conclusion, given the multiple possibilities suggested in these chapters. Reflecting our desire to retain fluidity and diversity, as well as our recognition that there are multiple ways that a project like this could be framed, we became increasingly comfortable with the idea that the text would remain riddled with questions and uncertainties and we deliberately backed away from framing conclusive endings. Here we do not present a definitive overview or literature review or singular modes of engaging with the complex fields, concepts and methodological engagements located at the intersection with queer approaches. Rather, in this introduction, we offer the reader some contextualisation and insight into the possibilities for queering methodologies and methods.

---

on the expanse of social sciences, we hope that it will open spaces to articulate the tensions and possibilities of queer methods and methodologies in the broadest sense.

So, What is 'Queer'?

While we do not adhere to any specific school of thought about what it might mean to 'queer' methodologies and methods, we do want to provide some background or context for the chapters that follow. Charting a route through the various bodies of literature engaging with queer approaches in search of a coherent lineage for 'queer' thinking is a perilous and not necessarily useful undertaking. 'Queer research' can be any form of research positioned within conceptual frameworks that highlight the instability of taken-for-granted meanings and resulting power relations. Queer inflected perspectives, approaches and conceptualisations have been taken up, disputed and reworked in different disciplinary contexts, reflecting the traditions of knowledge production in those disciplines. Genealogies of queer theory reveal considerable disagreement over its relationship with and debt to philosophy, women's and lesbian studies, second wave and postmodern feminism and gay and lesbian studies (e.g. Jagose 1996a, b, Richardson et al. 2006, Sedgwick 1990, Turner 2000, Warner 1993, Weed and Schor 1997, Sullivan 2003). Whatever one's stance on queer theory's historical lineage, contemporary queer theory remains in continuous conversation with innumerable bodies of scholarship, however contested or collegial such exchanges might be. What is important for present purposes is how queer conceptualisations have intersected in a general sense with the research design and knowledge production in the social sciences. As the chapters in this book demonstrate, queerly crafted scholarship in both the humanities and the social sciences has pushed analyses in new and exhilarating directions.

Queer approaches of various sorts not only became visible in the HIV/AIDS activism in North America in the 1970s and early 1980s, it also surfaced across a number of disciplines receptive to the problematic of postmodern thinking – architecture, literary theory and criticism, film studies as well as sociology, philosophy and geography (cf. Bell and Valentine 1995, Butler 1990a, b, 1993, De Lauretis 1991, Reed 1997). Most scholars would concede that queer theorising initially gained greater visibility more quickly in the humanities than the social sciences. Work in the humanities challenges the conceptualisation of the modern Enlightenment subject as rational, unified and stable. Within postmodernist theorising, broadly conceptualised, scholars took critical aim at claims about a universal human condition and the linear tale of a progressive human history as artificial, improbable and unduly homogenising of the human experience. The philosophy of science literature in particular turned its critique to the notion of the supposedly unassailable 'objective researcher' inexorably uncovering a knowable reality through reliance on a relational theory of truth – a critique becoming increasingly visible across disciplinary boundaries (Jagose 1996b, Law 2004, Sullivan 2005). Further, the nature of the 'subject' of research, previously envisioned as a unified, coherent and self-knowledgeable individual, is redrawn as contingent, multiple and unstable; constituted within historically, geographically and socially specific social relations. Seemingly fixed attributes of the self, such as sexuality and gender, are re-imagined as social constructs rather than biological certainties and their contingent appearance and interconnection taken as a matter of analysis and investigation (Jackson 2001). For many, queer theory takes up these realignments and works specifically to unwrap the commonly taken-for-granted and normalised connections between sexuality and gender in order to render visible their contingent connections. As Gorman-Murray et al. argue (this volume), 'the notion of queer asserts the multiplicity and fluidity of sexual subjects ... and seeks to challenge the processes which normalise and/or homogenise certain sexual and gender practices, relationships and subjectivities' (99).

Queer theory challenges the normative social ordering of identities and subjectivities along the heterosexual/homosexual binary as well as the privileging of heterosexuality as 'natural' and homosexuality as its deviant and abhorrent 'other'. Many queer theorists argue, in concert with various feminist, gay, and lesbian scholars that normative understandings of sexuality (and gender) are central, organising principles of society, social relations and social institutions and are designed to preserve this hegemonic ordering (Sedgwick 1990, Sullivan 2006). While queer scholarship is most often interested in examining the experiences of sexual/gender minorities, some scholars argue for a 'queering' of heterosexual relations as well as including a rigorous analyses of the category of heterosexuality, its disciplinary processes and the heterosexist assumptions embedded in much social science scholarship (e.g. Hubbard 2007, Sullivan 2003, Thomas 2000).

Much queer scholarship has made good use of the interdisciplinary debates on Michael Foucault's work detailing how sexuality itself is a historically specific concept as well as a regime of disciplinary knowledge structuring society and social relations (Foucault 1978). His attention to teasing out the available knowledges and systems of meaning in circulation in any one historical period (and place, one might add) shifted research foci from a consideration of the constitution of subjects and their subjectivities to a focus on 'discourses', institutions and practices that discipline and reinforce certain understandings about gender and sexuality. For many queer scholars, the disciplinary effects of the heterosexual/ homosexual, man/woman binary understandings of sexuality and gender and a consideration of alternative practices that do not fit into hetero/homo categories are central. A growing body of multi- and interdisciplinary scholarship explores desires, practices and identities that defy the dualities of social categories and unsettle the epistemological and methodological assumptions underpinning much of the work on gender and sexualities – that there is a 'man', 'woman', 'lesbian' or 'homosexual' to be studied as the object of research (e.g. Browne, Brown and Lim 2007, Butler 1990a, b, Corber and Valocchi 2003, Fuss 1989, Garber 2001, Giffney 2004, Halberstam 1998). Queer scholars can argue for the 'playful' possibilities of unstable and indeterminate subjectivities and for transgressive practices that challenge heteronormative sexual and gender assumptions.

Not everyone is enamoured with queer theories deconstructive tendencies and critiques have emerged from numerous quarters. Those involved in forms of identity politics such as second wave women's or gay and lesbian and trans movements argue that denying the stability of the subject (women or lesbian) undercuts the ground on which political activism is built by denying the existence of a viable political subject (e.g. Hartsock 1990, Richardson et al. 2006). While identities may be unstable and shifting over the course of a lifetime (as Gorman-Murray et al. discuss in Chapter 6), great comfort is found in these identities given they serve a central organising stability in many lives.

With the increasing political and social assimilation of some lesbians and gay men through legislative means such as gay marriage, LGBT human rights legislation, pension benefits and the ability to adopt children, attention is being paid to the notion of 'homonormativity'. Whilst this term is used in a variety of ways, it is most easily introduced as the privilege (social, economic, political, racial, classed, gendered etc.) that those who were once sexual 'dissidents' now are supposed to experience (Duggan 2002, O'Brien 2008). Such legislative 'gains', it is argued, in fact privilege certain forms of 'homosexual' expression and regulates bodies and practices within neoliberal privatised norms; closing off contestation of normativities themselves. These arguments play out virulently in North America where the institution of 'gay marriage' is read as a homonormative institution that regulates, normalises and assimilates same-sex couples, valuing monogamous 'wealthy' couples over other forms of queer kinship (Warner 1999). Contestations of homonormativity point out that the homonormative/queer binary often implicit in these critiques, problematically neglects how we are all complicit in the reproduction of power relations (Oswin 2005). Moreover, it can essentialise (and demonise) white gay men who are assumed to experience particular forms of privilege without examining the experiences of those who are presumed to occupy these subjectivities (e.g. Elder 2002, Nast 2002).

Certain strands of queer theorising, in rejecting a representational theory of 'truth', use various forms of discourse and textual analyses to consider how power relations are constituted and maintained in the production of social and political meanings. With this initial focus on discourse analysis and cultural critique, some scholars argue that queer approaches, while interesting theoretically, are largely detached from the blood, bricks and mortar of everyday life. Trans scholars, for example, argue that using trans people to illustrate the fluidity of gender/sex is problematic and an appropriation of an assumed lived experience that generally does not actually engage with trans people themselves (Namaste 2000, Prosser 1998, Stryker 2006). Queer theorising arguably does not lead to effective changes around the material inequalities in everyday life (although this could be questioned by the cultural materialist strand of (still textual) queer theory). Such a critique has less purchase in the social sciences where scholars often deploy queer approaches in their examination of the material experiences of their subjects. Further, some scholars contest the supposedly liberating possibilities of queer 'playful', 'fluid' and transgressive practices and behaviours (Browne 2004, Nash forthcoming). As Yvette Taylor argues (this volume), these playful transgressions are tied up with the material possibilities of everyday life and often left largely unexplained is how the ability to experience the variability of a self is embedded in power relations that limit and/or open up certain possibilities and not others. Critiques contend that the material possibilities of being need to be firmly linked to the economic, social and historical contexts (Richardson et al. 2006).

Queer scholarship, then, in its contemporary form is anti-normative and seeks to subvert, challenge and critique a host of taken for granted 'stabilities' in our social lives. 'Queer' is, in Law's (2004) terms, a way of knowing that is a 'situated inquiry' that relates to specific ways of knowing in particular locations. Yet queer rarely recognises its own location and how it travels. Much queer theorising originated in the Global North with its particular social and historical contexts and its uncritical engagement with gendered and sexual lives in other geographical locations is not necessarily appropriate or helpful (Gorman-Murray et al. 2008, Johnston and Longhurst 2008, Liinason and Kulpa 2008, Waitt and Markwell 2006). Social science and queer intersections need to recognise the location of both of their key defining terms and their various ways of knowing (even where they are widely and diversely used). Yet, queer travels in a variety of ways across disciplines, disciplinary fields or places. This is a significant point because although there has been some investigation of how queer travels throughout the world, there has been little attention paid to the reworking and reconfiguring of queer even within the space of one institution (see for example Baldo 2008, Cruz-Malavé and Manalansan 2002, Mertz 2008, Viteri 2008). As these and other writings highlight, there is a geography to queer thinking, theorising and identification that often leaves unrecognised the situatedness of academics from the Global North who become 'international', transcendent and adopted, whilst those from 'elsewhere' are bound to their location. Acknowledging the geographies of queer thinking can also bring into view the micro-spatialities of an academy that reflect rifts despite the tropes of interdisciplinarity.

Queer(ing) in this Collection

Despite being able to recite a somewhat cogent and coherent pedigree for 'queer' scholarship, what we mean by queer, we argue, is and should remain unclear, fluid and multiple. The impossibility of foreclosing debate around the meanings of queer is evident in the depth and breadth of its usage in the following chapters. But while we might argue about the impossibility of placing boundaries around a 'true' meaning of queer, what is meant by queer is often policed informally in situations where certain forms and approaches are deemed more authentically 'queer' than others. Such determinations of 'the' authentic approach to what is 'queer' work to dictate what 'queer' (and in turn 'queer research') can and cannot do. The orthodoxies of what queer is, who can write it, how it should be written (what language terms etc.) can go uncontested. Those who challenge the 'right' form of 'queer' engagement can be dismissed as 'essentialist'/'outmoded'/'simplistic'/ 'under-theorised'. Yet keeping queer permanently unclear, unstable and 'unfit' to represent any particular sexual identity is the key to maintaining a non-normative queer position. This is not a simple task in an academy that increasingly embraces 'queer' contingencies while simultaneously requiring specific rules of rigour, clarity and truthfulness; all the while generating queer celebrities who supposedly 'get it right' (see Heckert, this volume). Wilcox (2006) understands this assertion of, and search for, authenticity as a form of queer fundamentalism, drawing parallels between religious fundamentalism and those who adopt literal and doctrinal views about queer theory. Such fundamentalisms, in our experience, are usually based on texts by (mainly US and UK-based) queer 'celebrities', who themselves would mainly reject such dogma (see also Browne, Munt and Yip 2010). The imperative to define 'the right kind of queer' is apparent in the academy and in the reviewing procedures for book proposals and articles, in informal discussions and often in conference discussions. Such processes are largely subterranean, neatly side-stepping reflection or engagement, while having the very real effect of proscribing how the term 'queer' can be used and understood. We experienced this form of boundary-keeping and authenticity claims in the first round of 'reviews' of the proposal for this book. (We were told quite specifically that we needed to both define the term 'queer', and define it in a particular way.)

In our initial proposal, we used the term 'queer/ing' to highlight the questioning nature of our project and the way in which queering the research process can shift perspectives and ideas (see also Detamore, this volume and Gibson-Graham 1999). In response, one reviewer wrote:

> *Queer/ing*: It is not clear from your proposal how you are using the terms 'queer' and 'queering'. I understand that contributors use the terms in a vast array of ways but you need to clarify in a paragraph (300–500 words) how the collection more broadly understands these terms and the questions raised by their usage.

Such a comment reflects the impulse to find commonality and coherence where often there is none. Our response to this comment reflects our commitment to leaving the defining up to the authors, while sensitising us to the impulses of some to seek and enforce certain definitions.

> *Our response*: These terms will not be clarified, as to clarify and define these terms is to limit their usage just to these understandings. We are allowing authors to use and define the terms how they choose. Rather than policing queer, we think such a definition is inappropriate. We will not be reifying this slippery concept and its plethora of possible uses and its temporal and spatial contingency within 300–500 words.

The position we have taken for this project is one of not clarifying, and this may be seen by some (more traditional?) scholars as reflecting a lack of 'theoretical sophistication' and a failure to neatly box up our thinking. When we realised this, we began to think about the importance of opening up academic processes and discussing reviewing protocols in detail, to explore the internal 'boundary policing' that often takes place, yet is often ignored, overlooked or silenced. Who can speak? How? Using what terms? Our collection both expands on these questions and leaves them permanently unclear. Such a tactic is intended to keep current sets of meanings associated with queer in circulation while also allowing room, we hope, for others that are as yet unknown, unasked or unacknowledged.

For us, queer is a term that can and should be redeployed, fucked with and used in resistant and transgressive ways, even if those ways are resisting what could, and some would argue already has, become a 'queer orthodoxy' (Browne et al. 2010, Wilcox 2006). We did not enforce any particular definition onto 'queer' or onto the authors included in this collection. Rather we asked each author to enunciate clearly their own understanding of 'queer' within their research. Therefore, while there is no common understanding of queer amongst the contributors, one can discern a commonality of approach. The pages of this book testify to the ways that refusing to specify, delimit and define can be queer, and that queer dogmas can be contested by offering other ways of exploring (mainly gender and sexual) difference. In crossing between theory, methods and methodologies, many of the chapters transgress the supposed 'sophistication' of queer theorising by questioning its necessary usefulness and offering other ways of knowing and doing.

Perhaps ironically, in not proscribing how authors should use 'queer' in any particular way, there was an assumption by a number of authors that we would do this work in the introduction, again through a search for commonality, coherence and consistent 'themes' or meanings. In a traditional sense, a 'good' introduction should 'clarify the terms', draw out similarities and highlight differences (perhaps even determine 'errors') in understandings. Many authors resisted our direction to define 'queer', nervous, as we were, of pinning down this concept. We worked hard to be clear that what we wanted was not a definition of queer itself but an understanding of how queer was being deployed by the author. Several authors believe there is a coherency to queer, or a knowledge of the term that connects us all, and used footnotes rather than the main text to outline their use of queer. Most authors use queer to do particular things, to create specific spaces and to open up particular lines of enquiry. The lack of coherence across the collection indicates the diversity of queer theorising and its refusal to be bounded, controlled or defined.

Social Science Methods/Methodologies:
The Possibilities and Plethora of Queer Methods and Social Lives

Thinking about social science research involves initially recognising that this field of research can be interrogated in terms of its distinct parts – methods, methodologies and 'the social'. There is a logical progression in the research process whereby a researcher, in taking up an ontologically theoretical position on the 'social' then takes up a set of epistemologies that drive the choices regarding methodologies and methods. Nevertheless, ontological, epistemological, methodological and methods-related considerations necessarily intersect, overlap and are engaged in mutual and contingent constitution. This is an inter/cross/trans disciplinary conversation, as this book highlights. For some authors, their disciplines are read as 'queer' from the outset. Boellstorff (this volume), for example, asserts that anthropology is queer in part because it investigates everyday lives and cultures that are nuanced and complex. Valocchi (2005) argues that ethnography, as a methodology, enables the intersections of sociological and queer theories, because it allows for openness, flexibility and change. Green (2007), however, questions the need to interlink what he understands as the distinct fields of sociologies (concerned with the social) and queer (deconstructionist) theories. These do not have to be integrated or intersected and rather can focus on distinct issues/conceptualisations. Plummer (2005: 371) argues that the differences between critical humanism and queer theory should not be completely reconciled, arguing that 'contradiction, ambivalence and tension reside in all critical enquiries'. We would contend that across social research, there is the potential to variously deploy and rework 'queer', as well as to critically engage with and contest theories, concepts and ideas that have developed in the humanities and through particular forms of textual and linguistic analyses (Gamson 2003, Plummer 2005, Seidman 1995, Valocchi 2005, Warner 1999). However, what forms these engagements might take, or how they might be categorised, necessarily remains permanently blurred, contingent and multiple, and following Plummer, nor do we seek to resolve contradictions or tensions.

We will now move on to consider various strands of methods, methodologies and social research, glancing at huge areas of writing, thinking and critique to give the reader an overview of some of the key issues underlying much of the book. After a brief discussion of methods and methodologies, including feminist and queer engagements with these, the proposal for 'new social research methods' will be outlined. We briefly address how contestations of 'the social' relate to queer contestations of stabilities and normativities. In this section, we attempt to flag some of the wide ranging areas touched on in discussions of queer methods/methodologies. There is, as always, far more to be said and done.

Methods/Methodologies: Is there a Queer Method?

This book does not offer technical guidance on research design nor is it intended to introduce research methods and methodologies as they are practiced in the social sciences.[2] We begin our discussion with a consideration of the intersections of methods and queer thinking. Research 'methods' can be conceptualised as what is 'done', that is, the techniques of collecting data (interviews, questionnaires, focus groups, photographs, videos, observation, *inter alia*). By contrast, methodologies are those sets of rules and procedures that guide the design of research to investigate

---

2 Although, increasingly such texts have explicit references to queer theory, particularly where these address qualitative research. See for example Filax et al. 2005, Gamson 2003, Plummer 2005.

phenomenon or situations; part of which is a decision about what methods will be used and why. Methodology can be understood as the logic that links the project's ontological and epistemological approaches to the selection and deployment of these methods. Most of the chapters in this book seek to place research techniques and methods, and the underlying epistemologies and ontologies that guide them, into conversation.

In addressing queer and social science research methodologies, we usually refer to qualitative research, making quantitative research notable by its absence (Browne 2008, Gamson 2003, Valocchi 2005). In the 1970s and 1980s, the conceptual distinction between methods and methodologies enabled feminists to address the impasse regarding the existence and desirability of so-called 'feminist' methods. Methods understood as feminist were initially qualitative as their take was to recover the reality of women's lives rendered invisible through the masculinist use of quantitative data (see for example Harding 1987, McCormack 1987, Wilkinson 1998). Nevertheless, feminists also argued the necessity for qualitative data to support or demonstrate, for example, inequalities in income, access to services or poverty rates and so on (Lawson 1995, Moss 1995a, b). Feminists contended that methods themselves had no inherent epistemological or ontological qualities; rather how they are deployed in the pursuit of certain forms of knowledge produced data that supported feminist ways of knowing, and contested masculinist forms of knowledges (see for example Maynard 1994, Stanley 1990, 1997, Stanley and Wise 1983a, 1993). However, feminist researchers also considered the fact that these methods assume a 'humanist subject'; one who is deemed able to accurately recount lived experiences and observations 'authentically'. In working through these concerns, feminist researchers struggled to grapple with critiques of the 'knowing' subject and the 'objective' researcher; the power relations and ethical concerns in the research process in documenting marginal lives as well as problems with notions of truth and authenticity – struggles that became increasingly familiar for researchers across disciplines (cf. Burt and Code 1995, Haraway 1991, Harding 1986, 1987, Hesse-Biber and Leavy 2008).

Given how queer approaches undermine the once stable sexual (and gendered) subject now conceived as fluid, blurred and contingent, the prevalence of qualitative methods in queer scholarship is perhaps unsurprising (Gamson 2003, Plummer 2005). Arguably, it is illogical to 'count' subjects once one has argued that a 'countable subject' does not exist – the methodological problematic we described at the beginning of this chapter and one haunting qualitative as well as quantitative approaches. However, this form of thinking does not predominate in popular cultures where the knowable 'gay and lesbian' figure is increasingly one to be counted and regulated (Brown and Knopp 2006, Browne 2008). Not surprisingly then, where statistical data is gathered on sexuality, mainly through market research or census data on 'couples', it usually finds white, affluent, middle class, men who live in specific areas (see Badgett 2003, Brown 2000, Brown and Knopp 2006, Browne 2008, Duncan and Smith 2006, Fish 2008). This gives a very particular picture of sexual and gender difference and is dependent on finding individuals prepared to identify with particular sexual variables ('gay', 'lesbian', 'bisexual' and so on). This obviously becomes increasingly complicated with more nuanced and non-normative understandings of gender and sexuality, particularly in relation to queer identities (see Browne, this volume). Contesting the supposed veracity (and truth-making processes) of statistical data techniques as well as the power relations that can inform 'quality' data collection, Plummer (2005: 336) notes that queer can be disloyal to all forms of conventional disciplinary methods; and that includes contesting the norms of social science research. Queer can challenge the supposed coherence, reliability and generalisability regarded as a central concern to some social scientists (see also Halberstam 1998). Yet, while queer approaches might contest the possibilities of quantification of subjects, there is a danger in then asserting that queer epistemologies, methodologically, require the use of qualitative methods only, or must always contest traditional and conventional techniques. As some of the contributors in this collection argue, queer approaches should overtly grapple with the contradictions that arise without definitively endorsing one set of methods over another.

One could argue that there is, in fact, no 'queer method' (that is, 'methods' specifically as research techniques), in the sense that 'queer' lives can be addressed through a plethora of methods, and all methods can be put to the task of questioning normativities – a political positioning that infuses research processes with ethical considerations.[3] In particular, where queer is taken to destabilise particular understandings of the nature of the human subject and subjectivities, power relations, the nature of knowledge and the manner of its production, a 'queering' of methods themselves might pose particular difficulties as well as possibilities for traditional data collection methods (Gamson 2003, Green 2007, Plummer 2005). 'Queer research' could promote a particular understanding that simultaneously constitutes and destabilises conventional research considerations. Thus, are there data collection techniques or methodologies that are not 'queer'? Does 'queer' fundamentally alter the realms of identities, 'the social', and conceptualisations of realities such that social science research methodologies are defunct for these ontological and epistemological forms? Does social science research that investigates lesbian, gay, bisexual, trans and otherwise 'queer' lives need to locate itself within anti-identitarian queer epistemologies? What place do traditional social science methods, and quantitative research have in understanding the messiness of sexuality and gender in the contemporary world? In this context then, what we might mean by queer research is also problematic. Is research 'queer' if it is undertaken by queer researchers? Is such research about queer subjects and/ or research that employs a queer conceptual framework? And what does it mean when we speak of a queer methodology or a queering of methodologies? These

---

3   These links are apparent even where the methodologies deployed, driven by a particular philosophical positioning, upset the conventional norms of data collection, such as Halberstam's scavenger methodology (1998).

questions are at the heart of the chapters that follow; while some are addressed, many more remain unanswered.

What is 'the Social' in Social Science Research?: Multiple Methods, Multiple Politics

The terrain of social (science) research methods is disparate and contested. The conjoining feature of this area of study is usually the focus on 'the social' and conceptualising 'the social' has moved through different phases in academic thinking. Recently (including within queer thinking), 'the social' has come under critical scrutiny, with some suggestion that queer theories are/can be disarticulated from the study of 'the social' (Green 2007, Seidman 1995). Such social science contentions imply that queer theoretical work is important, but is disengaged from understandings of contemporary experiences of sexualities and lived socialities. Increasingly, it is argued there is no one 'social', but many socials operating in diverse ways and across multiple scales. In this era of globalising forces, the 'social' meanders across and through its more traditionally understood territories and exceeds its old spatial boundaries (Beck 2000). Some proclaim the death of 'the social' in favour of conceptualisations linking notions of associations, assemblages and other terms that direct attention away from the idea of the social as coherent. Recent scholarship also contests the notions that the 'social' has any necessary materiality or that particular social structures and constructs can be used to explain other phenomenon or outcomes. The social, it is asserted, cannot be reduced to human interactions and a growing body of work addresses the non-human, including the place of objects, animals, environments, materials and so on (see for example Giffney and Hird 2008, Latour 2005, Law and Hassard 1999, Murdoch 1997). Law (2004: 2) argues that social science methods can only ever partly capture the mess of social worlds, requiring us to rethink 'the realities of the world using methods unusual to or unknown in social science' (see also Graham, this volume). In a similar vein, Latour (2005) attributes the need to refocus attention to a 'sociology of associations' because of the success of social sciences, and Plummer (2005) argues that with the advent of societal change, research techniques should also alter.

There can be no doubt that reconceptions of the social have prompted the proliferation of 'new' and 'innovative' social science methods seeking to (re)present the messiness of social life, attend to affects, and to work beyond particular representational concerns (see for example Anderson 2002, Macpherson 2009). These methods seek to investigate that which cannot be reduced to, and at times contest, traditional forms of data collection. In addition, such methods question the place of social 'science' in understanding social lives by challenging the tenants of social science research, such as rigour, clarity and the possibilities of 'knowing' social life. Consequently, social research methods may not necessarily adhere to any 'scientific' structures of knowledge.

Strategies of data collection need to address this understanding of social worlds, including various forms of observation, visual materials and engagements with auto-ethnography as well as exploring the intersections of humanities and social sciences through art and textual analyses (see for example Boellstorff 2007, Halberstam 2005, Holmes-Jones and Adams this volume, Power 2009, Volcano 1999, Volcano and Dahl 2008). However, there is a danger that investigating social worlds in this sense returns us to textual analyses that proclaim the messiness of everyday life, without involving the people and materialities present in the creation of these studies.

Clearly, the desire to foster progressive social change through research is not necessarily distanced from the contestations of the social. Scholarship recognises the researcher's place not only in constructing 'socials', but also in questioning, rethinking and reworking them. 'The field', 'the social' and other presumed stable objects of social science enquiry into sexual and gendered lives are implicated in and by queer theoretical approaches and the ways queer is read through and in these social contexts (see Jackman, Nash, and Dahl, this volume). Lewin and Leap's (1996) edited collection *Out in the Field*, notes that issues of reflexivity, and the ethics involved in carrying out fieldwork about sexualities, illustrate that not only are methodologies always informed by those that 'collect' the data, but that collected data has implications for the researchers themselves. More than this, social science research itself is implicated in the reconstitution of 'the social' (Browne 2003, Dahl, this volume, England 1994, Law 2004).

Looking at the wide range of queer scholarship that has developed since the early 1990's, it is clear that 'queer' approaches are deeply engaged in questioning the existence and 'knowability' of the social, particularly in various socials normative claims. The entanglements of methods, lives and research moves beyond 'explaining' the social, making it clear that queer theorising and social research fields are mutually constituted. If sexual and gender studies (and broader social theorising) create social fields, it follows that destabilising such theorising, including through queer theorising, and creating new social methods can create transformative politics through research (Law 2004). This mode of politics is one of the many ways that power relations and associated hierarchical constructions of social lives can be contested through research. Participatory action research, for example, encompasses and develops new social research techniques with reworkings of established forms of data collection (Kindon et al. 2008). By recognising not only the messiness of social life, and the place of the research/ researcher in (re)creating it, such research can provide a place for those who otherwise tend to be marginalised, disenfranchised and excluded in the process.

Many of the chapters in this collection are concerned with relations (and crossovers) between researcher and participants bringing together the questioning of stable social lives, the research practices that, in part, create them and power relations engaged in recognising and constituting social life through social research (see chapters by Gorman Murray et al., Dahl, Nash and Heckert, this volume). The complex place of the social in/of 'the field' also comes under critical scrutiny, as power relations and taken-for-granted norms are interrogated. Most of the chapters in this collection explicitly or implicitly seek to address the place of research in effecting social change, but no coherent 'queer' or social research agenda is proposed. Rather, these chapters illustrate how research engagements can take multiple forms and serve a plethora of purposes and politics.

This book interrogates conventional social science research, as well as pushes the boundaries of what might constitute 'queer' objects of study. We see the questioning of 'the social' as an opening; one of the many ways of exploring the messiness of social lives, experiences, power relations and hierarchies. Such investigations, however (as with queer engagements with identities, sexualities and genders), should not create orthodoxies, forcing closure around multiple socials, methods and the myriad ways of knowing the mess of social life.[4] In light of this, you will find that in the chapters that follow, authors often both depart from the norms of social science research methods as well as the emergent orthodoxies of queer theorising.

In keeping with our approach that resisted the imperative to define 'queer', we did not impose any criteria relating to methods/methodology on our authors nor did we suggest what we meant by 'social science research' to the authors. Instead we asked the authors themselves to clarify what they meant by methods, methodologies and social science research. Again, rather than finding coherence, this book illustrates some of the breadth of this field and the diverse appropriation and understanding of often taken-for-granted terms such as ethnography, the researcher, participants and the field. Allowing authors to grapple with these issues led to useful and productive discussions that we hope will continue beyond the pages of this book. We are clear that in intersecting queer and methods and methodologies, we are not proposing a solution to the tensions created through placing these into conversation, converging them or reworking each in relation to the other. Once again questions remain, including whether it is, or continues to be, productive to talk of something called queer methods and methodologies.

There is no Structure:
The Road Map of *Queering Methods and Methodologies*

In creating this book, we sent out personal invitations to so-called 'queer celebrities' and those we knew were working in this area. We also put out an open call for contributions and interventions. This approach resulted in chapters from a wide variety of disciplines, including sociology, anthropology, women's/gender studies, communication studies and geography reflecting both the coherence and

---

4 Creating singular 'correct' methods/methodologies is not also the intention of authors such as John Law. Thus, other, or 'new' ways of knowing and methods can operate alongside and compliment more conventional forms of data collection. However, in putting these into conversation with each other both are affected by the interaction.

distinctions across disciplinary boundaries as well as within them. Because of the diversity of the contributors, in addition to the differences we have discussed above, there is no one praxis, orthodoxy or way of intersecting queer and social science research methods. Instead, the coherence of the chapters pivots on the centrality of queer theory in social science research.

As with most editors, we struggled to squeeze chapters into structures, recognising that they escape confinement, overlap, and contest each other in diverse ways. At the book proposal review stage, any structure we tentatively and uncomfortably proposed was unravelled by reviewers who rightly pointed to the artificiality of our selected boundaries and categories. We found it a struggle to create an order for the chapters, not because they do not fit together, on the contrary the chapters overlap and complement each other but do so in ways that defy neat categorisations within overarching themes. As a result, we decided to work with a more open and fluid structure allowing connections, synapses, overlaps and disjunctures to be drawn out by the reader (see also Moss and Falconer-Al-Hindi 2007 who produced a number of separate contents lists to deal with this very issue). This rhizomatic approach is also reproduced in certain chapters throughout the book (see Dahl, Heckert, Gorman-Murray et al. and Jones and Adams).

So how did we ultimately decide to organise the book? We played with the idea of drawing names out a hat (or letting the dog decide), producing a completely random structure not beholden to any academic protocols or personal preferences. In the end, we concluded we needed to work with and for those who may not be intimately familiar with the issues raised in this collection, and to create a structure that leads a reader through the material in a way that allows them to grapple with this complex arena. The chapters placed at the beginning of the book discuss issues and approaches that frame key concepts and ideas related to intersections between queer approaches and research design. The middle chapters discuss various queer approaches in research design; drawing on and reworking a number of central themes and considerations. The final chapters focus on a radical rethinking of queer theorising and social science methods and methodologies in new and provocative ways. So while there is an 'order' to these chapters, such order reflects our concern to further the reader's understandings rather than thematic or categorical decisions.

We begin with the work of *Alison Rooke* who considers the well-rehearsed critique of queer theory's so-called textualism and of sociology's continued attachment to scientific methods. Calling for an affective and erotic approach to research, Rooke appeals for a 'queer sociological ethnographic perspective' that considers queer theories of sexual subjectivity and a queer ethnographic approach. By paying attention to everyday, lived realities of hetero and homo-normativities, she argues ethnography offers cogent insights into how lesbian identities and sexual subjectivities are necessary, negotiated and always being reformed. Further, she notes, we need to question the possibility of there being a stable ethnographic 'self' and an achievable 'distance' that critical ethnographers supposedly attain during the writing up period. Rooke argues that a reflexive approach requires that we understand that the 'field' has fluid and flexible boundaries (to which the ethnographer is emotionally (inter)connected) and recognise the always becoming identities and subjectivities ethnographers occupy. This highlights the productive possibilities lurking in the silences of ethnography and how a queer reflexivity helps us consider the erotic in knowledge production – an argument illustrated through her experiences as a 'lesbian' queered through the course of her fieldwork at a LGB (Lesbian, Gay, Bisexual) community centre in London.

Jamie Heckert continues the exploration of the (re)making of the researcher through an impassioned account of how he 'becomes queer' in the research process; an experience he links to his desire to explore forms of 'methodological anarchism'. For Heckert, this is a process of letting go of the traditional research boundaries, including those between theory/data, researcher/researched, homo/hetero. Drawing on Deleuze and Guattari, he asserts that 'becoming queer' is always in process, never stable, fixed or predictable. Through the sharing of rhizomatically interconnected stories, Heckert formulates an understanding of a 'queered' methodology that is not reserved for the 'transgressive few'. Rather, he asserts we all fail to attain normative standards of sexual/gender performance and conceptualises the individual as 'a multiplicity interconnected with other multiplicities' (48). If this is the case, the researcher becomes both subject to and the subject of research, highlighting the interconnections that create the possibilities of becoming queer, becoming anarchist.

Lorena Muñoz continues this reflection on the unstable positionality of researcher and researched and the shifting nature of the 'field' in her consideration of 'whiteness' in queer research. She critically reflects on the presumptions researchers can bring to the field and how a consciously queered methodological approach can open up unexpected avenues of enquiry. In exploring Latina experiences of street vending in downtown Los Angeles, Muñoz argues that employing a 'queer of colour' methodology allows her to slip subject positions, as a researcher, between her queer and Chicana identities. So doing, she argues, can 'enable us to reconfigure fluid racialised, sexualised and gendered methodological constructions in the field' (58) rendering visible what often remains unseen. Exploring her own nuanced and multifaceted identities that interweave personal and public selves, Muñoz examines her own complicity in reproducing Latino vending streetscapes in Los Angeles that often reiterate heteronormative assumptions and trans/national imaginaries.

While we need to be attentive to the queered positionality of a researcher in a queer methodological approach, we cannot lose sight of other aspects of the self beyond gender and sexuality in play in queer lives. In conjunction with Alison Rooke, Andrew King, Ann Cronin and Yvette Taylor assert that queer methodological approaches must be attentive to issues of intersectionality including a concern with class, age, racialisation and ethnicity as well as gender and sexuality.

Yvette Taylor draws our attention to how queer research approaches often inadvertently centre the socio-economically most privileged by neglecting interrogations of class. Taylor notes that queers' much-touted ability to assimilate and/or transgress normative boundaries is not freely available to all. She argues that queer methodologies are often 'deployed by/for/with queers' (69) in ways that exclude or render invisible certain queer lives. What is required, Taylor argues, is a re-orientating of queer methodologies towards critically investigating the silences of material (im)possibilities, particularly for those who do not occupy positions of middle class ordinariness. In comparing working class and middle class interviewees' experiences of parenting, Taylor demonstrates that a queer methodological approach, driven by intersectional analyses, highlights that the possibilities of queer fluidities are limited to those with the resources to step out of, assimilate or transgress the 'system'. In this instance we can see how queer methodologies that attend to the possibilities and limitations of intersecting sexual and classed normativities highlight how some queer lives 'may not be that queer at all' (83).

In a similar vein *Andrew King* and *Ann Cronin* take as their starting point the use of the term 'LGB' (Lesbian, Gay and Bisexual) in public policy initiatives focused on older people in the United Kingdom. The uncritical use of the term LGB in these contexts can fail to recognise the contingency of sexual identities that refuse containment within these categorisations. They argue that a more thoughtful understanding of how lives are lived requires a queer rethinking that is attuned to the fluidity and incoherency of lived experience to better understand how older adults might reflect on their experiences over their life course. The authors consider how categories of 'older lesbians, gay men and bisexual adults' are formed and, using Judith Butler's work, contend that identities are political in that they reproduce as well as transgress hegemonic norms. Utilising membership categorisation and narrative analyses, the authors explore how participants represent themselves and their social worlds. In attending to the complexity of self-identifications, actions and experiences, we become aware not only of the signification of our research categories but of how, when and where people deploy these categories. This approach troubles straightforward associations of sexuality and age and seeks to avoid repeating hetero-normativities and other power relations in how we undertake research.

The 'field' is a complicated place, made more unstable by the shifting positionalities of the participants (both the researcher and researched), and by the inherent difficulties in finding common understandings across sometimes vast political, social and cultural divides. *Andrew Gorman-Murray, Lynda Johnston* and *Gordon Waitt* seek to interrogate the 'queerness' of communication through a reflection on the use of interview-based research methods with sexual minority communities and participants in Aotearoa, New Zealand and Australia. The three authors, in refusing one authorial voice, use a conversational approach to explore questions of insider/outsider and the complications of sexual subjectivities in postcolonial settler societies. They argue for a greater account in queer research of the power relations, positionalities and differences embedded in sexual minority populations. In a vein similar to both Rooke and Heckert, the authors argue that 'a queer research context' must allow for a plethora of possible subjectivities to emerge and attention must be given to 'queer silences'. The fluidity and spatial contingency of researcher-researched subjectivities is highlighted as well as the need for attentiveness to 'the fractured constellation of ethnicised-sexualised hybrid identities' unfolding in postcolonial settler locations (107). In paying attention to the 'queering of communication', the importance of spatiality and the mess of methodologies, the authors assert that the fluidity of sexualities and ethnicities in research processes changes researchers as much as it creates knowledges.

Continuing a focus on the queerness of the 'field' and the research process, *Michael Connors Jackman* argues that the critiques of various forms of literary and textual analyses found in much queer theoretical work, can be fruitfully brought to bear on more traditional anthropological assumptions about the 'field'. Jackman questions the here/there, field/academy binary, and the presumptions made about where the field actually 'is'. Analysing the them/us of scholars/informants dualisms, Jackman examines the 'dynamic desires' in play in the 'field' and how they reveal 'intimate details' that can question the supposed 'rigour' of fieldwork and the nature of the 'field' itself. Reminiscent of both Dahl's and Heckert's chapters, Jackman argues for an intense appreciation of how sexuality is continually managed in the 'field'. In reconsidering the role of desire, Jackman moves to open up conversations that account for the traditional academic and emotional de/linking of sexuality and erotics imposed on research encounters. Jackman concludes by suggesting that while ethnography is an important 'import' from the social sciences to queer studies, we need to undermine the inherent heterosexuality of 'the field'; arguing for a range of replacement conceptualisations including the idea of queer publics and assemblages.[5]

Catherine J. Nash also explores the shifting nature of insider/outsider relationships and the unstable nature of the 'field', drawing on her experiences talking with transmen about their everyday lives in LGBTQ (Lesbian, Gay, Bisexual, Trans and Queer) space in Toronto. She reflects on the unexpected instabilities in a researcher's subject position that can occur over the course of the interview process and, in fact, during a single interview. Nash also considers the importance of spatiality in the research process and the importance of being attentive to the historical and cultural specificities of the field. Wading through the political and social debris that contextualises her discussions with transmen's use and experience of queer/lgbtq space, Nash simultaneously notes shared histories, distances and divisions that characterised her interviews. For Nash, as well as

---

5   As we noted earlier, it is important to consider the 'location' of queer theorising. Jackman's discussion, for example, illustrates the particularity of the North American scholarly context where queer studies has emerged as a separate subdiscipline in many American universities and colleges. Jackman's argument would not have much logical consistency in the United Kingdom, for example, where queer studies does not have such disciplinary specificity and queer approaches have a much stronger interdisciplinary application.

Dahl and Heckert, the politics of knowledge production are a central focus and a queer methodology can engage with the struggle to recognise the permanent instability of researcher-researched relationships, insider/outsider status as well as the intersubjective political and social processes in the research process.

Ulrika Dahl draws on her research practice with femmes to argue for a queer feminist ethnography. Together with Nash, Dahl is motivated by the queer political stakes of ethnographic research and explores femme lives and experiences as a neglected aspect of queer gendered engagements. She considers what it might mean to conduct femme-inist research that seeks to reframe the meaning of femininity. Questioning the home/away dichotomy that can structure conceptualisations of the field, Dahl unsettles hierarchies associated with research academies, calling for a queer anti-normative critique of the processes and practices of writing. Drawing on her *Femmes of Power* book (2008), Dahl discusses the work she has done together with Del LaGrace Volcano to create participants as co-researchers. Grappling with issues such as anonymity, the reduction of research participants to theoretical points, sameness within femme-ininity and intra femme-politics and community, she points to the possibilities of queering ethnography by co-producing knowledge in order to rethink the meanings of femininity. 'Tuning into the frequency of femme-on-femme research' (164), Dahl calls for a commitment to sisterhood and the creating of community through research that does not stand outside of that which it studies/creates.

Extending the consideration of politics of intimacy taken up by Heckert and Jackman, *Mathias Detamore* places ethical questions at the centre of queering social science research. 'Queerying' the liberal individualised ethic of consent, Detamore seeks to engage with an ethics as method that is queer as it queerly queers research/researcher relationships (see Gibson-Graham 1999). Taking to task Institutional Review Boards (IRBs) in the United States, Detamore argues that the research process is risky, intimate and innovative, creating new sets of possibilities that should be approached through a queer ethics as method. The politics of intimacy becomes a political device, one that queers the institutionalised dominant bureaucracies, and is best seen through participatory action research. Moving beyond emancipating subjugated voices and towards 'something that looks much more like kinship' (178), Detamore points to the mobile negotiation process in research relationships that cannot operate outside the social and the personal. Researchers are affected by research kinships, creating 'mutually entangled vulnerabilities' which can 'craft new ethical constructions that transform and shape alternative social worlds' and advocacy (168). In taking ethics seriously, Detamore argues for 'sober perseverance' in using ethics as methodological tools for creating methods.

Shifting our attention away from questions about the 'researcher' and the field, *Mark Graham* asks us to reconsider the materiality of 'things' – an area that is recently gaining attention (see Giffney and Hird 2008). Drawing on the work of Karen Barad (2003, 2007) and her unusual fusion of ideas from feminism, quantum mechanics, queer theory, post-structuralism and philosophies of science,

Graham argues we need to consider how the research object is brought into being. We can do this, he asserts, through the research process itself, using a queer and naive methodology that is gullible and open to new suggestions in productive ways. This more 'worldly' method can follow lines of flight to reconsider how sex-gender-sexuality 'cuts' in ways that render them indeterminate and 'available for alternative cuttings' (192). To do this, he examines the giving of a 'gift' and the unlikely and unremarked materialities that surface when we queer our methodological approaches to research in this way. Arguing for methods that explore the queerness of materiality, Graham concludes with a call for humility that recognises that strategies and objects that can be used for queer ends, can also reproduce normativities and complicities.

Stacey Holman-Jones and *Tony Adams* begin by criss-crossing the role of autoethnography in constructing 'knowledge of subjection', and the place of stories of (unremarkable) ease and pleasure such as those found in a coffee shop encounter. Drawing parallels between queer theory and autoethnography, they position autoethnography as a queer research method. Queering the writing process, they use 'I' to encompass 'us' and 'we', in ways that understand such subjectivities as always becoming and potentially interlinked; offering the possibilities of writing 'ourselves into new ways of being and becoming' (198). Exploring the multiple definitional possibilities and uses of autoethnography, they use the device of the 'hinge' to examine connections that are tentative and yet necessary in both being and being heard. Beautifully written, the chapter interlinks poetics and prose, making autoethnography performative and activating queer into queering. Queer autoethnography allows for journeys of self-understanding that are relational and not restricted by the limits of categories while proposing challenges to normative ideologies and discourses. For Holman-Jones and Adams, queer auto-ethnography seeks to create transformation and liberation in ways that recognise and embrace fluidities and contingency, opening up more ways of being in the world, that is a political venture.

Tom Boellstorff asks us to consider the intertwined and relational nature of the 'data-theory-method triangle' where the relationship between theory and data is best viewed as a methodological problem. In considering his own ethnographic scholarship in Indonesia as well as the virtual world of Second Life, he explores what he calls the 'queer valence' of his methods across these two different field sites. He does so through an exploration of two theses that could be regarded as queer in a methodological sense. Using notions of emic (insider's point of view) and etic (outsider's point of view) theory, Boellstroff argues that one element of a queer methodology might be to upset this distinction and allow for the emergence of theory from both 'within' and 'without'. Second, he argues that a queer method might 'surf binarisms', that is, might 'recognise the emic social efficacy and heuristic power of binarisms without thereby ontologising them into ahistoric, omnipresent Prime Movers of the social' (223). As 'queer techne', that is, human action that alters the world through crafting, these methodological styles offer the possibility of overtly (re)politicising queer studies and a 'reframing of intersectionality in terms of method as well as object of queer study' (230).

Lastly, *Kath Browne*'s chapter takes us back to one of the fundamental divides in social science research, namely, distinctions between qualitative and quantitative methods and methodologies and the perceived difficulties of 'counting' queer subjects – the potentially problematic issue detailed at the beginning of this introduction. Browne notes there is a shortage of critical engagements with the 'quantitative' in queer scholarship and her chapter takes up this issue through a consideration of 'the messy processes' of quantifying sexualities through a 'sexuality question' designed for governmental social research in England and Wales. In doing so, she attends to both the limitations of anti-normative queer conceptualisations and the messy possibilities that arise when one attempts to craft quantitative sexual identities questions for social science research. The productive tension, in holding together the utility of identity politics categories with the destabilising deconstruction of those self same categories, highlights the disruptive possibilities and limitations in the sexual categories created in social governmental research.

And Finally, or Just the Beginning?

This book, in allowing for the diverse possibilities of queer, explores the limitations and potentials of queer engagements with social science research techniques and methodologies. Plummer (2005) associates the conceptualisation of 'sexualities as problematic', with a 'queer turn' in research styles. This 'queer turn' is a central discussion point of this book, and yet the book acknowledges its ties to feminist scholarship, lesbian and gay studies and women's studies, as well as social science research that foregrounds relations between people (and people, places and objects). In turn, we refuse a future within delineated boundaries. Thus, rather than attempting to overthrow 'the old' and lay claim to new (queer?) thrones, this book strives to do something different. We remain respectful of that which has forged the way for this form of social science and queer thinking to emerge. By refusing to establish or reinforce a queer canon or any social research/science 'party line', the book illustrates some of the methodological and theoretical innovations that arise from combining theories developed in particular contexts with research concepts and techniques that are equally culturally and spatially specific. It does this without offering any coherence or standardisation, challenging any form of queer/social/research fundamentalism. Thus, rather than sounding the death knell of any particular form of activism, identity, method, practice and so on, we are arguing for opening up a plethora of ventures and adventures.

This is not to say we have 'got it right'. We see this book as limited, partial, and imperfect in many ways. We know that as readers, you may come with expectations of what 'should' be in such a collection, what 'should' be said and how. We suspect these expectations will only ever be partly met, if at all, and we would ask you to consider what you can do to augment work such as this. The version of queer, social (science) research and methodology you identify with (adhere to?), may influence the way you read each chapter, (in)forming your views, perhaps reiterating some prejudices. We ask you to think about what feels 'comfortable' in the chapters that appeal to you (and what does not), why that might be, and then to dwell on other ways of knowing, doing and using the permanently flexible concepts of queer and social (science) and research. We hope this book will foment thinking and scholarship in these areas, furthering the engagements with the intersections, overlaps, divergences and coherencies between queer theorising and social (science) methodologies and methods. We envisage this will require compromise, losses and gains on all sides, such that 'pure' social science research/queer theory will be muddied and disorientated. Thus, rather than offering a definitive ending, this books seeks to create infinite openings.

Chapter 1

Queer in the Field:
On Emotions, Temporality and
Performativity in Ethnography[1]

Alison Rooke

Introduction

Reflecting on a year of ethnographic fieldwork conducted in and around a lesbian, gay and bisexual (LGB) community centre in London, this chapter argues that queer ethnography does more than use ethnography to research queer lives; it also takes queer theory seriously to question the conventions of ethnographic research. More specifically this includes addressing the assumed stability and coherence of the ethnographic self and outlining how this self is performed in writing and doing research. To *queer* ethnography then, is to curve the established orientation of ethnography in its method, ethics and reflexive philosophical principles.

This chapter draws on research concerned with the ways in which working-class lesbian and bisexual women experience and negotiate the meanings of their sexual identities on an individual everyday basis, and the ways identity categories are institutionalised at a subcultural level. As part of this research, I conducted ethnographic participant observation in and around a London LGB community centre. The centre functioned as a lens to see the field of sexual geographies through, rather than constituting a focus of study per-se. At the Centre, I took part in a range of activities, including volunteering at the centre, carrying out mental health outreach, running sexualities discussion groups, and a series of photography workshops with lesbian and bisexual women. In this chapter, I discuss some of the epistemological, ontological and ethical dimensions of ethnographic research which were raised in this process. The chapter begins by setting out a case for an ethnographic approach to the study of sexuality working between the critique of queer theory as overly concerned with textual criticism and the attachment to methodological scientificity within some schools of sociology. This is followed by a discussion of some of the historical critiques regarding ethnographic research and of the textual normativities at the heart of ethnographic writing. The chapter then

1   This chapter draws on concepts and arguments that were published in an earlier version in Lesbian Studies ('Queering the Field: On the messy matters of ethnographic research', *Journal of Lesbian Studies* 13(2) April–June 2009).

goes on to explore some of the tensions in ethnographic research and writing as the ethnographer moves from affective participant observation to a distanced writing up, offering a critique of the temporal and spatial fictions of ethnography. Against this background, I close my chapter by arguing for the queering of ethnography, appealing for an open discussion of the affective and erotic dimensions of knowledge production which continue to be written out in the writing up process.

The emergence of queer theory in the early 1990s was characterised by a shift from empirical research into lesbian and gay lives, which had been a distinctive feature of the field of lesbian and gay studies, toward readings of literary and cultural texts, often with a French poststructuralist Foucauldian and Lacanian emphasis (see for example the work of Judith Butler 1993a, b, 1996, 1999, Teresa De Laurentis 1991, 1993 and Diana Fuss 1991, 1995). Sociological criticisms of queer theory have circulated around queer's tendency towards philosophical abstraction and textual criticism, its employment of an under-developed concept of the social, and its lack of engagement with the material relations of inequality (See Seidman 1993, 1995, 1996, Warner 1993, and McRobbie 1997 for further discussion). I do not want to rehearse these positions here. Instead, in this chapter I am advocating a queer sociological ethnographic perspective that brings together queer theories of sexual subjectivity and an ethnographic approach to researching identity categories and the practices which generate them. I chose to conduct ethnographic research into lesbian and bisexual women's everyday lives in a deliberate attempt to counter the tendency towards high abstraction and a reliance on theory that had characterised queer. Queer is, after all, connected to emotions as much as it is a body of theory. This is an attempt to work in a theoretically engaged way by grounding analysis in materiality, lived experience and empirical research. This is not a question of prioritising the sexually flexible or post gay identities but one of paying attention to the complexity of intersubjectivity in constructions of the self, in terms of lives as they are lived at the level of the everyday and in the double hermeneutics (Giddens 1987) of the research and writing process. I did not want to 'throw out the (queer) baby with the bathwater' and dismiss the insights of theories of performativity and selfhood, or fail to recognise the workings of language, discourse and signification. Abstraction does have a purpose; it offers complex ways of seeing beyond the immediate, surface understandings of a situation and moves our thinking beyond the immediate confinements of empirical realities. However, there is, I believe, a strong case for a queer ethnography that hones queer theory and qualifies it within the context of everyday life.

Ethnographic 'Intellectual Effort':
Between Methodologies and Everyday Lives

In sociological training, ethnography is generally discussed on methods courses. However, ethnography is not merely a research method. The postmodern turn within anthropology and sociology (Atkinson and Hammersley 1989, Clifford

1988, Geertz 1973, Marcus 1986) recognises that ethnography is not defined by techniques and procedures (such as the length and intensity of participant observation, the combination of semi-structured interviews, historical analysis, questionnaires, surveys and the use of a research diary) but rather by the kind of intellectual effort it is. Geertz (1973), for instance, states that ethnography should consist of seeking to 'converse' and produce 'thick description' – that is, understanding and describing what is going on in a culture and the meaning of what is going on to both oneself and informants. From this we can see that ethnography is an intellectual approach rather than a method; a theory of the research process which is defined by its relationship to certain theoretical positions. One of the strengths of ethnography is the way that it seeks to link structure and practice, micro and macro-analysis, historical, economic, political and cultural factors. Postmodern critiques of ethnography (specifically within anthropology) have led to what has been described as an interpretive turn (Geertz 1973) recognising that ethnography is more than mere cultural reportage, relaying the truth or 'reality' of a situation, stressing its role as a cultural construction of both the self and the other. As Geertz puts it, ethnographic writing involves the 'construction of other people's constructions of what they and their compatriots are up to' (Geertz 1973: 9). Similarly for Clifford (1988) anthropology is an invention, not just a representation, of culture. Postmodern ethnography has carefully acknowledged its limits, interrogating the politics of the research process and the conditions of the production of ethnographic texts. This has led to a reduction of and deconstruction of claims to 'knowledge' and a critique of an assumed ability to definitively represent cultures. Ethnographic truths are recognised as inherently 'partial – committed and incomplete' (Clifford and Marcus 1986: 7). A parallel deconstructive turn regarding epistemology is found within feminist debates which have also interrogated the politics of knowledge production within scientific disciplines, raising questions of the relationship between the knower and the known, and the gendered nature of research, in an attempt to create new subject positions of knowing (Code 1991, 1993, Grosz 1993, Harding 1991). Both of these critiques eschew the 'god-like' position of detached, rational, objective observer and a neutral positivism, and see the production of knowledge as a discursive and political activity. Both have demanded attention to reflexivity and intersubjectivity, addressing the researcher's own ambiguous position.

One of the distinguishing characteristics of ethnography is its relationship to theory. As Willis and Trondman (2000) argue, theory should be employed when it offers some insight into ethnographic evidence rather than prioritising theory and then seeking to find evidence to 'prove its validity'. Furthermore, they argue that ethnography should seek to promote 'theoretical informed-ness', 'sensitising concepts' and 'analytic points' as a means of 'teasing out patterns from the texture of everyday life' (Willis and Trondman 2000: 4). Ethnography then, offers the possibility of reshaping and fine-tuning theory by offering knowledge of the world of practice: the way that people make sense of the understandings available to them. It is a way of grounding theoretical comprehension in a located social context. An ethnographic approach to sexuality then, acknowledges that gender and sexual identities, and the meanings that circulate around them, are more than merely discursive formulations. They are daily realities and practices that have real consequences.

Ethnography is a methodology which has been subject to considerable criticism due to its epistemological underpinnings and its representational conventions. These have been central to the debates of reflexive anthropology (associated primarily with the work of Clifford and Marcus (Clifford 1988, 1997, Clifford and Marcus 1986, Marcus and Fisher 1986) as well as Geertz (1988) and Taussig (1987). Matters relating to ethnography as a methodology, including issues to do with the power relations of research, the textual construction of the classed, racialised and gendered other, ethnography's assumed lack of scientific rigour, the limits and possibilities of knowing, and knowledge production, the discipline's emergence in the conditions of colonialism and imperialism, have all been thoroughly interrogated. Ethnography is undoubtedly methodologically untidy, and university bookshelves are filled with some of the anxious writing which this messy methodology seems to produce. Due to its intensely social and at times intimate character, ethnographic research is filled with ontological, epistemological and ethical dilemmas. And yet, rather than packing up shop and leaving town, ethnography seems to be thriving as both a method of research and as mode of representation.[2] Today ethnography, at its best, continues to be a genre of sociological and anthropological writing which has the power to communicate the irreducibility of human experience with pathos. It is a mark of the skilled ethnographic scholar that he or she is able to witness and make sense of the complexity of the social world. Indeed, the best ethnographies do not just offer nuanced, up-close accounts of lived experience, they also produce socio-cultural analyses which have a grounded sense of the social world as at once 'internally sprung and dialectically produced' (Willis and Trondman 2000) probing the ways that social lives are caught in the flow of history, the discourses that surround us and the webs of meaning we weave.

In carrying ethnographic research into lesbian lives, I offer an account that interrogates the everyday dimensions of lived experience in an attempt to pay critical attention to the direct and subtle workings of hetero- and homonormativity. I wanted to analyse the ways in which the changing meanings of the identity category 'lesbian' are discursively produced in socio-historical context, and in particular the ways that women live in relationship to the meanings of the category 'lesbian'. In an attempt to offer a productive space of praxis from which to think through the 'necessary trouble' of identities (Butler 1991), I aimed to combine queer, postmodern and poststructural theories of knowledge production and the self, with a commitment to ethnographic understandings of identity categories.

---

2   Ethnography is a research method which has travelled beyond the academy, being increasingly popular with corporations concerned with matters such as the ways people use technologies, for example the Ethnographic Praxis in Industry Conference 2005 held at the Microsoft Campus Seattle Washington.

This approach allows me to theorise the ways in which contemporary sexual subjectivities are discursively produced while simultaneously doing justice to the ways in which identities, such as lesbian, are lived with intersubjective complexity. It is the descriptive nature of ethnography that allows for the nuanced communication of experience and enables ethnography to offer a way of exploring the intricacies and nuances of lived practice in a specific temporal and spatial context; how people live through the problems and pleasures of daily life, how they live in relationship to the identities available to them.

Between Here and There: The Normativity of Ethnographic Time

I now want to move on to consider how we might question some of the normativities of ethnography. After all, queer as a body of theory is not limited to thinking about gendered and sexual subjectivities. Rather it is a philosophical commitment to contesting the logics of normativity. Queering ethnography therefore necessarily involves exploring the normative logics of ethnographic research and writing. This includes interrogating the fictions of ethnographic time and space and the intersubjective nature of the field. In a discussion of queer time and the ways in which postmodern understandings of temporality and spatiality are normative Judith Halberstam (2005a: 6) argues that our sense of time is not merely one of natural time internalised, but rather a complex consequence of living within (post) modernity which is a 'social construction forged out of vibrant and volatile social relations'. Research practices contain their own temporal normativities. Our sense of waiting, haste, (im)patience, boredom and industry make up the everyday temporalities of research practice. One of the defining characteristics of ethnographic practice is its disciplining temporal progression as the researcher moves from periods of participant observation during fieldwork, to the process of writing up the research. This places varied demands on the researcher: participant observation involves 'deep hanging out' (Clifford 1997) and immersing oneself in the field, while 'writing up' demands that we extract ourselves from the webs of entanglements we wove, in order to achieve the critical distance required to write up our analysis (often with externally imposed deadlines). This move into the 'writing up' period classically follows a scholastic convention of presenting a self who is now detached and distant from the fieldwork situation in both emotional, spatial and temporal terms. These aspects are part of the fiction and normativity of traditional ethnography. The fiction of the field being *elsewhere* is particularly apparent when fieldwork takes place close to home. In traditional ethnographies the ethnographer goes off to a distant and (presumed) strange culture, dwells amongst the people in a particular village or neighbourhood that he or she hopes to understand and describe. He or she then returns from the field changed in the process and through 'writing up' makes some sense of both their embodied rite of passage and the culture that it took place within. This is more problematic when the field is close to home. Presenting it as a strange, or unfamiliar culture can be a fiction. Doing one's fieldwork close to home (both the location of home and the ontological home of comfort and belonging) problematises the idea of the field as a space/place physically and temporally bounded. It requires that we think of the field as having fluctuating boundaries which are continually expanding and contracting. (When a participant calls me six months after my fieldwork has ended am I momentarily in the field again? If I bump into a participant when I am out shopping in the local high street and have a chat is that a moment of fieldwork? Should I just ignore that last text message now that I am not in the field?) My own research, situated close to home, highlighted how the process of crossing the fictional borders between the field of the university and the fieldwork site of the LGB centre blurs the edges of what I thought of as the field.

The temporality of the field has also been interrogated by Hastrup (1992: 127) who argues that 'the field world has neither a firm past nor a distinct future because its reality is intersubjectively constructed and depends on the ethnographer's presence in the field'. Therefore, when the ethnographer leaves the field, she carries its immediacy, its presence, with her. The 'field' becomes a spatial, temporal and sensory capsule, which is constantly revisited through notes, transcripts and memory in order to make sense of it and to find its broader sociological significance and meaning (if we follow Geertz's proposition that the task of interpretive ethnography is to find the sociological or anthropological meaning in the ethnographic encounter). Producing ethnography requires a constant crossing between the 'here' and 'there', between the past, present and future: from being 'in the field' while thinking about the future point of writing up, to the point of writing and revisiting the 'ethnographic past'. Even when we are 'there' we are 'here' and vice versa. Acknowledging this temporality is to queer an otherwise normative rational version of ethnographic time. Furthermore, this back and forth movement also leads to an existential splitting; an experience of being in two places at the same time. This experience has been interrogated in feminist debates regarding research ethics, methodologies and epistemologies. As Haraway states 'Splitting, not being, is the privileged image for feminist epistemologies of scientific knowledge' (Haraway 1991: 193). Queering ethnographic temporality demands that the ethnographer finds a way to be as fully present as possible when 'there', while keeping a mind on the exacting demands of later being 'here'. Similarly at the point of writing up, reflecting on the process of fieldwork and making sense of it theoretically, she is required to revisit the ethnographic past of fieldwork. If the 'field' is intersubjectively constructed by the ethnographer, we might argue that he or she is the *only* person who inhabits the field *as* 'the field'. The informants may be in the same place at the same time but their experience of it is different to that of the ethnographer. The challenge to ethnographic scholarship this brings is illustrated beautifully in the following passage by John Berger:

> What separates us from the characters about whom we write is not knowledge, either objective or subjective, but their experience of time in the story we are telling. This separation allows us, the storytellers, the power of knowing the

whole. Yet equally, this separation renders us powerless: we cannot control our characters after the narration has begun. ... The time and therefore the story belongs to them, yet the meaning of the story, what makes it worthy of being told is what we can see and what inspires us because we are beyond its time. ... Those who read or listen to our stories see everything as through a lens. His lens is the secret of narration, and it is ground anew in every story, ground between the temporal and the timeless (1991: 31).

The people we write about, those whose stories we aim to tell, embody and live in their own time and their stories go on long after we have left the 'field'. The ethnographer's challenge is to grapple with the meaning of the story in that moment, to tell it with honesty and an ethical commitment to doing it justice. It is not so much that the ethnographer is armed with a theoretical and methodological toolbox, possessing a superior 'objective' knowledge. Indeed, ethnographic knowledge is 'partial, committed and incomplete' (Clifford and Marcus 1986: 7) but this partiality is a strength, not a flaw; it is a way of acknowledging and interrogating our social and political situatedness as researchers.[3]

Beyond 'Establishing Rapport'

Butler reminds us of how our sense of self is made through the inevitability of loss, and the ways in which we are connected and indebted to each other:

Let's face it. We're undone by each other. And if we're not, we're missing something (Butler 1993a: 31).

She points towards an ethic and ontology of vulnerability. Qualitative social research is filled with interpersonal encounters, haptic human connection, closeness, understanding and interpersonal engagement. The affective process of gathering ethnographic 'data' depends on sensory involvement which, in an attempt to convey and make some sense of embodied experience, takes emotions seriously. This challenging emotional process is described eloquently by Ruth Behar discussing her anxieties when moving from research to writing:

Loss, mourning, the longing for memory, the desire to enter into the world around you and having no idea how to do it, the fear of observing too coldly or too distractedly or too raggedly, the rage of cowardice, the insight that is always

---

3   There is an often-unacknowledged overlap between postmodern ethnography and feminist critiques of research methodologies. Both reject the stance of the natural observer, recognise the intrusive and unequal nature of research relationships in the field, are self conscious of the potential for distortion and the limitations of the research process, and both recognise that they are producing 'partial truths'.

arriving too late, as defiant hindsight, a sense of the utter uselessness of writing
anything and yet the burning desire to write something are the stopping places
along the way (1996: 3).

Scholarly ethnography relies upon this ethical connection. However, this is often
at odds with the kind of distanced, rational and reasoned texts produced in a
sociological discipline that prioritises distance, and offers methodological skills
training that emphasises quantitative and systematised modes of data storage
and analysis, combined with theoretical abstraction. In the process of conducting
ethnographic research I found myself repeatedly caught between intense
phatic engagement (participation) and a kind of cool intellectual detachment
(observation). Postgraduate research training and sociological methodological
texts had not prepared me for the complexity of these affective intersubjective
encounters. I felt a deep unease when attempting to keep my feelings to myself
and retain some objectivity while trying to engage and understand my informants'
experiences through an 'ethic of listening' which combines emotions and intellect,
in what Bourdieu (1999) describes as 'intellectual love'.[4]

Although much ethnographic writing has focused on emotions as culturally
variant constructions – legitimate and important forms of understanding for both
informants and ethnographers (see Rosaldo 1989, Coffey 1999) – little writing
on the emotions of ethnographic fieldwork acknowledges the extent to which
ethnography is a form of emotional work, or emotional labour, with its own hazards
and difficulties. The concept of emotional labour, as developed by Hochschild
(1983), was first used to describe the way in which workers (specifically women in
the service sector) manage their own feelings in order to induce feelings in others.
Hochschild describes various levels in the performance of emotional labour: surface
acting and deep acting. Surface acting entails managing outward appearances and
pretending 'to feel what we do not ... we deceive others about what we really feel,
but we do not deceive ourselves' (Hochschild 1983: 33). 'Deep acting' means
'deceiving oneself as much as deceiving others. We make feigning easy by making it
unnecessary' (Hochschild 1983: 33). In order to establish these affective connections
that ethnography hinges upon the ethnographer must have a degree of emotional
competence, and an ability to convey genuine interest, express care and respond
appropriately if the desired outcome of establishing feelings of trust is to be achieved.
This is sometimes glibly described as 'establishing rapport' in classic anthropology
texts. It is on the basis of this emotional labour, which produces bonds of trust, that

---

4   Bourdieu's ethical listening aims to offer the research subject an opportunity 'to
testify, to make themselves heard, to carry their experience over from the private to the
public sphere; an opportunity also to *explain themselves* in the fullest sense of the term'
(Bourdieu 1999: 612–15). The encounter with the researcher, when framed within the ethic
that Bourdieu suggests, can offer up a unique opportunity for self-examination. This is not
without its problems (See McRobbie's (2002) critique of *The Weight of the World* and the
limits of Bourdieu's project of 'social pedagogy').

informants 'open up' to give clear accounts of themselves. Significantly, the self-explanations offered to the ethnographer are offered on the basis of the informants' understanding of the *kind of person* the ethnographer is. In my own research I take the standpoint that rather than inhabiting the position of 'modest witness' (Haraway 2004) I need to consciously present myself with honesty as a white working-class lesbian and a researcher. Looking back I can see that it was, in part, due to my embodied situatedness in the subject positions of 'working class' and 'lesbian' and my communicating some shared understanding of the pleasures and difficulties of lesbian lives, that informants were willing to disclose their life experiences and self understandings to me. However, whilst emphasising similarities and shared experiences was productive, it is also necessary to acknowledge that simultaneously playing down my educational background, my professional training and the class mobility this brought, also formed part of my interaction with informants, brought about by an awareness that these 'differences' might jeopardise the 'rapport' I sought to develop. This was an experience of constantly managing my outward appearances and the aspects of my self I wished to share and at least attempting to manage my own, sometimes difficult, feelings.

Ethnography's Epistemological Closet?

If the emotional and intersubjective aspects of carrying out ethnographic research have often been selectively written out of ethnographic accounts, the work of the erotic dimension of fieldwork is almost invisible. Historically anthropologists and sociologists have been fascinated by the sexual and intimate lives of others, however, their own erotic subjectivity has been notably absent as a site of critical scrutiny. As Kulick points out, this has been due in part to anthropology's 'disciplinary distain for personal narratives' and cultural taboos about discussing their own culture's sex, while constructing the often 'exotic sexualities of others' (1995: 20). This silence is productive in that it works to preserve the bounded subjectivity of the (usually male) ethnographer, set the limits of legitimate critical enquiry, whilst at the same time suppressing 'women' and 'gays'.[5] As Newton points out, (2000) in a discussion of homophobia in academia, this silence works to keep heterosexual male subjectivity out of the lens of critical enquiry. Sexuality continues to be the dirty secret kept in the epistemological closet of research ethics, and will remain so as long as the erotic equation in fieldwork is 'written out', rather than 'written up'. In the spirit of a feminist and reflexive ethnographic project, paying attention to the work of emotions and erotics in ethnography is, in part, a push to question the way in which the ontological and epistemological boundary between the 'knower' and the 'known' is produced and maintained in the discursive production of 'us'/'them'. As Marcus points out, 'the ethnographer's

---

5   For more discussion and examples of ethnographic texts which do interrogate these matters see Kulick and Willson (1995) and Newton (2000).

framework should not remain intact if the subject's is being analytically pulled apart' (1994: 50).

Queering ethnography is a task which requires that we approach with caution, and make clear, the normative logics of ethnographic practice. This includes undoing some of the textual conventions which create the ethnographer as unproblematically stable in terms of their gendered and sexual subjectivity. It also requires that, as part of a reflexive research process, we examine the consequences of taking seriously the complexities of understanding queer subjectivities. As ethnographers of queer lives, while we are busy deconstructing the discourses and categories that produce our informants' subjectivities, we might consider the extent to which we ourselves are willing to be 'pulled apart' or undone? Are we willing to risk relinquishing our often unspoken attachment to the categories that offer us a sense of ontological security? To illustrate, when I set out to conduct my fieldwork, I was keen to conduct feminist research which was collaborative and dialogical (Skeggs 1997, Stacey 1988, Stanley and Wise 1983a, 1983b, 1990, 1993). I naively assumed this would be fairly unproblematic to put into practice. However, my undeclared attachment to ethnographic distance and the comfort and authority it offered was repeatedly made obvious to me while carrying out my fieldwork. So for instance, I realised, over time that one of my 'informants' was friends with one of my former lovers. When in conversation she made it apparent that she knew some of the details of our relationship break-up, I realised I was comfortable to be known in some ways but not in others. What may be simply gossip in the space of a bar or a party, impacted on my identity as an ethnographer and an academic at the community centre. The field was a space where my personal boundaries and my stable sense of self were gradually undone. This is best summed up in Geertz's assertion that 'You don't exactly penetrate another culture, as the masculinist image would have it. You put yourself in its way and it bodies forth and enmeshes you' (1995: 44). Such a gendered and sexualised metaphor also draws attention to the sexual subjectivity of the ethnographer, a matter which continues to be surrounded by a slightly embarrassed, uneasy silence.

Doing Identity in the Field

Queer theory, specifically the work of Butler (1993a, 1996, 1999) and Foucault (1977), has decentred and fragmented the research subjects' subjectivities.[6]

---

6   I am thinking specifically here of Butler's theories of performativity and embodiment which imply that adopting 'gay' and 'lesbian' identities is to base one's identity on a sexuality which rests upon fixed gender differences rather than acknowledging gender as performative, and as having no ontological status which stands apart from the acts that constitute it. Sexual subjectivities then are culminations of performative acts which all work to hold sexualities in place. And Foucault's theories of the discursive production of sexual subjects whereby those adopting or claiming 'lesbian' and 'gay' identities within

However, the self that is producing much cultural research still remains distant and stable. So for example, much anthropological reflexive writing has at its centre a somewhat disconnected self that is bounded, integral and stable through space and time. As Willson points out:

> Many ethnographers go to the field with the illusion that their identity, like their body, is discrete and impenetrable, that although their public persona is controllable and flexible, they have an inner identity, a kind of holy ground like a silent pool of water that nothing will touch (1995: 256).

Perhaps as a way of countering this tendency, Probyn asks 'just what exactly a self-reflecting self is reflecting upon?' (1993: 80), suggesting that the reflexive self should be 'both an object of enquiry and the means of analysing where and how the self is lodged within the social formation' (1993: 80). I want to argue here for an intellectual commitment to queer theory which employs a methodology characterised by epistemological openness and attention to one's own subjectivity, positionality and embodiment. Queering ethnography requires a methodology that pays attention to the performativity of a self which is gendered, sex, sexualised, classed and generational in the research process. It demands that the ethnographer work from an honest sense of oneself that is open and reflexive, rather than holding on to a sense of self which provides an ontologically stable place from which to enter into the fieldworld and subsequently come back to. This queer reflexivity offers a means of theoretical manoeuvring by exploring the connection between ontology and epistemology. This is a position which offers the possibility of articulating the relationships between researcher/writer and the texts we produce, the possibilities of knowing and the worlds we construct in our writing.

Following on from writing on the emotional dimensions of carrying out fieldwork, the performativity of erotics in the field is a potentially useful source of reflection and knowledge making. Queer reflexivity requires drawing attention to the erotics of knowledge production. My own fieldwork, which had at its centre the issue of lesbian selfhood and spatiality, provided a space for reflecting on my own investment in a certain version of lesbian identity. I was in, and of, the culture I was writing about. The extent to which I could establish relationships with informants affected what I could research and the limits of my study. My access to the LGB Centre was negotiated through my cultural and social capital. I had friends who had worked or volunteered there in the past and also knew some of the workers, a little, socially. Although I was a 'cultural insider', inhabiting

---

this can be understood as being caught up in what he describes as a 'reverse discourse', thereby accepting the labels that discursively produced them in the first place. Although this may be a simplistic rendition of the barest bones of queer theory, it does reflect the looser readings of queer theory and a reflection of a cultural sensibility which has problematically been described as post-gay and heteroflexible. See Blackman (2009) for a discussion of the methodological consequences of these tendencies for researching lesbian lives.

the ethnographic imagination often left me feeling like an outsider looking in. In this field I was consciously aware of the investment in, and political necessity of lesbian, gay and bisexual identities. Within the Centre's work around sexual and mental health issues and support, questions of sexual identity were at the fore and the conceptualisation of 'sexual identity' was distinctly different from the discourses of sexuality in my day-to-day academic life. In the latter sexual identity often felt incidental and part of a bygone debate hinged on identity politics that perhaps we as good postmodern scholars should have moved beyond. Outside of the academy and in the 'field' I was self-conscious of my performing of my lesbian credentials and the ways that my participation in discussions of sexuality and sex, my camp sensibility and bawdy sense of humour, demonstrated a certain ontological security. These conscious repetitive performative displays of my lesbian cultural capital (Rooke 2007), which I had accumulated through years of practice in bars, clubs and working in women's projects in the past, contributed to my acceptance and inclusion. To illustrate, while helping out in the Centre's office, I became acutely aware of the quick repartee, casual flirtatiousness, and sexual innuendo that constituted the sexuality of the office space.

The conditions of my inclusion in this space were contingent on my ability to join in on it or willingness to be the butt of jokes. My lesbian identity had been formed in a specific place and time: London in the 1980s and 1990s. At the start of the fieldwork situation, I felt that I had a stable sense of myself, the meaning of my sexual identity and a future trajectory based on that ontology. However, throughout my fieldwork experience, I was forced to examine my own presumptions and consider the extent to which my particular sense of my lesbian identity, which reflected my experience of the cultural politics of the lesbian feminist culture where my lesbian identity had been formed, was colouring my perception of the issues coming out of the research; whether the issues of importance to me were actually relevant to the women I was engaging with. These difficulties were often guiding principles in pushing my analysis forward. And, more generally, they challenged my preconceptions of contemporary lesbian identity. By thinking and writing reflexively and through a queer lens, I became increasingly vigilant to the ways in which the ontological category of lesbian that I inhabited was not universal. This is not simply a case of 'lost objectivity' or 'bias'.

> [C]ould it be that the subjection that subjectivates the gay or lesbian subject in some ways continues to oppress, or oppresses most insidiously, once 'outness' is claimed? Who or what is it that is 'out', made manifest and fully disclosed, when and if I reveal myself as a lesbian? What is it that is now known, anything? (Butler 1991: 15).

> Substantial groups of women and men under this representational regime have found that the normative category 'homosexual', or its more recent synonyms, does have a real power to organize and describe their experience of their own sexuality and identity, enough at any rate to make their self application of it

(even when only tacit) worth the enormous accompanying costs. Even if only for this reason, the categorization demands respect (Sedgwick 1990: 83).

One of the challenges and possibilities of engaging with queer theory is the ways in which it challenges epistemological and ontological comfort in and coherence of identity categories. As Butler and Sedgwick illustrate, the category 'lesbian' is as necessary as it is problematic. The category continues to have salience and political import, as well as the power to oppress. This resonates with my reflections on the performativity of my subject position as a lesbian researcher during my fieldwork and how it could be seen as productive in that it enabled the connection I was seeking in the research process. However, about halfway through the fieldwork process, and quite suddenly, the security and perceived authenticity of my subject position as a lesbian was questioned by myself and others when my own subjectivity was somewhat 'queered'. I began a relationship with a female-to-male transsexual, who was in the process of transitioning. I met this man in the research process and initially mistakenly read him as a lesbian. Our erotic relationship flourished over discussions of lesbian, gay and queer theories, conversations of gender norms and queer communities in the course of my fieldwork. Concurrently my theoretical interest in the logics of exclusion within contemporary lesbian cultures was experienced with more immediacy. These difficult changes brought about a new basis of understanding with some participants as well as associated ethical dilemmas. For example, several months into my fieldwork, I began facilitating a 'sexualities discussion group' for women beginning to come to terms with their sexual desires for other women. I facilitated this group with Centre staff and other volunteers. The women who attended the group were mostly working-class. Several of them were mothers who were either married or divorced. On a weekly basis in group discussions women struggled with the stigma they associated with lesbian identities. I found myself experiencing a fresh sense of empathy in this space. In group discussions I shared my experience of coming out as a lesbian, albeit twenty years earlier; however, I now felt a more immediate appreciation of the anxieties of many of the women in the group. I was also struggling with coming out again to friends and family. Discussions that focussed on fears of telling family and friends, anxieties about being misinterpreted and possibly rejected by friends and the fear of social stigma now had more urgency and resonance for me. I was acutely aware of the necessity of identity and the enormous personal costs that go with identifying with the category and yet I was simultaneously conscious of the ways in which identity is an unfinished narrative, that the coherence that it offers does not do justice to many queer lives which are often conflicted, contradictory and defying the coherence these categories offer. While I knew I had a lot to offer women who were struggling with the shame and stigma of being a lesbian, I also felt my participation in the group was somewhat inauthentic because I was presenting myself as a lesbian supporting other lesbians when actually I no longer felt that I fitted easily within that category. My self-presentation began to feel increasingly like a partial, unfinished narrative. I was encouraged by the other facilitators to share experiences of my first coming out and remain silent on the second. However, my growing awareness of, and commitment to, trans politics meant that I was uncomfortable about being evasive about my partner's trans identity (and more generally this was not always possible due to his gender ambiguous appearance while he was going through his transition). Overall, these circumstances caused me to question the status of my insider knowledge and what it *does*. I began to feel more marginal and less a 'cultural insider'. I asked myself, what conflicts of meaning would be overlooked if I denied my ambivalent situation? I wondered whether I should present myself as the confident secure lesbian role-model that some of these women sought? What would I say in the group if people asked whether I was in a relationship? Should I confuse the apparent coherence and authenticity they sought from me? By writing about these dilemmas would I be indulging in 'banal egotism' (Probyn 1993: 80)? Was I merely reflecting on others in order to talk about myself? My ethnographic fieldwork brought my sexual subjectivity, and that of the informants I worked with, into sharp focus. It forced me to ask myself whether the personal cost of being on the margins of some of the more conventional understandings of lesbian identity would be too great and jeopardise my project.

These dilemmas point to an understanding of the ethnographic self which is as contingent, plural and shifting as that of many of the informants we are concerned with. Paying attention to this provisionality is a matter of questioning the self at the heart of ethnographic accounts found in the social sciences, asking how we connect with others, the purpose of reflexivity, and the importance of honest and rigorous considerations of the vulnerability of the observer (Behar 1996, Moreno 1995). Reflexivity then, is not merely intellectual and epistemological 'navel gazing' (Babcock 1980, Okely 1992) but rather a matter of acknowledging one's subject position in the power relations of research, and interrogating 'a discursive arrangement that holds together in tensions, the different lines of race, and sexuality that form and reform our senses of self' (Probyn 1993: 1–2). This is a 'theoretically manoeuvring' self rather than a stable, coherent and impenetrable individual.

Conclusion

A central task of queer ethnography is writing and researching in a way that does justice to the ways that people live their gendered and sexual subjectivities with complexity. It is also an undertaking which requires that we question the conditions of knowledge production when theorising queer lives. One of the challenges of the craft of ethnographic writing is finding a way of clearly articulating what the often hidden work of ethnography involves. Integral to this task is an account of what goes on within the field *and* within the ethnographer. This is not the kind of sociology that one finds by looking in the 'how to do it' textbooks on sociological qualitative methods. The craft of ethnographic research is often what is left out in sociological texts. My argument for queering ethnography can be located within wider debates about the nature of the sociological imagination. In this chapter I have set out some of the ethical, methodological and ontological difficulties of researching the meanings of lesbian identities ethnographically with a commitment to queering some of the scholastic conventions of ethnography. The issues raised by the discussion of queer ethnography set out above; its temporality, the ethics of intersubjectivity, the emotional nature of research, the limits of the queer self, and reflexivity and, more broadly, the relationship between ontological and epistemological locatedness. The professional 'rite of passage' that is the ethnographic journey is not merely a matter of stepping out of the academy and into the messy social world of the 'field'. We bring the academy with us, in the form of our understandings and our aspiration to develop what Mills described as a sociological imagination.[7] An ethnographic journey is one which requires that we embrace the queerness of the situations we often find ourselves in. This can lead to an ethnography that recognises experience as a nodal point of knowledge, providing useful information about the self, subjects, and the spaces they inform and are informed by (Probyn 1993). Often, my experience of ethnographic fieldwork has been one of journeying without a map, moving within and between categories, slipping out of the comfort that the identities 'lesbian' and 'researcher' offer. It is also an experience that requires that I engage with the instability and challenges that this brings and the consequences for theorising: emphasising the importance of being able to move beyond that location, out of our mindset, theoretical orientations and preconceptions.

---

7   C. Wright Mills, writing in 1959, made a plea for the development of the kind of sociological imagination which pays attention to the relationship between private troubles or the traps of everyday life, and those matters which become public issues. One of the strengths of the sociological imagination (Mills 1959) is that it can ground postmodern philosophical speculation in the materiality and intimacy of everyday life.

Chapter 2

Intimacy with Strangers/Intimacy with Self: Queer Experiences of Social Research[1]

Jamie Heckert

I didn't want to write a queer Ph.D. Queer and me – we didn't have a great history. It was a word I had used as an identity label after I decided neither gay nor bi were for me. My desires never seemed to fit other people's expectations of those words. Queer struck me, at the time, as somehow more radical, more slippery, more transgressive. Besides, I was used to thinking of myself as a dangerous outsider. Having grown up a gender deviant atheist geek in a very small, very straight town this felt familiar. The thing is, dangerous outsider can be a lonely position. Besides, I didn't *get* queer theory. Foucault scared me. I got a lot of security from thinking of myself as smart and when I didn't understand much of anything we read in my undergrad queer theory discussion group, I was spooked. These memories and feelings came alive for me again a few years later when a fellow postgraduate student told me that what I was doing *was* queer, that I *should* be reading queer theory.

Simply allowing memories and feelings to arise without trying to contain or control them was not the way I'd learned to live, nor was it what I was learning as a sociologist in training. Unable to acknowledge my fear, I fell back on a well-known emotional strategy in academia. I sneered. What I was doing wasn't queer – it was better, even more radical. It was *anarchist*.

> 'How does it feel to be free?' She asked.
> 'I like it' said Wilbur. 'That is, I guess I like it'. Actually, Wilbur felt queer to be outside his fence, with nothing between him and the big world.
> 'Where do you think I'd better go?'
> 'Anywhere you like, anywhere you like' said the Goose.
>
> E.B. White, *Charlotte's Web*

Like Wilbur, I had (and still get) mixed feelings about living outside certain fences. I learned somewhere along the way a practice of scholarship that depended

1   This chapter would not be what it is without the editorial labours of Kath Browne and Catherine Nash. I thank them for the careful feedback and challenging questions that helped me hone this piece through many drafts. I also deeply appreciate the support and inspiration I received from colleagues during my fellowship at the AHRC Research Centre for Law, Gender and Sexuality at the University of Kent.

on putting diverse thoughts into boxes and judging them.[2] This was theory as battlefield. As Foucault once put it, reversing a famous aphorism, 'politics is the continuation of war by other means' (2003: 15). And war, I knew from my life in militaristic cultures in the United States and United Kingdom, is much more comfortable on the winning side. How would I know which side I was on without a fence, a border? How could I assess right and wrong, whether I was right or wrong, without boxing and judging? How could I live without relying on these strategies? I'm still learning. I'm becoming-queer.

* * *

Looking back, I can see how I crafted stories both of how my methodology fitted into conventional sociological practices of qualitative research *and* how it overflowed these disciplinary borders (Heckert 2005). I wanted both integrity and security at the same time. How honest, how daring, could I be and still get my Ph.D.? How queer can one be in a university?

I can no longer see any clear border between anarchist and queer. Perhaps this is because I understand both terms as referring not only to a refusal to grant legitimacy to borders, whether those of classes, nations or sexualities, but also as ways of becoming, of learning to experience the unreality of borders, to know profoundly that they have no independent existence. To learn that their continual construction is *utterly dependent* on everyday forms of policing, conformity and obedience can be a part of learning to cross them, to bridge them.[3] Likewise, neither term stops at the appreciation of individual transgression; both recognise that to either undermine or overflow borders is a collective effort.[4] I am also practising non-attachment[5] toward powerful, linear, masculine cultural stories

---

2   This is what Deleuze and Guattari call 'overcoding', which they say 'is the operation that constitutes the essence of the State' (2000: 198). We all code – putting labels on things in order to communicate with each other, to make sense of the world. Overcoding is imposing the right way to make sense of the world – the truth or the law which must not be questioned.

3   Queer comes from the German *quer* – to cross. Bridge refers to the writings of radical women of colour whose experiences do not fit into separate boxes of race, class, gender and sexuality (Moraga and Anzaldúa 1981), as response to the despair felt by an anarchist who came to imagine that social transformation was divided from individual transformation (Bookchin 1995) and, finally, to the joy I feel standing suspended over flowing waters.

4   On queer as a collective effort see Butler 2009 and Mattilda 2004.

5   A concept found in various spiritual traditions emphasising the benefits of an open relationship with thoughts and desires (prefiguring Foucault's critique of a truth of the self found in either). I'm particularly taken with a version of this in the Tao Te Ching: 'So the unwanting soul sees what's hidden, and the ever-wanting soul sees only what it wants' (Lao Tzu 1998: 3). What visions, what possibilities, what lives remain hidden when the mind is focused on, driven toward, success? What would it mean for you, for me, to let go?

that emphasise achievement, accomplishment, success. Neither anarchist nor queer, as I see them, are concerned with these linear stories and their (continually postponed) happy endings. Nor do they attempt that subtle ruse of power, to claim that history is ended, that democracy is achieved or that life involves accepting official stories about economics, politics, intimacy. Instead, both may refer to the erotic potential of everyday life, to the ongoing joyful awareness of being alive, even when it hurts; an awareness that life itself is exuberant and *always* escapes, overflows, undermines or disregards all attempts to impose categories, to discipline.

How then, does one do research with joyfully undisciplined exuberance? One source of inspiration for me is Judy Greenway's description of a 'methodological anarchism that relinquishes control, challenges boundaries and hierarchies, and provides a space for new ideas to emerge' (2008: 324). She advocates a juxtaposition of stories: of self, of research subjects, of audiences. In doing so, she enacts the anarchist ethic of prefiguration (Franks 2003, Gordon 2008): prefiguring possible future social relations by putting into action directly anarchist values of deep equality, radical transformation and listening. Intertwined with Greenway's methodological anarchism, I draw on Deleuze and Guattari, among others, to consider methodology as a practice of becoming-queer. For me, this has involved continually learning to let go of borders: between theory and data, researcher and researched, hetero and homo, right and wrong. I am learning to cross, to connect, to realise that I don't need fences. Becoming-queer, I am learning to be 'comfortable with uncertainty' (Chödrön 2002). This is never finished, accomplished, achieved – those favoured words in a society of control. Becoming queer is always in process – experienced only in the present, in presence.

Like their friend Michel Foucault, Giles Deleuze and Felix Guattari reject sex, or anything else, as the truth of the self. What appears to be true about someone is an effect of actions and connections. Being is always a *becoming,* never an achievement, a truth, an actor pre-existing the enactment. What I love about becoming-queer is the way it sidesteps any efforts to make queer into a new disciplinary category. It takes the power out of voices asking, am I queer enough? Is she really queer? No one IS queer. Anyone might be becoming-queer. Another thing I love about becoming-queer is that it foregrounds connection, the profoundly ecological basis of life itself (Hird 2004). Rather than attempting to diagnose and transform a situation which exists, becoming-queer is a reminder that life *is* transformation.

> [O]ften I intended my teachings to serve as a conduit to radicalization, which I now understand to mean a certain imprisonment that conflates the terms of domination with the essence of life. Similar to the ways in which domination always already confounds our sex with all of who we are, the focus on radicalization always turns our attention to domination (Alexander 2005: 8).

Becoming-queer turns our attention to life itself, remembering that the becoming of the self is always already a social transformation.

* * *

In this chapter, I share a number of stories from my experiences of becoming-queer, of methodological anarchism. These stories are not true, for I am in agreement with the notion that there is 'no such thing as a true story' (Chödrön 2002: 17, see also Stainton Rogers and Stainton Rogers 1997). Nor do they follow a single line of direction or desire; they connect to each other in many ways. They form a rhizome (see below). In sharing these stories, I do not have a simple message or a particular argument to convey. Like Ursula Le Guin (2009: 129), 'I wish, instead of looking for a message when we read a story, we could think, "Here's a door opening on a new world: what will I find there?"'

Understanding Sexual Orientation

I set out in my Ph.D. research to understand sexual orientation (Heckert 2005). I knew the mainstream categories of gendered desire – hetero, homo, bi – didn't work for me anymore, and I knew that I wasn't alone in this. Involved in sexual health education work with young people, in LGBT and queer politics as well as anarchist and feminist networks, I had come to see the everyday ways in which the very idea of sexual orientation affects people's capacities for intimacy and honesty. I had also learned from my own earlier frustrating efforts to tell people involved in sexual identity politics that they were doing it wrong. I wanted to develop a more compassionate approach, including compassion for my younger self who took inspiration from LGBT Pride. If sexual orientation categories are problematic, or even oppressive, as queer theorists suggest, why do (some) people hold on to them? What do they/we get out of having them? Are these categories and the hetero/homo border that gives them structure losing the apparent coherence they may have once had?

To explore these questions further in order to develop a deeper and more subtle understanding of sexual orientation as a phenomenon which is inseparably personal and political, I sought out individuals who I expected would also have complex, troubled, queer relationships with sexual orientation and I listened to their stories. I invited as 'interview partners' (Klesse 2006: 579), people who saw themselves as being in 'mixed sexual orientation identity relationships':

> I am interested in the diversity of people's experiences, so my definition is broad. You would qualify for inclusion in this research project if you are in an ongoing romantic and/or sexual relationship where *the way in which you identify your sexual orientation, either now or in the past, is different from that of a current partner*. Sexual orientation identities do not have to be limited to traditional

categories like bisexual, gay/lesbian and heterosexual. They can be much more diverse (http://sexualorientation.info).

For many, sexual orientation is taken for granted as a natural truth. Although I suspect that no one's life really fits entirely in these boxes, the lack of open discussion and questioning of this is the effect of the ubiquity of the hetero/homo division (Sedgwick 1990). Of course, this division (itself merely the continuous effect of particular social relations) *is not determining*, and many people, in many situations, question the reality of sexual orientation. I expected that 'mixed relationships'[6] would be one situation that would encourage both the questioning of the hetero/homo division and the capacity to openly discuss the questioning of sexual orientation and categorisation with a stranger (me). Such perspectives, I thought, would be interesting for understanding how sexual orientation is produced, how people experience it, and how it might be undermined. Saying that, I have a memory of a supervisor asking me why I was so sure these stories would be suitable for my research. I wasn't sure and I couldn't explain to him why I wanted to do this. Listening to my intuition, I was making a queer methodological choice.

I was also inspired by other work on relationships that cross borders. Gloria Anzaldúa's (1999) writing about living in the borderlands taught me to think of borders in new ways – and not just as those of nation-states. Another research project that inspired me was on the white birth mothers of African descent children in Britain (Winddance Twine 1999) which found that these women became very active and effective anti-racist educators because of their relationships with their children. Similarly, Kandiyoti (1994, cited in New 2001) suggests that Muslim men who support anti-purdah arguments do so because of the importance of their relationships with their mothers. Joan Nestle, a lesbian feminist, wrote a passionate defence of women's right to enjoy sex with men based on the mutual understanding she developed with her mother. Although at one point she hoped her mother would abandon the men who often abused her and instead choose lesbianism, Nestle came to accept her mother's decisions. 'We faced each other as two women for whom sex was important and after initial skirmishes, she accepted my world of adventure as I did hers' (1983: 470). Like the Zapatista's often repeated call for 'a world where many worlds fit', Nestle's story of freedom and acceptance of others' relationships (whether labelled personal or political, local or global, social or economic) fuelled the border-crossing impulse of my research.

---

6   There are numerous ways to approach the question of sexual orientation as a normative construction of gender, desire and intimacy always already intertwined with other normative and hierarchical constructions (of e.g., class, race, age, ability and aesthetics). Tam Sanger (2010), for example, was writing a Ph.D. thesis at the same time as me looking at 'mixed relationships' in terms of transgender and genderqueer identities which also beautifully troubles the idea of sexual orientation.

Listening to people's stories of mixed relationships, I hoped, would provide an opportunity to further explore how intimacy or love might offer inspiration at a time when I had become deeply dissatisfied with politics defined by identity. This dissatisfaction stemmed in part from reactions that I, and others I have cared about, have had when our own erotic relationships crossed borders of sexual orientation. These concerns were echoed in popular representations of sexuality at the time. Films such as *Chasing Amy* (1997) and television programmes like Channel Four's *Bob & Rose* (2001) acknowledge the possibility of mixed relationships. Both also demonstrated the risks attached, including being labelled a traitor. Similarly, the cover story of one issue of *Marie Claire* (2001 UK edition) was advertised as '"I was gay, but now I'm married with a kid" One woman's story'. It addressed a mixed relationship and other stories of changes in people's sexual desires and identities (Maguire 2001). Similarly, in a *Guardian Weekend* magazine article entitled 'My Crime against the Lesbian State', comedian Jackie Clune wrote about becoming lesbian and how she 'achieved gayness for 12 years, and [how] most of the time it was wonderful' (2003: 26). At the same time, she had real problems with what she calls the 'Lesbian Police' promoting a very particular idea of lesbianism. When she decided to go straight again, she was labelled 'Most Disappointing Lesbian of the Year' (2003: 29).

In addition to setting the stage for developing a research project, these representations of sexuality in the media might also say something interesting about social change. With some notable exceptions, the predominant representation of 'mixed' relationships in twentieth century Anglophone culture is that of the gay or bisexual husband who cheats on his unknowing wife. While a more historically grounded study would be needed to address this question thoroughly, I believe it is fair to say that many would find it difficult to imagine a research project like this one taking place 20 years ago; popular understanding of sexual desire has changed so much in this time, perhaps due to a postmodern cultural shift (Roseneil 2002), a question I return to shortly.

Finally, the focus on mixed identity relationships is part of a long (and queer?) sociological tradition of examining the 'unusual' in order to better understand the 'usual'. As I mentioned above, I expected that stories coming out of mixed identity relationships would likely question the truth regime of sexual orientation. Although I did not make the connection when I first chose to focus on mixed identity relationships, the experience of questioning truth regimes and producing different possibilities is part of experiencing anarchy. On the non-hierarchically organised women's peace camp at Greenham Common, Sasha Roseneil wrote,

> There was no ethical framework readily available to tell them how they should live together and how they should confront the threat of nuclear war. ... Women at Greenham had to invent their own set of values to guide their actions. ... Greenham was a *liminal* space, a created world where many of the rules and values of the rest of society were consciously questioned, reworked, transformed or discarded in favour of a new set of beliefs (2000: 114–15).

Roseneil suggested that the Greenham experience was in many ways part of living in an 'uncertain postmodern world, where tradition has less and less hold over us, [and] we are increasingly forced to create our own codes for living' (114). Following on from this one might also suggest that mixed relationships are a very postmodern phenomenon. Indeed, the recent rise in cultural representation of mixed relationships might support this argument. At this point, I am more in agreement with those who argue that postmodernity (Newman 2007), and thus queerness (Tuhkanen 2009), is not bound to a particular historical moment, but is a practice that can be found anywhere. It seems to me that we all make it up as we go along, regardless of time or space. Some just have the 'benefit' of imagining that they are not – that they are following essential truths or unquestionable traditions. Like the women at Greenham Common, people in mixed relationships do not have that 'benefit'. Arguably they may experience a degree of freedom that is exceptional in the contemporary world rather than indicative of a contemporary period of postmodernity.

Like Greenham Common and other anarchic spaces, the experiences of people in mixed identity relationships may highlight how carefully controlled and traditional everyday life can be. Their 'unusual' experiences of negotiating the borders of sexual orientation highlight the extent of representation – of telling people who they are or what they (should) want – in everyday life. At the same time, participants' diverse practices of resistance to sexual orientation may be more obvious, more coherent, more open or more comfortable than those practised by many other people, but as no one is entirely capable of constantly living up to the gendered and sexualised standards of normative sexual orientation, resistance must also be ubiquitous. Practices of queerness are everywhere.

Queering Theory

Crucial to Deleuze and Guattari's project of an anarchist alternative to '"State philosophy" [which] is another word for the representational thinking that has characterised Western metaphysics since Plato' (Massumi 1999: xi) is the advocacy of rhizomic rather than arboreal understanding. The individual tree, they suggest, is the model upon which representational philosophy is based. It has a central trunk from which stem binary divisions of branch and root. The existence of a centre imposes both unity and hierarchy. Each branch and root is unified by the trunk, and each is defined in terms of its position in relation to the centre (e.g. the 'normal'). Rhizomic thought is Deleuze and Guattari's alternative to the centralised and hierarchical metaphor of the tree. Unlike the tree with its trunk, the rhizome has no centre. 'Any point of a rhizome can be connected to anything other, and must be. This is very different from the tree or root, which plots a point, fixes an order' (Deleuze and Guattari 1999: 7). Without a centre, the rhizome lacks the determinism of hierarchical arbourescence: there is no correct order. Furthermore, the centreless multiplicity of the rhizome contrasts sharply with the singular unity of the tree. Defying the dichotomy of subject/object, multiplicity is the effect of relationships themselves. 'Puppet strings, as a rhizome or multiplicity, are tied not to the supposed will of an artist or puppeteer but to a multiplicity of nerve fibres, which form another puppet in other dimensions connected to the first' (1999: 8). In other words, Deleuze and Guattari reject the notion of the independent subject, but see the 'individual' as a multiplicity interconnected with other multiplicities. Importantly, a rhizome is also nomadic, and 'never allows itself to be overcoded' (1999: 9), trapped by categories of discipline, borders of control. The nomad is continuously, creatively, joyfully queer.

Like many others who have found the rhizome to be valuable in developing their queer (e.g. O'Rourke 2006, Storr and Nigianni 2009) and anarchist (e.g. Call 2002, Kellogg and Pettigrew 2008, May 1994, Sullivan 2008) projects, it helped me understand how to describe my experiences of methodology. I often worried I was doing something wrong: I couldn't make sense of my experiences in terms of my training in chemistry, psychology or even sociology. I heard from various sociologists that my work was 'too political', that I should have known exactly what I was looking for when I interviewed people, or that I should develop an analysis by 'listening to my data'. My experience of research, however, cannot be fitted neatly into separate boxes with borders between theory and data, storytelling and practice; it has been rhizomic, anarchic, queer. And I keep learning to queer these borders, to be open to uncertainty.

> There is an old – and I believe convincing – argument that most of us theorise a fair amount of the time as we go about the business of living our lives, whether that living involves writing books or painting houses or changing bedpans. We ask how and why the world works as it works, why it does or doesn't change. … It should not be such a daunting task, for instance, to integrate materials from anecdotes and interviews and everyday life with theoretical encounters of the footnoted kind. The point is not to treat street theorising as 'raw data' that remains TBE – to be explained – but to approach street theorising as a wellspring of explanatory devices and rhetorical strategies in its own right (Weston 1998: 144–45).

In this statement akin to Greenway's (2008) methodological anarchism, Weston challenges the arboreal logic of grounded theory with its dichotomy of theory and data. In the research project I initiated, interviewees' narratives have inspired the theoretical development of the work, not simply as illustrations of high theory, but as theoretically sophisticated in themselves. Becoming-queer, for me, has been in learning to see that I don't need this distinction between theory and data, opening my eyes to new possibilities. Erica helped me see this, for example, when she spoke eloquently about the connections between anarchist and queer in a way that transcends (or undermines) this distinction:

The freedom, the freedom to be yourself without any dictate from hierarchy because it's still hierarchy. ... Sometimes it's the State that dictates what you should do and what you can do and what you can't do, according to who you fuck or who you love or whatever but it's just like all the unspoken hierarchy that I think are the worst ones anyway because they're the origin of the structure. Yeah, *all the sort of having to conform to certain things and what we lose, what we give up on just for the safety of conforming. ... that's ... part of what I'm really fighting against every day.* In all sorts of different levels, not just at a sexual level. But I don't separate sexuality from the rest of it. ... a lot of my more articulate anarchist thinking developed around the time that I was struggling with the gay scene and when I dropped out of it and I was getting my head around sexual orientation (Heckert 2005: 143, my emphasis).

Long before I began to understand the works of Butler and Foucault, I was heavily influenced by much more accessible theory. Libertarian, sex-positive women writers have influenced my thinking on gender, sexuality and politics since I first encountered pornography as a teenager. As the advice columnist for *Penthouse Magazine* and author of *The Happy Hooker*, Xaviera Hollander is hardly likely to be considered a theorist to be cited in serious scholarly work. But what is the political impact of maintaining a silence on her influence? bell hooks has voiced similar concerns regarding the ongoing de-legitimisation of a range of work by women that does not use academic language or style:

Work by women of colour and marginalised groups of white women (for example, lesbians, sex radicals), especially if written in a manner that renders it accessible to a broader reading public, is often de-legitimised in academic settings, even if that work enables and promotes feminist practice. Though such work is often appropriated by the very individuals setting restrictive critical standards, it is this work that they most often claim is not really theory. Clearly, one of the uses these individuals make of theory is instrumental. They use it to set up unnecessary and competing hierarchies of thought which reinscribe the politics of domination by designating work as either inferior, superior, or more or less worthy of attention (hooks 1994: 63–4).

While uncritical of capitalism, Xaviera Hollander's column supported and encouraged people to explore a wide variety of sexual desires and practices without regard to the rules of 'sexual orientation'. Indeed, some pornographic writing provides a space in which the relationship between gender and desire is often very complex. Just as gay pornography has been crucial for many men resisting compulsory heterosexuality (Preston 1993), so too has pornographic nomadism influenced my own theorising. Other, less stigmatised but still clearly non-academic forms of cultural production also influenced the theoretical development of my Ph.D. research. In particular, the anarcha-feminist science-fiction writings of Ursula LeGuin (1999, 2001), Starhawk (1993) and Marge Piercy (1991, 2000) present inspiring alternative realities where relationships of gender, sexuality and authority are radically different. So too has the music of politically engaged songwriters, too numerous to mention, pieces of queer, anarchist and feminist communication in the forms of zines, leaflets and web sites, conversations and other miscellaneous movements of theory that have passed through me without necessarily having been carefully documented and cited as 'theory'. Rather than confessing poor scholarship on my part, I mention these examples to acknowledge, in hindsight, the debts that my theory owes to the labour of many people whose theoretical efforts are unlikely to be granted the same social status as academic or intellectual work.

As well as preferring a broad and open definition of what constitutes theory, I like to read around. As a Ph.D. student, I was both intimidated and bored by the notion of doing literature reviews. Intimidated because I knew it was impossible for me to gain a so-called mastery of all the fields of literature my research intersected and I suffered that common fear in academia – not being good enough (Heckert forthcoming). Bored because I really love variety and spontaneity – I could not face carefully reading what I was supposed to read. I took inspiration from Black Consciousness activist Steven Beko's title 'I write what I like' (cited in Sullivan 2005), and decided to read what I liked. Ecological direct action (Do or Die Collective 2000, Jordan 1998), anarchist literary theory (Cohn 2007, Le Guin 2004) and writings at the intersections of anarchism and poststructuralism (Dempsey and Rowe 2004, May 1994, Rousselle and Evren 2010) have all queerly excited my sociological imagination. Mine was a 'promiscuous reading',[7] a practice of the 'queer art of cross-pollination' (Halberstam 2008), of citing texts differently (Butler 1993a).

I also love remembering that I can queer any supposed border separating theory from practice. To theorise *is* a social practice. Like any other practice, theory has effects – whether that be to challenge or to contribute to relationships of domination (or, as often is the case, both simultaneously). Likewise, the sharing of theory can also be a practice of freedom or a practice of domination (hooks 1994). Other forms of social practice necessarily involve theory – the everyday practice of understanding what one's actions mean and why one does them. The theorising that shaped this project is not all inspired by the writings of philosophers and pornographers, by the thoughts and feelings of the participants, but also by my own participation in various social practices including intimate relationships, teaching sex education, and political activism (see Heckert forthcoming).

Becoming-queer

I recently gave a talk where I was very open about my emotional experiences of attempting to work within universities. I emphasised care of the self through mindfulness or presence. One of the participants in the discussion that followed, an

---

7   Teixeira, R. Personal communication, 15 March 2008.

established academic who expressed her own doubts about continuing to be able to work in academia, said she didn't like care of the self, that to her it just meant 'getting by': a way to cope with, rather than transform, oppressive relationships.

For me, 'getting by' has often involved a certain denial of self. I would strive to be the good researcher: rational, capable and strong. At the same time, I wanted to be a good activist: challenging hierarchies, carving out transformative spaces, being one of the good guys.[8] I have since noticed powerful overlaps in the disciplinary identities of activist and academic. Both are rife with the imposter syndrome – characterised by the worry that one isn't *really* an academic or an activist, that one is not good enough, and imagining that others will realise and see through the charade. Getting by, to me, means doing what you have to do to keep up appearances, to survive. Maintaining these often conflicting performances is draining.

Of the 16 interviews I completed, four included stories of childhood sexual abuse. Even more common were stories of sexual harassment, homophobic violence, and numerous other forms of abuse for not conforming to the borders and judgements of gendered and sexualised categories. What did I do with the feelings and memories these stories triggered for me? Mostly, I ignored them. I got by. I was professional. And my strategies for getting by included learning to stop paying attention to my body, my fear, my shame, even my hunger. Dizzy with hunger, I was distracted from pain. I nearly passed out at one interview. I didn't tell anyone at the time. The same went for overeating. The jeans I wore at the beginning of my postgraduate studies had a 32 inch waist while of the suit I bought for my viva and job interviews was a 38. Speaking with others, I understand this is a common experience.

Buddhist theorist and teacher Thich Nhat Hanh argues 'the practice of the healer, therapist, teacher or any helping professional should be directed towards his or herself first, because if the helper is unhappy, he or she cannot help many people' (cited in hooks 1994: 15). This did not fit with much of what I was learning from either anarchists or academics. In fact, it is inconsistent with the phallicised Christianised cultures (Winnubst, 2006) in which I have lived, where it is believed to be more blessed to give than to receive.

As I wrote my Ph.D., I was often more concerned with giving than receiving. I have a memory of expressing concern to one of my research partners that I might be exploiting them by taking their stories. She reminded me that by listening, I was giving something as well. Giving and receiving, receiving and giving: an anarchist economics of research and a compassionate queering of borders between self and other.

> When one carries out an ethnography, one observes what people do, and then tries to tease out the hidden symbolic, moral, or pragmatic logics that underlie their actions; one tries to get at the way people's habits and actions make sense in ways that they are not themselves completely aware of. One obvious role for

---

8 I use the masculine 'guys' purposely here to indicate what I now, with the help of feminist critique, see as the gendered nature of pervasive discourses of activism.

a radical intellectual is to do precisely that: to look at those who are creating viable alternatives, try to figure out what might be larger implications of what they are (already) doing, and then offer those ideas back, not as prescriptions, but as contributions, possibilities – as gifts (Graeber 2004: 11–12).

* * *

For Deleuze and Guattari, philosophy should be 'utopian', 'so as to summon forth a new earth, a new people' (Deleuze and Guattari 1994: 99). In researching others' stories, this might be expressed through the anarchist/poststructuralist argument that our subjectivities are the result of our practices (Ferguson K. 2004, May 2001). How might the always already embodied, emotional and relational practices of research involve practices of the self, or a care of selves, that allows possibilities unimaginable before? How might research create space for becoming-queer? Though the summoning forth of a new earth was ambitious for a Ph.D. project, I aimed to make a modest contribution. In terms of new people, the interviews alone had some effect. Bourdieu (1999) once described the interview as a process of creating a transformative space, which changes both the interviewer and interviewee. I know that I have been transformed. While I have not asked all the participants for feedback on their experience, those with whom I have spoken to since have expressed appreciation for being listened to and for new stories which helps them experience life differently. After sending Erica a draft of the story I crafted from her stories (see Heckert 2005: 137–48), she wrote to me:

> I got the draft in the post this morning. It's fine as it is, I'm actually really impressed and can't wait to read the whole thing! It's a powerful experience reading my own words in print, not just in a do-I-really-talk-like-that kind of way, but also being confronted with what I said, and finding that it's, well, true, I really did mean it, I still mean it and live it and intend to carry on. Because if that is me, then I am someone. It strongly counteracts that vague sense of unreality I've had all my life. So strongly in fact, that I don't think I could have handled it a few years ago! I'm glad I met you, and that you asked me to take part in this project, and that I said yes. I'm glad my interview helped. I'm glad you're writing this thing.

Space to share stories, to hear/read one's own stories and stories of others is what is transformative about methodological anarchism – it creates space for new possibilities to emerge. In this way the interview itself is potentially a gift to the interviewee as well as to the interviewer. For this to be the case, the interviewee must have the opportunity to speak about what is important to them as well as what is important to the interviewer. I encouraged participants to carry on talking about issues that seemed particularly important to them. I listened to stories when I was not sure whether or not they related to my own research aims. At times, this seemed like a potential weakness. I thought I should have a better idea of what I was researching and what I wanted to know. The most interesting stories were not born of a purely instrumental logic – they came from moments of connection. By this I mean those moments where I am able to set aside identities and ideologies, those forms of psychic armour that constrain as they protect. I grow softer, listening with empathy to stories from another person's world. And they grow softer in the telling, knowing that they are being heard, knowing that they need not defend themselves because there is no attack, no critique. What is labelled weakness may well be a source of strength (Lao Tzu 1998).

I crafted from their stories new stories, gifts. I do not claim the authority to tell the truths of the lives of these individuals. Rather than representing lives, I am re-presenting stories that have been presented to me. My role is less that of the social scientist; I see myself more as a gatherer and a teller of stories.

> For literature, in contrast to science, thought is inseparable from language; 'writing' is aware of itself as language. Certainly what Barthes says about science rings true for much sociological writing which regards itself as a scientific representation of reality, and hence not writing (*that* is for fiction). Notions of truth in sociology are connected with the idea of a reality that is a presence, there to be represented: sociological text is a transparent bearer of the truth of the world. ... Writing disturbs 'reality', and any truth grounded in reality; it also disturbs the notion of an objective observer, outside social relations. The only reality we can discuss is culturally produced. And the scholar – one who uses language – is *in* language, the sociality of language; the scholar is culturally produced (Game and Metcalfe 1996: 90).

In the intimacy of gathering stories, of crafting new ones, I take part in this production of myself, and in the production of others.

* * *

When I try to get by, imagining myself capable of controlling situations, capable of living up to the masculine ideals of the university, I am less capable of listening openly to the stories of others, less capable of non-violent communication. I have learned that a deeper listening to others comes with a deeper listening to myself (Rosenberg 2003). Care of the self, for me, involves the practices that enable a letting go of the fantasies, the masks, the identities that arise out of defence in the war of all against all that characterises the State (to invert Hobbes). While I used to imagine that being anarchist, or being queer, meant a disconnection from others, I know now that becoming anarchist, becoming queer, is something different: a deepening awareness of the connections that always, already exist. Care is the gift I give myself so that I am more capable of giving and receiving with others; of creating together our own boundaries and overflowing imaginary borders (Heckert 2010). This is how I become queer.

Chapter 3

Brown, Queer and Gendered: Queering the Latina/o 'Street-Scapes' in Los Angeles.

Lorena Muñoz

Asi que eres como yo [lesbiana]? Pero como? Tu familia te accepta? Tienes pareja? Huy si hubiera sabido esto desde antes, te hubiera invitado a mi casa desde hace mucho [So you are like me [lesbian]? But how? Does your family accept you? Do you have a partner? Well, if I had known that from the beginning, I would have invited you to my house a long time ago].[1]

Introduction

Herminia, a Latina street vendor in Los Angeles, anxiously welcomes me for the first time to her two-bedroom apartment in a Latino immigrant-receiving neighbourhood in South Central L.A. Although I have informally interviewed her on many occasions at her place of work – the street – this is the first time she has opened up her home to me. I immediately notice that Herminia is dressed very differently from her usual street vending attire. Here the floral shirt and floral skirt, chosen to blend into the street vending landscapes are, replaced with a men's button-down shirt and pants. Herminia lives with her two sons and Maria, a janitorial worker. Maria has a daughter that she had to leave behind her when she journeyed to the United States and who lives with her relatives in Mexico. The two women not only support their household, but provide economic assistance to Maria's parents and daughter in Mexico as well. I met Herminia three years prior to this visit. She is one of the thousands of Latina vendors in Los Angeles and one of the vendors in my study which looked at the production of informal street vending landscapes in Los Angeles. In this visit, hesitating at first, Herminia tells me nervously that Maria is her life partner. She did not want to tell me, since she never imagined that I could understand what she pointedly called 'that part of her life'.

It was when I told her that I was also gay, that the interview shifted. The interviews that followed my disclosure re-conceptualised my own field practices that were primarily based on feminist geography methodology. I realised that as a 'queer' researcher, I presumed street vending landscapes as hetero-normative

---

1   Herminia, Latina immigrant vendor in Los Angeles.

spaces. Because of this assumption, I chose not to prioritise my Latina 'queer' identity in the field. The moment when Herminia disclosed, I had to renegotiate my own subjectivity, reflexivity and identity construction as part of my larger efforts to understand the everyday economic spatial practices of Latina vendors. In this chapter, I will explore how I was pushed by Herminia's revelation to reconceptualise my own Chicana queer reflexivity and subjectivity. These experiences allowed me to attempt to queer the identities and subjectivities of the vendors in their everyday spatial practices. Thus, I turned to the possibility that queer of colour methodology would allow vendors like Herminia to be visible as 'queer' women in vending landscapes. I will further explore the queer of colour critiques of white-queer epistemologies, which call for a new methodological practice that understands queer of colour sensibilities, identities and subjectivities in space.

Queer, Feminist and Other 'Field' Practices

Over the past 20 years feminist methodologies in geographies have provided certain tools that have re-centered feminist field-methods against traditionally centered ontologies (Bondi 1992, Duncan 1996, England 1996, Gibson-Graham 1994, Hanson and Pratt 1995, Katz 1994, Kwan 2002, Massey 1994, Moss 2002). In the *Professional Geographer's* edited collection of 'Women in the Field' (1994) feminist scholars in geography contested, redesigned, analysed and provided feminist ethnographic frameworks on 'doing' field work (England 1994, Gilbert 1994, Katz 1994, Kobayashi 1994). Currently, these particular feminist methodological tools have re-centered the marginalised 'other' by making space for multiple voices and the everyday realities of women, children, people of colour, immigrants, and indigenous populations; groups previously silenced and relegated to invisibility as disempowered identities (see Kobayashi 2004, Kobayashi and Peake 2000, Mohanty 2003).

My purpose here is not to provide a historical development of feminist methodologies in geography, nor to engage with research methods debates in Human Geography. My focus instead is to highlight some of the limitations of doing fieldwork without a racialised queer consciousness and the possibilities that open up when we employ that consciousness. It is clear that contemporary qualitative feminist scholarship has provided tools and mechanisms to navigate complex power relations in the field. That said, these particular frameworks often reinforce gender and sexual categories even as they seek to redefine categorical structures. As of yet, such methodologies have not allowed for the rendering of gender and sexual categories as fluid embodied identities (Browne 2006, 2007a, Halberstam 2005a, Muñoz 1999). Additionally, certain feminist epistemologies and field practices stem from heteronormative social constructions and expectations (Browne 2008). My own field experiences attest to these assumptions. The story of Herminia uncovers certain challenges in the field when heteronormativity is assumed.

Recently, fixed heteronormative assumptions in space have been challenged by the emergence of queer geographical analysis. Queer geography emerged in the 1990s as what Knopp (2007a: 22) highlights '[as] a self-conscious intellectual movement ... It highlighted the hybrid and fluid nature of sexual subjectivities, and it reimagined the geographical dimensions of these accordingly.' Current queer geographies have contributed significantly to the reconceptualisation of 'queer' geographical imaginations across disciplines (for discussion see Knopp 2007a) and provide nuanced possibilities for the ways we think about and do fieldwork. A growing number of studies about complex queer identity formations in space (politics, bodies, performance, narratives, reproductions, and so on) deconstruct a multitude of normative categories and queer theory also reconceptualises the lens through which we view and contest normative categories (Binnie 1997, Brown 2004, Browne 2004, 2006, 2008, Valentine and Skelton 2003). 'Queer' is a highly contested term (Luibhéid and Cantú 2005), and as a geographer, I embrace it as a term that (re)defines non-normative categories of multiple sexual, gender and other marginalised identities as fluid. These identities are reproduced and embodied in spaces where normalisation is contested as an ontological practice. In other words, it challenges the heteronormativity that informs our way of seeing and systematically categorising life processes (Rodríguez 2003). Therefore, queer methodologies speak to redefining ontological views, which frame everyday realities that, within normative categorisations, have been rendered as marginalised, silenced and oppressed (Sandoval 2000, Haritaworn 2008). Although, this particular emphasis may also be limited in scope, since queer methodologies as they have developed within academia can run the risk of also constructing 'homonormative' categories that speak to privileged white gay experiences (Puar 2002). 'Queer' sensibilities are theorised and understood through lenses that are largely academic, western, white, and privileged. Binnie (2007: 34) writes that this homonormativity is characterised by,

> the increasing visibility and power of affluent white gay men (which) has been accompanied by the marginalisation of the politics of both lesbian feminism and sex radicalism, and has highlighted the exclusions within queer communities on the basis of race, class, gender and disability.

Given this limitation of queer epistemology, how can we understand and reconstruct practices in the field that do not exclude or marginalise 'queer' of colour sensibilities? These identities are always in the process of being and becoming and thus queer theory alone fails to provide a framework which explores Latino immigrant queer experiences like Herminia's.

While trying to understand 'queer' Latino immigrant spaces of flexibility, it is also necessary to grapple with the notion that 'queer' is not a translatable term in Spanish (Rodríguez 2003). As Viteri (2008) suggests, Latinos in the United States with transnational border crossing identities often understand 'queer' to be associated with white and therefore in conflict with their own Latino identities.

The street vendors in my study that self-disclosed as lesbian (only after I disclosed my own queer identity) did not know or understand the meaning of queer and, since I could not translate the term, they did not use it to describe themselves. However, 'queer' became my own lens of understanding their way of flexing heteronormative space. Although, Herminia will not call her practices 'queer', she describes herself as 'being' in non-normative space by affirming '*no soy derecha* [I am not straight[2]]'. Thus, the 'queer' gaze is my own and not Herminia's. It is no surprise that 'queer' often equates with white by Latino immigrants in the US, as this mirrors contemporary criticism of queer theory as an academic project directed (created) by overwhelmingly white scholars (Binnie 2007, Eng et al. 2005). I would argue that while there are possible omissions and misunderstandings by using a 'queer' lens, this gaze renders visible spatial practices that would have been rendered invisible otherwise.

I suggest that queer of colour critiques arise to question white queer sensibilities as well as the white queer understandings of 'queer' voices of the marginalised other. Queer of colour epistemologies, such as Gloria Anzaldua's *Queer Mestizaje* (1999), Luibheid and Cantu's *Queer Migrations* (2005) and Ferguson's *Queer of Color Critique* (2004), among other contemporary works, enable us to reconfigure fluid racialised, sexualised and gendered methodological constructions in the field. Queer of colour epistemologies offer (also with limitations) a more expansive framework for understanding the fluid constructions of race, class, gender, sexuality and ethnicity in space and place. Queer of colour methodology can facilitate understandings of 'pseudo' heteronormative spaces as fluid temporal queer space, such as the production of Latino street vending landscapes, thus, including multiple positionalities, identities and perspectives of the marginalised 'other' in gendered, classed and racialised spaces. Hence immigrant queer spaces contain messy, fluctuating, multiple trans-border identities, that can be made visible only through flexible field practices.

Invisible Latino Queer Spaces

The story of Herminia is not unlike thousands of Latina immigrants who reconfigure public space into informal economic landscapes. Street vending in Los Angeles is reconfigured, organised, and supported through the daily practices of Mexican and Central American immigrant women street vendors. Street vending is seen as unskilled work but it involves complex mechanisms of human capital development to deal with the daily economic challenges. Women vendors tend to be entrepreneurially savvy; they are constantly reinventing and reconfiguring vending practices while also performing 'street-childcare' and accessing networks on the street. In addition, women vendors navigate complex systematic vending

---

2 This is the literal translatation of *derecha*. Where as 'queer' is untranslatable 'straight' is less problematic.

practices and constraints not only set forth by the state and its apparatus, but also by local gang members who claim rights to public space (see Muñoz 2008). Most research on the informal economy describes street vending as an economic activity of last resort. In this way, street vending is conceptualised as a simple survival strategy situated outside the standard system. Because women are shut-out of formal employment opportunities, they turn to selling their wares on the streets. Yet, women vendors have proven to have agency and choice, not only in terms of their formal and informal employment choices but also the agency they have in reconfiguring the craft of street vending as part of their economic strategies (Muñoz 2008).

For the past five years I have formally and informally collected research related to the production of informal economic street vending landscapes in Los Angeles. In particular, my interest focused on Latinas' reconstructing of public space as informal economic spaces in Latino neighbourhoods. Through qualitative methodologies, I conducted 'field' ethnographies using oral histories, participatory observation, interviews, photo-documentation[3] and photo-elicitation.[4] As a researcher, I knew that entering the 'field' was in a way entering a part of my own everyday lived spaces. At the time, I was living in a Latino immigrant neighbourhood in Los Angeles, which also served as one of my research sites. I did not choose to live there because it would be a great experience immersing myself in the field, nor to somehow legitimise my research; it was where my social networks 'placed' me. I rented a storefront, illegally converted into an apartment, owned by a relative of my sister's mother-in-law. The apartment, although with various apparent code violations, was an affordable option in a neighbourhood that, like for many of my neighbours, felt familiar; in more ways than one it felt like 'home'.

My personal background is inextricably linked not only to the vendors in my study but also with the spatial complexities of my everyday life, as my grandmother was a migrant worker who crossed the Tijuana-San Diego border undocumented. She worked full-time in cannery factories in San Jose, California, and part-time as a fruit vendor. I remember accompanying her while she sold (primarily) strawberries in her Mexican neighbourhood. I grew up in Mexico where purchasing food from vendors was an everyday practice. I would purchase food from vendors outside

---

3   Photo-documentation is one mode of visual representation used here to understand complex relational processes that are displayed in the same place, at the same time, and for comparing different time intervals as well. Street vending landscapes are extremely mobile in nature. The vendors are always dependent on moving, lest they be shut down by city code enforcers. Also, customers, new vendors, and 'street childcare' are all part of this moving and variable landscape.

4   Photo-elicitation is a method that serves as a way of flexing power relations between the researcher who is photo-documenting the landscape, and the subject who is being photo-documented. Photo-elicitation was used as a tool to extract further information beyond gathering data orally, or capturing data not disclosed in the interview, while involving the participants in the analysis of the visual data. The subjects' interpretations and perspectives speak via their own explanations of their recorded landscape.

my school, after church on Sundays, on holidays, outside clubs and bars, and on the beach and in the parks. Once I arrived in Los Angeles, I would purchase food from vendors that worked on my block. I established a friendly relationship with some of the women vendors, long before I started collecting data for this study. I was a 'regular' to the vendors on my street who not only sold prepared foods, but also fruits and vegetables. My identity is shaped by transnational migratory spatial practices; the continuous border crossings with my family in search of work inevitably resulted in an interrupted education experience and negotiations of living in new immigrant receiving communities on the United States side of the border. As I negotiated cross border spaces, I did not prioritise my own queer identity. Thus, my identity as a 'queer' feminist intersects in conflicting ways with my identity as a cross-border Chicana. Herminia's disclosure invited me to create more fluid and flexible ways of seeing. My normative gender performance, often a privilege, does prioritise certain embodied identities over others. This moment gave me an opportunity and a challenge to reconceptualise my lens as a researcher. Unless I am in explicit 'queer' spaces, I usually represent an embodied straight Chicana immigrant identity while I navigate hetero-normative spaces.

My ability to speak Spanish with a 'Mexican' accent also 'placed' my identity with the Mexican street vendors as a community member. This was not entirely the case with vendors from El Salvador and often it took me longer to establish trust with women vendors from Central America. I had a couple of uncomfortable incidents in which vendors from El Salvador, after hearing me speak, accused me of collecting information for the police. It was only after I spent time as a participant observer that they consented to the interviews. In Melissa Gilbert's research (1994), the participants were all women, and Gilbert notes that what set her apart was not gender but her own privileged position as a white academic. I would argue that in my particular case, as described earlier, I did not feel that racial and class privileges set me apart from the women I interviewed, but my apparent ethnicity/nationality did. It was the fact that I spoke Spanish with a Mexican accent that brought to light the silent ethnic conflicts and sentiments that some Mexicans and Central Americans have in Los Angeles. This is similar to what Gillian Rose (1997) describes, as her middle-class English accent set her apart from her interviewee who was male and Scottish. The sentiments are deeper than simple gender and ethnic differences however; there are multiple, complex layers of historical experiences that shaped my research study of immigrant experiences in the settlement and transmigration processes. For instance, immigrants from El Salvador, who migrated to the United States via a step-migration process, often encountered difficulties in crossing the southern border of Mexico, where many immigrants suffered atrocities at the hands of Mexican officials and civilians (Hamilton and Chinchilla 2001, Menjivar 2000). Also, the settlement processes in Los Angeles can be a point of conflict among Central Americans and Mexicans, since the Latino immigrants who settled in the Los Angeles metropolitan area prior to the 1980s were predominantly Mexican. Hence, the Central American immigrants' context of reception was, in a way, shaped by the existing, longstanding generations of Mexicans living in Southern California (Menjivar 2000). Amelia, a street vendor from El Salvador that sells 'popusas', a traditional delicacy from her region (thick, handmade corn tortillas shaped and stuffed with cheese, pork, or beans, among other ingredients), said in an interview that while she personally does not dislike Mexicans in her neighbourhood, her family members make fun of her for having Mexican friends. She added that it is always a negotiation with her family to justify her choice of partners if they are Mexican.

While I was reflective in the field about the complex layers of socio-economic, cultural, and racialised processes that shape and inform street vending and how language, regional accent and transnational immigrant identity formation would provide a framework in which to think about my field methods, I was not prepared (at first) to uncover multiple ways in which street-vending landscapes informed 'queer' practices that shape, restrict and flex street vending in heteronormative spaces. I was, however, conscious that as a Latina immigrant whose identity is shaped by trans-border experiences (much like the participants in my study) I had to be aware that it was not my story I was telling, it was the vendors', while also knowing that I could not completely remove myself from the research. This process required me to be constantly reflective in the field about my own positionality. I became aware that I, a Latina with trans-border identities like the participants in my study, was actively and dialectically co-producing data with the subject participants (Haritaworn 2008). How I collected, edited and analysed the data was not void of my own ontological assumptions. I knew that some of the vendors that sold on my block were going to connect with me, but not on issues of sexuality. I was aware that I needed to negotiate my queer identity in 'straight' Latino public spaces in the same manner I negotiate it in my everyday life. Being queer is linked to my academic identity, but it is negotiated differently in my own Latino communities. If I wanted to conduct fieldwork in my own community, I needed to constantly negotiate and prioritise certain fluid identities over others to minimise barriers. I am clear that my own normative gender performance embodies 'straight' privilege, as I am also clear that my Mexican accent in some instances created barriers with vendors from El Salvador. This attests to the complexities of negotiating multiple identities in the field. Being Mexican both created barriers and opened doors, and my gender performance did the same. Thus, queer of colour methodology helped me re-frame the analysis to acknowledge how I, as well as the participants in my study, was complicit in producing the 'pseudo' hetero-normative Mexican trans-border imaginaries that shapes Latino vending street-scapes in Los Angeles.

As stated earlier, gendered street-vending practices, as well as public-space in Latino neighbourhoods in Los Angeles, are heteronormative representations that shape and inform street vending practices as well as the lives of those who create and consume these landscapes. Informal vending practices are dialectically informed by immigration and migration processes that are gendered, racialised, classed and sexualised (Pichardo 2003, Viteri 2008). When I started approaching street vendors to participate in my study, I was not entirely clear if my experiences as a granddaughter of a Latina immigrant street-vendor, and my connection to the vendors as a neighbourhood resident and customer, would be enough of a connection for the vendors to let me in. I was completely aware of my privilege as 'the researcher' and a doctoral student. I was also aware that I needed to negotiate with caution the fact that I am queer. I say this, based on my own upbringing, having been raised as a transnational child, and having all of my family reside in Mexico. I have personally experienced in present day Mexico a level of invisibility and un-familiarity of queer women. In the Mexican imaginary, narratives regarding homosexuality (since queer is not precisely a translatable term), are overwhelmingly representations of homosexual men. The representations of the *puto* and *maricon* (the effeminate male character) proliferate in Mexican social constructions of homosexuality. Female homosexuality is still invisible, relegated to exist mostly in private spaces, and in some cases considered socially immoral and punished by social marginalisation. Chicana lesbians are considered *malinchistas*, or traitors, to our culturally and religiously assigned gender roles of mother and wife (Anzaldúa 1999). The notion of the *marimacha*, the butch 'maria', is the most dominant representation of Lesbians in Latino communities and is still considered a derogatory term (Rodríguez 2003). Although, there are spaces where queer women actively create communities, particularly in large urban spaces, they are still largely invisible in public spaces. In Latino immigrant communities in Los Angeles, queer women are present but their public embodiment of their queerness is for the most part invisible. Private spaces however, are constantly (re) negotiated and (re)constructed to embody the multiple fluid identities of Latina immigrants. Vendors like Herminia, take part in the reproduction of socially constructed heteronormativity in the ways she lives and performs in both her home and work-space.

This was true for me earlier on in my field research as I realised I would have to navigate assumptions and expectations of heteronormativity. It became clear to me that heteronormative discourses were informed differently among men and women vendors, although in many situations they enforced the same expectations. Often, in search of social connections, both male and female vendors asked me about my 'husband' or 'children' which implied that I was straight and/or a mother. I am neither; thus I disappointed some vendors who then would volunteer words of encouragement to comfort me, as Lupe a Latina street-vendor stated 'no te preocupes, ahorita estudia, cuando termines veras que te encuentras un buen hombre y te casas [don't worry, now just study, when you finish you will see that you will find a good man and you will get married].' Even male street vendors would provide opinions based on my unmarried status. Don Luis a street vendor whom I got to know very well, would reassure me that 'a ti te han de sobrar pretendientes no? ... que diera por tener un hijo soltero de tu edad [you must have a surplus of men courting you? ... what would I give to have a son your age ...]'. Interviewing male vendors proved to have more barriers than interviewing women vendors. The male vendors were eager to 'help' me by allowing me to interview them; they were friendly and they would say how proud they were that I, a fellow

Mexican, was enrolled at the university. They called my work 'homework', taking pride in the fact that they could help me with it. Most of the men talked at length about their hard work, dreams, and stories from 'back home'. Yet, when asked about paying rent to local gang members for protection, not one of them admitted doing so, even though the female vendors confided in me that they did. Culturally, I interpreted this negation to the male vendors not wanting to show me (being female and Mexican) weakness on their part. In addition, the male vendors emphasised their success and ability to sustain their families economically and talked less about their struggles than the women did. Most women vendors were very forthcoming about their struggles, fears, abuses, and disappointments, much more so than the male vendors. With these obvious barriers based on cultural gender identity constructions, I was hesitant to further complicate interactions by disclosing my queer identity or asking questions that would 'queer' the interview.

Also, these particular statements are produced by heteronormative gender dynamics that define gender and family structure in 'imagined' Mexican families (Hodagneu-Sotelo 1994, 2001, Rodriguez 2003). I say imagined, because the everyday lives of Mexican immigrants in Los Angeles break with such gender expectations that are often more romanticised than real. That is, stories of men migrating alone or with their families dominate; despite the fact women have continually crossed the United States – Mexican border in search of work, single and not necessarily leaving a child or a husband behind. These imagined narratives construct transnational migratory identities (Hondagneu-Sotelo 1994, Hamilton and Chinchilla 2001). Mexican women have also migrated to the north of Mexico to work in maquilas without a male counterpart (Bank-Munoz 2008), and there are a number of Mexican immigrant women living in Los Angeles who are queer, lesbian, out, activist, closeted, living dual lives, etc., whose gender processes shape the everyday reality of immigrant women. My reaction to questions or statements posed by the vendors about my non-married status, were also informed by the imagined narratives that constructed my own expectations of public space in immigrant neighbourhoods. Hence, I constructed questions for my interviews to uncover the ways in which Latina street vendors (re)create vending landscapes. The feminist methodological framework I utilised when I first entered the field was a reflection of my own perspective and investment as a researcher that shared an immigrant-transnational identity with the Latino vendors in my study. I also was convinced (at the time) that being queer was a private identity and that it was being brown, Chicana, bilingual and bicultural that constituted the important connections I had with the vendors in my study. I perceived that my queerness had nothing to do with vending landscapes as I also interpreted them as heteronormative spaces. It was comfortable to be Chicana, bilingual, bicultural, transnational in these spaces, yet it was Herminia's story that disrupted the romanticised heteronormative construction of Mexican imagined narratives that allowed me to see that my methodological lens was limited. In other words, I too separated, like Herminia, my personal life from my work life.

Reflecting on this, I ask what would it have looked like if I had challenged the narratives provided by the vendors in my study and consequently disclosed my own queer identity? Would I have understood the production of Latino vending landscapes in other ways? I did have the opportunity to find out with Latina vendors. I was only able to retrieve information that Herminia sold outside Latino gay bars because I disclosed I was queer. For the previous three years, I had only interviewed Herminia during the day when she sold in the garment district to garment workers south of downtown Los Angeles. This new gaze allowed me to understand the negotiations of selling in queer spaces at night, which led me to different interpretations of the space. Herminia has personal connections to selling outside gay Latino bars; she is Latina, an immigrant and lesbian. She also sold outside one of the few gay bars that cater to Latina immigrants on certain days of the week; her choice to sell in that particular sidewalk at night is more complicated than a safe/unsafe dichotomy. It was not until I disclosed my queer identity that Heminia supplemented her story with details omitted in previous interviews. Without this information I would have interpreted her everyday economic life choices differently. This new information reframed all the data in ways that attest to multiple fluid positionalities, subjectivities and identities in space.

What does my experience as a researcher tell us about how we construct a queer methodology when we are conducting research in a 'pseudo' heteronormative space and with perceived heterosexual subjects? When I disclosed as a queer of colour researcher, doors opened to information I could not have accessed if I was a researcher who was not conscious of the possibilities of queer presence in these landscapes. Yet, based on the complexity of racial, ethnic and class privilege constructions of the home countries of the participants in my study, would it have been easier for Latina vendors to talk to 'white' female researchers they read as not *derecha* (straight)? Was it that I served as a mirror for my participants, as the vendors where a mirror to myself, therefore both of us end up being complicit in the construction of heteronormative public space? It was only after my visit to Herminia's apartment that she opened up about her selling at night outside Latino gay bars and that she also frequented a 'ladies night' in the same bar. Herminia stated '[vender] afuera de los bares gay's pues no hay peligro si hay puro maricon [[selling] outside the gay bars, there is no danger since there are only "faggots"]'.

Heminia's statement about selling in 'queer spaces' reifies the constructions of the male homosexual from 'back home' as representations of 'maricones' as effeminate males, and emasculating gay Mexican men as not being 'machos' or simply not being 'real' men and therefore gendering the sidewalks. Herminia also states that ('no hay peligro') 'there is no danger' selling in sidewalks outside Latino gay bars. For Herminia, selling there is safe because she perceives that she will not be a victim of gay bashing. However, her choice of selling in an obvious queer space was also about feeling connected to the space. In her own words,

> Yo se que hay otros lugares a donde ir en dias que son para las mujeres, pero como que no son para nosotras son de otra clase ... ahi es donde van nuestras

amigas que son lesbianas tambien, aunque se llena de vestidas, pero hasta ellas son como mujeres no? la verdad que otro lugar asi no hay por aqui [I know there are other gay bars that have ladies night, but these are not for us these are from another class ... there [the Latino immigrant bar] is where our lesbian friends also go, although it fills with drag queens, but they are also like women no? to tell you the truth there are no other places like that around here].

Herminia and Maria frequent the bar on 'ladies night', where they have built a community and network outside their private space. Although lesbian or 'women' queer spaces in Los Angeles County are not invisible in cities like West Hollywood, a 'gay city' or in the media (such as *The L Word* – a lesbian drama on Showtime based in West Hollywood), these are spaces of not only class privilege but white privilege. In these spaces Latina immigrants like Herminia are only represented as flower vendors and/or bathroom attendants. Certainly, queer spaces as spaces occupied by other than gay white males are understudied. Even studies on the invisibility of lesbian spaces often create an archetypal 'Lesbian' who is devoid of race, and/or ethnicity (Podmore 2006).

Herminia also talked about sharing the bar on 'ladies night' with drag queens. Her statement that drag queens are 'like' women identifies the space as female centred and thus safer. However, Herminia's experiences of safe space for women are complicated. In Latino gay bars she feels connected to drag queens who she understands as biologically male. It is in heteronormative vending spaces that are considered masculine that she also feels the most uncomfortable being not *derecha*. In one space – the bar – she is safe as a woman and safe being not *derecha*, in the other space – street vending landscapes – she only feels safe if she performs as a gender conforming Latina. She flexes her identity in both spaces for economic reasons but in the bar she has a sense of belonging. The invisibility of these queer spaces (gay bars) in Latino neighbourhoods makes them safe spaces. Unlike 'lesbian nights' or 'ladies nights' in non immigrant gay bars, the gay bars in Latino immigrant neighbourhoods that cater to women one day of the week tend to be invisible in the landscape to both the white queer gaze and 'straight' Latinos. Thus, they are 'free' from both the racism that sometimes accompany the white queer gaze and the homophobia that sometimes accompany the Latino gaze. That invisibility is an extension of the same social constructions that create street vending landscapes as perceived heteronormative space.

Conclusion

Through the story of vendors like Herminia, who embodies her gender and sexuality in the streets differently than at home, I discovered how performance is rooted in the imagined Mexican identity that informs vending landscapes in Los Angeles. However, this multiple spatial embodied performance is not limited to Herminia or other Latina vendors who create multiple fluid identities in work and at home I, as a researcher, also prioritised particular identities in specific spaces. When conducting research, I was performing my Latina, Chicana, brown, immigrant, transnational, Mexican identity, while making a conscious choice not to disclose my queer identity. It seemed clear to me at the outset that from the multiple complex historical layers I would have to negotiate with vendors in the street (such as language, regionalism, national identity, class and gender to say the least), my queer identity would be an added barrier. However, Herminia proved that my queer identity is simultaneously a barrier *and* an opening to multiple ways of seeing. Thus, it was reflexivity and openness to possibilities beyond my expectations that allowed invisible spaces to become visible. By re-framing the methodology in the field and disclosing my multiple identities to some vendors, I was able to see the 'queer' Latino street-scape.

So what possibilities and limitations do queer of colour methodologies offer? First, I must say that at this point there are more questions than answers. Drawing on the story of Hermina and my own experiences in the field, I would argue that queer of colour methodology goes beyond deconstructing heteronormative discourse. 'Queer' often results in constructing homonormative, white, western queer epistemologies. By expanding the possibilities of queer of colour subjectivities, which are largely marginalised, excluded and silenced, I call to understand and reconstruct practices in the field. Those re-shaped practices are informed by queer sensibilities of people of colour, whose identities and spatial practices are always incomplete.

Second, queer of colour methodology can expand the possibilities of further accepting and understanding that researchers co-create data with their subjects, thus adjusting the lens so that multiple ways of 'knowing' and 'being' become visible. Through my own field experiences, I became aware that I was not divorced from co-creating the data. This realisation helped me re-frame the analysis to acknowledge how I, as well as the participants in my study, were complicit in producing 'pseudo' heteronormative Mexican trans-border imaginaries. This process, although messy, complex and fluid, requires us as researchers to better understand 'queer' of colour sensibilities in space and across borders.

Finally, I want to emphasise the importance of the work being done within queer of colour critique in its challenging of white queer deconstruction of heteronormativity, pointing out how it excludes the marginalised racialised 'other', and thus reinforcing homonormative privilege. They have also called to transform and reconfigure fluid racialised, sexualised and gendered epistemologies therefore rendering visible the marginalised 'other'. Yet, limitations still arise while utilising a queer of colour critical lens. Can only researchers of colour use this lens? Is there a way to construct 'queer' methodologies while conducting research in heteronormative spaces where there is no apparent 'queer' subject? I proceed with caution in order not to suggest that everything is 'queer', yet I do suggest that heteronormative space is not absent of queer social constructions. Thus, spaces we perceived to be heteronormative are actually 'pseudo' heteronormative. By challenging my own social constructions, (reified by my own Mexican imaginaries)

I opened up to the possibilities of uncovering and reconstructing flexibilities of everyday lived spaces. The journey I embarked on in the field was necessary for me to uncover that when Herminia's 'queer' identity is invisible in the landscape so is mine.

Chapter 4

The 'Outness' of Queer: Class and Sexual Intersections

Yvette Taylor

Introduction

Queer theory and methodology has been associated with explorations of difference and the contestation of rigid categories and normalising discourses and practices, speaking instead of the fluidity of spaces and identities in the process of always 'becoming' (Browne 2008, Haritaworn 2008, see also Heckert this volume). While queer theory has sought to undermine universalisms and meta-narratives, its frequent failure is in unpacking intersecting material dimensions, with the result that the resources through which sexual selves can be known and articulated are effaced. As the field of sexualities studies expands and becomes increasingly diversified, queer could usefully engage in a more empirically-grounded focus on material inequality. Yet, class is not a 'difference' which can be easily incorporated into a queer framework, where notions of deconstruction sit uneasily alongside that which often is still not named, complicating ideas of (sexual) multiplicity and situatedness. Queer itself may also be guilty of making uneasy generalisations and exclusions (Haritaworn 2007, Puar 2007, Heaphy 2008), problematically, and ironically, centring the most privileged. If a critique of queer (theoretically) has provided such an assessment, the challenge methodologically is how to research and illuminate such dynamics and, specifically here, to put class into such considerations, alongside sexuality.

In still struggling with (research) articulations, I'd like to explore the 'critical differentials' (Gabb 2001) in processes and experiences of 'being' and 'becoming'. To do so I raise questions, from a methodological and theoretical concern, about who gets to 'be'; which versions of ourselves (sexual or classed) get to speak and who can have voice and legitimacy within this (Adkins 2002, Skeggs 2003)? I aim to focus upon the substantive – and frequently neglected – issue of intersecting sexual and classed lives as holding promise for developing queer methodologies. While the sexual subject has frequently been deemed the central focus of queer research, where a queer methodology may be understood as that deployed by/ for/with queers, there is scope to extend its focus, asking what is to be gained or lost in searching beyond queer's direct reference to the sexual. Queer approaches have arguably reinforced rather than challenged such specificity, failing to place conceptualisations of 'queer' within the social landscape inhabited by, and illuminated through attention to, social actors and their material realities (see Haritaworn 2007).

Methodologically, my concern is in making visible, the utilisation of 'stories' or, conversely, the absence of (legitimate) tales, where the 'ordinariness' of privilege can also be made visible in such articulations and silences. This seems a concern of, yet a failing within, queer research where the classing of sexual subjectivities and materialities has largely gone un-interrogated. And in this chapter I suggest that queer could usefully re-orientate itself to a more empirically-grounded focus on material (im)possibilities. Theoretically, this challenges explorations of 'difference' as formulated within queer scholarship, and while some (sexual and classed) subjects may be in a reflexive process of always 'becoming', for others the categories of sexuality and class are experienced as unequal and far from fluid. 'Stratifying homosexualities' are empirically demonstrated here in the ways that (middle)classed subjects can speak in voices that are heard, achieving mobility, subject-hood and even 'ordinariness' which may not be all that queer.

In this chapter, I draw upon my research on lesbian and gay parents from working and middle-class backgrounds to situate the complexities, complications, and important intersections emerging from absences in queer agendas. I include empirical data in the form of participants' narratives in demonstration of the methodological issues detailed above, regarding the concern with dangerous absences and the foregrounding of 'reflexivity' within sexuality studies. When the 'straight and narrow' version of parenting continues to circulate, where deviance is still projected onto – and responded in – lesbian and gay parenting narratives and experiences, even in the context of social, cultural and legal change, the question is who can resource and achieve mobility, subject-hood and even 'ordinariness'? How should these processes be understood and situated within feminist and queer methodologies? Rather than solely highlighting my own positionings, I aim to situate intersections of class and sexuality within the interview encounters and narratives themselves; this is where positionality can be politically situated, rather than personally repeated in situating myself alone. Such a situation surpasses and opposes a queer framework and the (dis)engagements within this framework are elaborated upon throughout.

Class and Sexuality

While much has been written of the dangers of ignoring class in researching and theorising sexuality, it remains somewhat sidelined and absent in contemporary work on sexualities, which has weighty consequences for the understandings and knowledges produced (for exceptions see Skeggs 2001, McDermott 2004, Moran 2000, Taylor 2007, 2009b). The reluctance to acknowledge the significance of social class to sexual lives hides inequalities in experiences, practices and meanings of everyday lesbian, gay, bisexual and transgender (LGBT) lives. As a consequence, the academy tends to reproduce a middle-class LGBT experience as universal – rarely has such privilege been made visible or 'deconstructed', absent too from 'queer' accounts of sexual fluidity and change. In this context, Plummer's (1998: 612) call for the need to research 'stratifying homosexualities' is relevant indeed; yet while queer research has illuminated sexual subjectivities, imaginings and practices, it has rarely attended to the stratification of sexualities, particularly in terms of the interconnection between class and sexuality, where queer scholarship may also be guilty of making uneasy generalisations and exclusions (Heaphy 2008). Like Weeks et al. (2001) and Clarke (2001) I seek to be attentive to the socio-historical circumstances allowing for and necessitating a critique of the limitations in sexuality studies. This involves looking critically at how queer research in its aspiration to undermine normative constructions in drawing up the 'outsider position' from which it formulates its critical stance, may ignore the implicatedness queer has in establishing its own norms, boundaries and 'outness'.

In this chapter I aim to point towards some of the dangers of ignoring class in queer methodologies; empirical data is presented in order to best illuminate presences and absences, interrogating 'who gets to talk', who and what is rendered (in)visible in sexualities studies. I focus on the interconnections between class and sexuality in the telling of 'selves' in the interview encounter, probing at whose story holds weight and value; I demonstrate this in the presentation of interview data based on in-depth interviews with lesbian and gay parents from both middle-class and working-class backgrounds. The issue of 'who gets to talk' is partly about what we ask, as researchers, and to whom and why – from the questions we construct to where we go to 'find' our interviewees: the fascination with how I 'found them' (working-class lesbians), however, suggests a (dis)location between lives included against those still excluded, even as this exclusion is 'intriguing' (Taylor 2004). The movement here from research practice, the interview encounter, and academic dissemination extends my concern with who gets to talk – and who gets listened to, moving from a specific methodological approach and 'moment' to the general creation of academic knowledge.

Consider why, when presenting my own research, the polite yet slightly subdued nods received when stating 'Working-class' are met with decidedly more enthusiastic ones when I finish my seemingly contradictory and definitely confusing statement with 'lesbians'? This enacted separation, occurring between a nod in the right direction, a wink of approval and a gasp of doubt, wrongly detaches these terms. 'Who gets to talk', to be heard and legitimised (or not) is revealed in such conversational cut-offs (Taylor 2005). However, I resist the temptation to write-in all of these moments as personal slights emphasising instead the value of interrogating such moments as research encounters, and arguing for reflexivity in (research) *practice*, rather than a reflexivity in *being* (a researcher), where researchers' frustrations and 'movements' are foregrounded at the expense of the 'researched' (Adkins 2002, Skeggs 2002). The sole 'situation' of the researcher is often over-done and in probing at whose story has weight, I will include interrogation of my own positioning and investments – this is certainly relevant, yet 'where I am' in this chapter may also be viewed as deliberately 'absent' at times, where my methodological commitments push me to present my *findings*. I was indeed present in constructing research questions, in undertaking the fieldwork, in analysing the results and I include this as a methodological issue, pervading research design and outcomes, rather than solely as a reflexive self-positioning. Where research provides the spaces for lives to be narrated, it should be attentive to the opening and closing of dialogue, to the classing of 'talk' and to the subject positions mobilised or refused in and beyond the interview encounter.

Queer and Feminist Methodologies

Feminist researchers within the social sciences have long developed methodologies addressing debates about sensitivity, values and ethics, researcher 'status' and position, and the relationship between the researcher and the researched. The risk in easy replacement of the 'feminist' with the 'queer' is the dismissal of complications where gains and intersections are lost in misrepresentation and invested struggles in declaring whose side you are on: 'feminist' or 'queer'? This question has been posed, and variously answered, in attempts to intersect feminist and queer theory; the 'intersection' being disputed, theoretically and methodologically, with the 'queered' disciplines situated in the humanities rather than social sciences (Richardson et al. 2006). My purpose here is not to extensively chart the theoretical 'outness', and exclusion of queer theory, since this has been commented on elsewhere (Jackson 1999, 2001, Ahmed 2004, Taylor 2005); in fact readers may not find this chapter to be a particularly queer one and this situation is both awkward and deliberate (and I will return to this).

In teasing out similarities, compatibilities and intersections between feminist and queer theory, such a project itself must deal with past, and ongoing, dichotomies and hostilities, lashed out on both sides of the theoretical fence. The purpose of breaching such a fence lies in the extension of political possibilities, but may also require giving up 'old certainties', and losing a comforting, entitled confidence –such as the notion that I automatically have a good feminist empathy, even 'insider status'. Yet the critique of universalising (feminist) research agendas depicts feminist theory, methods and politics as naively innocent, unable to theorise complication or multiplicity; as the inadequate and replaceable predecessor of a later, more complex and developed queer theory.

My purpose here is not to lay absolute claims to such concerns as feminist and/or queer; in re-visiting such re-runs the trick, methodologically, may in fact lie in not being bound by claims, concessions and negations but rather to find a way through, around and with identities, experiences and practices (Taylor 2009a). Arguably this contests and extends the research of feminist and queer methodologies. I start with my own (dis)identifications and (mis)positioning, though these, like the investment in 'for' or 'against' certainties, come with a weight, an expectation: an (awkward) 'story to tell'.

Stories to Tell? Situated Selves

I have been somewhat guarded in writing this piece on queer methodologies, sniffing out the authoritative academic air and considering whether such a piece would carry or fall flat, whether it would be a useful addition or a personalised 'moan', where I have already taken up considerable, complaining space (Taylor 2007). What had I to add with my research on classed and sexual lives? (And when was I going to put that particular project to rest, to get on with something more 'new' and 'interesting'?) Identities and inequalities are frequently and variously cast as embellishments or deletions, the component parts of 'class', 'gender' and 'sexuality' to be added or scored out in furthering sociological agendas (Skeggs 1997, Hennessy 2000, Jackson 2001). While it is relatively easy to paint a picture of myself as a mere observer of these debates such a portrayal both ignores and highlights my own professional and personal positioning and implicatedness within this. The intersections that I chart in my research are also personal passions and pains, unsolved by the rolling of eyes, academic or otherwise. This is why it has been both difficult and easy for me to talk about class, and for that matter, sexuality: I am simultaneously positioned as entitled and unentitled to capitalise upon such 'past' experiences; what right do I as an academic have to talk about class inequalities, to lay claim to a working-class identity? Another possible issue is that the 'sexuality' part in this connected experience is seen as relatively unproblematic and such separation makes re-connection difficult, as does the assignment of some experiences to the past and the foregrounding of others to the present.

This is not, however, meant solely as personalised confession, whereby research reflexivity is achieved in 'coming out' on paper. Skeggs (2002) argues for the turning away from self-telling, and authorising oneself (being), in order to instead prioritise research reflexivity in practice (doing), albeit noting that lesbian, gay and feminist politics have used similar self-telling strategies in order to make political claims. The classing of such 'stories' is crucial here to her contention where it becomes 'a matter of positioning and access to the means of telling. It is also about the ability to be heard' (2002: 352). Feminist research has insisted on practices that involve a 'self-situating' to avoid over-arching universalism, yet an easy insertion of identity ('lesbian', 'working-class') may risk replacing critique of the resources required to tell (legitimate) stories, tending towards 'self-promotion' rather than signalling responsibility and accountability in and throughout research(ing). Adkins (2002) also reiterates this point, critiquing the misplacement of researchers' introspective reflexivity as signalling 'good' research, positioned against a 'bad' lack. Such an approach, for Adkins, posits 'a mobile relation to identity on the side of the knower in relation to the known' (2002: 340) which fails to consider uneven distributions of reflexivity in relation to class and gender.

LGBT accounts have been situated in the reflexive individualisation thesis proposed by Giddens (1991, 1992) and Beck (1992) where the self is (re)made under conditions of choice, fluidity and 'risk': 'we are, not what we are, but what we make of ourselves' (Giddens 1991: 75, see also Heaphy 2008). This idea of the reflexive self may be over emphasised, centring the experiences of the privileged (Skeggs 1997, Adkins 2002). Similarly, the positioning of individuals as 'reflexive' is one which does not acknowledge that reserves necessary for the making of the 'self' are unequally distributed: 'the resources required for self-fashioned and 'empowered' sexualities are underestimated' (Heaphy 2008: 2). In this assessment, Heaphy suggests that LGBT research valorises and reaffirms an exclusive experience, generating normative assumptions of universal sexual subjectivity as self-making and self-determined. This fails to engage with the power-based differentials of, for example, social class. In seeking to situate selves and engage with the multiplicity that queer invites, I will now therefore seek to attend to the 'complexities' and 'complications' in articulating varied – and unequal – positions.

Complexities and Complications

This section draws upon data from the British Academy funded project 'What would the parents say?' based upon 60 in-depth interviews with lesbian (n=46) and gay (n=14) parents in the UK, aiming to draw attention to 'who gets to talk' and the ways these voices are rendered legitimate – or otherwise: what stories can be heard, what resources are required to sustain their articulation, what stories are excluded and at what expense? The sample ranged from 18-63 years old, with approximately half of interviewees identifying as 'working-class' and half as 'middle-class' (see Taylor 2009a). Broadly, the project explores intersections between class and sexuality in lesbians' and gay men's experiences of parenting and the everyday practices and pathways navigated therein, from initial routes into parenting and household divisions of labour, to location preferences, schooling choice and community supports (Taylor 2009b). It seeks to situate parents as both sexual *and* classed subjects, interrogating the relevance, transmission and accumulation of class and sexual (dis)advantages, highlighting both a challenge for – and an engagement in – queer methodologies.

Although a now growing field, much current work on lesbian and gay kinship still overlooks the significance of socio-economic status (Weston 1991, Bernstein and Reimann 2001, Sullivan 2001). Even where there has been attention to gendered dynamics and constraints, class, as a crucial component of parental 'choice' and experience, has been neglected (Gabb 2004, 2005, Ryan-Flood 2005, Lindsay et al. 2006). This research is situated between unconnected and competing positions; frequently lesbian and gay families are positioned at the vanguard of transformations in intimacy while often still empirically absent in such declarations: they are misplaced in this dual over-emphasis (as agents of social change) and sidelining (under-investigated when compared to the research on heterosexual families). Such a critique in itself is suggestive of the need for more empirically grounded research interrogating the 'queer tendencies' now named in relation to family change and intimate transformations (Klesse 2006).

That said, the concept of the family, however fluidly defined, continues to be both a corner stone of societal value and a yard stick against which concepts such as 'normativity' 'worth' and 'properness' can be measured and judgments made (Stacey and Biblarz 2001). The complexity of family relations has long been acknowledged, but when issues such as class and sexuality are mixed in, these already murky waters can become opaque. From the transgressive queer to the everyday 'ordinary' there is a need to avoid positing lesbian and gay families as an alternative ideal *or* as an acceptable 'norm' (Carrington 1999, Ahmed 2004). A focus on the possibilities and impossibilities which (dis)allow transgression prevents a reading and reduction of lesbian and gay parented families as transformative or assimilative for '"transgression" must be psychically, emotionally, materially, socially possible' (Ahmed 2004: 153). Here, assimilation and transgression are not choices available to individuals, easily practiced and achieved; rather they are complexly inhabited and refused, structured and reproduced.

Class and sexuality intersect in interviewees' material and subjective positionings, apparent in naming and doing family across everyday social spheres. The stories which interviewees tell of their lives are classed: where some self-position as agentic, reflexive subjects, actively transforming their lives in 'coming-out' and claiming space, others speak of the uneasy shifts in class positioning, slippages and rejections, of stepping outside the system. The ability to name, practice and resource such a side-step, a different way of being, often relies upon reserves of capitals, mobilised in occupying and securing familial territory. Where some can outline their distance from normative categorisation and practice, feeling a positive sense of difference, others sought to position firmly with the 'ordinary'; 'difference' *and* 'sameness' could be strategically claimed and rejected, but these processes were still reliant upon and reinforced a sense of the 'other' as profoundly classed. Others still are hesitant to tell their story, feeling that there is no story; this is teased out in comparing sexual lives which are always also classed. Methodologically, the case is in comparing middle-class and working-class interviewees, of putting class back in to the study of sexual lives. This speaks to complexities and complications, often explicit within queer understandings, yet strangely absent in relation to class and sexual intersections. Such methodological concerns must move beyond the dynamics of my own reflections, motivations and mis-placements, to include care and attention to the research *practice* of fieldwork, analysis and presentation.

Class is indeed complex; many have felt, known and theorised this complexity, even as class analysis is derided as simplistic, confusing and no longer relevant

(Skeggs 1997, 2003). In seeking to speak to both working-class and middle-class parents, I wanted to explore the inter-relatedness as well as the inequality between these lived in categories, between being and always becoming classed. I wanted to explore the difference of class, as a lived in, structuring experience, reproduced and ruptured in relation to sexuality. Interrogating middle-classness is difficult given its 'neutral' status, where my comparisons and contrasts between 'working-class' and 'middle-class' lives at times felt similarly difficult even disturbing. Queer discussions of 'homonormativity' often call for an interrogation of class privilege, but rarely delivers on this empirically (Haritaworn 2007, Puar 2007). In trying to interrogate this particular normative construct, I wanted to be respectful to interviewees' lives. And attentive to inequalities painfully experienced and grappled with.

In conducting this research, I have wrestled again with my own frustrations, and though I don't necessarily want to reflexively foreground these, I do want to make them explicit so that the knowledge that I construct and produce here can be situated. Such frustration frequently posed an interrogation of personal and professional positionings *vis-à-vis* interviewees (Almack 2007), particularly in relation to sexuality, gender, class and parental status (see Taylor 2009a). For example, I do not have children and such a fact at once disrupts an alignment of 'sameness' based on sexuality (see Lewin 1991, Weston 1991). In problematising 'insider status' there may be a range of significant factors that structure the differences between researcher/researched and the production of knowledge therein. These personalised disjunctures and mis-fittings can act as realisations and re-articulations of the long-standing feminist declaration of the 'personal as political', while full political engagement requires a move beyond individual placement, reflexivity – and frustration – alone. So, in highlighting the personal as (still) political I want to endorse and query this wise saying, asking who gets to talk – who can be listened to, recognised, legitimised? In other words: Whose personal?, Whose 'political' (Skeggs 2002)? These questions are posed to the queer theorist, aiming to highlight the 'outness' of queer, where queer may be guilty of generating exclusions, and erasures.

As a researcher I have been challenged by the apparent desire for 'sameness', understood not only as a desire for access to the same privileges and entitlements of heterosexual parenthood but to the same processes of legitimisation: an 'ordinariness' desired and enacted by middle-class interviewees cannot be understood as 'queer', nor perhaps can the sidelining of working-class parental experiences, also experienced through 'normative' spaces, yet constantly positioned as still 'failing' (classed and sexual) standards. Privileges, resources and entitled expectations were frequently mobilised in, for example, the securing of a 'good' school, in telling 'good' parental tales and in generally presenting as good subjects and citizens, manifest also in desires to undertake civil partnerships. To act, present and tell the self in such ways is a difficult thing to do when parenting 'credentials' are fraught and challenged in everyday encounters; once secure middle-class positions are seemingly eroded. But the classed differences here may be in their resurrection and reappearance, in and beyond the interview encounter (for these are not 'just' stories). It may well be painful to present, and be queried, as the 'proper' parent. But the knowingness, even naturalness of such proper presentations, and the materialisation of these across social spaces, did secure advantages for middle-class parents, directly speaking to (and against) queer commentary on 'homonormative' lives.[1]

Where discussion of sameness/difference has been situated between heterosexual parents and their non-heterosexual counterparts (Weston 1991), a consequential *classed* difference appears in the ways that middle-class interviewees could be 'rescued' in terms of 'just' doing things that 'make good sense', using the resources that they had and seeking to accumulate more. Rarely, if ever, are working-class parents able to easily align with such classed sentiments of 'good sense'. Nor are they able to mobilise material resources to secure and legitimise their parenting, whether that be in negotiations with social and educational providers or in movements away from – or towards – specific locations, school and communities. Below, I draw upon a case study of two interviewees' lives, deliberately avoiding a polarised picture of working-class and middle-class interviewees (such stark contrasts are, however, evident in the data). The differences that I present are also ones which I have been forced to reconsider and readdress in light of accounts of the complexity of middle-class lives, as a rarely named, 'ordinary' status.

Researching comparative classed lives forces consideration of the best methodological approaches to cast light upon connected categories (such as working-class, middle-class) as they are lived out, inhabited and re-produced. Both Valentine (2007) and McCall (2005) highlight the use of the case study approach, which seeks to take an individual's experience and then extrapolate to the broader social location embodied by an individual. This is an approach I will use in discussing the intersection of class and sexuality, hoping to illuminate the research application of 'intersectionality' and the benefits and possibilities of this for queer methodologies. The reader may judge if the intersectional efforts are mired in confusion, where intersectionality stalls and breaks down, or if the coming together of different axes of difference and inequality illuminates the mutually constituted lived-in experience of class and sexuality. While the sexual subject has been the central focus of queer research, there is scope to extend its focus, probing at what is gained in searching beyond queer's literal reference to the sexual (see for example Puar 2007 and Haritaworn 2007, 2008). Queer methodologies may seek to empirically explore the relevance of multiple positionings, normativities and intersections.

---

1 The notion of 'homonormativity' speaks critically to the developments in sexual citizenship, extending only to *certain* citizens while cementing exclusions, renewing and even heightening the boundaries of (un)acceptability between the 'dangerous queer' and the 'good homosexual' (Duggan, 2002). In other words, to be 'homonormative' is to embody the idealised version of white middle-class monogamous coupledom, where the only 'difference' is sexual status.

Privileges and Disadvantages: Across and between Social Class

Consider these two interviewees' experiences and accounts of being a lesbian mother and a gay dad: Abi's (36) and Geoff's (44) different stories cast light upon the varying privileges and disadvantages, intersecting classed, sexual and gendered (im)possibilities. These stories may be perceived as oppositional and indeed there are times when this seems the most plausible tale, a drastic difference and an evident inequality in routes into parenting and of family life more generally, buffered by, or isolated from, social supports and networks. Yet accounts are inevitably rendered more complicated, in the messy inhabitation, contestation and replication of social categories, forcing attention to the 'differences that matter' across time (Ahmed 2004). Class, gender and sexuality intersect here, where social ropes elevating status may be taken-for-granted, necessary and disappeared at different times, particularly highlighting the constructedness and contestation of 'middle-classness'. Such accounts blur the coherences of a completed narrative tale, to be neatly depicted in analysis, yet they both cast light upon stories of 'worth', stories which can be told and legitimated, even as they are hard to hear.

In using these two interviewees as case studies I wish to highlight the tangled webs navigated by Abi and Geoff, but would also like to point out that while I see the worth in considering the location embodied by these interviewees, I am also conscious that these two interviewees don't stand for all the complexities and complications in lesbian and gay parental experiences. Again, their accounts don't emerge, disembodied 'from nowhere', to be summarised in print. Of course Abi and Geoff embody a history, presence (and anticipated future) with journeys before and beyond parental pathways and such paths exemplify transitions and tensions across time, intersecting class, gender and sexuality.

Differences – and distinctions – are captured in the readable 'success' of Abi who identified as middle-class, with postgraduate qualifications and a professional career, as contrasted with the 'struggle' of Geoff who was unemployed and had experienced periods of homelessness as a result of 'coming-out' and exiting the heterosexual family unit. Not only do Abi's and Geoff's material locations differ, but their routes into parenting and their 'coming out' narratives also differ; where one is a story mostly of ease and acceptance, the other tells of secrecy and the living of a 'double life' for many years. For Geoff, the category 'gay dad' was claimed and contested throughout the interview, seemingly fractured by not being 'real' enough (a real man, a real father, a real gay man), not having been 'out' long enough, not knowing the 'right' contacts and communities, and generally not quite fitting in.

This sense of being out of place had, unfortunately, been all too realistic given a period of homelessness, following an episode of mental and physical breakdown. Geoff's sense of reaching 'breaking point' was told through the initial denial of access to his two sons, as well as through material hardships. Abi's emotional stress was perhaps no less painful or fraught on a personal level as she struggled to finance assisted insemination over an 18 month period. Her involvement in everyday childcare arrangements and schooling experiences differed from Geoff's ongoing exclusion from these areas, although, for Abi there were difficulties in establishing parental credentials to educational providers and in balancing work/care commitments with her female partner and co-parent. Privileges and disadvantages reappeared and disappeared in the negotiation of familial and institutional spheres.

Commonalities in Geoff's and Abi's accounts exist in the re-telling of mobility. For Abi, this occurred in terms of an upward mobility from what she described as a 'lower middle-class' upbringing to a financially secure 'middle-class' existence. Conversely, Geoff described a 'descent' in material terms and in familial and societal esteem, moving from a middle-class heterosexual family where he was the main breadwinner to a current single, unemployed status. The lack of employment was also explained in terms of 'getting better', demonstrating his expectation of also 'getting on' (again), contrasting perhaps from a long-term sense of fixity and despair. The pondering of how much these individuals have moved, what they have lost or gained in their travels seems somewhat of a blunt calculation, failing to capture the disturbing upheavals and everyday efforts in 'getting by'. This refocuses the material factors constraining and enabling (sexual) agency. It seems clear that Abi and Geoff came from differently (middle)classed backgrounds; for Abi this inspired a desire to live differently beyond the 'lower middle-class' dynamics she described her childhood through, where a desperate 'hanging on' to privilege has been replaced with a financial certainty. In contrast, Geoff described the relative ease in previous years and of expected – and fulfilled – educational and employment gains.

While Abi determinedly rejected classed-specific 'conformity', Geoff's prior everyday existence through such dynamics meant that for him there was a lot to lose in 'coming out' and rejecting this. Yet having more does not necessarily mean more potential loss and neither Geoff nor Abi are likely to describe themselves as entirely 'without'. Geoff's 'fall from grace' tells of personal, family – and societal – gendered and classed disappointments in him 'failing' to be the traditional family provider. But Geoff's continued reluctance to re-establish contact with his sons and his ex-wife potentially mirrors a typical tale of 'absent' fatherhood, where the necessary 'escape' from family life was articulated as something he just had to do – for himself. Abi's upward mobility, to a different strata of middle-classness, also tells of her refusal to 'fit in' to normative gendered roles, a struggle she 'wins' in attaining a more 'cosmopolitan' (liberal, diverse, middle-class) city lifestyle. Abi has gained formal and legal recognition of her civil partnership, while Geoff has had and lost a more valued recognition (heterosexual marriage). Survival, strategies and struggles exist in Abi's and Geoff's accounts, problematising (middle)class and sexual reproductions. There are reversals and refusals within their accounts, which speak of privileges lost *and* gained, similar to the broader interview sample.

Interviewees experienced and related classed experiences and identifications differently. Consequentially, for some, positioning in class terms was a 'story to tell', with a coherent, if disrupted narrative of upward mobility, moving away from that which had been constraining – whether this was articulated as a movement away from working-class or middle-class positionings. Others pointed to the variety and instability within what could be considered 'middle-class' where sexuality meant standing somewhat outside the edges of the box. Being 'outside the box' was some people's everyday reality and didn't merit comment, it 'just was', whereas others talked through and actively centred this 'mis-fit' in a very 'agentic' self-reflexive positioning. Having something to tell, whether that be a story of not fitting in, of moving up or down in terms of social estimation and materially, may be contrasted with a matter-of-fact sense of things being how they are, necessitating a 'getting on' with it, where there is 'no story' (McDermott 2003). As Byrne has argued, discourses of class and gender are 'implicated in these different renderings of the self' (2006: 45). The 'outness' required of queer identification (Fraser 1999, Hennessy 2000), misses out the classed and sexual hesitancies and silences, even as a queer methodology holds potential for highlighting such ambivalences; and yet the structuring of these possibilities and utterances is also a problem for a queer methodology, where 'fluid' slippages must be set against personal and institutional regulation. The further that class and sexuality are unpacked empirically, the more light is cast on who can and cannot step outside fixed boundaries and binaries.

(More) Stories to Tell ...

The telling of stories, of selves, can rely upon a mobile version of identity and agency, to be queried as specifically classed; Jacqui, for example, has a 'story to tell' regarding her class mobility, moving away from a 'disadvantaged' background, in pursuit of educational achievements. Interestingly this gain is also expressed as a potential loss, signified by the 'pretensions' standing against a materiality which can still be evidenced:

> I would say I'm working-class with middle-class pretensions (laughter). I'm definitely working-class. In my family, it was never said that we could go to university or we could do anything like that, you know, you've stopped school, you finish school at 16 and you went out and got a job, that's it (Jacqui, 43, self-defined as working-class, in middle-class employment).

Others also reflected on the possibilities of upward mobility, commenting on their own changing educational and employment opportunities. Differently, Steph (54, middle-class) spoke of deliberately moving away from a 'boring and very conventional' suburban middle-class upbringing. In highlighting the variety of middle-classness, from tedious tradition to a tolerant liberalism, some interviewees spoke of being a bit 'outside the box' of middle-class standards and signifiers, although these were often still invoked as well as rejected. This is evident in Ann's (38, lower middle-class) account of being a 'bit unconventional' but being a 'Guardian reader' nonetheless. Ann's stepping out of the mainstream is directly related to her coming-out, claiming a new sense of self.

The variety of class led Lorna (42, middle-class) to ponder on the mixture of sentiments, loyalties and politics constructing her own sense of class, where her objective employment and educational positioning as a middle-class professional contrasts with a sense of unity in being in the Socialist Workers Party for many years. Lorna asked if I wanted a '5000 word essay on the subject' (I did not), again highlighting the story to tell here, where the conclusion is that she most definitely wants her child to be middle-class 'I'd say I was middle-class because I aspire for him to be as good a person as he can be'. The moral and material weight of class resulted in an avoidance for some who, aware of its all encompassing nature, desired to stand outside, to get away. Rachel (40, middle-class) considered class to include 'belief system' as well as 'how you're going to pitch yourself socially', meaning that 'the further into it I sort of go, the more I would actually want to jump out of the system completely'. Queer 'deconstructions' have to grapple with the way this 'jump out' is resourced and reflexively articulated.

In contrast, the sense of 'no story' to tell was apparent in working-class respondents' sense of the 'obviousness' of their class position, where there seemed nothing else to say; why state the obvious? It wasn't that these accounts were any less complex but their expression simultaneously co-existed with their sidelining, rather than reflexive foregrounding:

> I would put myself in working-class, just I don't know, just your basic I'm just, I'm not like an upper-class, you know. I wouldn't class myself as being middle-class either. I don't know as low as you can get, no I don't know. I've never classed myself as anything, you know. I've never really thought about it really. Oh lower-class (Jody, 40, working-class).

Jody negotiates the extremes of class, eventually placing herself as 'lower-class', while Karen was very definite, highlighting her position at the 'bottom' of the class spectrum as a result of financial circumstances:

> I would say the bottom of the bottom, I mean when I was very young there was the five of us lived in a one bedroom flat ... We didn't have any money, we didn't have anything, everything was always hand-me-downs and it was *not* a good quality of life ... and I think the thing of seeing yourself a little bit further down had already set in my mind and that's why I lived sort of the way I do to better myself for me and my baby (Karen, 22, working-class).

Karen tells of obviously knowing and feeling her class position and of the desire to do better. Parental desires and possibilities were often articulated as another manifestation of class, apparent in both Stacy's and Clare's accounts of accessing rights, services and networks, 'trading on privilege', even as Stacy still centres self-determination:

> Yeah, I think, let's be honest, I'm probably from a middle-class background. I think if you go on what my parents are, I would say that my dad is probably upper middle-class. He used to have a very well paid job, but I don't think that that does determine class, I think you determine your own socio economic group or whatever. I think probably I must be middle-class, in that, you know, the job I do, the type of house I've got, the aspirations I have for my children that sort of thing. I think it's much easier to be, this is going to sound awful, a middle-class lesbian with children, than it would be to perhaps be a working-class lesbian with children, because I just think it's just terrible stereotypes, but I think, within my social circle anyway, because of the kind of people I mix with, they probably are quite accepting of the fact that I'm a lesbian, you know, so I think that has helped really (Stacy, 33, middle-class).

Stacey situates herself as a self-determining individual, reflecting too on the ease that comes with this. Similarly, Clare speaks of negotiating various clinicians, nonetheless feeling capable of claiming rights with her partner, as well informed and articulate subjects. They have the knowingness, resources and confidence to move in and claim space:

> We're scary, you know? Yeah, we are both articulate and we've come from countries where we are used to having our rights and we know how to find out information for ourselves. The health visitors don't like us, they are afraid of us. We just look like the sort of people who could get really annoyed and make complaints and be a nuisance. And I know that's resource-based, but not everyone has that and that's just really unfair that we trade on that privilege (Clare, 32, middle-class).

The stories we present are 'performed' and regulated in different institutional and interpersonal moments; yet, as Clare articulates, there are classed strategies and successes within such enactments. This highlights the situation 'beyond' sexuality where, as parents, interviewees necessarily interact with a range of institutions, across various places, negotiating judgments and norms: queer methodologies hold promises in terms of uncovering such normativities, where class and sexuality can be seen as (still) absent intersections in queer frameworks.

While class positionings and privileges were expressed in moments of parental negotiation and intervention, respondents' broader social networks, families and friendship groups also provided a classed gauge where who they were in class terms was made (in)visible in who was – or was not – around them; 'We don't really have acquaintances of any other class so it is difficult for us to comment on whether or not it matters' (Cathrine, 28, middle-class). Nigel (43, middle-class) tells of coming to realise that 'classes can mix', the experience of which begins to challenge and erode his own assumptions and 'pretentions'. While Nigel has revised his opinion, Peter (43, middle-class) notes his 'luck' in being able to move exclusively in 'fairly cultured and liberal circles' amongst individuals with 'very liberal middle-class values'. Such sentiments cast light upon classed boundaries, which may not be understood as simply 'different' but rather as fundamental to how we see 'us' and 'them', where such distinctions may also be upheld within sexual (and academic) 'communities'. This research on lesbian and gay parenthood, in exploring sexuality and class, provides some space to begin connecting these often separated areas, urging research reflection (in practice) on the political challenge in naming – and changing – such inequalities, where queer methodologies may seek to empirically explore the relevance of multiple positionings, normativities and intersections.

Conclusion

Ignoring class in researching and theorising sexuality has consequences for – and limitations to – the knowledges produced; where queer has aimed to challenge universalisms, in favour of multiplicity and difference, the inattention to class inequalities, both theoretically and methodologically, has meant that queer re-enacts other exclusions and boundaries. In reconsidering methodological approaches that illuminate the classing of queer lives, the reproduction of middle-class LGBT experience as universal can be made visible and 'deconstructed', holding promise for queer methodologies which challenge, rather than re-center, privilege. Here, I focused on the interconnections between class and sexuality in the telling of 'selves' in the interview encounter (and in academic spaces), probing at whose story holds weight and value; I deliberately demonstrated this in the presentation of interview data based on in-depth interviews with lesbian and gay parents from both middle-class and working-class backgrounds. I did so, rather than (only) presenting my 'queer' and classed 'self', or 'reflecting' on my methodologies without reference to my findings. I propose that Plummer's (1998) call for attention to 'stratifying homosexualities' should be given critical attention in explicitly including class as part of our methodological and theoretical framing, demonstrated here in the ways that certain classed subjects can speak in voices that are heard, thus achieving mobility, subject-hood and even 'ordinariness', which may not be that queer at all.

Chapter 5

Queer Methods and Queer Practices: Re-examining the Identities of Older Lesbian, Gay, Bisexual Adults

Andrew King and Ann Cronin

Introduction

The relationship between ageing and sexuality is contentious; older people are frequently represented as either being sexually inactive or not having a sexual identity. Aside from the issue of ageism, such a representation also occludes the lives of those who have been defined by their sexuality: people who identify as lesbian, gay or bisexual.[1] Until recently, the lives of this group of older people had received little serious study (Cronin 2004, Heaphy 2007). This is despite the finding that they comprise an estimated 1 in 15 of the users of one of the UK's largest charities for older people (Age Concern 2002). Research has now begun to develop across different regions of the UK (see for example Communities Scotland 2005, Davies et al. 2006, Heaphy and Yip 2006, Stonewall Cymru and Triangle Wales 2006) demonstrating that despite similarities with older heterosexuals, older lesbian, gay and bisexual adults do have specific needs and issues, some of which will be discussed in this chapter. However, much of this literature represents 'older lesbian, gay and bisexual' as a largely stable, fixed, taken-for-granted identification. This appears to be at odds with other perspectives within the humanities and social sciences that contend that identities are unstable, multiple and produced contextually. In this chapter we consider this tension and its implications for methodology. Overall, we argue that developing and using methodologies to examine how older lesbian, gay and bisexual identities are produced or accomplished is important if we are to continue developing thinking that moves away from essentialism and avoids reinforcing existing heteronormative understandings of older age.

---

1   Whilst the identities of older transgendered people are important and certainly something we intend to examine in future research, the material we discuss in this chapter is focused on older people normatively gendered into male and female who identify themselves as lesbian, gay or bisexual – bearing in mind that trans people can also identify as lesbian, gay and bisexual.

The first section of the chapter begins by discussing the representation of older lesbian, gay and bisexual identities that emerges in previous research; a category of people who are similar yet different from older heterosexuals. In the second section we trouble, or queer, this identification, considering insights from queer theory, the post-structuralist feminism of Judith Butler, together with the sociological perspectives of ethnomethodology and conversation analysis. We then outline how we are developing a methodology in our own research that adopts these insights and that uses both membership categorisation analysis and narrative analysis, although for reasons of brevity we focus our discussion in this chapter on our use of the former. We outline and give examples of this work before discussing its advantages and disadvantages. Finally, we discuss the impact that taking the notion of 'queering' seriously has had on our own methodological practice and its potential for a wider application.

Older Lesbian, Gay and Bisexual Adults – Queer, but not Necessarily Queered

While the sociological study of sexuality can be traced back some 40 years, sociological studies and considerations of older lesbian, gay and bisexual adults did not appear until the early 1980s (Quam and Whitford 1992). Additionally, there has been a 'queer absence' (Cronin 2004) in studies of old age and particularly in social gerontology. As we noted earlier, this omission has begun to be addressed and slowly a representation of older lesbian, gay and bisexual adults has begun to emerge, which indicates certain similarities as well as differences in their lives as older people when compared to heterosexual people from the same age group. For instance, statistical evidence reviewed by Badgett (1997) shows that gay men, like heterosexual men, are more likely to have material advantages in older age; the likely result of a lifetime of gender discrimination in pay. Hence, older gay and bisexual men are more likely to have better pension provision than older lesbians and bisexual women, who have more in common with heterosexual women in terms of financial status. Gay men are also more likely to be living alone (Hubbard and Rossington 1995) due in part to bereavements and because they are less likely to have dependent children. Conversely gay men are more likely to be caring for older relatives than their heterosexual or lesbian counterparts (MetLife 2006). More generally, several studies report that older lesbian, gay and bisexual people are more likely to either experience, or expect to experience, discrimination from health care practitioners (Hunt and Minsky 2005, Keogh et al. 2004, MetLife 2006). In addition, their concerns about residential care are based not only on a loss of independence, but also a fear of homophobia (Tolley and Ranzijn 2006).

The above is a short exegesis of the literature looking at older lesbian, gay and bisexual adults. What is interesting about this research is how the identity category of 'older lesbian, gay and bisexual' is represented as a determining factor in people's experiences. In effect, it indicates that because people are lesbian, gay or bisexual they experience a different older age to heterosexuals. Much of the research on older lesbian, gay and bisexual people's experiences has been conducted for and by policy makers and practitioners (notable exceptions include Cronin 2004, Harrison 2006, Heaphy 2007, Heaphy and Yip 2006, Kurdek 2005). However, Heaphy (2007: 194) suggests that this research suffers from an epistemological problem: 'a problem that stems from the conceptual significance afforded sexual identity as the key determining factor of lesbian and gay experience. A more sophisticated understanding is required of social constraints and possibilities as they relate to non-heterosexual living and ageing.' What Heaphy is pointing to, and something that we would emphasise, is that much of the research intended for policy makers and practitioners perpetuates a view of identity, of the subject, as fixed, stable and by implication, essential. This, it seems to us, occludes much of the important work that has emerged from the sociological study of sexuality that views sexual identity as both socially constructed and highly situated or contextual (Seidman 1996, Weeks 1989, 2003). In essence, whilst not eschewing the significance of the aforementioned studies for developing affirmative policies relevant to people who identify as older lesbian, gay and bisexual adults, such studies may unwittingly, by quickly translating or 'black-boxing' (Latour 2005) subject positions, occlude the processes by which they are produced. Furthermore, such a position risks the charge of reinforcing heteronormativity because it does not adequately analyse or disrupt its production. It is our contention that we need a more sophisticated understanding, and indeed methodology, to examine how and why the identifications 'older lesbian, gay and bisexual adults' are produced in certain contexts. It is for this reason that we have turned to ideas in the humanities and social sciences that trouble the notion of stable, fixed and essential categories of identification.

Queering Older Lesbian, Gay and Bisexual Adults

The troubling of stable, essential identity categories has emerged from a range of approaches within the humanities and social sciences, but for us, most notably in queer theory, the post-structuralist feminism of Judith Butler, and within sociology from ethnomethodology, conversation analysis, and narrative analysis. What distinguishes these approaches from others within LGBT studies is their focus on the active production of categories of identity in relation to wider social and cultural norms, such as heteronormativity.

Queer theory is a diverse and sometimes contradictory body of work that takes the deconstruction of categories of identity and knowledge as its central analytic task (Fuss 1991, Green 2007, Seidman 1995). Queer theorists maintain that adopting taken-for-granted categories of identity, whether they are considered the product of an essential biology or a process of social construction, has the effect of obscuring differential experiences and re-affirming existing inequalities. Queer theorists seek to demonstrate that identities are unstable, fluidic fictions that are the effects of regimes of power/knowledge, which regulate bodies and desires (Jagose 1996, Seidman 1996, 1997). Indeed, Sullivan (2003: vi) argues that *to queer* is 'to make strange, to frustrate, to counteract, to delegitimise, to camp up - heteronormative knowledge and institutions'. Queer theory, certainly in its radical deconstructionist guise (Green 2007), maintains that heteronormativity is a discourse that normalises and governs the identities that it brings into being. Thus,

> [t]he language and law that regulates the establishment of heterosexuality as both an identity and an institution, both a practice and a system, is the language and law of defence and protection: heterosexuality secures its self-identity and shores up its ontological boundaries by protecting itself from what it sees as the continual predatory encroachments of its contaminated other, homosexuality. (Fuss 1991: 2)

Because heteronormativity is the ideology of sex/gender that permeates Western societies (Rubin 1993, Sedgwick 1993), the approach adopted in many studies of older lesbian, gay and bisexual adults, that equality is a fundamental goal which is attainable through negotiation and conflict resolution around identity categories, would be problematic for queer theorists. This is because that approach pays too little attention to the disciplinary power of heteronormativity. It is, therefore, important that a methodology that utilises queer theory considers how 'older lesbian, gay and bisexual' in ways that relate to and draw upon heteronormative presumptions is produced. What is needed is a methodology that is itself 'queered'; that is, attuned to uncovering heteronormative presumptions in empirical data. However, queer theory does not encompass a methodological programme *per se*, although it is clear that those seeking to adopt its central tenets will seek to question, or trouble, taken-for-granted understandings and ways of knowing (Dilley 1999, Seidman 1996); in particular, to question the notion of a stable, objective, fixed and essential subject of research. This deconstruction is something that is also central to the work of the post-structuralist queer feminist theorist, Judith Butler.

Explicitly drawing upon the writings of Foucault, Derrida and Austin, Butler contends that discourses, or bodies of knowledge, constitute subjects (Butler 1990a, 1993b, 1997b, 1999, 2004). To this end, she asserts that categories of identity are performative: they are brought into being through discursive practices that constitute what they name. Butler's famous example is how biomedical (and heteronormative) conceptions of gender produce a subject position from which a subjectivity is constituted. As Butler (1993a: 232) suggests,

> [gender] is thus not the product of choice, but the forcible citation of a norm, one whose complex historicity is indissociable from relations of discipline, regulation, punishment. Indeed, there is no 'one' who takes on a gender norm. On the contrary, this citation of the gender norm is necessary in order to qualify

as a 'one', to become viable as a 'one', where subject-formation is dependent on the prior operation of legitimating gender norms.

Like Queer Theory more generally, this position stands in marked contrast to the notion of older lesbian, gay and bisexual adults that we discussed in the previous section of this chapter. In effect, it helps us to recognise that the citation of 'older lesbian, gay and bisexual' is performative, bringing those identifications into being in specific ways for specific purposes. Furthermore, recently Butler has examined how performativity actively de-subjectivises selves and she has applied her analysis of such linguistic and symbolic violence to topics as diverse as Gender Identity Disorder and the so-called War on Terror (Butler 2004, 2005). Considering the ways in which discourse constitutes the management of identity, she demonstrates how discourses and discursive practices can be both constraining *and* enabling. In essence, their citation may constitute subjects, but this is never complete. Agency, difference and resistance emerge through performative enactment. Thus, using this perspective, we can view older lesbian, gay and bisexual identities as multiple and complex, always beyond attempts to fix or stabilise them.

In spite of her assertions and corrections (Butler 1993a, 1999, 2004), Butler's conception of discourse has been criticised for being too deterministic (see for example Benhabib 1995, Hood-Williams and Cealey-Harrison 1998). Indeed, her work has been criticised for ignoring materiality and employing an approach that is 'merely linguistic' (Benhabib 1995, Hood-Williams and Cealey-Harrison 1998, McNay 2004). However, for us, the value of Butler's work is her demonstration that identities are inherently political; to elaborate on their performativity is to establish 'as political the very terms through which identity is articulated' (Butler 1990a: 148). With respect to older lesbian, gay and bisexual adults, this would mean treating these identifications as political, as identities that because of heteronormativity both reproduce and transgress existing norms.

One problem with Butler's work is its tendency to be theoretical and abstract. Therefore, for it to be useful in social research more generally it has been suggested that it needs to be grounded in a methodological programme attuned to examining how people accomplish identities in specific settings (Fenstermaker and West 2002, McIlvenny 2002a, 2002b, Moloney and Fenstermaker 2002, Speer 2005, Speer and Potter 2002). For instance, McIlvenny (2002b: 9) refers to the effect of queer theory and Butler on the study of identity as 'more a manifesto' than an empirical programme. Indeed, the suggestion made by McIlvenny and others here is that the sociological approaches of ethnomethodology and conversation analysis may have considerable purchase in this enterprise.

Ethnomethodology is a branch of sociology that studies the methods that the members of any particular social situation or context use to make sense of and order their understandings of it (Garfinkel 1984, Heritage 1984). In so doing, it examines how these members draw upon their tacit knowledge of 'how the world should be'. Moreover, it asserts that in outlining 'how the world should be' members offer accounts: descriptions of something or someone that is tied to the situation in which it is uttered (Heritage 1984). This means that understandings are both indexical, tied to the context of their use, and yet form part of members' background expectations about the social world, a 'natural attitude' that reflects wider social and cultural norms.

To demonstrate how members account for and order their social realities in this manner, ethnomethodological studies have attended to members' sense making procedures: for example, in his study of Agnes, a male to female transsexual, Garfinkel observed how Agnes had to learn to 'pass' as a woman, despite being socialised as male (Garfinkel 1984). In a series of interviews with Agnes, Garfinkel (1984: 130) noted how she selectively glossed her biography to make it appear to others that she was a 'normal natural female'. Although Garfinkel's study has been subject to criticism (for a useful discussion see Speer 2005), not least because Garfinkel's own gendered understandings influenced Agnes' interactions with him, his study of Agnes does demonstrate how taken-for-granted categories of identity and the meanings attached to them are produced and utilised in social actions and settings, including research settings themselves.

A concern with how identities and meanings are produced in specific settings is also central to conversation analysis. This methodology was developed by Harvey Sacks, who was himself influenced by the ethnomethodological programme of Harold Garfinkel and the micro-sociologist Erving Goffman (Silverman 1998). Conversation analysis has since become a broad research programme that focuses on various aspects of naturally occurring talk, or talk-in-interaction, including turn-taking, overlaps and pauses, and categories and their associated attributes and activities (Silverman 1998). For some, this approach is overly descriptive, politically naïve and so concerned with the minutiae of social interactions that it fails to account for wider issues of structure and power (Billig 1999, Coser 1975, Hilbert 1990, Kitzinger 2000, Pollner 1991, Speer 2002). However, like Garfinkel, Sacks noted that much sociological research proceeded on the basis of applying 'undescribed categories'. That is, researchers tend to use categories such as age, gender, sexuality, class, ethnicity etc as resources to analyse social problems, such as social change or the effects of power, rather than treating them as topics in and of themselves (Zimmerman and Pollner 1990 [1970]). From the latter perspective, social research methodologies should be attuned to the artful practices used by people to construct the aforementioned 'undescribed categories', rather than eliciting 'facts' that are the outcomes of being members of these categories. In relation to older lesbian, gay and bisexual adults, this would mean treating these categories of identity as accomplishments, exploring how they are constituted by people themselves in specific settings and how they are interrelated with other aspects of self that they make relevant in their talk.

So far we have argued that much of the research that has been conducted into the lives of older lesbian, gay and bisexual people has implicitly relied on a conception of research that can be described as 'fact eliciting'. Arguably, adopting such an approach has produced useful and interesting findings that have informed policy and legal debates as we noted earlier. However, we are concerned to examine how and why the categories of identity and knowledge related to older lesbian, gay and bisexual adults are accomplished by members, considering how and why certain discourses are drawn upon, utilised, challenged and transformed in their talk. We have sought, therefore, to queer the categorisation of 'older lesbian, gay and bisexual', rather than viewing these categories as *a priori* social facts. In attempting to undertake this task, methodologically, we are drawing here upon membership categorisation analysis.

Queering our Practices, Taking Membership Categorisation Seriously

Membership categorisation analysis 'pays attention to the situated and reflexive use of categories in everyday and institutional interaction, as well as interview, media and other textual data' (Benwell and Stokoe 2006: 38). Enabling the investigation of 'culture-in-action' (Baker 2000: 112), membership categorisation analysis shows how cultural understandings are carried by discourse and are reproduced and transformed in their use. It can be used to analyse specific instances of the categorisation of people, places and events, but it is also attuned to detailing how these instances link to wider discursive norms and practices. In short, it is attuned to both micro and macro levels of analysis.

Membership categorisation analysis has been used to analyse gender, crime, organisational structures and stigmatised identities, amongst other topics (Eglin and Hester 2003, Llewellyn 2004, McKinlay and Dunnett 1998, Nikander 2000, Stokoe 2003a, Stokoe 2004). Stokoe (2004), for instance, demonstrated how gender categories became interactionally relevant in a student workgroup, rather than simply determining the interaction in advance. She showed how the categories used by the students in their talk resulted in the positioning of the only female member of the workgroup as the scribe. In effect, through the talk-in-interaction the group reproduced normative gender roles, although not without a degree of argument and re-categorisation. Stokoe argued that this reveals the critical nature of membership categorisation analysis; it shows the micro-political dynamics of categorisations in talk and uncovers how power structures are manifested and contested in local settings.

Membership categorisation analysis examines how categories are grouped into certain collections, called membership categorisation devices, and how they are bound to specific activities or attributes, referred to as predicates. The combination of membership categories, membership categorisation devices and associated predicates in a narrative or account is artful; that is, people do not passively reproduce normative combinations of these, rather they deploy them in specific situations to do specific things. Hence, the male students in Stokoe's study (2004) used them in a series of interactions to reproduce gender roles in their workgroup, while trying to appear to be egalitarian. In addition to reproducing or transgressing norms and roles, categories can be combined to establish moral and behavioural precedents. Sacks (1995) demonstrated, for example, how a navy fighter pilot artfully used categorisations in an account of a bombing raid in order to justify the killing of other people involved in the conflict. Similarly, McKinlay and Dunnett (1998) examined how gun owners constructed their identities as 'average' in opposition to a discourse that positioned them as dangerous.

We have sought to utilise membership categorisation analysis (both on its own and in combination with narrative analysis) in our own research in order to examine how heteronormative presumptions about ageing and sexuality are reproduced, challenged and transgressed in the narrative accounts of people who identify themselves as older lesbian, gay and bisexual adults. We conducted policy-based research, interviewing 20 older lesbian, gay and bisexual adults who we recruited via newspaper adverts, flyers in public settings, including those in the LGBT community, and online LGBT forums. Analysing the accounts of these people with membership categorisation analysis presented us with a means of exploring how they categorised themselves and their social worlds, given that they have already been categorised by participating in the research as older and lesbian, gay or bisexual. Later in the chapter we will point to the queer move associated with undertaking this analysis on the policy-based data we generated.

Membership categorisation analysis has however been criticised, even by those who are adherents of conversation analysis (Eglin and Hester 2003, Horton-Salway 2004, Housley and Fitzgerald 2002, Stokoe 2003a, 2003b). One problem noted is that membership categorisation analysis can become overly concerned with the content of categories, neglecting to attend to their sequential organisation (Housley and Fitzgerald 2002, Schegloff 2007). People develop the meanings of categories and their associated attributes during the course of an account. Without attending to this level of analysis, membership categorisation analysis is not very different from thematic and grounded forms of analysis that are more traditional in qualitative research. Ways of avoiding this have been detailed elsewhere (King 2010, Stokoe 2003a, Watson 1997), but we contend that narrative analysis (Earthy and Cronin 2008, Riessman 2008) is particularly useful here since it is attuned to examining narratives as a whole, their sequential exposition, rather than isolating certain features. In order to demonstrate some of these points, we now turn to an example drawn from our own empirical data.

The extracts outlined below come from an interview conducted with a 73 year old man who we will call Ernest. The interview began with a question concerning sexuality.

> Interviewer: We all use different terms to describe our sexuality so it would be helpful for me if you could tell me how you describe your sexual identity?
>
> Ernest: Right er well I feel it's a very important issue, well it is for me. I'm a gay man but my gayness is not what I would call my primary characteristic. My primary characteristic is that I'm male and er I would do everything that I would expect an ordinary male to do except that when it comes to sex then I'm going

to prefer to have sex with other men but that's the only way I consider myself to be gay.

Here the interviewer's question makes the membership categorisation device 'sexuality' a relevant resource for Ernest to categorise himself. This does not mean that Ernest will always categorise himself according to this device; indeed in his response he makes it clear that his understanding of this identification is more complex, what we might describe as 'doing' rather than 'being'. Initially he categorises himself as a 'gay man'; a category that is consistent with the membership categorisation device, 'sexuality'. However, rather than ending his description at this point, Ernest then turns this categorisation into a predicate, 'gayness' and in so doing makes his membership of this category something of note. Ernest then emphasises the other device that 'gay man' belongs to: gender. He asserts that 'male' is his 'primary characteristic'. What distinguishes Ernest from being an 'ordinary male' is something he 'does': he 'has sex with other men'. It appears, to an extent, that the categorisation work that Ernest is undertaking uses heteronormative understandings/assumptions at this point – heterosexual men, men who don't have sex with other men, are 'ordinary'; conversely, gay is not ordinary. This appears to be confirmed when he provides an account of why 'gay' is not his primary characteristic:

> I've never lived erm I've always been around other gay people but I've never lived in an exclusively gay community. I've never been in an exclusively gay relationship although I've had quite a few fairly long-term gay relationships but er I wouldn't consider anything like a civil partnership or anything in a formalised way. I have been married but that was purely for erm immigration purposes while I lived briefly in America and that didn't succeed at all (laughs) it wasn't a very rewarding experience.

In this section Ernest is outlining what he associates with being gay and problematises his own membership of this category by dissociating himself from certain attributes that he considers mark membership of this categorisation: membership of a gay community, an exclusively gay relationship and civil partnerships. However, it is not possible to simply classify Ernest as 'closeted' from this statement since he makes it clear he has always associated with gay people and has had 'long-term' gay relationships. Moreover, he makes it clear that his attachment to the heteronormative activity, 'marriage', was both instrumental and unrewarding.

Previous research has indicated that older lesbian, gay and bisexual adults, like Ernest, who grew up in an era before male homosexuality was decriminalised, are more likely to attempt to 'pass' as straight than those older lesbian, gay and bisexual adults who grew up after decriminalisation (Rosenfeld 2002). Other forms of thematic analysis might well categorise or code this section of Ernest's account as an example of passing. However, we contend that the categorisation work evident in these sections of Ernest's account indicates a more complex representation. In effect, Ernest subtly and artfully situates himself as 'gay', but not 'typically' gay. Whilst this can be viewed as heteronormative, since he appears to suggest he passes as 'straight', it also can be viewed as 'queer': Ernest is actively rejecting existing categorisations and situating himself as different. This may well be the result of a lifetime of passing, *but* it may also be a more subtle practice of transgression that having spent a lifetime of avoiding being categorised (and in some cases pathologised) is indicative of how Ernest views his sexuality - as something he does rather than something he is. Any researcher or practitioner who simply categorises Ernest as 'gay', or for that matter as a 'man who has sex with men', would miss this more complex understanding.

This complexity is also evident in a latter extract from Ernest's interview where the topic of age was made relevant. In a discussion that follows a question where he is positioned as 'someone who can comment on services for older people', Ernest refuses to let himself be categorised as 'older':

Interviewer: What about service provision for older people do you think?

Ernest: There again I have very rarely got myself involved and not classifying myself as gay I don't classify myself as er old I just don't think in terms of age … so that's [his voluntary work] brought me much more in to focus on the needs of older people and what older people talk about er which is mainly sitting around chatting about the old days (laughs) it's not really my scene but you know you listen and you try and be as helpful as you can.

Ernest's response explicitly makes clear that the category 'old' is not applicable to him. Nonetheless, his voluntary work has made him 'think' about what older people need and their behaviours: their talk, 'chatting about the old days'. He also dissociates himself from their 'scene'; an interesting attribution since it *implicitly* references the 'gay scene' which he has already made clear is not relevant to him. Whilst we cannot assume that Ernest does not want to talk about the old days because they hold memories that are painful, his suggestion that his role was to 'listen' and 'be helpful' again dissociates him from membership of the category 'older person': they talk, he listens. Ernest, who we might categorise as 'older' according to normative models of ageing, artfully positions himself as different. Again, this has implications for researchers and practitioners who might be attempting to recruit older people for research projects or who wish to provide services specifically aimed at the category, 'older' people. In essence, therefore, categorical membership matters and how people chose, at certain times and not others, to categorise themselves matters more.

We do not wish to generalise or proselytise from one account; whilst Ernest's account was different from others in our corpus, it certainly had similarities: a desire not to be easily classified; to be similar yet different from other LGBT people; a desire not be classified as 'old'. Our use of Ernest's account in this chapter is simply to demonstrate the use of our methodology in considering the complexity of older lesbian, gay and bisexual identities. We have, therefore, sought to take the notion of queering seriously, something that we will now consider in more detail.

Qualifying Queer Practices: Some Observations and Conclusions

We contend that analysing people's categorisations of themselves and others, of people and events, represent a first step in demonstrating the instability and the performativity of older lesbian, gay and bisexual identities. We have argued that this is because we did not feel that the extant literature related to older lesbian, gay and bisexual people considered the unstable, complex and fluidic nature of identity that is apparent from work in the humanities and social sciences, particularly in queer theory, the post-structuralism of Judith Butler, together with ethnomethodology and conversation analysis. In developing a methodology to take account of these insights, we have drawn on membership categorisation analysis and narrative analysis. We think that these are particularly useful in this respect as they take the notion of queering seriously. In this chapter we have attempted to demonstrate how this can be done and why it is important. We believe that the methodological approach we suggest can help to extend previous research, examining the production of older lesbian, gay and bisexual identities *in situ*. In future, this form of analysis could be used in other, more naturalistic, settings, such as care homes, day centres or public meetings. In these instances, research could attend to the conditions of possibility that these settings afford, or deny, to members in how they accomplish their older lesbian, gay and bisexual identities.

Our methodology also attempts to queer the categorisation 'older lesbian, gay and bisexual' itself: to explore the discursive resources that people use when they are asked to identify with these categories. This is what Baker (2000: 112) refers to as the exploration of 'culture-in-action', asserting that attending to membership categorisation involves considering 'how discourses are called on and how they are invoked in the mundane activities of talking, hearing, reading and writing'. Our methodology is designed to show how people use and transgress heteronormative models of sexuality and ageing, producing complex representations of themselves and their life course. Thus, we contend that this troubles, or queers, simplistic notions and equations of age and sexuality with exclusion, marginalisation or isolation. While these will be factors in some people's lives, they will not be applicable to all. Attending to how people construct their selves represents a first step in exploring these complex issues.

Finally, in this chapter we have also queered the data we originally collected and the reason why it was collected, which was primarily to inform the development of local government policies and to ascertain the needs of older lesbian, gay and bisexual people. Our analysis and discussion here queers, or troubles, its original purpose. Indeed, our argument is that any qualitative data can be re-analysed using queer methods. Overall, therefore, we have sought to avoid generalisations and fact production, focusing instead on the processes by which certainties (and uncertainties) are produced. Whilst we consider that we are still developing our methodology, we hope that others will consider utilising some of the insights we have provided here in different contexts. Taking a queer turn in approaching methods and methodological practices is important if we are to avoid replicating (hetero)normative understandings, power relationships and occlusions in our research.

Chapter 6

Queer(ing) Communication in Research Relationships: A Conversation about Subjectivities, Methodologies and Ethics[1]

Andrew Gorman-Murray, Lynda Johnston and Gordon Waitt

Prologue

In this chapter we critically reflect on the use of interview-based research methods with sexual minority communities and participants – such as in-depth interviews, focus groups and ethnographic conversations – seeking to interrogate the 'queerness' of communication in these research relationships. Queerness is used here both to represent lesbian and gay lives as they exist outside of normative heterosexuality, and how communication works across and subverts subjective binaries in research relationships, such as insider/outsider. Moreover, the notion of queer asserts the multiplicity and fluidity of sexual subjectivities. Our discussion emphasises how sexual subject positions proliferate through the inflection of sexuality and gender with race, ethnicity, postcoloniality, culture, class and life-course changes – entanglements which have a powerful resonance in the empirical context of our work 'down under' in Aotearoa New Zealand and Australia. We argue that this fracturing of sexual subjectivities has critical implications for communication in interview-based research with sexual minorities.

Drawing on our situated experiences, we consider the perils, problems, possibilities and successes of communication between researchers and participants of differing sexual subjectivities in the research process. In this discussion, we lead by example, deploying a conversational approach and rebounding off each other's experiences. Initially, we advance calls contesting the insider/outsider dualism, discussing how notions of 'insider' and 'outsider' do not neatly map onto our experiences of communication in interview-based research with sexual minorities. Subsequently, we focus on the inflection of sexual subjectivities with ethnic-cultural heritage in the postcolonial-settler societies of Aotearoa

1   Acknowledgements: We sincerely thank Kath Browne and Catherine J. Nash for inviting our contribution, their stimulating and encouraging feedback on earlier drafts, and allowing us to write the chapter in a 'queer' manner.

New Zealand and Australia, contemplating how these entwinements complicate research relationships and conversations. Through this dialogue we call for greater account in queer research of the power, positionality and difference inherent in sexual minority populations and communities, and equally for more awareness of the contingent role of (national and regional) locality in the formation of sexual subjectivities.

Andrew: Effective communication is fundamental for achieving useful outcomes in any research project which involves working with particular (sets of) communities. This certainly includes work with sexual minorities – homosexuals, gay men, lesbians, bisexuals, transsexuals, and other non-heteronormative subjects – who often feel misunderstood by the wider societies in which they live, thus experiencing a 'breakdown' of effective communication at a societal level. Much has been written about the place of communication in social research, from treatises on qualitative techniques such as in-depth interviews, focus groups, ethnographic dialogue and oral histories (Bennett 2002, Silvey 2003, Dunn 2005, George and Stratford 2005), to more reflective work on understanding the networks of power and positionality of and between 'researchers' and 'research subjects' (England 1994, Rose 1997, Dowling 2005, Howitt and Stevens 2005). This range of work indicates that effective communication in the research relationship is not only a matter of good rapport and question-and-answer within the research setting, but also requires critical reflexivity on the part of the researcher about their own power and subjectivity in relation to those they are researching.

Consequently, in this chapter we critically reflect on our use of interview-based research methods with sexual minority communities and participants, notably in-depth interviews, focus groups and ethnographic conversations. We are particularly concerned with processes of communication and comprehension between sexual subjects – ourselves and our participants – in these research relationships. While researchers often speak of 'research subjects', both researchers and research participants are, in fact, subjects, in that both researchers and participants enter the research relationship from the perspective of their own subjectivities. Subjectivity refers to the social traits of individuals, which are always spatial and multiple in that, as individuals, we have classed, gendered, sexed, aged and rac(ialis)ed characteristics, amongst others. Subjectivities, however, are not simply held by individuals. Rather, the way certain social attributes are valued (or devalued) is a matter of wider social and cultural norms which 'position' attributes differently in networks of social power – hence the related term 'positionality'. These realities play a critical role in communication in the research setting, as Robyn Dowling (2005: 25) argues:

> Collecting and interpreting qualitative information relies upon a dialogue between you and your informants. In these dialogues your personal characteristics and social position – elements of your positionality – cannot be fully controlled or changed because such dialogues do not occur in a social vacuum. The ways you

are perceived by your informants, the ways you perceive them, and the ways you
interact are at least partially determined by societal norms.

Dowling (2005: 25) goes on to contend that 'critical reflexivity is the most
appropriate strategy for dealing with subjectivity'. By this she means that
being aware of your own subject position, your positionality in relation to each
participant's subject position, and how these might interact, is a useful way to start
interrogating how the process of communication – entwined with networks of
social power – affects the research project and its outcomes.

In this chapter we emphasise the 'queerness' of interview dialogue and
research relationships between sexual minority researchers and participants,
and advocate why thinking 'queerly' about such communication is a vital part
of research ethics when working with sexual minorities. 'Queer' is a term that
has been widely associated with particular sexual subjectivities (Jagose 1996a,
Sullivan 2003). Specifically, the notion of queer asserts the multiplicity and fluidity
of sexual subjectivities, and moreover, seeks to challenge the processes which
normalise and/or homogenise certain sexual and gender practices, relationships
and subjectivities in contemporary society (Browne 2006). One challenge in queer
academic scholarship is the difficulty in effectively communicating and achieving
understanding across an increasingly wide range of sexual subjects, each with
their own experiences, practices, relationships and subjectivities. While those who
variously identify as homosexual, gay, lesbian, bisexual, transsexual or otherwise
non-heteronormative share a range of common experiences around legal, political
and social constraints, there are also significantly different lived experiences of
oppression and exclusion between these groups. Indeed, it is common for processes
of normalisation to operate within homosexual populations (Browne 2006).

Recognising the multiple and fluid contours of subject positions, we seek here
to explore differences and difficulties in communication, dialogue and relationships
between researchers and participants of differing sexual subjectivities in interview-
based research, interrogating where commonalities and challenges arise. This is
where our conversation takes an even queerer turn, moving beyond the analytical
linking of queer with only sexuality and gender. Rosemary Hennessey (1995:
86-7) insists that the queer project marks 'an effort to speak from and to the
differences and silences that have been suppressed by the homo/hetero binary, an
effort to unpack the monolithic identities 'lesbian' and 'gay', including the intricate
ways lesbian and gay sexualities are inflected by heterosexuality, race, gender,
and ethnicity'. Eve Sedgwick (1993: 8–9) also issues a strident claim about the
possibilities of queer theorisation of subjectivities, particularly emphasising the
nuances of postcolonial contexts: 'a lot of exciting work around 'queer' spins the
term outward along dimensions that can't be subsumed under gender and sexuality
at all: the ways that race, ethnicity, postcolonial nationality criss-cross with these
and other identity-constituting, identity-fracturing discourses'.

Sexual subjectivities are thus sculpted not only by sexuality and gender, but
also race, ethnicity, postcoloniality and class. These possibilities have particular

resonance in the empirical context of our work – the postcolonial-settler 'down under' nations of Aotearoa New Zealand and Australia. In this sense, the fracturing of sexual subjectivities along lines of gender, sexualities and ethnicities has a palpably place-specific dimension: with their racially, culturally and socioeconomically diverse indigenous and immigrant populations, the Antipodes provide a pertinent context to explore communication and comprehension in interview-based research across proliferating and politically-charged sexual subject positions. We have conducted research projects which have engaged us with varying sexualised places and people, such as Pride festivals and tourist spaces (Johnston 2005, Waitt and Markwell 2006, Gorman-Murray et al. 2008) and lesbian and gay homes (Johnston and Valentine 1995, Gorman-Murray 2007a, Waitt and Gorman-Murray 2007). Our scholarship has not always foregrounded these differences but, ethically, receptive communication demands sensitivity to difference. Given our own diverse sexual subjectivities, we believe a critical conversation is the most effective means to prompt this intervention, eliciting experiences of research relationships and interview dialogue, exploring the complexities of place, embodiment and identification in conducting research. Through this exploratory conversation we call for a queering of communication in interview-based work within geographies of sexuality, and follow this up by reflecting upon some of our research experiences involving colliding constellations of gender, sexuality, race, ethnicity, age and class, *inter alia*. Gordon will begin these reflections, discussing how insider/outsider relationships are complicated by understanding interview-based research as a spatially-situated practice.

Gordon: I argue that queering communication in interview-based research through rethinking the subjectivity of the researcher in spatial terms is crucial for keeping methodological discussions alert to the dualisms that often shape understandings of these practices. Rather than positioning the researcher within the dualism of either 'insider' or 'outsider', queering communication keeps alive the importance of being alert to how narratives are always told *in situ*, to a particular audience. Many take comfort in arguments constituting the position of the researcher within the insider/outsider binary. Unaware of arguments that warn against how the concept of 'insider' fixes subjectivities within essentialised attributes, they take comfort in thinking within the normative dualism that suggests researchers who share the subjectivities of their participant as 'insiders' may have access to ideas, experiences, attitudes and practices denied to 'outsiders'. Claims of research credibility and dependability are made through calling upon the subject position of an 'insider'. In this case, the assumption of credibility is based on the notion that say a differently-abled woman interviewing a differently-abled woman, a gay man interviewing a gay man, a lesbian interviewing a lesbian, or a surfer interviewing a surfer, has access to understandings, attitudes and experiences that an 'outsider' may not. Drawing upon arguments which queer the researcher's subjectivity I suggest that each time claims of rigour in qualitative research are made by privileging a particular aspect of the researcher's subjectivity as an insider, a 'credibility fallacy' is committed by ignoring how subjectivities and space are relationally co-constituted.

Queering the researcher's subjectivity requires responsiveness to feminist arguments that demonstrate how subjectivities are negotiated spatially (Probyn 2003). Queering of subjectivity requires rethinking credibility in terms of the way that all narratives are told in circuits of social power. When all research contexts are thought about in spatial terms as circuits of social power, then the researcher becomes alert to the relational processes in which the interconnections and interactions between individuals are made. The crux of 'queer' within the social relationships of conducting research is therefore twofold; for the queer scholar it becomes a case of remaining alert to how subjectivities are an outcome of a relational process and to how a queer methodology must facilitate telling and interpreting narratives that do not inadvertently impose meanings rather than seeking to rework and create new meanings. The spatially-situated interactions of research help to constitute not only the context and the subjectivities of the researcher and participants, but also *how* narratives are told. How narratives are told frames how meanings are shaped. Hence, a queer research positionality requires sustaining a research context that enables the exploration of the various possibilities that interviews provide rather than those constituted through a pre-established system. This is not to suggest that the narratives are defined in abstraction. Clearly, there are forces at work that give meaning to the social relationships of the interview. But rather than these meanings being preconfigured – as in conventional understandings of the social relationships of semi-structured interviews configured by the dichotomy of insider-good/outsider-bad – the meanings of narratives are actively determined through the unfolding interactions of the interview.

To illustrate the importance of queering communication through thinking spatially about circuits of social power, I use my research on the relationship between home and travel in Townsville, Queensland, Australia. The broad objective of the Home and Away Project was to investigate the relationship between non-heteronormative subjectivities, travel and home-space in a tropical regional centre. I conducted interviews with thirty men and women who live in Townsville (see Waitt and Gorman-Murray 2007). From the start, the intersections between age, class, gender, regionality, nationality, ethnicity and sexuality constituted the spaces in which stories were told. I suspect, to many of my participants, I was initially a 'researcher from Wollongong working with the Queensland AIDS Council and the Townville Gay and Lesbian Task Force'. While I only stayed in Townsville for three weeks, recruitment relied heavily upon building community partnerships over the previous months and positioning participants as co-researchers. The vocabulary of co-researcher was deliberately deployed to move research practice beyond the dichotomy of insider/outsider. The 'co-researcher' is not a panacea but a plea to think outside the dichotomy of researcher/researched. Collaborative research projects with communities of diverse sexualities are not easy or unproblematic; sometimes it is difficult to accommodate differences across age, income, sexuality, gender and HIV-status. Hence, while claiming equivalence as a guiding principle,

I was faced with how I am embedded in forces that shape my everyday life. People in this study were both younger and older than me (I was 40 years of age), most had not travelled beyond Australian metropolitan centres, and they had different employment experiences to mine. To explore the relationship between travel, home and sexuality I often had to elaborate on what 'being gay' meant for me and my own experiences of home, travel and migration. Co-researchers did not assume that my understanding of 'sexuality' was similar to theirs. Notably, these differences often became central to *how* and *where* stories were told during the data gathering process.

Co-researchers most willing to talk about Townsville-as-home to a researcher from an Australian university beyond the metropolitan capitals often told stories of how they negotiated or unsettled the regime of heterosexuality in this provincial centre. Some were stories of community activism, others were coming out narratives. Many included illustrations of how normative assumptions of sexuality were reaffirmed and/or reconfigured through space. For instance, stories revealed how naturalised assumptions of heterosexuality were often remade by a number of enactments including: how they walked in the street, who they spoke to in public places, what they said, and where they showed same-sex affection. In other instances, stories were told about reconfiguring everyday assumptions about sexuality in Townsville through opening 'gay' venues, organising meeting places amongst friends, and cruising for sex in public places. In these, Townsville was ambiguously positioned as offering both opportunities and constraints for exploring same-sex-attraction. These stories were commonly told over a series of meetings, in a number of different locations. After initial meetings, I was often accepted into places co-researchers called 'home' – including cafes, pubs and houses. Here, they drew upon a range of material artefacts that triggered memories to illustrate their home-stories. In these less formal and more empowering social contexts, co-researchers repositioned my subjectivity in various ways. Across interviews I often felt and heard myself being constituted as both 'expert' and 'naïve', as 'listener' and 'storyteller', and 'confidant' and 'stranger'.

Reflecting on *how* and *where* the stories were told to me by how co-researchers positioned me differently within the spaces of the project requires revisiting the ethics of the research as a negotiated process, rather than the formal research procedures of a Human Research Ethics Committee. In the context of a conversation in which two people were making sense of their lives, for whom was the participant's intimate knowledge intended? Were stories shared with me positioned as confidant rather than as researcher? Equally, on the one hand, in not re-telling particular aspects of their stories, how did I become complicit in remaining silent about the dominant regimes intersecting around heterosexuality, class, and ethnicity in Townsville? On the other hand, the differences in lived experiences, and complexities of sexualised subjectivities, revealed 'splinters' between different groups of lesbians and gay men. How might I negotiate the 'tensions' within these queer communities? In accounting for these questions of difference, a queer research positionality is produced through ongoing communication with participants. This collaborative process is not a panacea in itself, but continued engagement is a practical call to recognise the challenges of working with communities of diverse sexualities. The key, then, is how interviewing is a two-way process that does not recreate exclusions and power concentrations that mask the ways that boundaries of sexuality are blurred or reconfigured.

Queering communication also facilitates an awareness of how what may be termed 'queer silences' are introduced into projects. Learning to be alert to concealment is integral to the theoretical challenge posed by queer theory. Judith Butler (2002) has argued that 'frameworks of understanding' are socially produced critical sites of power. She and others have ably demonstrated the importance of singularised identity labels in many political struggles – including the Gay Rights Movement – in recovering a collective memory denied by official channels. These forms of 'strategic' or 'essentialised identity' are often the basis for temporary rallying points and many political struggles. Indeed, recruitment for queer projects often relies upon essentialised identities of lesbian, gay, bisexual, transgender and transsexual. Such recruitment processes have implications for what is then concealed and disclosed during an interview/conversation. Listening to my transcribed conversations from the Home and Away Project I became aware of how I could sometimes 'hear' silences through how several respondents constituted political formations of 'gayness' around my positionality in the project. When asking questions exploring normative frameworks of sexuality and the home, some participants utilised these political formations of 'gayness' as a rallying point, both strengthening and facilitating alliances. For other respondents, however, the singularised political formations of gayness worked to marginalise, particularly several young men who assumed I was not 'like' them. An example of this is illustrated by participants who categorised themselves as 'queer' and disagreed strongly with the 'identity politics' of 'gay'. Bodily movements suggested these co-researchers were less comfortable speaking to me and they tended not to tell detailed stories. Their transcripts were not structured as a narrative with a beginning, middle and ending. Instead, the transcripts from our conversations have an almost interrogative quality, with respondents giving one-word answers. Rather than dismissing silence as absent voices that should be present, consideration is given to how these 'queer silences' are also moments of disclosure. These queer silences in the Home and Away Project may have arisen from co-researchers' assumptions invested in normative frameworks of sexuality. The Home and Away Project made heterosexuality visible in Townsville, and those expected to tell how the regimes of heterosexuality work were men and women with a range of experiences of discrimination and subordination: people who were gay, lesbian, queer, bisexual or trans identified. Yet, in making heterosexuality visible, the project also ran the risk of essentialising non-heteronormative identities, setting aside the multiple intersections of sexuality with class, gender, age, and so on, that cohere around any individual. In other words, a recruitment process focussing on same-sex-attraction assumed sexuality was an important dimension of making sense of Townsville-as-home. This, then, is an argument that silences cannot be dismissed, but should be reflected upon in terms of frameworks of understandings about subjectivities.

Andrew: Gordon makes many important points about how 'insider' status does not automatically confer understanding between 'research-subjects' and 'researcher-subjects'. The corollary is that 'outsider' status does not necessarily mean poorer understanding in the research relationship. This is even more the case when we realise that, through the circuit of social power, the multiple and fluid nature of subjectivities means that we are all *simultaneously* insider and outsider. I began to recognise and appreciate the difficulties – and possibilities – this brings to research relationships with sexual minorities when I was conducting interviews for my doctoral project on gay and lesbian homemaking practices in Australia. I discuss that project here, thinking about how the insider/outsider binary did not neatly map onto my experiences of communicative comprehension and dissonance in interview dialogues.

I want to think first about being an insider – that is, a gay researcher interviewing individuals also self-identifying as gay or lesbian – although this positionality is refined and challenged in subsequent paragraphs. While I agree with what Gordon said above, I also think that being an insider helped generate good research relationships in my project. Despite differences wrought by gender, race, ethnicity, class, age, spirituality, politics, *inter alia*, my respondents and I shared a range of commensurate perspectives on and experiences from living in Australian society. Robyn Dowling (2005: 26) suggests that insiders might have an advantage because 'people are more likely to talk to you freely, and you are more likely to understand what they are saying because you share their outlook on the world'. This was often the case in my research relationships, and reveals how wider societal norms – about who's socially mainstream and marginal – help facilitate communication. Thanks to overarching heteronormativity in Australian society, my participants and I shared a common experience of marginalisation because of our failure to adhere to Australian sexual norms. We have a shared experience of the potential danger of public spaces, and a shared desire to find places where we can 'be ourselves'. We have a common experience of marginalisation *vis-à-vis* Australian laws which still do not grant us equality with heterosexuals in key social and legal institutions, including marriage, taxation and adoption. All of these conditions impinge upon and inflect our diverse-yet-collective gay and lesbian homemaking practices.

But as I reflect on this project now, this is also where insider/outsider positionality became more complicated. Perhaps our conversations weren't detailed and fruitful merely because we shared common experiences as gay men and lesbians. Rather, perhaps the research relationships were rich because we were gay and lesbian *homemakers* – with the classed dimensions and characteristics that entails – and this imbrication of sexuality, class and homemaking was fundamental for invoking communicative understanding and textured narratives. Indeed, some of my least informative interviews came from respondents most closely aligned with my own multiple subject positions – tertiary-educated, middle-class, younger (20s/30s) gay men with left-wing political views and involved in activism – *except* for their more limited investment in homemaking. I thought these respondents would provide rich data about using their homes for advocacy, support groups and political agitation, and thus reveal how campaigning for social justice might work across, and even collapse, the distinction between 'domestic' and 'public' spheres (cf. Staeheli 1996, Legg 2003, Blunt 2005). However, they were more interested in simply articulating broader political goals for gay men and lesbians than in reflecting on how their uses of home might support that work – or indeed, how their political goals might have a notable impact on gay and lesbian homemaking (e.g. same-sex marriage, civil union, taxation and adoption reforms). I now realise that while we may have shared perspectives about 'gay rights', we failed to understand each other about the role of homemaking in wider politics.

Here, then, the supposed benefits of being an insider were compromised by complexities of spatialised subjectivities; they were gay activists, while I was a gay homemaker. While not mutually exclusive positions on opposites sides of a public/private partition – indeed, much activism in Australia is precisely about 'homemaking entitlements' such as civil unions and the right to disclose domestic partnerships in the public sphere – in this instance different identifications with activism and homemaking led to a degree of misunderstanding in, and about, our communication. Although a speculative reflection on my part only, these participants might have questioned the value of academic research about gay and lesbian homemaking *vis-à-vis* political activism – querying if the production of such knowledge could be transferred to and effectively utilised in grassroots action for social justice – and consequently maintained a 'polite distance' in the research relationship. Given the current activist focus on legal prerogatives attached to cohabiting partnerships, I thought that more nuanced understandings of gay and lesbian homemaking could contribute to political claims, but due to communicative misapprehension during the interview process, the perceived breach between academic knowledge and grassroots activism was not overcome.

Consequently, it is important not to romanticise insider status. Even with those most closely aligned to my own subjectivity in terms of gender, age, class, ethnicity and politics, the research relationship and interview conversations were inhibited and we talked at 'cross purposes' (although this has other potentials, with researcher and participants exposed to each other's political positions and agendas). How much more serious might communicative dissonance be with those with quite different subject positions from my own, such as lesbians, older gay men, or those from different ethnic-cultural backgrounds?

Surprisingly, I found that communication often worked better across such divides: just as it is possible to misunderstand across sameness, it is also possible to understand across difference (Valentine 2002). Dowling (2005: 26), for instance, points to the advantages of being an outsider: 'people make more of an effort to clearly articulate events, circumstances, and feelings to the researcher'. In my case, some respondents carefully explained certain circumstances with which they thought I would not be familiar, or which lay beyond my own life experiences as a younger, middle-class, Anglo-Celtic gay man. For instance, some older respondents, recognising that I am part of the 'post-liberation' generation of gay men and lesbians, thoroughly described their experiences of growing up and coming out before the era of 'gay liberation' (occurring in Australia during the 1970s and 1980s), and how those experiences have subsequently coloured their meanings, uses and designs of home. Likewise, some lesbian interviewees stressed a lack of lesbian-dedicated commercial venues (against many for gay men) to frame their explanations of why home is an important site for identity-affirmation. Meanwhile, some respondents with Italian or Greek cultural heritage, recognising my Anglo-Celtic background, took great care to explain how and why their ethnic-cultural affiliations remain important to their homemaking processes – and how their homemaking practices re-unite their ethnic-cultural and sexual identities. In these instances, my different positionality was a means for drawing out further nuances of gay and lesbian meanings and uses of home, and for learning about how sexuality combined in different ways with other subject positions in those homemaking practices.

It is arguable that communication worked 'better' in these instances because both researcher and participants mutually sorted through our multiple subjectivities, sifting dissident sexuality to the top as the point of commonality akin to what Gordon suggested above about how designing a research project specifically for 'gay' and 'lesbian' participants can have repercussions for silence and disclosure in subsequent interview conversations. While acknowledging that these circumstances probably unfolded in certain research relationships, overall I don't think such hierarchical categorisations were the rule across this range of interviews. During discussions many of these participants spontaneously stressed – unprompted – the importance of ethnicity, gender and life-course changes to their senses of self and carefully indicated where these subjectivities entwined with sexuality in their processes of homemaking. In this way, through the opportunities presented by the interview dialogue, the participants took it upon themselves to highlight to me their 'intersectional' subjectivities (Valentine 2007) – entanglements of sexuality with gender, ethnicity, race, age, class and spirituality in individual sexual subject-formation.

Prompted by these richly-textured conversations, I am thinking more carefully about the confluence of ethnic, gender, age and sexual subjectivities at work in homemaking practices. For instance, in a recent paper drawing on this data (Gorman-Murray 2008), I investigated how material homemaking practices are used to reconcile individuals' ethnic-cultural, religious and sexual subjectivities over the life-course.[2] Like Gordon, I found the location of interviews vitally important in effective communication and, consequently, understanding how ethnicity, cultural heritage and sexual identity inflect each other in everyday domestic lives and lifestyles. The interviews were conducted *in* participants'

---

2   And across 2009–2012 I will explore older gay men's homemaking experiences as part of an Australian Research Council project on changing spatialities of masculinity and domesticity in inner Sydney.

homes, and given that life stories and memories are often palpably spatial (Moss 2001, Gorman-Murray 2007b), this location acted as a built-in 'spatial prompt'. In discussing their experiences and uses of their homes, interviewees drew on memories associated with the very setting of the interview, thus encouraging closer consideration of their taken-for-granted daily homemaking practices. Respondents could look around and consider 'on the spot' how certain parts of their homes were designed and used in particular ways, and be reminded about specific experiences associated with those spaces. Similarly, various material objects around their homes acted as triggers: respondents weaved their narratives around the objects at hand, detailing why they were important, evoking their meaningful connections to self and others. They talked about what the objects symbolised, why they were located in certain places, and how they related to other objects in their homes. I found that this was particularly important for prompting participants' reflections on the confluence of ethnicity and sexuality over the life-course, revealing their mutual influence in unfolding subjectivities and practices.

In this way, my experience of interview communication is queering my understanding of multiple sexual subjectivities in contemporary Australia, eliciting the entangling of ethnic-cultural heritage in sexual subject-formation. This rethinking is ethically important in Aotearoa New Zealand and Australia. While established as largely Anglo-Saxon and Anglo-Celtic English-speaking nations, over the twentieth century our countries have registered amongst the highest per capita intakes of migrants from non-Anglo backgrounds, such as the Asia-Pacific and southern Europe (Waitt et al. 2000). This shifting demographic composition overlies existing indigenous populations, and long-standing Anglo-settlers, to produce countries at once postcolonial and multicultural. Each cultural and ethnic group has brought their own notion of sexuality (which is itself in flux). This matrix of racial, ethnic and cultural differences has produced an array of inter-mingling and over-lapping sexual subjectivities based on the mutual inflection of ethnicity, cultural heritage and sexuality – including productive collisions between how sexuality is perceived in the homeland and 'host' land (Pallotta-Chiarolli 1999, Jackson and Sullivan 1999) and between indigenous and settler socio-cultural structures (Hodge 1993, Riggs 2006, 2007). Not surprisingly, then, Australasian scholars have been at the forefront of work exploring how sexuality is 'queered' by its criss-crossing with race, ethnicity and postcoloniality (Jagose 1996b, Jackson and Sullivan 1999, Sullivan 2003, Johnston and Longhurst 2008).

Thus, in the Australasian context, communication in research relationships must be 'queered' and ever-attentive to the fractured constellation of ethnicised-sexualised hybrid identities unfolding 'down under'. This is not to suggest that other subject positions don't also affect these entangled subjectivities (e.g., as noted, 'classed' and 'activist' subjectivities were keenly implicated in my research), but rather I stress the paramount importance of race and ethnicity in social relationships across postcolonial-multicultural Aotearoa New Zealand and Australia. In the subsequent discussion, Lynda elicits these intersections with regard to indigenous subjectivities in Aotearoa New Zealand. Parallel circumstances are at work across the Tasman Sea, in Australia, although inflected by geographical, historical and (post)colonial differences. Unfortunately, specific consideration of 'Aboriginal homosexualities' (Gays and Lesbians Aboriginal Alliance 1994), and the convergences and divergences between Aotearoa New Zealand and Australia, cannot be accommodated in the scope and length of this chapter. However, Lynda's discussion of Māori sexual subjectivities sufficiently exemplifies our collective concern with the intersections of race, ethnicity, postcoloniality and sexuality.[3]

Lynda: I would like to pick up on Andrew's points about researching ethnicity and sexuality 'down under'. Living and researching 'down under', it is impossible to understand gender, sex and sexuality without also considering issues of biculturalism, multiculturalism, racism, colonisation and postcolonialism. Subjectivities such as race, ethnicity and culture cannot be disentangled from the spaces in which we research sexualities. In a recent special issue of the *Australian Geographer* entitled 'Geographies of Sexuality and Gender Down-Under', Robyn Longhurst (2008) notes that there is a burgeoning literature in the area of sexuality and ethnicity and more specifically she points to research in Aotearoa New Zealand by Linda Tuhiwai Smith, Leonie Pihama, Clive Aspin and Glenis Philip-Barbara at the University of Auckland as a noteworthy example of this. This group embarked upon a Māori Sexuality Project from 2002–2004 'to support the consciousness, advance the practice of, and promote the availability of Māori understandings and definitions of Māori sexuality' (Māori Sexuality Project 2008). In 2007 the Aotearoa based company 'Huia' published an excellent book *Sexuality and the Stories of Indigenous People*, edited by Jessica Hutchings and Clive Aspin. However, even with this encouraging development there are still many opportunities for social scientists and others to engage with the intersections of sexualities and ethnicities. I agree with both Andrew and Gordon that engaging in these issues demands a greater sensitivity to difference and my research on sexuality and space has meant I have been acutely aware of ethnicity and sexuality as mutually defining subjectivities.

For many years I have been involved in researching Pride celebrations (see, for example, Johnston 2005, 2007) and as such I have been part of Aotearoa communities involving diverse sexual subjectivities.[4] As a pākehā (white New

---

3   For rich discussions that also address indigenous sexualities in Australia, I recommend Hodge (1993), Gays and Lesbians Aboriginal Alliance (1994), Clarke (1999) and Riggs (2006, 2007).

4   These diverse subjectivities are best expressed in Hamilton Pride's (2008) 'Who are we?' publicity pamphlet: 'Gay. Lesbian. Bisexual. Queer. Homosexual. Non-heterosexual. Transgender: A person who lives as the opposite birth gender. Transsexual: A person whose gender identity is opposite the birth gender. M2F: male to female transgender, F2M: female to male transgender. Transition: a term used to explain taking steps to change from one gender to another. Transvestite, Cross dresser: a person who enjoys wearing the clothes of their opposite gender but does not wish to live as that gender. Drag Queen: a man who dresses as a woman for entertainment purpose. Drag King: a woman who dresses as a man for entertainment purposes. Androgyne: person

Zealander), tertiary educated, woman who identifies as lesbian there were times during Pride research when I was simultaneously both an insider and outsider. As Gill Valentine (2002: 199) notes, in many research situations 'it is impossible for us to unpick how the mutual constitution of gender, class, race, sexuality works. ... Dualisms of insider/outsider can never therefore capture the complex and multi-faceted identities and experiences of researchers'. As Gordon has mentioned above, place makes a difference to the positioning of the researcher within the dualism of either 'insider' or 'outsider'; as geographers we are alert to how research narratives are always spatial, temporal and to a particular audience.

Part of my research on Aotearoa New Zealand's annual Pride festival (the HERO Parade and Festival held in Auckland) involved working with the Parade Director as a volunteer for six weeks prior to, and during, the festival. During this time I successfully gathered empirical material (focus group and individual interviews) from approximately 30 gay men, lesbians, bisexuals, queer youth, transgender, intersexed, and so on, people involved in presenting festival celebrations to the public. I was not, however, *always* 'successful' gaining empirical material and I will outline an example of what Andrew mentioned – a situation of communicative dissonance between me as the researcher and potential participants.

I invited all groups involved in the HERO Parade to be part of my research. One group who regularly used the Pride workshop space was Te Waka Awhina Takatāpui. They were a group of Māori gay men and transgender people who were constructing a large waka (a type of canoe usually associated with the arrival of the first people to Aotearoa) as their centre piece for the Pride Parade. They declined to be interviewed when I approached them (on two occasions) with my invitation to be part of the research project. With the hindsight of time, reflection and more research experience, I realise that my subjectivities as a pākehā lesbian was a crucial point of difference. While the Pride Parade was for all non-heteronormative forms of sexuality, sometimes the 'umbrella' of 'queer' was not enough to unite groups.

Concepts of sexuality, queerness, gender, and ethnicity do not translate easily into non-English languages such as Māori. While the word takatāpui tends to be used currently to embrace all non-heterosexual forms of Māori sexuality, it is a term that has a (pre)colonial history that is different from the history of the terms such as queer, gay or lesbian (see Aspin 2005, Brickell 2008 and Longhurst 2008). In a publication called *Ko Ia He or She* produced by the Hau Ora Takatāpui

---

appearing and identifying neither as female or male presenting a gender mixed or neutral. Intersex: a person born with both male and female genitalia. Takatāpui: an intimate companion of the same sex. Hinetau: drag queen. Hinehi: transgender. Tangata ira tane: a person who has the essence of a man. Tangata ira wahine: a person who has the essence of a woman. Whakaaehinekiri: recognise oneself as a female. Whakawahine: to be like a woman – used by male to female transgender Māori. Fa'afafine (Samoan), Fakaleiti (Tongan), Akava'ine (Cook Island).'

(Māori HIV Prevention Programme, New Zealand AIDS Foundation) the author
explains:

> In the language of our ancestors there was no pronoun to distinguishing gender
> such as he or she, there was ia, which as used to distinguish that person regardless
> of their gender. So was there a Māori word for Transgender? Were our ancestors
> aware that for some gender is not defined at birth? (Harris 2005: 3).

Such differences in understanding gender, sexuality and ethnicity between pākehā
and Māori were probably the reason that I did not make a research 'connection'
with the group Te Waka Awhina Takatāpui. The politics of race and indigeneity in
Aotearoa adds another layer of complexity to our subjectivities that goes beyond
the sometimes uneasy binary of lesbian/gay male. This example of communicative
dissonance didn't stop at our very different understandings of subjectivities. My
use of normative Eurocentric research methodology was probably another reason
people of the Te Waka Awhina Takatāpui group declined to be interviewed. At the
Pride Parade workshop I talked briefly to a couple of people involved in Te Waka
Awhina Takatāpui, and I left with them my introductory letter which explained my
research intentions and that I had gained 'ethical approval' from my institution
– the University of Waikato. This is standard research practice for many western
(white) academics. Put another way, I had adopted 'authoritative', normative and
Eurocentric methodological processes because of my institutional requirements.
Yet clearly, this is not always an appropriate methodology when conducting
research with Māori in Aotearoa.

    In this situation one way to 'queer' communications in research relationships
may be to adopt ideas, concepts and methods which correspond with Māori belief
systems. In Aotearoa researchers are often guided by an indigenous approach to
research called 'kaupapa Māori', that has an epistemological stance that distances
itself from traditional western concepts and practices and determines its own
agenda based on values, belief systems and actions accorded by Māori tradition.
The discourse of kaupapa Māori emerged as an alternative research paradigm out of
the dissatisfaction with 'orthodox' western methods which have in the past gained
the reputation for being incompatible, and in many cases, ethically inconsistent
with Māori understandings of place and people (Bishop 1998). 'Kaupapa Māori
is an attempt to retrieve space for Māori voices and perspectives ... it also opens
up avenues for approaching and critiquing dominant, Western worldviews' (Cram
2001: 40). Back in 1985 geographer Evelyn Stokes highlighted the need for
research methodologies that incorporate cultural frameworks. She argued there
is a need for trained Māori researchers and research to be conducted for Māori
with Māori. Kaupapa Māori research positions indigenous knowledges at the
centre, promotes Māori involvement in research, focuses on methodologies that
are appropriate for Māori and highlights mutually beneficial outcomes for the
researcher and the researched (Tuhiwai Smith 1999: 183).

Since 2007 I have become involved in another Pride organisation, Hamilton Pride (see www.hamiltonpride.co.nz). I work with this group because of a desire to support sexual minorities in our region. Hamilton Pride is an organisation that seeks to serve as a liaison between various sexual minority community groups as well as publicising, supporting and hosting Hamilton Pride events locally and nationally. Hamilton Pride aims to help people feel 'in place' and 'proud'. It provides a space for people to network with others, and it may assist people to explore new and changing subjectivities and places. In partnership with this group, I have started a research project called 'Hamilton Pride: Spaces of Sameness and Difference'. The project examines politics, subjectivities and feelings of 'belonging' for a diverse group of sexual minorities, including takatāpui. This research may queer communication through the establishment of a 'research whanau' (extended family). A research whanau is a way of organising research through decision making and participation that is consistent with Māori philosophy, values and practices (Tuhiwai Smith 1999). As this new research project unfolds we proceed with a commitment to ensuring that research activities are consistent with the spirit and intent of the Treaty of Waitangi[5] and seek to adopt an epistemological stance that distances itself from traditional western, colonialist, masculinist and heteronormative concepts and practices. It is vital to work closely with and for takatāpui in Hamilton Pride. Of particular concern is that sexual and gender subjectivities do not travel easily from pākehā to Māori knowledges, hence a research whanau provides a core space to organise the research, incorporate ethical procedures, report back to communities, and a way of debating ideas and issues which impact on the research project. A research whanau involving multiple and complex subjectivities associated with sexualities and ethnicities in the Hamilton Pride group may queer research communications and be a highly appropriate methodology in Aotearoa. Pride research led by, and with, takatāpui is more likely to be attentive to the way in which postcolonial places queer methodologies.

How, then, to conclude? As our chapter conversation has unfolded we found ourselves thinking more and more about our own and our participants' subjectivities. The sharing of our ideas about research experiences forced us to confront that it is not just *how* we do research that matters but also *where* we do research. Doing sexuality and space research in 'down under' postcolonial spaces has increased our awareness of subjective entanglements in interview-based communications – between researchers and participants, between participants, and between researchers.

Research concerned with subjectivities requires a great deal of self-awareness on the part of researchers, including an awareness of the limits to self-knowledge. Gail Davies and Claire Dwyer (2007: 257) remark 'it is hard, though perhaps not impossible, to imagine what a radically new form of qualitative research

---

5   The Treaty of Waitangi is known as New Zealand's founding document. It was first signed, on 6 February 1840 in Waitangi. The Treaty is an agreement, in te reo Māori and English, that was made between the British Crown and about 540 Māori rangatira (chiefs).

practice might look like'. We have looked hard at our methodologies and have found problems with some of our research practices. We have also found that some of our attempts to queer methodologies worked well. In general, we have used 'standard' qualitative methods – such as focus groups, interviews, and ethnographies – yet we have identified changes in the way these methods can be conceptualised and executed. These changes might start by questioning identity categories and examining how certain western sexual and gender subjectivities travel (or don't) into other knowledges. To facilitate queer conversations in our postcolonial nations we may need to be part of a 'research whanau', and/or work with indigenous Australian communities with goals to transform the way in which research methods are employed.

Andrew, Gordon and I – like many social scientists concerned with social justice, equality and difference – seek to challenge research processes which may normalise and homogenise certain sexual practices and knowledges. We have worried about our methodological approaches, and whether we have been 'appropriate' when working with participants that are both similar and different to us. Communication 'worries' of this kind are the stuff of academic labour: we negotiate them, whether in micro-level, routine decisions about our interactions with others, or in more major ways that may have a decisive bearing on the lives of those both within and beyond the academy. Consequently, queering the academy may change those who do research as much as it may change the production of knowledge. Indeed, queering methodology within and beyond the academy has been as much about finding new ways of *being* as about changing research practices. Our sexuality and space research is undertaken in powerful, western and conventional institutions (our own and many of the institutions in which we research). Queer academics, and academics conducting queer research, repeatedly confront and struggle with profound tensions between working in heteronormative institutions whilst seeking to challenge such norms. The same can be said of the tensions that arise due to privileged – classed, raced, gendered – positions of some sexual minority organisations and individuals. Queering communications may be a useful tool to understand further power relations created and dismantled during research. We are committed to complex and critical understandings of reflexivity and self, opening up explorations of non-rational, non-(hetero)normative and non-colonial dimensions of research relationships.

Our discussion about sexuality and space research has highlighted the multiplicity and 'mess' of methodologies (see Law 2004 on 'mess in social science' and the introduction to this collection). Despite the difficulties, we think there is value in examining and queering communications in order to make sense of – and mess with – the way in which geographies of sexualities intersects with gender, race, ethnicity, age and class. We look forward to reading more about queering communications as research practice and about researchers queering their communications.

Chapter 7

The Trouble with Fieldwork: Queering Methodologies

Michael Connors Jackman

New work on methodologies in sexuality studies has emerged from a range of academic disciplines with different, and sometimes conflicting, approaches to doing research. In bringing together the interpretive strategies from the humanities and methods from the social sciences, the question of methodology has become central to how scholars develop and execute research plans, as well as how they conceptualise the who, what, and where of carrying out research. Though my focus aligns primarily with anthropology and the cognate disciplines, I am concerned with the pan-disciplinary problem of crafting research plans and the production of knowledge. Questions of how queer studies should construct its object of study must be posed not only in terms of theory, but also as part of a larger concern with methodology and the politics of representation. Drawing on anthropological work on sexuality and new approaches to methodology, this chapter queries how *fieldwork* and *ethnography* are being conceptualised in queer studies. In what follows, I examine some of the methodological problems associated with carrying out ethnographic research, in connection to my own work with gay and queer artists in Atlantic Canada. The problem of 'the field' as a concept in the social sciences must be given some attention if we are to develop new queer methodologies that might incorporate ethnography as a theoretical and methodological tool.

The core of this chapter concerns how ethnography is being employed as a research method in queer studies. Though field research can help scholars to examine the active role individuals play in producing meaning, it can prove problematic for queer studies, for it assumes a point of origin that demands muted sexuality. In addition to showing the limitations of the field as a concept, I point to some preliminary ways to refigure fieldwork in queer studies such that studies of sexuality might benefit from the nuanced and intimate understanding that ethnography provides. In the first section of this chapter I examine how the field has been theorised in anthropology and the complications involved with its use in queer studies. Secondly, I discuss how the boundaries of field sites interact with the erotic subjectivities of researchers and informants. Part of the trouble with the field, I argue, is that the maintenance of its boundaries can often silence the dynamic play of desire that shapes fieldwork relationships. In the final section I draw on some of my own experiences with decision-making and desire during fieldwork. Proposing a reorientation in how ethnographers conceive of desire, I consider whether ethnographies of queer publics and assemblages might hold the promise of expanding our existing understanding of sexualities cross-culturally.

Part I

Queer Ethnography?

The problem of defining what queer signifies is almost as difficult as explaining what is not queer. In fact, as there are no final answers to what counts or fails to count as queer, it might be added to a list of what Walter Bryce Gallie (1956) has called essentially contested concepts.[1] In a recent issue of the *Graduate Journal of Social Science (GJSS)* devoted to queer studies and methodological approaches, Tiina Rosenberg (2008) offers a critical overview of the usage of 'queer' in academic debates in Sweden since the emergence of 'queer theory' in the early 1990s. This genealogy is distinct from the circulation of the term in the United States and much of Euro-American scholarship, and as Rosenberg notes, the concept of queer continues to connote a range of meanings for different audiences even today (2008: 14). However, the term 'queer theory' and with it the term 'queer' can be traced to Teresa de Lauretis's 'Queer theory: Lesbian and gay sexualities' (1991) and, at the time of its appearance in gay and lesbian studies debates came to refer to a reinvention of how we understand the sexual (1991: iv). However, since the early 1990s queerness and queer theory, as critical categories, have themselves undergone considerable reinvention and there are no all-encompassing definitions to be had. My use of queer follows from Michael Warner's introduction to *Fear of a Queer Planet* (1993), in which he describes the term as having 'the effect of pointing out a wide field of normalization, rather than simple intolerance, as the site of violence … "Queer" therefore also suggests the difficulty in defining the population whose interests are at stake in queer politics' (1993: xxvi). It is this undecided and doubling aspect of queer that makes it a potentially useful methodological guide. As it presumes no necessary object, research carried out in the name of 'queer' might hold the possibility of remaining unfixed, fluid, and dynamic, thereby resisting a simple reduction of research findings to mere formula. Though queer studies became quickly institutionalised after the publication of de Lauretis's first mention of the term queer theory, the question of what queer means remains just that: a question.

As a question, queer has continued to develop, unravel and grow since its inception almost two decades ago. In the previously mentioned collection on methodologies from *GJSS* there is an effort to redirect the focus of queer

---

1   Following Gallie (1956), I wish to make the argument for the use of contested concepts as always in need of remaking. Because they allow for multiple interpretations, they can be deployed to different ends depending on the aims of those who draw on the concepts.

studies, and to reconsider whom *queer* designates, by emphasising the bias of United States scholars in studying cross-cultural and transnational sexualities (see Liinason and Kulpa 2008). The articles presented in the volume centre on the problem of studying sexuality in a global world where sexual identities and practices in seemingly remote locales are informed by, and sometimes themselves also inform, the construction of sexualities in distant cultural contexts. This work follows from and expands upon earlier studies of globalisation and sexualities by Elizabeth Povinelli and George Chauncey (1999), Dennis Altman (2001), Martin Manalansan IV (2003), Evelyn Blackwood (2007), and Tom Boellstorff (2007b). The move towards a global perspective has brought to the fore some of the deeply held colonial and ethnocentric assumptions about the categories of analysis deployed in studies of sexuality that have pervaded and shaped anthropological enquiry and much of the social sciences.

In an attempt to foreground international and transnational sexualities and to locate them within a global framework of unequal power relations, some have turned their attention to the study of diasporas. Among such recent works that explore the interconnectedness of racism, sexism, and homophobia amongst diasporas is Gayatri Gopinath's *Impossible Desires* (2005), which interrogates the complex intersectional relationships between race, gender, and sexuality in South Asian diaspora cultural production in the United States, Canada, and the United Kingdom. Gopinath's work shows the innovation and vibrancy of those involved in creating cultural products specific to their experiences as members of diasporas, yet studies of this sort rely heavily on cultural artefacts (books, films, music) as indicators of wider social phenomena. The methodological approaches taken up by Gopinath are indeed queer in so far as they challenge common representations of South Asian diasporas as heterosexual. Yet it is her recasting of radical and materialist feminism, in the mantra 'queerness is to heterosexuality as the diaspora is to nation' (2005: 11) that provides a serious critical perspective on the unequal power relations between fixed and fluid identities. Redirecting Catherine MacKinnon's attack on patriarchy in Western society, Gopinath's text shows the potential value of a queer diasporic reading practice. Indeed, this is the principal focus of her text, a work that deploys 'a queer diasporic reading practice that traces ... multiple and contradictory meanings' (2005: 26). A critical reading practice is central to any rigorous study of cultural life, but one must also consider the broader social conditions that enable such readings.

A common response to literary and cultural studies of sexuality by those who focus on informant-based research is to disregard such studies in favour of quantitative and empirical work. While there exist epistemological limitations to those textual analyses which do not consider the context in which texts are produced and read, this critique holds no water if we consider that literary scholars and social scientists draw on many of the same methods, tools, and perspectives to analyse language, cultural products, or archival materials. This critique of ethnography is by no means new, and was central to what was dubbed the *crisis in representation* in anthropology. The debate, which peaked in the late 1980s, was characterised by a general concern with objectivity in academic research and the authoritative voice in ethnographic accounts. As outlined in James Clifford and Eric Marcus (1986), the rise of reflexivity within anthropology as a discipline developed as anthropologists turned to literary theory to explore the problems of interpreting social reality (1986: 6). The interpretive turn links back to Clifford Geertz's *The Interpretation of Cultures* (1973), as well as Dick Cushman and George Marcus's now classic essay 'Ethnographies as texts' (1982). Clifford and Marcus's piece in particular shows how the complex relationship between experience, writing, and the reception of ethnographic works is often erased from the final ethnographic record in order to maintain the objective stance of the researcher. They call for a redefinition of ethnographic texts as experimental accounts of fieldwork, arguing that ethnographers must account for both the production of fieldwork accounts and their anticipated reception by a range of different readerships. In order to do so, researchers must recognise the role of the ethnographer as mediator and interpreter of cultural texts.

Ethnographic approaches specific to the study of sexuality are fraught with similar problems of representation, authorial authority, and objectivity, but they can nonetheless offer insight into the dynamics between researchers and informants. Indeed, their potential to expand the scope of seuxality research is part of the reason some have proposed employing ethnographic methods. As sexuality involves bodies, feelings, emotions, and human interaction, it is important to recognise the exchange and dynamics involved in human-to-human relations. Notable among such proponents of ethnographic fieldwork as a research method is Elisabeth Lund Engebretsen (2008) who argues for the use of ethnography as a theoretical and practical guide to the study of sexualities cross-culturally. In this way, ethnography can offer 'a critical appraisal of current theorizing on sexual globalization and queer studies' and emphasise the situated realities of everyday realities by employing a 'multifaceted "thick" data that enables effective re-thinking of received analytical paradigms' (Engebretsen 2008: 112). While the use of ethnography in queer studies provides a way of critiquing ethnocentric and universalising tendencies in theoretical frameworks which presume pan-cultural sexual identities and practices and thereby privilege Euro-American categories as fully developed, the promise of ethnography should be met with some caution. Ethnography and its bedfellow, fieldwork, together imply the existence of the ethnographic field, and that field is as much a social and cultural construction as the identities and practices that commonly concern queer studies scholars.

Fields of Desire?

In much of the social sciences, fieldwork is a privileged research method. In anthropology the field is not only where a researcher does his or her work, it is what enables such research in the first place. How the field emerges in anthropological writing almost always charts how the anthropologist arrives at his field site. This is a distancing mechanism through which anthropologists establish the relationship between *here*, academe, and *there*, the field. In their introduction to *Anthropological Locations* (1997) Akhil Gupta and James Ferguson point to the persisting problem of defining the field, asking 'what of "the field" itself, the place where the distinctive work of fieldwork may be done, that taken-for-granted space in which an "Other" culture or society lies waiting to be observed and written?' (1997a: 2). Indeed, what of the field? What is it and what makes its study a viable research enterprise? The fact is, not all field sites are thought to make good places of study. There are subtle ways in which anthropologists discipline one another and police what kinds of field sites become acceptable.

On a number of occasions I have been both subtly and directly advised by anthropology professors that the likelihood of securing a teaching position in anthropology is significantly greater if one chooses to *go away* and travel thousands of kilometres to do fieldwork. Reading classic ethnographic accounts reveals this pervasive assumption that the farther one travels, the more authentic one's research becomes. This is one of the unwritten, yet powerful, rules that define anthropology as a discipline. The tendency towards travel is mapped out by Virginia Caputo as a devaluing of research 'close to home', in favour of 'real fieldwork' carried out somewhere else (2000: 22). She describes the dismissal of her own work as a expectation for fieldwork to be 'marked by travel, physical displacement, intensive dwelling in an unfamiliar setting away from home, an experience of initiation, and movement in and out of a field' (2000: 22). In maintaining its claim to the field as a spatiotemporal site with clearly identifiable and salient boundaries, anthropology lays a unique claim to the analysis of cultural difference. And to carry out fieldwork among people of the same cultural group as oneself is to undermine the integrity of the discipline. Those who choose to take this route are sometimes seen as traitors to the discipline and are thereby awarded the title 'native anthropologist'. For Kiran Narayan (1993), the notion of the native anthropologist implies a fractured allegiance to the discipline of anthropology. To be classified as such is to be accused of identifying too strongly with one's informants. While this is true for many researchers whose political and religious affiliations or ethnic backgrounds are shared with informants, a similar argument can be made for sexual orientation. Kath Weston (1997) writes of her own professional experience in anthropology as one of nativisation, by which the lesbian anthropologist who chooses to study gay men and lesbians comes to be regarded as an authentic member of her informant group. Weston describes this process as the effect not of authorial intent on behalf of the researcher, but of power relations in the wider society (1997: 172). It is in response to these tendencies that Gupta and Ferguson advocate decentring 'the field' as the singular, privileged site of anthropological knowledge, in an effort to reconfigure it as one element in a multistranded methodology, not unlike what Donna Haraway has called 'situated knowledges' (1988: 37). Still, some fields are thought to be better sites than others for the purpose of situating oneself.

Up to this point I have offered a critical overview of queer as it has been theorised in studies of sexuality, and ethnography as anthropologists have used conceived of it. In the next section I point to one of the most troubling aspects of fieldwork: getting there. Recounting my experience with mapping the boundaries of the field for my Master's research, I show that my attempts to go to the field and to get involved in the everyday lives of informants conflicted with the realities of fieldwork, eventually leading me back to my point of origin. It took several trips to and from my field site to come to the realisation that the boundaries of the field as I had defined them were preventing me from getting fully involved in my research. Reviewing work on erotic subjectivity in the field, I show that such boundaries generate a false sense of locality in fieldwork and serve to downplay the role of erotic dynamics in fieldwork.

Part II

Following the Field: In or Out?

> The morning comes too soon. When I wake it is late, but I have slept very little. My head aches from the night before. I telephone Jude to ensure that we will not miss our flight to St. John's. We are going to St. John's for the opening of The Rooms, a new arts centre housing the provincial archive, museum, and art gallery of Newfoundland and Labrador. The Halifax airport is at least a half-hour drive from where we are, so we had best to get going. Moving along the highway, north beyond Dartmouth, we chat about local artists and mutual friends. When we pull up to the door for Departures we quickly grab our bags from the car and scurry into the airport. We had not the time to pick up a paper on the way to the airport, so it came as a surprise when Jude directed my attention to a headline in the Halifax Chronicle-Herald: 'Harper: Same Sex Debate Not Over.' Today Bill C-38, The Civil Marriage Act, receives its first reading in the Canadian Senate. Today, 25 June 2005, would mark a noteworthy shift in Canadian history, though it seems to affect us all in different ways.

> As we check in at the airline counter I try to make myself presentable. We show identification to a very grumpy airline employee who glares at us, her eyes filled with something resembling judgement. She asks if we are flying together or separately. We confirm that we are indeed travelling together. After we check in our baggage, Jude lets out a high-pitched guffaw. 'Oh! I hope the poppers aren't in my carry-on!' he laughs. I wonder if the receptionist understands what poppers are. Regardless, she looks at Jude and looks at me and looks disgusted. The flight to Newfoundland is smooth, but I am in poor form from the night before. As we topple onto the runway in St. John's I think about Pierre. We left him quite late the night before, so it is possible he has missed the ferry in North Sydney and will arrive late for the official opening of The Rooms.

Luckily, Pierre makes it in time for the opening reception. Looking around I see a few familiar faces of St. John's artists devouring food and wine amidst the crowd of overdressed money with carefully sculpted hair. Midway through the event I run into my dear supervisor who stands out against her surroundings. She asks me, point blank, what I am doing back in St. John's, which I take to mean: 'Aren't you supposed to be in the field?' A wave of guilt washes over me. I avoid confessing that I am, indeed, a lazy fieldworker. In the world of academia one can feign ignorance, and on occasion with proper documentation be excused from obligatory meetings. One might even receive a pardon for cutting class if one can offer an elaborate explanation of computer failure, highway robbery, or unseasonable tempests linked to global climate change. But, there is no excuse for skipping the field. Fieldwork is to be carried out for a specified period of time in the field; you are either in the field or out of it.

I return to Halifax shortly thereafter to continue interviews and participant observation. As the plane sweeps over the marshy wilderness of Newfoundland and into a speckless sky, I wonder why I have stayed so long. When the seatbelt sign fades to grey, I insert my headphones and disappear into the clouds. Am I in or out of the field? Am I approaching or leaving my field site?

Travel is an integral part of research, and regardless of whether movement occurs across a vast global expanse from Toronto to rural Indonesia, between one urban centre to another, or within one's own residential area, all research requires the movement of the researcher from his or her originary position into that of the data. Also when the objects of study are texts, these form a field of study in and through which the researcher moves. However, for many researchers who study the lives of people of a particular historical period, geographic area, or cultural background, the field can become a reductionist synonym for that group of people. In my experience, the decision to explore a specific geographic field site initially brought me to Halifax to carry out fieldwork, just as it was this sense of place that punctuated my return. However, it was the desire to follow informants that lead me to St. John's. It was as though my field consisted of the people I had met, rather than their place of residence. This tendency has lead critics like Ellen Lewin (1991) to regard the researching of lesbian and gay culture by anthropologists as a troubling enterprise. Critiquing how lesbians and gays in anthropology have been represented in ethnographic accounts, Lewin writes that field accounts often assume a kind of immutability in the identities of informants. Lewin calls for a more nuanced rendering of lesbian and gay collectivity that avoids representing such cultures as bounded with fixed memberships (1991: 790–91).

The issue of membership lies at the heart of criticisms levelled at anthropologists who assume egalitarian relations between members of social groups. The discipline requires that the researcher maintain a sense of being an outsider whilst learning the intimate details of the group he or she studies. The *we* of social science literature is in most cases taken to mean *we scholars* in opposition to *them, the informative yet unreflexive purveyors of collective knowledge.* Most scholars who produce such studies will acknowledge that group membership is never given or static, but produced. The problem with studies of social groups is not that the findings of researchers have missed the complexities of everyday life that shape what it means to be gay or lesbian in a particular time and place. Rather, the linchpin in the machinations of field research is the framework itself, which assumes an unadulterated point of origin: one of muted sexuality.

The dynamic play of desires and conflicts is relegated to the margins of ethnographic accounts. And though one is supposed to withhold judgement in carrying out fieldwork, this act of withholding seems to constitute a fixity in the aims and goals of research. This would seem to contradict the truism that research can be unpredictable and, much like travel, incredibly disorienting. Indeed, one must face the battle of balancing research plans with the uncharted waters of exploration. After weathering out the storm of uncertainty, the researcher is rewarded with precious data, which he brings back to the university to show his friends. Thus, it is hardly surprising that critics like Susan Sontag (1966) have brought disciplines like anthropology to task for figuring the researcher as heroic explorer. But the issue of suspending judgement throughout the tumult and confusion of fieldwork does not solely concern the depth and breadth of one's research. The merit of scholarship is to be determined by the rigour and discipline of one's research, but the value of such work can be very easily called into question if one reveals too much about the intimate details of fieldwork.

Muted Eroticism in the Field

In *Taboo* edited by Don Kulick and Margaret Willson (1995), a path-breaking collection of texts on erotic subjectivity in the field, fieldwork emerges as a research practice that anthropologists always struggle to translate into ethnographic accounts. Field experience is fraught with theoretical concerns, ethical dilemmas, and a wide range of financial and temporal constraints on how anthropologists conduct their research. Anthropologist Don Kulick (1995) writes that the central taboo of anthropology, contrary to studies informed by psychoanalysis and Freudian concerns with repression, attachment or fetishism, is not the incest taboo. Rather, what remains silent and unspeakable is a persisting reluctance to acknowledge the erotic subjectivity of fieldworkers. Kulick writes that this silence 'works to keep concealed the deeply racist and colonialist conditions that make possible our continuing unidirectional discourse about the sexuality of the people we study' (1995: 4). Ethnographic accounts of sexuality tend to assume that the answer to the question of whether the anthropologist should have sex while in the field is a flat 'no' – end of story. The question of whether to document and analyse one's own feelings of attraction is a different kind of issue. It is much broader in scope and has lasting implications beyond the fleeting field encounter. This failure to account for aspects of erotic subjectivity ignores how feelings of lust, longing, and desire can stay with researchers long after 'leaving the field' and into the drafting, writing, and editing of ethnographic accounts. Kulick underscores the centrality of desire to every aspect of ethnography, arguing that erotic subjectivity *does* things (1995: 5).

The presence of eroticism in academic writing is neither new nor striking in and of itself, but it has yet to be fully explored by ethnographers. For this reason, Kulick contends that we must not foreclose the possibility of an ethnography of the erotic subjectivity of fieldworker-informant relations, as it can 'call into question the boundaries of self, threaten to upset the researcher-researched relation, blur the line between professional role and personal life, and provoke questions about power, exploitation, and racism' (1995: 12). While arguing that this form of writing *can* be epistemologically productive, he warns that there is a danger in producing yet another exoticizing discourse that reproduces colonialist legacies (1995: 23). Evelyn Blackwood (1995) echoes this concern for writing a new kind of ethnography that could capture the complexities of researcher-informant relationships. She urges anthropologists to remember that ethnographic experience is not simply about an identification of positionality or subjectivity. Rather, Blackwood contends, 'we occupy multiple positions and identities that transform over time, forcing us constantly to reconstruct who we are in relation to the people we study' (1995: 55). To presume that one's sexual positioning stays the same throughout research periods fails to recognise the intersubjectivity of all informant-based research. The shifting relations between researchers and informants are indeed central to the research process, and it is for this reason that ethnographic studies could help broaden our knowledge of queer sexualities. It is not *travel to* a particular field site that enables new avenues for enquiry, but *travel along with* informants that can provide in-depth analysis of the push and pull of sexualities and erotic tensions. To recognise the uses of ethnography for queer studies researchers must allow social categories and relationships to develop and change throughout fieldwork.

This focus on the positioning of researchers is further explored in Ellen Lewin and William Leap's introduction to *Out in the Field* (1996). Discussing sexual identity management during fieldwork, they describe the experiences of lesbian and gay anthropologists and their heterosexual colleagues as markedly different in terms of how each is expected to handle their personal identities in the field. Where heterosexual fieldworkers are taught to manage aspects of themselves when they enter the field, Lewin and Leap find that lesbians and gay men already know a great deal about filtering their personal lives for different audiences. 'Fieldwork', they write, 'is seen as different from daily life at home' (1996: 12) and the management of identity is an ongoing aspect of what it means to carry out anthropological research. The authors argue that the ordinary life course of lesbians and gay men 'depends precisely on this sort of management on a regular basis' (1996: 12), and is for them a foremost component of conducting field research. Along with considering the limits of US American sexual identity categories, the authors question the position of gay and lesbian anthropologists in relation to traditional frameworks for fieldwork (often somewhere far from the anthropologist's home) and the implications of this positioning for how they construct ethnographic interpretations (1996: 17).

Preliminary as the conclusions of the essays in *Out in the Field* may be, the text remains the only significant roadmap available to lesbian and gay anthropologists who seek direction in documenting the peculiarities of their experiences as fieldworkers. Will Roscoe's contribution to the book stands out as insightful, as it explicitly identifies the implications of identity politics in shaping academic research. In keeping with an emphasis on discursive relations attributed to Michel Foucault, he notes that anthropologists participate in making culture whenever they attempt to represent it. He explains that if discourse 'constitutes its objects of knowledge, as Foucault has shown, then writing lesbian and gay culture cannot be disentangled from constructing it' (1996: 203). This recognition of the co-construction of experience through field research is shared by Kath Weston (1998) who argues that to negate the shared constructedness of identity in the field is to overlook the difference between the colonialist's '*my* people' and the activist's '*my people*' (1998: 205). While the first maintains a hierarchy of racial and labour relations, the second indicates 'the limitations of the nationalist vision of an imagined community that undergirds identity politics' (1998: 205). In either case, the assumption of community identity obscures the construction of that entity.

In Lewin and Leap's follow-up publication *Out in Theory* (2002) the intersection of identity politics and academic critique becomes more apparent, and reveals some of the limits of identitarian endeavours. Beyond providing a space for new research on sexuality and anthropology in which new theoretical work might emerge, Lewin and Leap's text narrowly defines the scope of the collection in terms of the sexual identities of individual anthropologists. The editors reject 'queer' as an umbrella term for the anthology, in part because the authors in the collection have not drawn on queer theory to articulate research claims, but also because the contributors identify themselves as gay and lesbian, rather than queer. The play of identity politics in the making of disciplinary territory is important in so far as the negation of lesbian and gay identities is injurious within a heterosexual academic context.

In order to expand upon existing work on the ethnography of sexualities, it is critical to go beyond identity-based explorations of sexuality. This involves, as I have been arguing throughout, both a reexamination of the role of desire in fieldwork and a redirection in the aims of ethnographic research that moves beyond the limits of the field. In the final section of this chapter I give an account of some of my encounters with informants to show the intimate relationship between desire and ethnographic knowledge. In doing so, I consider whether ethnographies of queer publics and assemblages might hold the potential for expanding our existing understanding of sexualities in various social and cultural contexts.

Part III

Desiring Ethnographies

The power relations that operate in shaping the field as a space within which the ethnographer must resist giving in to the urges of carnality and reject the sexual advances of informants is one of the central problems of doing ethnography in a narrowly defined field. In at least two instances, I found myself navigating the uncertain territory of advances, and I found myself without a useful resource on how to respond. During interviews with Abe, an artist in his fifties, he frequently reminded me that he was very fond of young guys. I doubt that I am wholly incorrect in interpreting his comment to mean: young guys *like me*. These advances and my response to them were pivotal in shaping relationships with informants, but the experiences also taught me that questions of identity only go so far in mapping the range of desires that shape fieldwork encounters. Bodily impulses and feelings of intimacy can be key to both the formation of amorous linkages, as well as the investigation of friendship networks.

I recall a conversation with Pierre, an artist in his fifties, in a café in Halifax one afternoon. He was telling me about the history of *The Body Politic*, a Toronto-based leftist gay liberation magazine distributed internationally from 1971 to 1987 through the voluntary efforts of innumerable activists involved with *Pink Triangle Press*. Pierre recounted that many of the members of the group had been romantically involved with one another during the early days of the magazine. Going into more detail about the relationships between writers for *The Body Politic*, Pierre divulged, with pride, that he had stolen the boyfriend of one of the magazine's key writers.

I laughed out loud on hearing the news. I had read works by this writer whose boyfriend had been whisked away. Thinking such information should be kept private, I responded, 'Well, I'll be sure to omit that from my notes.' Pierre gasped in disbelief, 'No!' He explained in no uncertain terms that to write a history of the magazine or a history of gay life in Canada, one must explain, in detail, who has slept with whom. From his view, the gay friendship networks of Toronto of the 1970s provided a foundation for the development of activist efforts. As my research was not explicitly concerned with a history of gay relationships in Canada, at least some of the details of informants' sex lives have remained a mystery to me. In reflecting on this history of relationships some time later, I considered my own position in the web of relations and wondered where the limits of the story would lie in my ethnographic account. As the work of Bronislaw Malinowski (1929), as well as more recent anthropological work, confirm, it is perfectly acceptable to document the sexual lives of informants, which means that a study of relationships, break-ups and hook-ups would be an appropriate anthropological endeavour. But the researcher is not permitted to explain, or even suggest that he or she might have been involved in such activities. What is perhaps even less acceptable is an acknowledgement that anthropologists are sexual beings – that they are not passive objects of their informants' affection, but subjects of desire as well.

It was not until midway through my fieldwork in Halifax that I was forced to more seriously assess my own personal investment in the messiness of sexual attraction and researcher-informants relations. I met Peter at a conference dealing with issues of HIV treatment and AIDS services in Nova Scotia early in the summer of 2005. Peter was visiting Halifax from a rural community in Nova Scotia and seemed overjoyed to be in the city. Likewise, I was excited about attending the conference, as it would provide the opportunity to meet people involved with AIDS service organisations across the province. During the conference, I spent much of my time with Peter and others involved with the same organisation. As everyone was extremely friendly and inviting, I did not initially interpret Peter's attentiveness as anything more than everyday amity. However, by the end of the conference it had become apparent to me that Peter was pursuing me. There were several competing reasons why I did not want to pursue any kind of serious relationship with him that came to me in the form of questions: Was I restraining myself because I wanted to be a good fieldworker? Was I dissuaded from pursuing any kind of romantic engagement with him because such actions might have compromised the aims of my research? Or did I simply not find him attractive? Whatever the case, Peter's admiration went unrequited and the only polite way of dealing with his advances while staying engaged in my research was to affect an air of indifference.

It was late at night on the last day of the conference in a gay bar in the North End in Halifax that we said our goodbyes. The conversation involved me explaining that I had to go home while Peter urged me to stay out and have another drink. After making several attempts to leave, I indicated that I had to go home. Reluctantly, he turned to me and in a soft voice questioned, 'I'm sorry to ask this. I shouldn't ask, I'm sorry ... but, are you positive?' I doubt that the question would ever have arisen if I had flatly rejected Peter's initial advances. In fact I'm quite certain of the fact. But this would have foreclosed the possibility of forming any kind of informant-researcher relationship. The engagement proved important some time later as I puzzled over the ethics of pursuing or rejecting romantic advances. Is the only appropriate response to an informant's expression of extra-scholarly interest a flat no? As Allison Bain and Catherine Nash note in their study of Toronto women's bathhouses, the relationship between insiders and outsiders can become difficult to separate when carrying out fieldwork where researchers are themselves active participants (Bain and Nash 2007: 31, n.1). Yet more conservative voices purport that researchers should refrain from entertaining even the possibility that sex and research could mix. As ethics review boards continue to remind us, researchers are bound by institutional and professional guidelines, which proscribe sexual activity during research. Still, the question of where to draw the line is necessarily complex.

The encounters with Peter and Pierre, while seeming tangential at the time, contributed significantly to how I was forced to reconceptualise the field. The questions we asked one another and the kinds of expectations, opportunities, and limits we laid out for each other were part and parcel of what constituted my ethnographic field. These shifts should be essayed as ways of thinking about how we imagine our fields of enquiry. The field that came into view through my research is one that kept expanding to include new kinds of experience. Yet my own sense of professionalism and ethics largely prevented me from reciprocating the advances and romantic feelings of others. The field of eroticism and identity that took shape through interviews, conversations, and social events consisted of men who aligned themselves with distinct and overlapping political projects linked to several interrelated historical periods. In holding onto a fixed view of who counts as a research participant, it is easy for researchers to foreclose the possibilities that field research holds for exploring tangential and potentially informative encounters. As Irigaray writes, '[w]e haven't been taught, nor allowed, to express multiplicity. To do that is to speak improperly', and in our attempts to extract salient research findings, we oft run the risk of exhibiting 'one "truth" while sensing, withholding, muffling another' (1985: 210). The truth about researcher-informants relations that often remains muffled in ethnographic studies is not that erotic subjectivity exists and informs such relationships, but that the field, as it is conceptualised in the social sciences, requires the censoring of ethnography for desire and the denial of eroticism in fieldwork encounters.

The field that I found myself in was an undeniably sexualised one, largely because the non-normative sexual desires and identities shared by informants and myself rendered perceptible the erotic quality of our relationships. In growing closer to certain informants, I found myself negotiating the web of erotic relations spun through our interactions, which forced me to consider how to translate my experiences into an ethnographic account in which I would not open myself up to accusations of being a native anthropologist.

Potentials for Queer Ethnographies

New work on queer methodologies offers a more inclusive and comprehensive understanding of relations between researchers and informants, between informants and even between researchers by focusing on the role of desire in shaping those relationships. How desires enter into the researcher's purview is integral to how he or she imagines the aims and limits of research. In losing sight of the dividing line between work and desire, the connections between desire, meaning, and intention come to be seen as inseparable from one another. Of course, the blurring of professional and personal boundaries can be controversial, but the marriage of academic and personal life is by no means rare. Academics often reference their relationships in the acknowledgements sections of their books. No doubt the absence of thanks would be met with reproach, some harsh words, or quarrels over an evening meal. But this sense of intimacy often ends with a few words of acknowledgement.

Explanations of intimate relationships in an academic report serve not only to foreground the subjectivity of researchers and informants, they also provide a window into the active negotiation of the oft taken for granted categories of sexuality. As Evelyn Blackwood reminds us in 'Tombois in West Sumatra' (1998), the categories of gay and lesbian are neither universal nor culturally bounded; they exist somewhere in between the two poles. As a lesbian researcher, Blackwood explains her experience of first encountering tombois in the field and mistaking them for lesbians. Misinterpreting the identities of *cewek* and *cowok* as Sumatra's version of *butch* and *femme*, Blackwood shows how her own identification as lesbian provided a framework for her interpretation of sexuality amongst the women she met during the course of her research. It was through becoming romantically involved while doing research that Blackwood came to understand the full extent to which the sexual identities of her informants, her lover, as well as herself were relational and had no clear meaning outside of their enactment, meeting, and mingling.

As Blackwood's account and others attest, ethnographic research can be useful in showing the construction of identities in various cultural contexts. Hers is an example of what Engebretsen has called queer ethnography because it makes use of ethnography as theory and method in the study of non-normative sexuality. Yet the problem of representing desire, that of informants and researchers alike, remains troublesome if we continue to conceive of ethnography as something to be done in a faraway field. The possible alternatives to the field are multiple, and they must be if we are to fully explore the intimate dimensions of research relationships. In concluding this chapter, I would like to make two preliminary suggestions for alternatives to *field*work, each emanating from within queer studies. The first is a call for the study of queer publics, while the second is a related, yet arguably less clearly defined possibility for the study of queer assemblages.

First, Michael Warner's notion of queer publics proves useful as a conceptual tool, for it does not designate identifiable constituents and has no clear boundaries. To the extent that the queer public is relational, it must be understood as metacultural. In framing ethnographic research as an exploration of queer publics we can move through diffuse social forms without the expectation that they will be bounded in time and space as the concept of the field ultimately requires. As Warner's writing is concerned with the circulation of texts, which in turn enable shared reflexivities, this notion of publics is only partly tenable, beyond consciousness and reflective agency (2002: 14). The direction that studies of sexuality has and will take seems to follow Warner's lead in moving towards a less bounded understanding of sexuality and subjectivity than has been put forth in studies requiring delimited fields. This view holds for Ann Cvetkovich (2003) who argues that researchers of gay and lesbian history must pay careful attention to the diffuse feelings of connectivity that can, but do not always, forge social ties. She suggests seeing gay and lesbian researchers as collectors of stories and artefacts and active participants in the creation of archives. Blurring lines between emotional, political, and therapeutic cultures, Cvetkovich suggests an alternative approach to studying how affective experiences, in particular with reference to trauma, provide a foundation for the formation of queer public cultures (2003: 10). Such publics cannot be reduced to field sites, for they have no clear borders and no accepted memberships.

This vision of publics is shared by Lauren Berlant (1997), whose work considers the construction and nature of citizenship in the United States in studying the rise of what she calls 'public intimacy'. This intimate public sphere is what makes the personal political and makes public matters of citizenship and sexuality central to the construction of individualised subjectivity. Analysing how narratives of trauma have reshaped US citizenship, Berlant traces a transformation of national mass culture into a discourse of intimacy, sexuality, reproduction, and the family. Her text does, what she calls, 'a diva turn on citizenship, attempting to transform it from a dead (entirely abstract) category of analysis into a live social scene that exudes sparks, has practical consequences, forces better ways of thinking about nationality, culture, politics, and personhood' (1997: 20). These aspects of personhood and citizenship do not fit neatly into the field, as they encompass translocal and mediatised forms of social connectedness.

The second alternative is the study of queer assemblages, which involves a more radical reorientation in how scholars position themselves in relation to their work, as well as in how they imagine their research aims. As Jasbir Puar (2005) has shown, the question of how research designs account for splintering and tangential growth patterns has far-reaching implications for how researchers carry out their plans and what they finally write up as findings in their entirety. Puar proposes that scholars direct their attention to the study of queer assemblages, which she differentiates from the '"queering" of an entity or identity' (2005: 130), instead showing that 'queer praxis of assemblage allows for a scrambling of sides that is illegible to state practices of surveillance, control, banishment, and extermination' (2005: 131). Thus, the aim of queer research must neither be a simplistic queering of identity categories nor a documentation of the lives of queer people, but an intent focus on 'affective corporal queernesses, ones that foreground normativizing' (2005: 131). Her suggestion harks back to Warner's view that normalcy, not just heterosexuality, needs to be studied if we are to understand the production of non-normative sexualities.[2]

In new work on queer publics and queer assemblages, such as that of Puar, there is a potential for revitalising many of the theoretical and political aims put forth in earlier critiques of the field as a bounded locale, namely the documentation and commemoration of diverse sexualities. Work in this area suggests a growing

---

2   For a full discussion of the role of social norms in shaping queer sexualities, see Michael Warner's *The Trouble with Normal* (1999). Warner's critique has much in common with that of Puar, though where Warner's interest lies with the queering of heteronormativity, Puar's argument does not share the same conceptual framework with regard to political will. Warner seems to envision a radical practice of queering that would challenge normative sexuality, while Puar sees no such easy solution to the question of what is to be done about heteronormative regimes.

interest within queer studies in affective experience that has yet to fully manifest. Publics and assemblages are not mere substitutions for the field. Instead, they provide a means of resituating and re-envisioning ethnography. Where the prevailing assumption in the social sciences, and in particular within anthropology, is that researchers are fundamentally different from the people whom they study, ethnographies of queer assemblages could offer a way to study sexualities without presupposing the shape or integrity of desire.

There are no assurances in embracing these conceptions, for just as queer comes with no guarantee as a signifier of the undermining of normativity, new work on publics will prove useful to the expansion of theoretical endeavours only if the new terminology is not systematised as a frame of reference to lay claim to immutable boundaries. If disciplines founded on fieldwork and the experience of going to the field are to seriously critique the heteronormativity at their foundations, they must do so by examining the centrality of the field in creating and executing research plans and with it, the desires that the field conceals. I am not suggesting that social scientists must entirely do away with the concept of the field. Rather, researchers might do well to fully interrogate how the field, as the space of collectivity and sociality, has been theorised and put to work, so as to recognise its limitations as a theoretical as well as a methodological tool. The most useful import from the social sciences to queer studies is ultimately the practice and representational form of ethnography. However, to fully engage the potential of ethnographic enquiry, we must remain aware of the history of the field as a central organising concept in disciplines which continue to remain silent about the interplay of desires that shape relationships in research.

Chapter 8

Queer Conversations: Old-time Lesbians, Transmen and the Politics of Queer Research

Catherine J. Nash

Hi all,

I'm as reluctant as anyone to give my time to yet another researcher but I do think this one might produce something that could be useful to US re: grant applications for services WE want and need. She is an old-time lesbian, but has read quite a bit of trans academic stuff, listens well and has access to grants and academic credibilities (*sic*) (Research participant email, copied to the author and dated 19 July 2007, emphasis in the original).

Introduction

Several years ago, I began a small research project, interviewing transmen about their experiences in Toronto's gay village and other 'lgbttqq' and 'queer' spaces.[1] As part of that work, I relied on a few personal connections to solicit interest. The email quoted above was sent by one of my earliest contacts to 6 transmen in the local trans community.[2] In a few short sentences, the email's author succinctly illustrates the politically and socially complicated nature of the research – in this case, geographical research on the connections between places, identities and practices. In both its wording and tone, the email sketches out the unstable interconnections between 'the researcher' and 'the researched' and the sorts of assumptions that may be made about academic credibility, politics, and the possible reciprocities in the research process. Although the email raises many pivotal issues, this chapter focuses on the methodological complications that

---

1 'LGBTTQQ' is one of several acronyms in use in the Canadian context. It stands for 'lesbian, gay, bisexual, trans, two-spirited, queer and questioning.' 'Two-spirited' is considered a First nation's term referring to non-normative sexual and gendered individuals although the term remains a contested one, particularly in its appropriation by gay and lesbian political and social organisations.

2 The terms 'trans' and 'transfolk' are umbrella terms for an admittedly diverse and not necessarily commensurate series of embodied and/or gender variant subject positions and practices (Hines 2006, MacDonald 1998). I use the term transmen and transwomen to refer to those individuals who live gender variant lives and who may or may not have had medical interventions. While these were generally agreed-to terms used by the research participants, clarification and differentiation was provided by specific participants and this is included in the discussions.

surface in fieldwork including the changing nature of the 'field', the particularities of an 'insider/outsider' status and the production of knowledge. While the focus here is on expressly geographical research, these and similar issues surface in myriad ways across the social sciences.

Classical research in geographical studies of gender, sexuality and space considered newly emergent gay and lesbian spaces in urban areas including the distinctive downtown residential and commercial neighbourhoods that support gay and lesbian political, social and economic life (Castells 1983, Lauria and Knopp 1985, Valentine 1993, Forest 1995, Rothenberg 1995, Nash 2001, Podmore 2001). While trenchant critique has been directed at the arguably essentialist nature of these projects and for such projects' disregard for difference and for their failing to be reflexive about the political work such historiographies do, this research nevertheless brought questions of spatial marginalisation, resistance and subversion onto the academic agenda (Penn 1995, Bravmann 1997, Kirsch 2000).

For many academics interested in gendered, embodied and sexualised lives, myself included, our fieldwork is located, if not directly in our own personal social and political spaces, then in spaces where we are at least potential 'insiders' – gay men and lesbians comfortably part of the crowd. In my case, Toronto's downtown gay village has been both the site of my research and a place of social and political engagement for over 20 years. As Gorman-Murray, Johnston and Waitt argue (Chapter 6, this volume), conceptualising and negotiating 'insider/outsider' status is a complex business. Citing Valentine (2002: 199), they note 'it is impossible for us to unpick how the mutual constitution of gender, class, race, sexuality works. ... Dualisms of insider/outsider can never therefore capture the complex and multi-faceted identities and experiences of researchers'. Such a perspective rightfully problematises any straightforward claims to an 'insider' status. Research 'fields' themselves are unstable and constantly changing and in places such as Toronto, politically and socially stable 'gay' and 'lesbian' identities can now co-exist with queer notions of the self that disrupt the homosexual/heterosexual, masculine/feminine, male/female identarian binaries (e.g. Browne et al. 2007, Nash and Bain 2007a). Participants in variously understood gay, lesbian, queer and/or lgbtq spatial networks, cannot be assumed to be operating with similar understandings about their everyday lived experiences despite admittedly interlocking histories and geographies (Jeffreys 2003, Giffney 2004, Nash and Bain 2007b). As the above email makes clear, while particular subjects may come together in the same social or political spaces such as 'old time lesbian' geographers and transmen, they are not necessarily 'natural' or automatic confidants despite their presence in arguably 'queer' spaces and their longstanding, often intertwined community associations.

In this chapter, I begin by drawing on feminist and queer research to explore some of the methodological complications arising during my fieldwork on the experiences of transmen in queer or lgbttqq spaces in Toronto. In doing so, I hope to begin to think through what we might mean when we talk about 'queer' or 'queering' methodologies, given shifting ontological and epistemological understandings of ourselves as 'researchers' and of the nature of the 'field' at this historical and cultural juncture. Second, I consider several questions related to what we might call the queering of the field including questions about the instability of the researcher's 'insider/outsider' status. In the third section, I give some materiality to these questions through a discussion of these notions as they arose in my work with transmen and their experiences negotiating Toronto's lgbtq and queer spaces. Finally, I attempt to sketch out some other complications that came to light as part of what I see as the politics of so-called queer methodological approaches.

'Queering' Methodologies

While there are ongoing debates about the impact of queer theoretical and conceptual approaches on social science research, particularly around ontological and epistemological issues (e.g. Seidman 1996, Jagose 1996a, Kirsh 2000, Turner 2000, Browne et al. 2007), little consideration has been given to the related implications of these approaches for research methodologies. Scholars question whether some specific methods and techniques can be 'deemed queerer than others' (Binnie 2007: 33). Feminist debates about what might constitute 'feminist' research methodologies offer some direction to queer scholarship despite ongoing contestations over the specificity of their projects (Weed and Schor 1997, Richardson et al. 2006). Arguably, in a manner similar to feminist research agendas, what renders queer research distinctive is not only its underlying theoretical, epistemological and ontological starting points but its political commitment to promote radical social and political change that undermines oppression and marginalisation (Seidman 1996, Corber and Valocchi 2003). To paraphrase feminist authors Caroline Ramazanoğlu and Janet Holland (2002), queer scholarship is distinctive in its political 'take' on epistemology and ontology that enables critical explorations of disciplined normative truths about gender, sexuality and sex that are embedded in contemporary relations between knowledge and power.

While queer analytical perspectives offer a form of 'critical scholarship' that attempts to go beyond illustrating what is, (that is, unequal and unjust social relations based on gendered, sexualised and sexed categories), it also seeks to bring about material and social change (Sedgwick 1990, Warner 1993, Binnie 1997, Warner 2002, Corber and Valocchi 2003). Queer scholars arguably share a political and ethical commitment to radical and progressive social and political change that addresses unjust social hierarchies structuring social relations (Jagose 1996b, Turner 2000, Knopp and Brown 2003, Knopp 2007b).

While there is no quintessential queer perspective, queer analytical approaches employed by geographers are largely grounded in wider formulations of poststructuralist, postmodernist and Foucauldian ideas that dispute traditional appeals to ontological coherency, universal truth and causal connectedness that underlie modernist thought (Brown 2000, Knopp and Brown 2003, Browne et al.

2007). Queer perspectives assert a view of reality as fragmented and multiple and reject explanations that are grounded in the presumption of a directly knowable brute reality (Benko and Strohmyer 1997). Knowledge is, therefore, understood as partial, local and situated rather than capable of being woven into an over-arching grand narrative incorporating the entirety of possible human experience (Haraway 1991, Moss 2002). Locally situated knowledges about everyday lives and practices highlight the specificity of lived experience in a place while recognising the possibility of momentarily shared or collective meanings of social reality (Bailey 1999).

Queer theory, as it emerged in geographical research in particular, has taken on its own particular hue. Given that geographers have a particular concern with the material production and transformation of space, geography has arguably 'differed from other forms of queer theory that relied heavily on more discursive analyses and metaphorical understandings of space' (Browne et al. 2007: 10). In some ways it manages to avoid the critique of much queer scholarship that is seen to focus on texts, discourses and meanings rather than the lived, concrete experiences of everyday life (see for example, Harvey 1992, Brown 2000). Queer analytics conceptualize sexualised and gendered beings as historically and culturally constituted rather than as an epistemologically essential truth about the self reflecting a knowable reality. A queer geographical analysis, then, works to deconstruct and decentralise the binaries of male/female, masculine/feminine and heterosexual/homosexual that structure and organise social categories and relations in specific places as well as 'place' itself (Knopp and Brown 2003, Valocchi 2005, Browne et al. 2007). Such approaches challenge normative assumptions about sexuality and gender organised around the heterosexual/homosexual binary – a pivotal organisational system that structures understandings through the deployment of other 'derivative tropes' such as normal/abnormal, public/private and authentic/fraudulent (Valocchi 2005: 754). Queer explorations of lived experiences reveal 'the indeterminacy, contingency, malleability, and often oppressive nature' of these normative binary systems (Knopp and Brown 2003: 410). Looking 'queerly' for the non-conformative, sheds light on the possibilities and potentialities for lives lived in incongruent and conflicting relationships with normative systems of meaning – neither within nor without – but as a form of fluidity; a mobile instability in experiences, behaviours and practices of the self.

Spatialising queer epistemologies has meant (re)conceptualising how normative ontological systems of meaning might constitute places and, through that constitution, both enable and constrain the possibilities and limitations of lived experience in place. Queer activism seeks to open up spaces across the heterosexual/homosexual divide as locations for non-normative gendered and sexualised practices and identities (see for example Nash and Bain 2007a). This activist spatial 'queering' encourages 'moving beyond limited and normal male/female, hetero/homo divides' and clearly includes a queering of what might be thought of as traditionally gay and lesbian spaces as well as those coded heterosexual (Browne 2006: 888, Nash and Bain 2007a). Yet despite these admittedly optimistic imaginings, 'queer' has often become synonymous with gays and lesbians as a fixed identity category, thereby losing much of its critical edge, both theoretically and as a lived possibility (Browne 2006, Nash and Bain 2007b). The queering of space can be similarly problematic whereby aspirations of liberation and possibility give way to constraining disciplinary formulations structured through the political sensibilities and activist stance of its adherents (Nash and Bain 2007a).

In research design, 'methodologies' are commonly understood as the processes by which research is undertaken given a project's epistemological and ontological stance. The methodological process also involves the coherent maintenance of those stances through the selection and application of the technical methods of data collection. Methodology is further concerned with ensuring that these procedures lead to the creation of knowledges that can be regarded as 'valid' and 'authentic', raising questions not only about the 'authority' of the knowledges produced but also researcher accountability for the political implications of knowledge production (Moss 2002, Ramazanoğlu and Holland 2002). As Warner argues 'queer takes on its critical edge by defining itself against the normal rather than the heterosexual, and the normal includes normal business in the academy' (1993: xxvi). Arguably, the project of queering methodologies struggles to critically examine the way we as researchers 'do business' in terms of our potential complicity in normalising knowledge production.

Given this, what might a 'queer' methodology or a queered methodological perspective look like? In my research, using queer epistemological and ontological perspectives helps focus attention on how social categories of being, and lived experience, are constituted within certain historical, cultural and spatialized contexts, including normative ideas about what are deemed to be embodied gendered and sexual practices and behaviours. In my interviews for example with transmen, I am seeking to produce queer knowledges through methodological approaches that examine experiences and practices outside/beyond normative binaries to demonstrate the possibility of alternative ways of being and to make visible the normative, hierarchical regimes disciplining social relations in place. This research uses what might be considered classical qualitative technical methods of data collection including interviews, focus groups, and participant observation in 'the field', as the processes through which knowledges about queer lived experiences can be gained (see Browne, Chapter 14 in this volume for a discussion of quantitative techniques as well). Researchers interested in producing such knowledges often highlight the inequitable and uneven possibilities and opportunities that exist for various social relationships, ways of being and their geographical instantiation. These judgements can include political calls for action so perhaps, as Binnie suggests, 'rather than trying to prescribe certain methods as queerer than others, we should pay attention to the queering potentialities of different types of research' (2007: 33).

In producing knowledges about the specificity of queerly lived lives, researchers using various qualitative methods, myself included in the present example, directly interact with their participants in various fields, as embodied gendered, sexualised and sexed individuals and bring their own lived experiences to the research process (Limb and Dwyer 2001, Gorman-Murray, Johnston and Waitt, this volume). This raises classic questions about the nature of mutual production of knowledge across different ways of being in the world and the possibility of shared understandings across that difference. As Kath Browne asks, 'does one have to be queer to undertake queer research? ... do queer theorists have to live queer lives?' (2006: 890). Put another way, in the current historical and geographical context, as a lesbian researcher in an increasing 'queer' field, am I 'queer' enough?

Queering the 'Field': Insiders/Outsiders and the Production of Knowledge

In what follows, I consider the methodological implications of a queering of the notion of insider/outsider status and the changing nature of the 'field' in queerly constituted research with a particular focus on the particularities of geographical research on queer spaces. My discussion here focuses on geographical research, however social sciences research that embraces queer approaches would also face some of these dilemmas.

Scholars have long recognised that the nature of the 'field' itself is problematic. This is due to the field being constituted through relations of power that define participants and researchers in hierarchical ways that are neither stable not necessarily coherent. Also, the field itself is constantly shifting in its interrelated material and representational qualities (Gilbert 1994, Staeheli and Lawson 1994). As England (1994: 82) argues, the relations of power between researcher and researched 'may be reciprocal, asymmetrical or potentially exploitative' and, as the research process unfolds, may take on any recombinant formulation. Despite a researcher's best efforts, research processes also have the potential to recreate and reinforce the forms of social marginalisation and exclusions that our research seeks to transform (Kobayashi 2003). In our interaction with our research subjects, we seek to understand others' lived reality but our ability to do so is structured in part by the 'distance/difference between the researcher and the researched' and implies we cannot fully know and understand the lived experiences of others (England in Staeheli and Lawson 1994: 99). But as Staeheli and Lawson argue (1994), it is this space of 'betweenness' (the difference between us and them) that constitutes a possible site for partial and situated knowledges to be mutually constituted and produced (Haraway 1991).

Fully understanding the partial and situated aspects of knowledge production requires researchers to think through the 'distance/difference' between ourselves and others and its effects on our abilities to work out shared meanings of life experiences. As Ramazanoğlu and Holland (2002: 106) assert, 'making knowledge claims across difference means taking responsibility for interpreting the social existence of others and so is normative, personal and political as well as epistemological' (see also Young 1990). Feminist scholars have turned to the notion of reflexivity to address the implications of these possibly uneven and unstable power relations in the research process. Self-reflexivity entails, in part, a 'self-critical, sympathetic introspection and self-conscious analytical scrutiny of the self as researcher' – a process designed to consider the distance between participants and to recognise the fallacy of the supposed 'objectivity' in the research project (England 1994: 82). Nevertheless, a reflexive acknowledgement of one's positionality should not degenerate into 'a privileged and self-indulgent focus on the self' that, in the power of the doing, is the act that sets the researcher apart (Kobayashi 2003: 34). In undertaking a somewhat self-reflexive stance as part of this research process, I am seeking to engage in what Audrey Kobayashi sees as the redeeming aspects of reflexivity, that is, a reflexivity that encourages exchanges with other scholars, seeks to advance an activist agenda and seeks to promote discussion beyond the confines of any individual circumstance (Kobayashi 2003).

Jon Binnie argues 'we have witnessed many transformations in the sexual political landscape' in the last 30 years or so (2007: 10). While geographers may have initially envisioned public spaces as largely heterosexual (e.g. Valentine 1993), queer theoretical and activist practices demonstrate, among other things, that the boundary between heterosexual and homosexual spaces is far more permeable, unstable and opaque than originally conceived (Warner 1993). Further, more recent queer scholarship challenges the contemporary North American gay and lesbian movement's largely neo-liberal, assimilationist politics that prompts a particular homosexual 'domesticity and consumption' while excluding a non-conforming queer constituency (Duggan 2000, Binnie 2007). Geographers assert that this spatialised homonormative politics renders certain gay and lesbian spaces inaccessible to marginalised queers and forces conduct deemed 'unacceptable' underground (Duggan 2000, Rushbrook 2002, Bell and Binne 2004). Nevertheless, queer identities and practices have unevenly infiltrated and reconstituted some of those traditional gay and lesbian spaces – an uneven and partial transformation of the 'field', altering the terrain of the knowledge production.

The increasing visibility of transfolk in queer spaces is one of the many shifting and transformative practices (re)shaping sexual (and gendered) minority spaces such as Toronto's gay village (Nash 2006). Scholars continue to unravel (and contest) the social and political histories and geographies of trans individuals and considerable disagreement exists over how transsexual experiences and the 'transgender phenomena' are conceptualised (Stryker 2006: 3). Nevertheless, it is fair to say that transfolk have had a lengthy and often acrimonious association with gay and lesbian community places.[3] Certain strands of feminist and lesbian

---

3 A highly fractious body of research is emerging about the relationship between transsexual and transgendered individuals and gay and lesbian political and social spaces. The newly emerging field of trans scholarship is itself divided over the historical, cultural and social implications of trans lives and such debates mirror, in some respects, earlier contentious scholarship on the emergence of the 'homosexual' in Western society. For some, the transsexual is a historically fixed and largely essentialised figure visible

scholarship are notably vitriolic in their condemnation and outright rejection of transsexuals (e.g. Raymond 1979 [1994], Jeffreys 1997). Both transmen and women are often deliberately excluded from certain gay and lesbian spaces based on some perceived biological and/or gendered and sexed 'imperfections'. Lesbian events and places have been particularly vigilant in policing sexual and gender expressions (Ross 1995, Stryker 2006). The longstanding (and hotly contested) exclusion of transwomen from the Michigan Women's Music Festival, a 'women-only' event, for some 30 years is a notable example (Cvetkovich and Wahng 2001, Morris 2005).

Feminist scholarship has long debated the implications of 'insider/outsider' status and the power relations inherent in the research process. As Valentine notes, 'notions of positionality and reflexivity have raised troubling questions about the politics and ethics of whom is entitled to research particular topics' (2002: 117). Insiders are seen as 'sharing the same identities as their subjects' and as such having a 'truer access to knowledge and a closer, more direct connection' with the research participants (Valentine 2002: 117, Marshall 2002). Determining insider/outsider status is also a form of boundary making 'that is seen to circumscribe identity, social position and belonging and as such marks those who do not belong and are hence excluded' (Robina 2001: 101). This boundary construction, in itself, is an exercise of power relations that is at the heart of the ongoing and negotiated relationship between researcher and the researched.

So when an 'old time lesbian' sets out to interview transmen about their experiences in 'queer' or 'lgbtq' spaces, it is not at all surprising that such a meeting is saturated with the historical and highly charged political debris – a great deal of 'baggage' in more unscholarly language. When my correspondent used the term 'old-time lesbian' in his email cited at the outset, it served as a form of short-hand that not only staked out a certain positionality for me as the researcher but also suggested that those reading the email would immediately understand the meanings inherent in the use of such a term. In its terms, the email grants me some credibility by intimating that while being an 'old time lesbian' might be a liability, it could be overlooked (or perhaps forgiven) in light of other apparently more positive attributes – some knowledge of trans scholarship, personal attentiveness and access to funding. This partial 'insider' status is tenuously granted and just as easily revoked. So while the term 'queer' or 'lgbtqqtt' might initially seem

---

throughout recorded history if one is able to 'read' the record against the grain – an exercise that includes re-reading some 'homosexuals' as in fact being 'transsexuals' (Noble 2004, Stryker 2006). For many, the contemporary dominance of gay and lesbian political and social movements since the Second World War forced trans identities and practices underground through the political denial of any association between 'gender inversion' and homosexuality (Stryker 2006). For others, the queering of contemporary politics and practices generated the possibilities for gender variant existence, and practice, and arose because of the particularities of this historical and cultural moment (and place) (cf. Noble 2006).

to encompass lesbians and transmen as members of a sexual minority group, a complicated social history, and geography, undermines such assumptions. So, while I might be able to argue (or it might be assumed) that my longstanding membership in Toronto's queer community offers some commonality, and supports a claim to 'insider status', the email suggests a rather tenuous and not at all reliable positionality.

As a lesbian investigating gay and lesbian space, I arguably possess an 'experiential sameness' that entitles me to claim a shared understanding with participants and therefore a certain moral authority and authenticity for the knowledge produced through that process (Robina 2001: 102). As a lesbian academic, the historically specific and increasing presence of queer identities, ways of being and practices, and the ongoing queering of the research field (particularly of lesbian spaces), highlights the historically and culturally unstable nature of one's 'insider' status and the shifting relationships that develop with one's research participants.

Queer Conversations: The Politics of Insider/Outsider Positionality

As part of a larger project on the queering of space in Toronto, I conducted 15 interviews with transmen of various ages, and personal histories. All of my participants considered themselves to be Caucasian, were between the ages of 20 and 60, considered themselves middle class and most had some secondary school education. All had spent some time in Toronto's lgbttqq or queer spaces and in many cases we met in bars and restaurants in Toronto's gay village to conduct interviews. I share similar social and racial positioning with the research participants, being white and middle class, as well as a somewhat similar experience of gay, lesbian and queer social and political spaces in Toronto. Despite these apparent congruities, however, both the nature of the field and my insider/outsider status shifted considerably not only during the course of individual interviews but across interviews and throughout the research process.[4] In what follows, I discuss several of the many complications this shifting status has for the research process and the rather tenuous activity of collaborative knowledge production.

---

4 There are many issues in play in the interview process that are worthy of attention but beyond the scope of this chapter. The 'whiteness' of the participants speaks to the particular demographic composition of Toronto as a whole and the historical constitution of Toronto's gay village. It also speaks to both access to and the cost of sex reassignment surgery (SRS). SRS has not been funded in Ontario for over 10 years although it has recently been reinstated as a covered procedure in Ontario's public health care system (May 2008). Clearly, access to costly procedures is one factor influencing membership in Toronto's trans community. The education and life experience of participants is also pertinent as most were actively engaged in trans research and intimately familiar with lgbtq, queer and trans scholarship as well as the historical and cultural history of Toronto's lgbtq community.

I shared similar life trajectories with several of the participants. We had 'come out' and participated in a local 1970s and 1980s lesbian community when we were in our late teens or early 20s and remained thoroughly imbued with the political and social sensibilities of that time. This group of transmen had initially understood themselves as 'lesbian' in a way that only partly resolved an internal dissonance over their embodied sense of self and their gender/sexual identity (for further discussion see Devor 1997, Cromwell 1999, Diamond 2004). These transmen ultimately decided to undergo some form of medical intervention and/or sex/gender reassignment in their mid to late 40s and are currently living their lives as men. Many transitioned while trying to maintain ties to Toronto's lesbian community given that this community comprised their longstanding social networks and constituted what several referred to as their 'dating pool'. In these interviews, as researcher and researched, we shared a partial 'lesbian' history; one that encompassed experiences as lesbians in particular spaces marked by a lesbian feminist politics that included sports team fundraising, the ubiquitous (and much maligned) lesbian 'potluck' and product boycotts. During these interviews, my insider status was initially reasonably secure; having a shared experienced of a particular form of 'lesbian' life, both literally and materially, in 1970s and 1980s Toronto. Such a positioning facilitated the use of shared systems of meaning in knowledge production around a lesbian history which then grounded discussions about the participant's changing relationship to lesbian spaces.

However, the 'distance/difference' in our lived experiences and shared meanings grew, not surprisingly, as our discussion shifted to their experiences of living their lives as men. Having lived as women, these transmen could relate their new experiences as men by placing them in juxtaposition to their knowledges of lives as women. We were able to discuss how as men, they explored the new and distinctive ways they occupied and took up space in both heterosexual and queer locations. Participants noted that when they were understood unproblematically as 'men', they were usually treated with more deference and attentiveness in social interactions and were less afraid in certain spaces. Participants tended to attribute this awareness to their 'lesbian/women' past and some form of feminist sensibility. As our discussions moved beyond these experiences, such as in discussions about their experiences as men in largely male spaces (e.g. heterosexual bars or gay male bath house space), the distance between our life experiences and positionalities moved me towards a distinctive 'outsider' status. During the interview process, our ability to share understandings and convey new ones was constantly in flux and largely diminished as we approached the core focus of the research project, that is, transmen's experiences in queer and lgbttqq spaces.

While these transmen may have continued to find lesbian spaces both accessible (and sometimes necessary) in their lives, many experienced varying degrees of rejection and forms of disciplining and policing in these spaces. Many still regarded lesbians as part of their social circle, including as potential sexual partners. However, they also made clear distinctions between lesbian and 'queer' spaces with spaces defined as 'queer' being understood or experienced as more comfortable, accepting and less regulatory. When in these spaces, some transmen claimed a 'queer' or 'queerer' identity which they could explore in ways that they could not in spaces where normative masculine gendered and sexual behaviours were expected. Some participants remarked on the ambiguities and complications of moving between these different kinds of sexualised and gendered spaces – an experience many of us have, but for very different reasons. As a lesbian academic, I share with some scholars a concern over the loss of 'lesbian' spaces through both the presence of transmen in lesbian spaces and the 'queering' of space as a whole (e.g. Prichard et al. 2002, Casey 2004, Nash and Bain 2007a). Raising this notion of the 'loss' of lesbian space is to tread perilously close to emphasising that uncomfortable political and social divide between lesbians and transmen and is one I explored with participants but with great care. For transmen with a 'lesbian past' who considered themselves 'heterosexual', lesbian spaces (as well as gay, lgbtq and queer spaces) were no longer of interest. Unlike transmen who still claimed a queer identity in some places, this group of transmen do not understand themselves as living queer lives and identified solely as heterosexual men. Some viewed their lesbian identities as a minor deviation from a life lived as a heterosexual man. In these cases, while we shared some similar remembrances of lesbian political and social communities, these transmen did so 'at a distance' – recognising the similarities while remembering feelings of dissonance and association at the same time. In at least one interview, a participant expressed what might be read as dismissive masculinist contempt for specifically lesbian spaces; sharply shifting our interaction from one of shared systems of meaning to a prickly interaction between a lesbian feminist and a heterosexual man. Such sharp changes in researcher/researched positionality were disconcerting and laid waste to any notion of shared or collective experience. The situation also brought into crisp relief the divergent political views held by me as the interviewer and several research participants who (in my perhaps momentarily reflexive reaction) seemed to have uncritically embraced a masculine, heterosexual aesthetic.

When interviewing transmen with a lesbian history who identified as gay men after transitioning, a similar shift in the interviewer/interviewee relationship occurred. While similar experiences of lesbian space and community initially provided common ground for the interview, as well as a more open understanding of themselves as queer, the partial rejection of that space in favour of queer and gay male spaces complicated mutual understandings. Given I had never experienced certain gay males spaces such as gay bath houses and the public cruising scene in Toronto's network of parks, subway stations and washrooms, any notion of shared understandings underpinning insider status disappeared. In understanding transmen's experiences there were clearly certain places I literally could not go without considerable personal awkwardness and/or levels of subterfuge that could compromise the research process. Understanding gay male bath house space as 'queer' only makes that space partially accessible to non-gay male presence, despite the libratory intent, and highlights the power relations in play in notion of what the 'queering' of space means.

I also interviewed younger transmen for whom a 'lesbian' identity was not part of their past life experience and who had expressly rejected an understanding of themselves as 'homosexual' or 'queer'. These individuals only made contact with the queer community at time of transition and then usually through medical establishment recommendations. Federal and provincial funding in Canada for trans services is funnelled through longstanding gay and lesbian social service organisations. These organisations provide space, budget management, resources and programming for a local trans community that often has little politically and socially in common with the gay and lesbian community. This requires that some transfolk who have no historical social or political association with the gay and lesbian community have to access services through those organisations – for some this means experiencing their first contact with 'homosexuals' in uncomfortable personal circumstances. This highlights the awkwardly linked histories of transfolk and the gay and lesbian community due to historical and geographical coincidences. Scholars have demonstrated that many individuals living 'queer' lives utilise the language and identity categories in order to access trans services while not identifying in this way beyond those circumstances (Valentine 2007). Some trans activists debate whether a separate trans activism movement might be more appropriate (Whittle 2000).

Transmen without a history of interaction with the gay and lesbian community often utilised queer spaces to access services. This speaks to the historical association with transsexual and transgendered funding being provided through gay and lesbian social organisations despite the fact that transfolk have largely, in Canada, had little continuous or engaged connections with those communities.[5] For some, this was their first foray into queer spaces and they found those spaces both relaxing and somewhat complicated. On the one hand, these spaces where often perceived as 'safer' than heterosexual spaces where detection of their trans status posed a greater threat to their personal safety – a sense of place that I partly share. On the other hand, however, these individuals had little or no identification with gay and lesbian social life or politics. In these interviews, my lesbian status, my social and political history and identification as unproblematically female-embodied meant we were struggling to find the common ground that a superficial understanding of 'insider' might suggest existed.

Finally, several of my participants understood themselves as 'trans' in the very political sense of refusing a legible gendered, embodied, sexualised identity, opting instead to be 'read' as largely unintelligible to others within normative gendered, embodied and sexualised frameworks in all spaces. As well, many of my subjects

---

5   Several of the older transfolk I interviewed referred to longstanding and quite distinct trans social networks flourishing in the Ottawa and Toronto areas in the 1960s–1980s. These networks had little to do with the local gay and lesbian communities and often found them hostile to trans presence, largely due to the movement's rejection of gender 'inversion' as a factor in sexual orientation. There remains an important political and social history to be written about transsexual and transgender lives.

made conscious decisions about their presentation in particular spaces in ways that suggested an internal malleability in self understanding that was not totally familiar to me and sometimes marked a considerable gap between us. Some transmen also noted the existence of expressly 'trans' space and rejected the suggestion that such space could be understood as 'queer'. 'Transness' marked such spaces as occupied by individuals living lives outside or beyond hetero/homo, male/female and masculine/feminine binaries and marked me as an outsider in every sense.

In all of these interviews, the supposed 'queerness' of our respective identities initially supported varying conceptualisations of an 'experiential sameness' but it became clear this was a fragile 'sameness' and one that was redefined constantly within and between interviews. A queer methodology speaks to the need to 'queer' the positions of researcher and researched themselves through a recognition that the relations between them are perpetually unstable. In queering our thinking about insider/outsider status, we expect the slippery disconnections and reordering of our interactions with our 'participants' (and collaborators in knowledge production) and set out to deliberately explore that instability for what it might show about the queerness of our interactions.

A queer methodology arguably seeks out and affirms the impossibility of a constant between the research, the researched and the field. Often, researchers seek to address admittedly shifting interactions between researchers and their participants through appeals to ideas such as 'positionality' and 'reflexivity' which, in themselves, are terms alluding to an at least momentarily stable place from which to be reflexive and to consider one's position. The relational slippages that surfaced between an 'old time lesbian' and transmen over the course of individual interviews and within interviews themselves are queer moments that are potentially less productive when we attempt to inflict stabilising analyses based on 'positionality' and 'reflexivity'. Our queer exchanges are saturated with shared histories and geographies that brought particular meanings; collective memories and points of contestation that are worth leaving undone. By leaving them 'undone' we can 'undo' the interview process itself between historically, politically and culturally specific subjects whose intertwined connections bring 'baggage' to the table that saturates the research process from the first email seeking participants to the final research paper.

Continuing Complications:
Reflecting on the Politics of Knowledge Production

As Steve Bravmann (1997: 25) argues, queer theory can quickly and powerfully problematise a 'phenomenally wide range of constructed and arbitrary regimes of the normal'. It encourages us to re-examine what we do as researchers including the activities we undertake as a 'given' – interviews, focus groups, surveys and participant observation. What queer methodological approaches press us to do is to re-examine those methods and their deployment within the wider historical and political context of research on sexual minorities and the more intimate and constraining spaces of interaction in the field.

Although these comments should have resonance across the social sciences, queer approaches have had a particular resonance for geographers interested in gender, sexuality and embodiment (as well as class, age and race). Queer geographies seek to demonstrate that gendered, sexualised and embodied experiences and identities are socially constituted within power relations that order social relations and social spaces in hierarchical ways. In so doing, they hope to not only destabilise the presumed fixity of those experiences but to create the potential for lives lived beyond those bounded material and representational possibilities. For those whose focus has been on the evolution of particular urban spaces such as Toronto's gay village, the historical and geographical nature of the 'field' has changed dramatically in the last 30 years. When the 'field' also constitutes our personal social and political experiences, we need to consider the possible impacts of these changes on our scholarship. Arguably, with the queering of the field, insider/outsider status, methodological approaches and our own relationship as scholars, participants and 'insiders' alters as well. While we may all shelter under the 'queer' umbrella, there are important political, social and cultural implications waiting to be explored.

Chapter 9

Femme on Femme:
Reflections on Collaborative Methods and
Queer Femme-inist Ethnography[1]

Ulrika Dahl

But you don't *look* like a lesbian …
I am the double-take
The queerest of the queer
So secure in my sexuality
That tonight I'll wear a dress
Which hugs my waist and hips

But you don't look like a *real* lesbian …
So you tell me what's real
While I shake out my hair
Kick off my heels
Peel off your shirt and tie
And push you into the pillows

But you don't look like a *normal* lesbian …
You're damn right, I'm not normal
I'm a subverter of society
And all its expectations

1   As this article centrally argues, knowledge is a collaborative practice and I wish to acknowledge my intellectual collaborators on this piece, without whom I could not think or practice these methods and ideas. First and foremost, eternal gratitude to Del LaGrace Volcano and the femmes I continue to work with. Several events and people were crucial for developing these points over the course of its year of production: co-teachers Katie King and Malin Rönnblom and the Ph.D. students in the Nordic Research School in Interdisciplinary Gender Studies course 'Feminist Methodologies: Situated Knowledge Practices' in November 2008; participants in the workshop 'Queer Street Theory' at the conference *Feminist Research Methods* in Stockholm 4–6 February 2009, in particular Kath Browne, Vanessa Agard-Jones and E. Manning; the engaged scholars at the University of Sydney workshop 'Glocalizing Sex and Gender' in February 2009; two anonymous reviewers for *SQS*. Above all, Antu Sorainen, Kath Browne and Catherine Nash provided continued encouragement and editorial brilliance. This chapter is written within the project *Femme as Figuration*, funded by the Bank of Sweden's Tercentenary Fund and I dedicate it to Rosie Lugosi with endless gratitude, friendship and support in her fight against cancer. A version of this article is forthcoming in *SQS Journal of Queer Studies*.

So perverted, I love women
And that includes myself.
(Rosie Lugosi 2000: 12)

Introduction: The Queerest of the Queer

Despite the kinky associations of the title and the assertiveness of the opening poem, the primary concern of this chapter is *not* the queerness of girl-on-girl desire per se. Rather, inspired by queer feminist scholars Lisa Duggan and Kathleen McHugh's declaration that a femme scientist 'solicits loving, grateful collaboration' (2002: 169), it offers some reflections on the queer dimensions of conducting femme-inist ethnographic research with/in 'ones own community' and on the possibility of queering ethnographic writing. It seems to me that while queer theory is growing increasingly salient in interdisciplinary gender studies, to 'straight' science there is always something academically queer about the desire to be with and write about one's own, even if it is not a territorialized, localized or even always visibly recognizable stable community.

Since 2000, I have written around the particular topic of femininity and sexual politics in Sweden (Dahl 2003, 2006, 2008) as well as on queer feminist politics more broadly. As a self-identified femme (activist) and 'scientist', (to use Duggan and McHugh's terminology), I explicitly aim to rethink and re-present the meaning of femininity and that often means I am both subject and object of both research and activism. That is, I both participate in, and study, queer feminist movements that seek not only render to femmes visible, but to call misogynist contempt for femininity into question and to explore how femininity is queerly lived and practiced. In this work I am often asked about how I can study something to which I also claims political and sexual belonging; questions that suggest underlying anxieties around the issue of objectivity. The subtext, it seems, is that despite decade-long epistemological discussions, there is still anxiety around that complex issue of 'objectivity'.

Like Rosie Lugosi in the above poem, I want to be assertive and clear from the beginning: this chapter is a rhizomatic rather than linear discussion and a twist on what counts as proper, real and 'normal' ethnographic research. It is motivated by queer political hopes for the uses and potentialities of academic work. Like those of many of my queer and feminist predecessors, colleagues and students, my stakes in femme-inist ethnography originate in and are part of queer and feminist movements that extend beyond the ivory tower and our ever-so exciting 'theoretical' debates about the nature of gender, desire, aesthetics and politics. I take my departure in Duggan and McHugh's (2002) brazen manifesto that proposes that the femme scientist is in 'the third phase of research', beyond explanation and demonstration (the first phase) and beyond relativity (the second) and has an explicit aim. For me a central part of such an aim is to address collaborative methods and the politics of visual and ethnographic knowledge production and representation. I argue that a central value of queer studies resides in collaborations and conversations that aim to produce knowledge collectively.

In this chapter, I will first meditate on some existing queer feminist models for conducting research within subcultural communities to which one belongs, drawing on lesbian anthropology and interdisciplinary queer studies. I then address the false dichotomy of home/away and how it structures ethnographic knowledge production with the aim to rethink community through movements, networks and figurations rather than geopolitical boundedness. The central part of the chapter centres on my recent work with gender variant visual artist Del LaGrace Volcano and the subjects of our book *Femmes of Power: Exploding Queer Femininities* (2008) considering it as one example of how one might conduct such femme-inist ethnography. I particularly call into question the dichotomy between the theorizing academic and her 'informants'. Honing in on the issue of writing and textual representation, I discuss how femme-inist ethnography may contribute to a reconsideration and re-representation of not only *l'ecriture femme-inine*, as a way to write femme differently, but also perhaps the meaning of femininity within and beyond queer communities.

While I draw on more than 10 years of ethnographic work on and with different communities that I consider myself belonging to (Dahl 2004, 2005, 2007, 2008), in this piece I focus on what I call femme-on-femme. I argue that methodological frameworks of collaboration and co-production of ideas can queer research conventions and contribute to a reconsideration of what counts as theoretical work, particularly with regards to femininity and its place within queer feminism. In so doing, I want to further work that explicitly critiques the radical individualism, self-congratulatory nature and liberal understandings of both positivist social science and other projects that assume unified and coherent subjects and objects. I highlight the collaborative dimension of knowledge making and subject formation, because as the lesbian political theorist Shane Phelan (1989: 5) notes, as political and scientific understandings of the world, abstract individualism 'isolates us from one another, both as objects for analysis and as subjects engaged in social intercourse'.

Femme/inist Beginnings

I opened this chapter with a poem by Rosie Lugosi, a self-declared 'lesbian vampire queen' from Manchester, England and an internationally touring queer performance artist, not only because it captures audiences but because it addresses some of what initially drew me, a femme-inist ethnographer, to researching and writing about queer femininities in general and about femmes in particular. Over the past five years, Rosie has not only been a research subject, along with many other femmes in the transnational web of femme activism and cultural production that I have both participated in, studied and written about (Dahl 2006, 2007, Volcano and Dahl 2008), she has been an interlocutor, textual critic and close friend. I invoke her work to point to the impossibility of making pure distinctions not only between identities such as 'lesbian', 'femme' or 'woman', but also between subjects and objects of research. With the help of this poem, before we plunge into the politics and poetics of femme-inist ethnography, let me briefly explain how I use the term femme and how I arrived at conducting femme-on-femme research via feminist and queer ethnography.

In brief, the term femme (or fem)[2] stems from pre-Stonewall, Anglo-American primarily working-class subcultural contexts and has historically been used in reference to a feminine lesbian, most often coupled with a masculine lesbian, the butch (Nestle 1992, Kennedy and Davis 1993, among others). Today's meaning and use of femme often exceeds that of earlier eras, insofar as self-identified femmes are no longer (only) erotically tied to butches (although many are) and they do not always identify as lesbians or even as women (Volcano and Dahl 2008, Burke 2009). Some femmes, though not all, argue that it reflects a femininity 'taken back from being the object of the masculine gaze', that 'transgresses expectations of women, but also expectations of femininity' (Livingston in Burke 2009: 25). Many state that they *intentionally* seek to *queer* femininity. To most femmes I have interviewed, a feminine aesthetic – that is, clothing, garments, accessories, make up and so on, is central to a femme expression.[3]

Lugosi's poem can be read as speaking to the place of femmes both within mainstream culture and lesbian subcultures, and by extension to the associations of femininity with passivity, superficiality and normativity. According to most arguments in their deployment of classic feminine attributes don't *look* like lesbians (Walker 2001). Since the onset of lesbian and feminist theorizing and activism, femmes have variously been dismissed 'less feminist' and 'less queer' than others, either because in their desire for butch women they 'imitate' heterosexuality or because in their gender expressions they 'pass' as straight, which then is taken to mean that femmes are 'less oppressed'. The rise of queer studies and movements that celebrate masculinity in women have given substantial attention and merit to butch gender in the last decade (Halberstam 1998, Volcano and Halberstam 1999, Rosenberg 2000). Femmes, even though often politically controversial, have received less theoretical and visual attention, and even when they do, it is mostly in relation to their presumed butch partners.[4]

---

2   There are two spellings (femme; fem) and divergent histories of their respective use as well as different contemporary uses of the terms (cf. Volcano and Dahl 2008, Crocker and Harris 1997). These are also used and contested in diverse ways in different femme communities in Europe and North America. Space limitations prevent me from a longer discussion about this issue here and thus I use femme as the umbrella term. It should also be noted that the terms butch and femme are also used within middle class lesbian and queer contexts, but I find it important to acknowledge their working-class origins (Crocker and Harris 1997).

3   For a discussion of the somatechnics of femme fashion, see Dahl, 2009 '(Re)Figuring Femme Fashion' *Lambda Nordica* 14(3–4): 43–77.

4   There is, however, now a significant archive of diverse and powerful writings by and about femmes, including several anthologies such as Nestle (1992), Harris and

The lack of queer recognition is a theme that many femmes, like Rosie Lugosi, address and rework through their writing, activism and performance – within local and transnational movements that have grown in size and exposure around Europe, North America and Australia in the past five years or so. A central part of recognition *is* visibility and thus much contemporary femme organizing is concerned with this. Rosie's poem can thus be read as a by now classic queer activist strategy of resistance and anti-assimilation and of speaking back to powerful majoritarian and minoritarian identity norms (Rosenberg 2002). Simultaneously, as Rosie makes clear, femmes call into question the idea that we should be able to *see* who is queer (and who is not) (Walker 1993, 2001) and this, it seems to me, is central to the complexity of femme. That is, femmes are both like and unlike other feminine folks in the world.

Within this historically emergent subject trajectory, many femmes, like Rosie Lugosi, insist that 'loving oneself' is a radical act on the part of femme-inine subjects who so often face contempt and danger and are subjected to very structured and conditional appreciation in a racist and heterosexist world. While this is an important political move, consistent with feminist empowerment, and while countering outside criticism is central to femme activism, in this chapter I will argue that femme-on-femme research is no more a narcissistic project about studying 'oneself' or advancing a personal agenda, than any other research. Contrary to the objections I often receive regarding my potential to be 'objective' (and therefore, presumably, more scientific), I propose that claiming belonging in a femme movement enables *both* affirmation *and* self-critical scrutiny, which in this chapter concerns that of the research process itself. By calling the unity and stability of identity categories into question and reflecting on multiple relations of power at work both in the world and in research, my work aims to explore geopolitically, historically and (sub)culturally specific understandings of what it means to queer femininity in and across a couple of urban queer subcultural communities in Western Europe and North America; communities in which I myself dwell.[5] Chicana feminist theorist Cherrie Moraga notes that indeed, 'to be critical of one's culture is not to betray one's culture' (Moraga 1983: 108) and I propose that through a collaborative and differentiated understanding both of

---

Crocker (1997) Dawn and Kelly (2005) and Burke (2009) as well as memoirs such as Nestle (1987), Hollibaugh (2000), 'guides' such as Rednour (2000), poetry like that of Gomez (1988), Hardy (2000, 2006), Newman (1995), Pratt (1995). Among notable theoretical/academic discussions by and on femmes and (queer) femininity are Martin (1996), Walker (2001), Gopinath (2005), Rodriguez (2003), Cvetkovich (2003) and Tyler (2003). As is evident here and everywhere, this chapter, like my work and life as a femme, owes much to this legacy.

5 Those communities are located in Stockholm, Malmö, Copenhagen, Paris, Barcelona, Berlin, London, San Francisco, Atlanta and Sydney. Needless to say, the degree to which I am part of these communities differs over time and in depth, with Stockholm, London, San Francisco and, recently, Sydney, being the primary ones.

research, community making and subject formation, the method and effect of self-scrutiny changes.

Queer Feminist Ethnography and Studying 'One's Own Community'

In contemporary gender and queer studies, 'methodologies' are a central node in conversations about scientific legitimacy and coherence, as well as in those about feminist visions of a different kind of science. Indeed, methods are far more often subject to discussion and contestation among colleagues and with students, than the (queer) 'theories' that are increasingly canonized within interdisciplinary gender studies. It is certainly difficult, if not undesirable and impossible, for interdisciplinary fields of knowledge to agree on a box of methodological tools in the way that, for instance, many disciplines within the social sciences, including anthropology tend to do. However, those of us trained in traditional disciplines often find that it is social scientific and cultural research that deals with speaking subjects rather than texts or other representations that tend to register fundamental and epistemological questions and concern. In a field so explicitly concerned with questions of power then, is it possible and ethical 'to represent' others? Can one speak on anyone's behalf? Ethnography has grappled with such questions for a long time, and in what follows, I discuss some ways that ethnography has been used within queer studies, with particular attention to models for thinking about reframing the positivist assumptions about relations between subjects and objects of research.

Based in ethnographic work conducted in what is often presented as radically different cultures and distinct communities, anthropological cross-cultural analyses have been important in challenging understandings of gender and sexuality as universal, predetermined, binary and fixed. That said, the discipline of anthropology remains at least phantasmatically dominated by studies of non-Western contexts and research on sexual cultures within Western contexts is a fairly recent topic. Existing studies on North American queer subcultural contexts, including Ester Newton's (1979) work on female impersonators and on queer community formations (1995) and Kath Weston's (1991) work on queer family formations, have been groundbreaking both within and beyond anthropology. Many have become 'queer classics' as well as significant within activist work against sexism, racism and homophobia. Tracing a legacy of collaboration of research and activism, I here draw attention to two models; the collaborative ethnohistorical model of *Boots of Leather, Slippers of Gold* (1993) on a working class white and African-American butch-femme community and the interdisciplinary queer methodologies presented by Judith Halberstam (1998, 2003) in her work on female masculinities and queer subcultural formations. I chose these particular pieces of research because they offer inspiration for how I might conduct femme-inist research.

In researching and writing *Boots of Leather, Slippers of Gold* (1993) anthropologist Elizabeth Lapovsky Kennedy joined forces with Madeline Davis, a librarian/singer-songwriter and activist and together they built their long study drawing on their community involvement and friendships. Their motivation was political: in the early eighties, Kennedy and Davis note, 'the entire [US] feminist movement became embroiled in the debates about women's sexuality and its practices' (1996: 175) and in that moment, working class lesbians were not considered legitimate subjects, either of politics or of research. Their project, which took 14(!) years to complete, was guided by a wish to give voice and visibility to a marginalized community and to provide a commentary to the feminist movement of the time. Kennedy and Davis knew that they were writing from a marginalized perspective with respect to their professions as scholars and as feminists. Wanting to 'give back' to their communities was more important than the prospect of 'professional advancement' and, among other things, they shared their royalties with the oral history project that enabled their work.

Kennedy had done 'proper fieldwork' previously and notes that being in 'their own nation' (as they put it) and sharing a common lesbian identity and activist pasts not only contributed to, but shaped, their research process (1996: 175). Their point of departure was one of recognizing that aging working class butch and femme lesbians are marginalized in multiple ways; as pre-Stonewall lesbians, as carriers of 'old-fashioned' gender, and as working class. Kennedy and Davis chose to render the subjects of their study anonymous unless they wanted otherwise, largely as a measure of safety for their friends and as a way of not altering relations within the community. Drawing on collaboration, ethnohistory, interviews, community involvement and political activism, Kennedy and Davis produced a ground-breaking study of a butch-femme community which not only contributed to a rethinking of lesbian gender, it also provided a model for how queer scholars, myself included, might engage and produce knowledge with and for our own communities.

Judith Halberstam is another scholar who engages in collaboration with 'her own community'. Like many queer, feminist and cultural studies scholars, Halberstam questions the kind of research that assumes that 'truth' can be drawn from 'raw data' in survey (or other) form, but also argues that ethnographic methods of participant observation and interviewing have their merits for queer work. In her ground-breaking study *Female Masculinity* (1998) Halberstam cites anthropologist Ester Newton, well known for her work on queer communities in North America, as her butch academic role model, stressing in particular her influence with regards to crafting intellectual projects around issues that are also of great personal importance.

In *Female Masculinity* Halberstam introduces what she calls a queer methodology of interdisciplinary work that she famously defines a 'scavenger methodology that uses different methods to collect and produce information on subjects who have been deliberately or accidentally excluded from traditional studies of human behaviour' (Halberstam 1998: 13). A queer methodology, she argues, brings together methods that are often cast as being at odds and refuses disciplinary coherence (1998: 13). In other words, the queerness lies both in the subject of research, the eclectic array of 'data' and in the 'strangeness' of mixing methods from different traditions. This model is one of few 'concrete' methodological proposals for queer studies. To my mind, it is also queer in the sense it makes it possible to show how queer subjectivities are formed out of an eclectic array of (sub)cultural references and reworkings of popular cultural representations.

Throughout her work, Halberstam provides a model for the butch scholar to do research as a member of the communities she studies. Drawing on participant observation among drag kings she produces work that has proven both inspiring and useful to a wide readership; as is demonstrated through her popularity in queer subcultural press. At the same time, Halberstam's analysis in *Female Masculinity* depends on a distinction between what she does as a 'scholar' and what the subjects of the work do in *their* work. Halberstam also insists on mixing methods in part because conventional methods like interviews may or may not give 'interesting' answers to questions like 'why do you like to dress up in drag?' (1998: 243). In other words, she is not primarily interested in the subjective experience of performing drag, but rather in its representational effects and the effects of subcultural production. Queer theory has offered insights into the difference between the performativity of all gender and intentional performance that aims to subvert. Many scholars labour to point out how queer genders call the stability of all genders into question (cf. Butler 1990, Munoz 1999, Westerling 2006 and others). Yet, it seems to me that here Halberstam's own readings of cultural representations sometimes remain separate from those of her subjects, thus leaving intact the authorative voice that reads and explains representations. Is this an inevitable effect of research and writing technologies that continue to insist on single authorship? Or does it suggest that there is a limit to the value of interviews themselves when it comes to theorizing queer gender?

In her more recent work on queer temporalities and subcultural lives, Halberstam develops her points about modes and motivations for queer studies further and notes that 'minority subcultures in general tend to be documented by former or current members of the subculture rather than by "adult experts"' (2003: 321). Furthermore, queer subcultures are themselves marked by blurred distinctions between what Halberstam calls the 'archivist' and the cultural producers. Many occupy both positions or coexist in the same networks, and, as she puts it, 'new queer cultural studies feeds off of and back into sub-cultural production' (2003: 322) – and this includes her own work on female masculinities. In other words, work on queer subcultures tends to both rely on collaboration and furthermore, to challenge presumed distinctions between the researcher and her 'objects'.

It seems then, that most often in queer and feminist cultural studies, ethnography is *one* of many methods used by interdisciplinary scholars working on themes, issues, or identity formations rather than bounded communities. Halberstam's call for eclectic methodologies and her model for queer subcultural archival work is innovative, inspiring and useful for a project aiming to rethink the meaning of femininity within and through feminist theory, in queer communities and in subcultural productions of art and life. As Halberstam notes, subcultural formations and productions are characterized by a complicated relationship to 'experts' and studies thereof must take this into consideration. Questions of collaboration and authorship remain difficult to address, especially since academic knowledge carries a particular weight and we live in a culture that fosters celebrity worship including queer scholars and performers. It seems to me that the dilemma is mainly that academic technologies of analysis and interpretation often produce distance and that within queer studies as a whole, ethnographic work remains secondary to literary or theoretical work.

Femme-inist Figurations

Trained in cultural anthropology and simultaneously deeply informed by post-colonial and feminist critiques of a discipline that has strong roots in positivist and colonialist science, I continue to insist that at its heart, ethnography offers interesting tools for making both knowledge and community. I locate what I call femme-on-femme research as part of a feminist project and call upon a tradition of queer and feminist ethnography. To me a *femme-inist* ethnography is that which takes femininities, rather than women, as both objects and subjects of study. It is motivated by a wish to reconsider (and change) the meaning of *femininity* rather than to, as classic feminist ethnography has aimed, to 'improve' the conditions of women.

To that end, I approach femme not as a narrow subcultural lesbian identity category but as a historically emergent *figuration* (Braidotti 1994, Haraway 2004, Castaneda 2002). As Claudia Castaneda (2002) notes, a figuration is at once literary, material-semiotic and embodied, constituted through particular practices and interpretations, including scientific and feminist ones. To me this means that the femme figuration is not outside of feminist and queer theorizing, but rather emerges in dialogue with and as part of such labour. By putting this figure to work, I follow Rosi Braidotti who argues that 'the difference between a figuration and a classical subject position is an accountability of one's location – which is not the same as a self-appointed position – it is a collective and shared spatiotemporal territory' (1994: 12–13). Below I discuss how one might take accountability of one's location as a *femme scientist* through departing from the shared spatiotemporal territory of theorizing femme-ness. In contemporary femme activism, that territory is often made through differently situated engagements with feminist themes such as objectification, relations of power, critiques of normativity and visions of a femme-inine future.

Queering Community, Home and Academy

Let me now pause to ask: what does it mean, then, to study 'one's own community'? First of all, any study of a 'community' requires that we define that community – in time and space as much as in movement and this requires a discussion of how belonging to such a community is structured. Halberstam (2003) notes that the idea of community implies a permanent population, often tied to a neighbourhood, and that conventional family models often are the implicit building blocks of such communities. There is indeed a rich literature concerned with geographic perspectives on queer community formation, including critical perspectives on the making of 'gaybourhoods' and the changing nature of queer communities over time (Bell and Valentine 1995, Browne et al. 2007). According to Halberstam, a subculture differs from a community insofar as it is transient, extra-familial and based in oppositional modes of affiliation.

Both conventional and subcultural definitions of community carry strong connotations of familiarity and belonging, and often a sense of being 'at home', in the sense of being amidst that which is familiar, comfortable and affirming. In short: a warm, fuzzy feeling. As Miranda Joseph notes, 'identity-based movements invoke community to mobilize constituents and validate their cause to a broader public' (2002a: vii) precisely because of its affective connotations. In her polemic against the romanticization of community, Joseph instead argues that rather than primordial, 'communal subjectivity is constituted through practices of production and consumption' (2002a: viii) and that the rhetorical invocation of community is imbricated in and deployed by capitalism. In this chapter, the aim is not to fetishize (femme) community, but rather to propose that research is, as much as identity construction, part of these practices of production and consumption. As Joseph notes in her conclusion, if communities are made and enjoyed, then

> a great deal of agency resides with the producers of community to make our collectivities more disruptive rather than less. In order to do so we must read the social relationships in which our communities are imbricated and assess the implications of our political goals and strategies, of the actions we do in fact all take all the time (2002a: 172).

In writing about femme communities I thus depart from Joseph's insight that community is always already imbricated in, not outside of late capitalism. Those that I study are neither merely local nor is membership and formation stable over time, even if they are intimately tied to particular locations. Femme movements are not exclusionary but rather, like most subcultural communities, open to new members whose politics and aesthetics are recognisable. Simultaneously, like many queer community formations, they rework the meaning and implications of familial and sexual bonds (cf. Weston 1991). Conducting fieldwork within femme movements thus requires knowledge of local histories and the specificity of queer identity politics, but equally it needs attention to how, when and why certain ideas and people travel. Attending and conducting research at conferences, pride events, performances and other kinds of cultural events, private parties or clubs, reveals that community is made and remade through the events that bring people together. These events both create and reflect community and there it is clear that visible cultural clues, including aesthetics of dress and desire, as well as queer kinship networks, are central to generating a sense of being 'home' and 'being in one's community'. As such, even as they offer critiques of mainstream culture, femme subjectivities and the queering of femininities are always already constituted through practices of cultural production and consumption.

As Joseph's work indicates, social scientists have long been sceptical of certain romantic conceptions of community belonging as tied to a nostalgic sense of feeling at home, in the comfort zone and at ease with the order of things seeming familiar rather than strange. Postcolonial and feminist anthropologists in particular have challenged the masculinist and Eurocentric underpinnings in how tropes of 'home' and 'away' structure ideas of proper ethnographic work. As I've argued elsewhere (Dahl 2004), following Gupta and Ferguson (1997), anthropology and academia in general often assumes that one is (quite literally) 'home' in the academy (or where one studies) and 'away' in the field. These days and to many of us, these tropes are reminders of hierarchies that have been central to the making of a particular knowledge/power regime which excludes women, queers and non-Western subjects. As such, the (if ever phantasmatic) dichotomy of home/away points to the racial and classed markings of the academy and assumptions of who belongs there – because as countless scholars of colour, women and queers have noted, an academy that is often sexist, racist and homophobic is certainly not 'a fuzzy warm home' by default. Indeed, marginalized and critical academics have often created their own spaces of home both within and outside of academia, largely by choosing to foster different conversations and knowledge projects that are critical of the increasingly capitalist and certainly still colonialist makings of 'straight' social scientific research. Furthermore, feminists have noted that home is always already gendered and as such it is not simply the place of the familiar, the safe and the comfortable, but equally a place of violence, labour, and generational and gendered hierarchies (Martin and Mohanty 1986). At the same time others have argued that it is the place of both subjugated and of empowering knowledges (Sawyer 2008, hooks 1990, Young 2005). For queers, home as a familial space may well be a place where one is not welcome and thus making and redefining home is often central to the making of community, and this may not always be territorialized and localized.

Some readers may now object and argue that none of these tropes prevail in a post-modern academy. However, the frequency with which I get asked how I can be *both* a femme activist advocating for femme-inist strategies and femme visibility *and* study that very movement points to how what I here call tropes of home and away structure research and above all carry strong messages about the need for distance between analysis and immersion. The related and frequent question of whether my work can be seen as 'scientific' (rather than 'ideological' or 'activist') also suggests that the positivist roots of social science live on in the sense of privileging and encouraging analytic distance and that there is a continued split between theory and practice. Indeed, even within queer and feminist contexts, there seems to be a kind of hangover of objectivity hovering around knowledge production. The epistemological underpinning of anthropology's main methodology, 'participant observation', is of central importance here, as it builds on the idea that one is to 'become', not 'be' part of a community. The good anthropologist is close enough to explain it, but not 'too close' so that she loses distance and starts speaking on her own behalf. While anthropologists are frequently asked to speak on the behalf of subjugated groups, a clear distinction is made between 'activism' and 'science'. In that procedure, 'key informants', who are often presented as 'friends' but rarely as authorities, are central to the ethnographic project. These actors act as brokers and trixters – they are able to explain and translate the cultural context in question, but they are rarely understood as co-producers of knowledge. While much work has been done to unpack such epistemological starting points, this persistence of this legacy, I argue, still makes for rendering the queer scholar of queer phenomena a rather queer, as in improper, researcher. While projects concerning cross-cultural perspectives on same-sex desire and critiques of heteronormativity are often groundbreaking and important, I argue that if queer is about critiquing norms, then calling research and writing conventions that presume stable distinctions between subjects and objects into question should remain central to queer studies and methodologies.

It is clear that we are neither fully at home nor fully outside of any community we aim to study. Rather, as science studies scholar Karen Barad (2003) points out, research subjects and objects always already exist in the same universe and they are always in intra-action. However, as feminist theorist Nina Lykke (2008) notes in a discussion of Karen Barad's work, limitations and boundaries are necessary for scientific projects. Although classic methods often presume that the relation between them exist prior to the research process, Lykke proposes that we begin by defining and contextualizing both research subject and research *and* the relation and boundary between subject and object, but not once and for all but rather temporarily. Through doing this, we also make clear the particular stakes or interests we have in our work (Lykke 2008: 167). Furthermore, while Lykke argues that situating our knowledge is tied to 'siting' and 'sighting' – that is, to locating and situating the researcher and the particular technologies of research that are being used (including interviews, anonymity, encounters) – femme-inist ethnography involves a third dimension which I call *citing*. At best, queer ethnographers who work in 'their own communities' belong to both and manage to queer the research process itself by rendering the familiarity of research conventions strange (queer). To further this point, the remainder of this chapter discusses some dimensions of the work with *Femmes of Power* as one example of how collaborative science might be made and what the effects of femme-on-femme research are. It is not suggested as an exemplary model, but rather as an opportunity for reflection and hopefully an offer of inspiration which itself draws on the models presented by queer and feminist ethnographers that I have deployed here.

Femme-on-Femmes of Power: Starting Points and Encounters

Featuring over 60 people from 12 cities in seven countries, *Femmes of Power: Exploding Queer Femininities* is the result of more than four years of un-funded research and collaboration. Like Kennedy (Kennedy and Davis 1993) and Halberstam (Volcano and Halberstam 1999), but as a junior femme ethnographer (still a graduate student when we started) rather than an established academic, I was given an opportunity to collaborate with an artist/theorist on this project. Del LaGrace Volcano is not only an internationally recognized queer visual artist; working with him also presented an opportunity to apprentice with and learn from someone who has spent considerable time representing and reflecting on queer community formations and how they change over time.

Like many queer feminist authors and artists, Del and I were motivated by what we saw as a marginalization of a set of issues and subjects (femininity in general and femmes in particular) and by a desire to 'give something back' to our communities and allies. Like Kennedy and Davis, we understood ourselves to be community members and activists as much as we were identified as an artist and an academic. In some respects, the project can be seen as an example of the intimate and entangled relationship between queer research and cultural production that Halberstam (2003) discusses. Those featured have chosen to be visually and ethnographically represented and the book also further contributes to their validation, empowerment and representation. As a corrective move then, all visual attempts for recognition raise issues of representation, that is, who is being represented and who do they represent?

Unlike the members of the working class butch-femme communities in *Boots of Leather* (but like the drag kings featured by Halberstam (1998) and Volcano and Halberstam (1999)) our subjects do not share a common location. They are joined by an interest in queering femininity, by networks with each other, and in some cases, simply by participating in our project. Rejecting a more conventional social science model of assuming that there are clear and bounded definitions of any community studied, the book project did not follow a comparative and representative model where geopolitical categories like nation or city, or even ethnic or class identities, would be used for representative and generalisable purposes. Instead we began the project – like we both have done in our previous work (Volcano and Halberstam 1999, Dahl 2004a, b, 2007, Volcano 1991, 2000, 2007) – in our own transnational queer kinship networks and communities and by making photographs and conversation with friends and acquaintances. At the same time, along with the subjects of our work, we continuously analysed the demographics of our communities and asked ourselves about silences and gaps, using what could be called a snowball method where meetings led to more meetings and introductions. We also presented work in progress in multiple contexts and to our different communities and networks along the way. We continuously solicited and followed suggestions from friends and traced conversational threads between the femmes we met, making the very selection process itself a reflection on femme genealogies.

That said, like all ethnographic work, the book is a partial and situated account that draws on some of these networks. It's also important to recognize that this book's femmes of power are all in positions where they can be visually represented in a book like this and this represents a historical moment when to these particular subjects being (visually) represented in a book poses less of a risk and more of an opportunity for connection and recognition. This has its limitations and in some cases, work or family situations did prevent femmes who would have liked to be part of the project from participating. In that respect, the book can only offer a small glimpse into a particular network of queerly feminine folks to whom participation in a highly visualized project is desirable and possible.

As a femme-inist ethnographer my position constantly changed in the process and I often conducted participant observation in the process and the politics of the research itself. Our starting point was that within both mainstream and queer subcultural contexts, feminine matters tend to be laden with negative connotations of superficiality, objectification, sexualization and so on. However, our goal was more than a simple act of visibility, even if that is commendable in itself (after all, Volcano has been a central figure in rendering female masculinity visible); we wanted to explore alternative ways of representing femininity and feminine subjects. Volcano has developed what he calls a queer feminist methodology of making images *with* which is invested in making images with subjects who speak and speak back, rather than taking images *from* subjects who are given no voice (Volcano 2008: 14). As Del puts it: 'The process of production is as important as the product. Digital photographic technologies enable the subject to give immediate feedback on their own image and for those that don't reflect the subject as they want to be seen can be instantaneously deleted.'[6]

Through sharing many moments of making images with femmes, I was able to follow how collaboration works in the production of representation, and learn about the intimacy of photographic art and about the mutual trust that is required in order to produce a carefully framed image with many layers. Through 'participant observation' in the photographic sessions, I gained a tremendous respect for the femmes who were willing to partake in the project and for the labour it takes to make images under what at times were rather difficult conditions of cold, rain, snow, crowd intervention and so on. In many cases, the very production of the image turned into a public spectacle, which in and of itself contributed to the reconfiguration of public representations of femininity. Close readings of the images produced, which the book invites but does not offer, also reveal a tremendous amount of clues to the specificity of each subject's legacy and agency,

---

6   Personal communication with Del LaGrace Volcano, August 2009.

as captured at one moment in time in a particular location. In that respect, *Femmes of Power* is more of an ethno-archive than a conventional ethnography.

As a collaborative project, working on the book brought together our respective and different networks, which meant that we did not always work together. For instance, Wendy Delorme in Paris and Maria and Signe in Copenhagen (see Volcano and Dahl 2008) came to the project through Del's networks[7] and photographs were made before we met. The warm day I met with Wendy in Paris and the cold December day when I took the train across the water from Malmö to Copenhagen to meet with Maria and Signe have stayed with me as remarkable instances of the joy of femme-on-femme ethnography. Like many other conversations, ours had started beforehand on email and has continued both as dialogue and through participation in virtual communities and collaborations in queer subcultural spaces long after our first encounter. Curiously, these crowded café conversations were more like reunions between old friends. Beginning with mapping itineraries, people, places we share (largely European and North American queer urban subcultural locations), we quickly moved into intense and deeply moving conversations about our lives. These were loosely structured around femininity, feminism, femme-ness and desire, but more often turned into stories of being different, and of family, community and life dreams. With a sense of shared interest and community, all conversations within this project zigzagged across time and space and we built on each other's arguments, cited other femmes we know, compared stories and found common threads. To be sure, a femme-identified researcher who is interested in meeting other femmes from an explicit sense of belonging to the same community and being interested in similar things sets up assumptions about a certain sharedness, even if it is more of a vague familiarity or sensibility, rather than something that connotes the sameness of family resemblance.

What makes for such easy first encounters? What enables the trust? Like most of my collaborators, I've been interviewed by queer researchers and journalists on numerous occasions and the at times seemingly contrived and distant neutrality that have accompanied such encounters have often generated awkwardness, as if though the interviewer participating in conversation may 'pollute the data'. While sometimes my apprehensions about the power of representation make me hesitate to do so, I always return to the same thing: If I wish my allies and collaborators to let me ask them questions and write about them, then should I not be willing to do the same for others? If I belong also to a community of researchers, then should I not assist my colleagues? As an activist, I know what it feels like to be interviewed and, more importantly, represented by others and this is useful and humbling experience because as Sharon Traweek has reminded me, epistemic privilege has a lot to do with whether or not one is able not only to say *yes* but *no*

7　In my forthcoming book from the project *Femme as Figuration*, I will address the nature of these interlocking queer kinship networks further, but space limitations permits me from doing so here.

to being studied.[8] Clearly, I can say no, but conducting 'participant observation' in an interview situation could also serve to simultaneously queer the science of interviewing and make the complex process of scientific knowledge production even more visible. It has also meant that I have gained a deep understanding of the difference between being cited as a scholar and as an 'informant'.

Ethnographers are trained to assume that rendering 'informants' anonymous is simultaneously a technology of objectivity and *the* way to avoid potential negative consequences for the research subject, especially for those who are marginalized and who may experience a very clear and present danger of being subjected to discrimination and even hate crimes, such as in the case of Kennedy and Davis's (1993) work. However, a clear downside of anonymity is that it also serves to reproduce the hierarchy of a named author and the unnamed 'informant'. While full transparency is obviously impossible, rendering interview subjects anonymous actively reproduces the idea of the author as 'theorist' and the interviewee as providing 'illustrations' of the author's theoretical points.[9] After all, we rarely see references to anonymous research subjects in our bibliographies.

My starting point for femme-on-femme research was that we share interests and stakes in wanting to challenge the contempt for femininity that exists both within majoritarian society and to some extent, within feminist and queer spaces. *Femmes of Power* was not a project that assumed that the femmes featured were in need of help for their empowerment. These femmes are indeed often – but not always or in every way – empowered femmes, who produce their own representations and narratives and tell their own stories through performance, art, writing, activism and teaching. They are willing and able to engage, to represent themselves and to be represented, and they share not only language, concepts and ideologies, but also spaces of intellectual and activist conversation. But by viewing femmes as co-producers of knowledge on a topic that generally has been tied to objectification, passivity, superficiality and so on, I wanted to challenge what counts as theory as well as the master voice of the interpreter who so often has reduced feminine subjects to anonymous narrators, or their (queer) images to superficial 'illustrations' of theoretical points. Actively aiming to decentre the scientific voice opens up ways of remaining humble and moving in and out of different positions of authority in a conversation. Nevertheless, questions remain: how then does one represent (members of) one's own community? Is it possible

---

8   Lecture given on the 'Ethnographies of gendered mobilities and imaginaries' research course, Luleå University, June 2009.

9   To give but one example, once in an interview I was asked to 'stop talking' as I was 'getting to close to the argument she wanted to make' on the subject of the interview. I was puzzled, and it revealed a presumed difference between an 'informant' who provides 'data' and a 'researcher' who provides 'interpretation'. I was to speak about certain aspects of my personal life relevant to the subject but was not to provide 'arguments' or 'theory'. Many femmes who are used to being interviewed recount similar experiences and often express scepticism of researchers for that reason.

to queer the ethnographic genre? To explore these questions, I now turn to a discussion of femme-inist ethnography.

Femme-inist Ethnography: The Politics of Femme Representation

I'd love to live in a world where the sexual binary system is considered a silly tradition of thought; but we're not there yet. I hope my work helps to paint myself and others as 'Subjects', not 'Objects'. (Trina Rose, in Volcano and Dahl 2008: 172)

Like many queer academics, I come to and through both queer/gender studies and ethnography with a love of writing and with an explicit feminist desire to contribute to a rethinking of the who, the what and the why of social scientific knowledge-making. In a cheeky way, inspired by the visionary experiments of writing sexual difference, I also want to reconsider what *l'écriture femme-inine* might look like. That is, what happens if we queer writing conventions and what might it do for reconsidering the meaning of femininity? When our lipgloss speaks together, through this co-production of knowledge, can femme (science) reproduce femininity with a difference? As Kennedy and Davis note, 'power in matters of *interpretation* is at the core of the research hierarchy. In part this is because interpretation and writing in the Western tradition are predominantly individual quests. But in part this is due to the entrenched nature of the social hierarchies of race, gender, and class' (Kennedy and Davis 1996: 185–86, my emphasis). Can femme-inist ethnography make a difference?

With equal weight given to text and image, the format of *Femmes of Power* is not only unusual in that it is neither a coffee table art book, nor a classic text book; it is also a conscious experiment in visual and ethnographic representation. The aim was to try and undo the implied hierarchies between the 'academic'/ text and the 'artist'/image. And rather than letting images 'illustrate' text, or text 'explain' images, together with our designer Elina Grandin, we laboured to make them work *together*, with a hope for an added, less tangible, dimension in which the reader is another (imagined) collaborator. In some respects, this is yet another way to queer ethnography; rather than a straightforward social scientific account with illustrations, the book consciously leaves many matters of interpretation up to its reader. While it is inevitably up to the readers rather than the producer to determine the queer effects of this project, here I want to further the reflections on the methodological dimensions of this work.

While the subject/object distinction is itself an inherent problem of the liberal paradigm, the gendered technologies of representation that are employed in research have been central to upholding that dichotomy. For instance, the classic image of the anthropologist 'in the field' often features a fully dressed, civilized man interviewing a naked, squatting and subordinate 'native'. The scientist records a cultural history as told by a key informant and simultaneously engages in implicit or explicit civilizing missions. He becomes the author and the authority on the subject at hand. The relation of power is quite literal in such images. The ethnographer on a chair and the informant on the ground, and thus they map onto that which is subject and object, white and black, dressed and undressed. By contrast, let's consider Del LaGrace Volcano's image entitled 'the femme ethnographer at work' (see Figure 9.1). In the context of the other images in *Femmes of Power* this particular image looks less like an arranged portrait but like many of Del's images, it also works by way of referencing and citing; in this case the history of (feminist) anthropology.

Figure 9.1 The Femme-inist Ethnographer at Work 2006, Del LaGrace Volcano, from Volcano And Dahl (2008)

In an explicit critique of male dominated science, methods deriving from feminist epistemology have suggested that 'women' are better equipped to study 'women' (Harding 1986). Since the death of the unified subject of feminism, woman with a capital W, feminist scholars have become more interested in relations of power between women within the research process, particularly along axes of race, class, age, sexuality and geographic location. Furthermore, feminist ethnographers have also questioned and experimented with ethnographic form and scientific authority (Viesweswaran 1994, Behar and Gordon 1996, among others). Femme-on-femme might connote sameness but what exactly would that sameness be? Compared to the classic image of the ethnographer in the field, this image might be read as two equally positioned (as reflected in sitting next to each other) white women. Morgana Maye, the subject of this photograph, is roughly the same age as me, she is well versed in feminist and queer theory and at the time of this conversation pursuing a Ph.D. Given the centrality placed on race, class, age, gender and education, all this might suggest that femme-on-femme research is about equality through sameness.

Rather than assuming sameness or picking an example of a femme who might be considered 'different' along such axes of power to point to the politics of difference within femme research, let me instead reflect on the difficulty of reading visual clues. Reading the aesthetic codes of femininity we might ask what dress tells us about the spatiotemporal and socioeconomic dimensions of femme and what we need to now to understand them. Morgana's pearls, fur and silk dress might suggest a contemporary love of vintage, or it might suggest upper-class living. A queer feminist reading might see a casually, fashionably or rather scandalously dressed ethnographer, conducting an interview with a house-dwelling and very assertive femme in San Francisco's Castro neighbourhood and this uncertainty I argue, might be read as a metaphor for the feminized complexity of both visibility and class in the early 2000s. If we add other information – such as that I am Swedish and that English is not my first language, that we dwell in urban subcultural contexts in Stockholm and San Francisco that differ significantly in terms of size, history, diversity and range of options for consumption, entertainment and dating, and that Morgana is a sexual educator with a private dungeon, while I am a teacher of gender studies whose sexual practices are to be kept separate from my work, are we still 'the same'?

If we linger for a minute on this 'ethnographic encounter' itself, it matters that like many of our subjects, Morgana is accustomed to doing photo shoots. That is, she is not only extremely articulate about her understandings of femininity, feminism, and performativity, but she carefully and capably negotiated, and at times even orchestrated the photo shoot. Our initial encounter, like those with many other femmes in the book, was routed through a then shared lover. This to me points to the workings of queer kinship in the process of femme-on-femme research and yet our desires and sexual practices differ significantly in many other respects including that mine became to obey hers. A great admirer of the power of the feminine, I found myself fascinated and willing to go along with every step, which pointed to the complexity of femme-on-femme desire, if not (only/always/ ever) sexual, then at least in terms of appreciation.

Lastly, if we expanded the anthropological definition of 'studying up' (Nader 1982) beyond studying epistemic power and understand it to mean studying things we admire rather than things we do not have access to, this image to me also points to the awe with which I conduct my research. Many of the subjects of my research are well-known authors, performers and artists whose work I often cite in my writing. Femme-on-femme research is a queer part of such a trajectory. It is often said that an image says more than a thousand words, and this image may or may not signal our affects in the situation. Reading the subtleties of visual and textual representations in *Femmes of Power* does require a certain queer cultural literacy as they both engage and disrupt expressive and scientific conventions.

According to Clifford, 'ethnographic truths are inherently partial – committed and incomplete' (1986: 7). It seems to me that the idea of the detached and lone scientist as labouring away producing original ideas is itself a fiction held up by the conventions of anthropology.[10] Inspired by this idea – that ethnographic truths are always partial and that ethnography is by and large a poetic fiction and an experiment with form – my understanding of femme-on-femme ethnography stresses the dialogic, the non-original, and the fictional dimensions of both identities and ideas.

For instance, in the letter-portrait of Morgana Maye, I aimed to go beyond the eerie surface of the images of her and convey not only our encounter and my admiration, but how Morgana herself accounts for her own fictional invocations of a 1950s suburban housewife aesthetic. 'To me femme is about taking the things that oppressed me and using them' she said, while also insisting on being astutely aware and critical of the racist reality of the United States in the 1950s that it inevitably references.[11] Explicitly feminist and equally queer, Morgana insists that this aesthetic 'captures the essence of traditional female strength and beauty' and that 'the 50s is a decade of full-bodied women and absent fathers'. While Morgana, like Rosie Lugosi's poem suggested, 'doesn't look like a real lesbian' in her simulacrum of femininity, she also critiques contemporary beauty ideals and fantasies of a classic nuclear family. Rereading the 1950s as an era where the mother was the centre of the domestic universe, Morgana Maye also queers 'mommy' in her work as a professional dominatrix specializing on age play. Her industriousness and her own understanding of both 'mommy' and of femininity, she explained, is inspired by her own mother and best friend, whose entrepreneurship as a Mary Kay lady[12] taught her economic independence and to appreciate the magic in rituals of femininity.

---

10   In a recent set of reflections on the future of ethnography, David Westbrook (2008) sets up precisely this archetype and writes, consistently referring to the academic with male pronouns: 'consider the classic story: a young man leaves Paris or some such center for the "field", armed with a notebook, a bit of reading, rather inchoate beliefs in the importance of cultural specificity and underlying humanity, and an earnest yet pleasing manner. After some months or years of talking to, indeed living among, members of another culture, the young man returns and writes up his findings about life elsewhere – our ethnographer has mapped a culture, made it available to the world outside (or at least, made it available to Western academics)' (2008: 9). Whether any anthropologist ever lived up to this ideal or not it is clearly still there as something to measure oneself against.

11   For a discussion of the circulation of 1950s aesthetics and the politics of whiteness, see my forthcoming piece entitled 'White Gloves?' in *Gender, Culture and Place*.

12   In brief, Mary Kay is a brand of cosmetics sold through networks and via parties for invited guests that is now a global multi-million dollar industry. Like Avon and Tupperware, it has been one way for women who were primarily homemakers to make extra income

Does the letter-form, whereby the narrative is one of addressing the subject herself in an intimate way make for a better kind of partial account? While my aim with engaging my fellow femmes was to challenge the tradition of individualism within ethnography, a key part of interpretation is providing a narrative frame, which I did for the majority of the texts in the book. Obviously, I chose not only the narrative form but the citations and anecdotes in order to paint a particular picture – one which mixes interviews with long answers, brief thematic overviews and portraits which highlight admiration rather than deconstruction or explanation.[13] I'm not sure. But engaging my fellow femmes as theorists of femininity, featured with name and image, and in a dialogue where they had the final say on how they were represented not only reflected but aimed to generate community and conversation and it extended the dialogue between us through the writing process.[14] Duggan and McHugh (2002) propose that the femme scientist solicits loving and grateful collaboration, and this can be seen as an attempt to experiment with such an approach. As a whole the book aims to provide many voices and textual forms, with the hope that together they point to some expressions of an emerging figuration. In addressing the text to femmes and in refusing to do the explicit work of explanation, it also explores the boundaries of how one does or even values science and to whom one addresses oneself to.

The downside of not building text on anonymized accounts was that it was more difficult to address what some interlocutors have called 'the thorny aspects' of femme politics and community making. In particular, moments of critique of fellow femmes and other queers in some respects had to be downplayed as putting things in print can have powerful effects. It also meant that there were things that were said in interviews that did *not* end up in the book – as subjects changed their mind or decided other things than those that I considered significant were more important. While some critics are quick to point out the lack of attention to tension and disagreements as a shortcoming of the book – and once again, hinting towards the notion that this would make *Femmes of Power* less 'scientific'. To me this raises questions about the inevitable limitations of any kind of representational 'outing'. If there is some kind of 'truth' that nobody is willing to state publically, then what kind of truth is it? How might one address such issues in an ethical way?[15] If the aim of rethinking *l'ecriture femme-inine*, like the effort to correct the lack of visual representation of queer femininities, is also to write femininity

---

13   As the initiator of the book, Del was invested in the politics of textual representation and felt it important that other voices were represented. These authors were Pratibha Parmar, Kentucky Fried Woman, Amber Hollibaugh, Campbell Ex, Lois Weaver and Itziar Ziga. Rather than 'representing' any one particular authentic experience, these authors were also central interlocutors and dialogue partners in the process of making the book.

14   This approach includes this piece as well, where Morgana Maye, as before, has given consent and input to this discussion, corrected misunderstandings and altered terms she did not find accurate.

15   For one attempt to do so, see my forthcoming article 'White Gloves?' in *Gender, Culture and Place*.

differently, then is it not also worth highlighting moments of generosity, exchange, community and solidarity to counter the moments fraught by tension and strife? Returning again to the social hierarchies outlined by Kennedy and Davis (1996), it is clear that issues concerning power structures in society as a whole cannot be undone, but they may be ethnographically and representationally challenged.

Conclusion: The Future of Femme Science

In this chapter, I have attempted to reflect on the ethnographic practice employed in the work on *Femmes of Power: Exploding Queer Femininities* and to situate its motivations against a legacy of queer, feminist and 'straight' anthropological practice. While the project was informed by ethnographic methodological sensibilities and in particular by feminist ethnographic discussions about power and representation, it is clear to any reader that it is not a conventional ethnography. Rather, *Femmes of Power* might be seen as a form of queer archive containing photographs, interviews and snippets of ephemeral, fleeting moments of encounters (cf. Munoz 1996).

To conclude this rhizomatic meditation on queer methods, and return to the question of what 'real' and 'normal' queers and science look like posed by Rosie's poem at the outset, I want to invoke the wisdom of my fellow femme theorists. 'Femme is a frequency you tune into', mused Caroline, a London based femme, when she reflected on her particular understanding of desire, aesthetics, aging and body politics (Volcano and Dahl 2008: 30). As such, it is tied to an archive of feelings, a set of ephemeral, intangible dimensions (Munoz 1996). To Caroline and many other lesbian femmes, the desire for butches was the starting point for their own understandings of being femme but femme *movements* are built from a wish for solidarity with other femmes. Femme-on-femme ethnography, similarly, might be understood as, in part, a response to the privileging of masculinity (even if it is ever so delightful to many of us), as a tuning into a frequency of sisterhood and queer community and a yearning for femme community.

If Halberstam's (1998) proposal for queer methodology is about scavenging among methods and taking those most useful for the project at large, then it is perhaps particularly suited for studying communities clustered around the pleasures of closets and rituals of 'borrowing, stealing and trading', as Swedish drag artist Indra Windh put it (Volcano and Dahl 2008: 53). Like Halberstam's trajectory, my ongoing work on queer femininities draws on multiple methodologies; archival research, ethnographic engagements, participation in community events and politics. Beyond being humble and recognizing the power in copying the wisdoms of others rather than attempting originality, tuning into the frequency of femme-on-femme research has at once been an invitation to femme sisterhood and a recognition that neither my own position, nor that of my research subjects, nor relations between us are stable. Many femmes argue that engaging with femininity means undoing what French femme Wendy Delorme calls 'our inherited self-hatred and trust issues, because in most societies, women are raised to think they are worth nothing, aside from beauty' (Volcano and Dahl 2008: 106) and work against stereotypes of femmes as 'bitchy, stealing each other's boyfriends, being competitive ... a residue from straight culture', as Caroline put it (Volcano and Dahl 2008: 182). To me, this signals a commitment to sisterhood and solidarity, not a declaration of perfection.

Femme-on-femme is, I would argue not simply about existing within and reflecting communities, it is also a methodology committed to making community. It is about seeing research as part of, not outside of, social movements, and seeing the research process itself as something that works towards the formulation of community in its (researchers') execution. It draws on conversations and exchanges in closets and kitchens as well as in clubs and gutters, in internet communities and emails as well as in conference settings and panels. Like the vampire queen Rosie Lugosi, the femme scientist comes out at night and like queers of all kinds, she hangs out in public, in bathrooms and behind the scene. Like other queer researchers she scavenges and collects clips, fanzines, songs and pieces of clothing, and she records frequencies and energies. To that end, femme-on-femme means sharing not only ideas and writings, but sometimes also beds, resources and lovers ethically; it means seeing every encounter as an opportunity not to make scientific authority but to make community and it means recognizing the theorizing not only of femme 'scholars' but of strippers, burlesque artists and community activists through their live and living art. Above all, it means acknowledging that academics and our concepts are always already part of networks and not outside of them.

So is femme-on-femme research a narcissistic project of self-promotion and homogeneity? Is it about lack of scientific distance to oneself? Standpoint-oriented feminist researcher Gabriele Griffin (2009) recently argued that feminist research can be divided into those who study that which is different and those who study that which is the same and that both methods lead to both compromise and being compromised. Omitting the contributions made by theorists like Trinh T. (1990), Donna Haraway (1991) and Chela Sandoval (2000) with regards to the position of the in/appropriated other, the trixter and the differentiated consciousness of an oppositional subject, Griffin seems to argue that while feminists have been critical of studies of difference (read: with subjects whose power positions are structurally different), researching 'the same' often leads to emotional investments that blur scientific vision. I argue that femme-on-femme research is neither and both, and that a shared engagement with queer femininities works as a point of entry to opening up questions about the materiality and performativity of the feminine, not as a final destination or bounded entity.

Doing femme-on-femme research with folks who range in age between their late teens and their sixties, who come from diverse class backgrounds and belong to a wide range of ethnic communities, requires being mindful of the social hierarchies, especially in these times of sex, class and race war on an increasingly globally interconnected scale. It is not only important in terms of the relationship between an academic, middle-class subject (by professional default and social democratic aspirations) and the subjects of my work, but equally importantly in terms of understanding relations of power *within* femme communities and among femmes. As Halberstam (1998: xiii) notes, many queer researchers labour to tread the fine line of not letting the personal be too weighty while at the same time not becoming so theoretical that the work loses significance in relation to what is often very complex, marginalized and personal experiences. Like Kevin Kumashiro (2002), a queer scholar dedicated to anti-oppressiveness and a pedagogue interested in questions of methodology and with a long history of working with activists, I have investments in my own research and those certainly need to be scrutinized. In my case, it is the *potentiality* of reconfiguring femininity that interest me and to that end, I draw out dimensions that I find particularly innovative and interesting, rather than attempting to present a unified understanding of femme identity. If queer work is about breaking down boundaries and contributing to a methodology that also serves an agenda for social change and if writing something also participates in producing it, then femme-inist ethnography aims to address such questions of political investment, as I have done here.

Engaging and presenting the subjects of the study as co-producers of theories and ideas, *Femmes of Power* was an attempt to perform the approach of siting, sighting and citing – while keeping the very notion that we both coexist and need to be separate at the centre. I agree with Rosi Braidotti (1994) when she says that in our contemporary moment, we need political fictions as much as we need theoretical systems. To that end, femme-on-femme research, like femme work in general, is greedy but humble, visionary but not proscriptive, reproductive but with a pleasurable difference. Above all, it has an aim, which is to contribute to what Lisa Duggan and Kathleen McHugh call a *femme science*, 'addressed to the future, a future where femininity as we know it … will have been completely superseded' (2002: 186).

Chapter 10

Queer(y)ing the Ethics of Research Methods: Toward a Politics of Intimacy in Researcher/Researched Relations

Mathias Detamore

Prologue: 'God Damn It!'

During the defence of my qualifying exams,[1] one of my committee members asked me why I was studying sexual minorities in Appalachia[2] and what impact I expected my research to have on this underrepresented population. I struggled with the question at the time because, on the one hand, I have a distinct political project and, on the other hand, I recognise that rural sexual minorities are in a particularly vulnerable position, socially, economically and politically. I beat around the bush in wishy-washy postmodern fashion trying to resolve how a political agenda would not disrupt their cultural sensibilities and personal identities. All the while I was working through notions of how I did not want to harm my subjects, how being there could disrupt their lives, or dangerously expose them, and how I did not want to presume what they want or need in the way that only a relativist postmodern anti-strategy can. At one point during my ramblings, the committee member who

---

1 In the Department of Geography at the University of Kentucky, we write and defend our dissertation proposals prior to carrying out our qualifying exams. From this, three sets of qualifying questions are rendered from the text of our proposals considering history/philosophy, substantive area of research, and method/methodology. We write an essay, outlining how our research is pertinent, for each of these aspects of the discipline, and the essays are then orally defended. The guiding principle behind this method of qualifying is that we are juried on the particular areas of focus that we are researching and how they impact the discipline rather than a broader survey of the discipline itself without a contextual interrogation of our relationship to it.

2 My doctoral research in cultural/political geography is concerned with sexual minorities and how queer space is produced in rural and small town Central Appalachia. Specifically, my research seeks to uncover how/if sexual identity is claimed in these rural places; how social networks are formed by sexual minorities; whether these networks constitute community and, if so, how these communities/networks are maintained and negotiated across rural places. The political project I hope to encompass over the course of my research is to bring substantive awareness to sexual minorities that are not in metropolitan areas, but live, have sex and create social relations in small towns and rural places.

challenged me slammed his fist down on the table and said, 'God damn it – won't you just defend yourself. Say, these people are being shit on and deserve a political project that will benefit them socially!'

I took this to heart. I am trying to make political change happen. I do see that as far as rural sexual minorities in the United States are concerned, there is a deficiency in the academy and queer/social theory that deals with their struggles and realities. The bulk of research on sexual minorities has a metropolitan bias and it is time to recognise how sexual minorities in rural contexts articulate themselves socially, geographically, historically and so on (Bell and Valentine 1995, Kramer 1995, Phillips and Watt 2000). By doing this, I have come to realise that I am allowed to have a political project in my research and that while that political project is contingent and negotiated with the participants in my study, I am allowed to 'perform myself' as a social actor within the research through the reflexive implication that entangles me into the lives of my participants (Denzin 2003). The political economy of mutual desires, affects, aspirations, and investments of the population that I am studying is allowed to happen. I am not merely observing an American subculture in the Enlightenment sense of the 'gaze' (Rose 1993, Cosgrove 1984), but mapping out paths to alternative social worlds by engaging my research group along multiple vectors of political aspirations and kinship making (Povinelli 2006) that constitutes a new, if largely unrecognised, assemblage of researcher/researched relations.

Mapping the Purpose:
Drafting a Politics of Intimacy through an Ethics as Method

However, such a revelation that I will be calling a 'politics of intimacy' necessarily raises a particular set of questions about ethics/the ethical and method/ methodologies. Yet, before delving into these questions, the differences between 'the ethical' and 'methodology', and 'ethics' and 'method' must be distinguished to nail down a vocabulary for proceeding. For the purposes of this chapter and the questions that it will be raising, the ethical and methodological should be viewed as strategies that define a set of conceptual and material positions from which I will be arguing. The ethical and methodological are also at the heart of the approach through which I am attempting to queer methods for social science research. Methods and ethics are the deployable tactics of those strategies. A queer 'ethics as method', that I will be developing in more detail below and remains the primary focus for queer(y)ing the ethical in social science research should be recognised as a tactic to animate an exploration into a broader methodology of a politics of intimacy.

'Ethical formations', 'ethical constructions' and 'ethical terrains' are concepts I will be referring to in order to describe specific manifestations of tactical ethics. Ethical formations speak to the pre-existing ethical positionality of the researcher and/or the researched. Ethical constructions speak to the ethical entanglements and emerging intimacies produced through the researcher/researched relation. And ethical terrains speak to the political and social spaces that are produced and negotiated as a result of such entanglements. Other manifestations of ethics such as 'ethical standards', 'ethical regimes', and the like are interspersed throughout as necessary to highlight the political antagonisms present in a progressive politics of intimacy.

In human subjects research that social science concerns itself with, and that this chapter attempts to queer(y), the very formation of a research project is an ethical undertaking (Madison 2005: 80–90). It seems to go without saying that methods inherently engage ethical questions. The questions that we ask as we embark on human subjects research come from a set of ethical strategies which are usually normalised through liberal notions of 'consent' (Bain and Nash 2006, Bradley 2007, Butz 2008) and the types of 'harm' that conducting research might place on our participants (Mueller 2007). Why/how do we choose to research the human subjects we pick? What questions do we ask? How do we ask them? What types of interactions do we have with our participants while collecting data? How are we a part of that data collection? How do we organise, analyze and disseminate our findings? These are questions of method, all with ethical imperatives.

But if we flip the paradigm – certainly without dismissing its original orientation – and say ethics are inherently methodological, we end up with a set of questions about methodology where ethics can be understood as a deployable tactic. How do we frame the questions we ask and probe for responses? How do we negotiate an ethical terrain that places our own ethical formations under scrutiny, while investigating other ethical formations? What parts of ourselves do we subvert, highlight, lay exposed in light of the comingling of ethical backgrounds and confounding complexities that studying human subjects place before us? How do we negotiate our emotional lives with the entanglements and attachments of a living research project? These are all questions of ethics that are inherently methodological. This chapter will concern itself primarily with this latter set of questions as it contemplates and queer(y)s the ethical constructions and terrains that constitute researcher/researched relations.

Every time we engage human subjects in research, we face the values, norms and ethical formations of our participants. This is not to say that the values, norms and ethical formations of our participants are necessarily 'good' or unproblematic (Massey 1994). But, it does mean that the ability to form lines of communication, forums for negotiation, connections of understanding, perspectives on difference, claims for justice, the possibility to create new kinds of kindred alliances, and so on, demand that the researcher can establish trust and common linkages through a complex set of terms, both their own and their participants'.

It is in the rational flip of the ethical and the methodological, of ethics and methods, as a means to constitute complex researcher/researched relations, that the queer enters as a technique to explore such assemblages. An ethics as method is understood to be 'queer' in its ability to destabilise our assumptions about the ethical in research, disrupt the researcher/researched relationship and cultivate the intimacies necessary to shape new types of alliances and strategies for alternative social worlds. Tearing apart the machinery of normative ethical regimes that delimit a full range of possibilities in researcher/researched relations, and redeploying ethics *as* method lays bare these limitations while opening up a space for new opportunities in research.

This chapter is about a methodology of a politics of intimacy, deployed through a queer ethics as method for crafting and defending alternative social worlds. In this way, this chapter has three primary purposes. First, to contribute to new strategies in the conduct of methodologies for social science research implicating the performances and entanglements that the researcher is embedded in as a result of conducting research. Second, to outline an argument that supports the assertion that reimagining these relations opens up new ways of producing knowledge and creating political and kindred alliances for social and environmental justice.[3] And third, to bracket the obstacles that inhibit the constitution of these ethical constructions and the political moment in the academy that social science scholars must take up to defend academic integrity and freedom.

To do this, I first attempt to assemble a definition of queer theory that de/ stabilises how a 'queer' research ethics ought to be deployed. I draw on Gibson-Graham's (1999) term 'queer(y)ing' in an attempt to craft a productive intervention for queer theory that can be applied to the development of a queer ethics as method. I sketch out the growing potential of queer theory to surpass the boundaries of sex, sexuality and gender as it is gaining a broader intellectual purchase. This definition of queer theory then frames an argument that maps a queer ethics onto the methods for conducting human subjects research.

I then take this definition and stretch out its ethical imperative for social science research and its methods and methodologies by looking more closely at the ethical construction of researcher/researched relations and how they are impeded by the bureaucracy of ethical oversight, such as Institutional Review Boards (IRBs).[4] Namely, what do the ethical standards imposed by these bureaucracies limit? And by

---

3   I am placing social and environmental justice together as a means to get at their inevitable coexistence. While the arguments in this chapter seem to lead more toward social justice and ethics, environmental justice and ethics is often, if not always, tethered to the social. The access to environmental resources, the protection from environmental degradation, the cultivation of environmental suffrage, and so on, all lead back to social justice and therefore should never be too far behind.

4   While this chapter recognises that 'regulatory regimes of research ethics' exist all over the world (Martin 2007) such as the Research Ethics Board (REB) in Canada (Haggerty 2004) and the more recent University Research Ethics Committee (UREC) in the UK (Blake 2007), in an effort to focus this chapter and keep it in the sphere of institutional bureaucracy with which I am most intimately familiar, the scope is limited to IRBs in the United States. While not speaking to the particulars of individual bureaucracies, it is possible to link similarities across these different bureaucracies sketched out here in the American form. General commentaries to these bureaucracies will be noted as 'human subjects review boards', and specific examples will be noted as 'IRBs'.

limiting the design of research methods to those standards, what potential knowledges are lost, hidden or incomplete? How can the queer(y)ing of methods/ethics in social science research challenge a bureaucratic system that often hinders research articulated through the progressive use of ethical/intimate researcher/researched relations? Looking at participatory methods becomes an optic through which to explore ways for developing researcher/researched relationships that outline the types of alternative ethical questions that this queer ethics as method seeks to broach and also to explore what a politics of intimacy might look like.

Finally, I begin to sketch a queer ethics to establish the intimacies that endeavour to carve out a social and environmental justice politics that I advocate here. I will be drawing heavily on Elizabeth Povinelli's work in developing an ethics as method that draws upon and leads toward a politics of intimacy.[5] Intimacy is risk, and if the argument for an entangled, co-production of knowledge can be valued as a legitimate means to understand the multiple and nuanced circumstances that constitute human socialisation and experience, then the relationships that are established between the researcher and the researched are inherently intimate. The queer(y)ing of ethics promoted by an ethics as method requires the development of different types of intimacy between researcher and researched (Povinelli 2006). Whether the material intimacies produced through new ethical constructions can be considered 'queer' or 'not-queer' cannot be the focus of this chapter – the focus remains, how a queer ethics as method can get us toward a broader set of intimate possibilities.

Why Queer Theory?

The title for this chapter draws heavily on J.K. Gibson-Graham's 1999 piece *Queer(y)ing Capitalism,* in which they make a methodological claim to the fundamental ability of queer theory to make broader interrogations for radical politics and research. The quirky way in which the term 'queer(y)ing' catches the imagination, by deploying a double meaning that folds back on itself, elegantly manoeuvres the playfulness with which queer theory destabilises our social

---

5 While I briefly outline some of Povinelli's strategies in the penultimate section of this chapter, for further reading I strongly suggest her work on liberal multiculturalism (2002) and how that bleeds into her more recent work (2006) on carnality and intimacy. In these texts Povinelli examines the complications between what she defines as 'liberal settler colonies' and their Others. To do this, she interrogates the assumptions of liberal governmentality by placing the 'flesh' of the body under a critical spotlight to distinguish 'corporeality' as the 'juridical and political maneuver of the flesh' from carnality as the 'physical mattering forth of these maneuvers' (2006). In this way, and what ultimately become important here, she leverages a critique against liberal assumptions about intimacy through the contingencies and vulnerabilities of the flesh, to open up a space for other kinds of intimacies. There is neither space nor time to elaborate on these in this text, but the intimacies I am suggesting in this chapter are drawn directly from her work.

worlds and reinforces the seriousness of such a manoeuvre. The 'y' in parentheses excavates the inquisitiveness of the 'queer' by showing that 'to queer' – i.e. queering – is equally to adjudicate a query or question. This enables questions that fundamentally deterritorialise the function of the question itself to not only understand the nature of the question, but also the contexts, contingencies and contradictions that make the question worth asking. In this way, the possibility for alternative social worlds – their ethical constructions, politics and intimacies – materialise out of the destabilised and shifting fractures in dominant discourses.

Queer theory has, since its inception in the late 1980s and early 1990s, stretched the boundaries of sex, sexuality and gender; particularly in the ways these relate to queer bodies and the multiple possibilities in which sexuality and gender are/ can be deployed. Drawing on the 'post' turn in social theory, the social sciences and humanities, queer theory, through scholars such as Teresa de Lauretis (1991, 1990, 1987, 1986) who jokingly coined the term 'queer theory' as the title of a conference she organised in February 1990 at the University of California, Santa Cruz (Halperin 2003), Eve Kosofsky Sedgwick (2003, 1993, 1990), Judith Butler (2004, 1993, 1990), David Halperin (2007, 2003, 2002, 1995, 1990), Michael Warner (1999, 1993), Leo Bersani (2000a, 2000b, 1995) and others, has revealed the contingency through which sexuality and gender are deployed as subject positions.

As queer theory has come into its own as a set of academic discourses, its methodological potentials to interrogate not only the contingency and complexity of human subjectivity through an optic of sexualised/gendered constructions, but other social and political formations have become ever more apparent. Recently, a handful of other possibilities for queer theory have emerged alongside the realm of gender, sex, and sexuality (see for example Gibson-Graham 1999, Warner 2002, Puar, Rushbrook and Schein 2003, Butler 2005, Puar 2007, 2001, Floyd 2009), revealing the untapped potential and durability of queer theory to grasp a vast array of possible social worlds. Referring to Sedgwick, Gibson-Graham note that 'breaking apart these associations [that maintain normative understandings] is the theoretical job of 'queering' sexuality and its representations' (1999: 81). They then go on to interrogate conventional understandings of late capitalism. In this way, the queer is that which disrupts the norm, disarticulates its representations and finds new, shifting and unstable ways to imagine how these disruptions and disarticulations fit together.

By highlighting Eve Kosofsky Sedgwick's 'Christmas effect', Gibson-Graham is able to methodologically show how queer theory can/should apply to applications beyond sex and sexuality to interrogate the political, economic and other aspects of social life. For Sedgwick, the 'Christmas effect' is the depressing set of circumstances which brings the multiple voices such as the Church, State, markets, media, and so on into a monolithic voice aiming toward the expectation of a similar predictable outcome – in this case Christmas. She likens these predictable outcomes to the predictability that society places on sexuality. In this, a similar constellation of sexual attributes such as biological sex, gender identity, masculinity or femininity, sexual orientation, sexual fantasies, political and/or cultural affiliations, and so on, align to result in linear, staid understandings of what one is supposed to result in. It is assumed that if you are straight, you are straight and your sexual determinations are determined by oppositional dyads (masculine and feminine), procreational functions and the like. Likewise, it is assumed that if you are gay, you are gay and your sexual determinations are determined by your masculinity or femininity and the expectation that your desires will mirror heterosexual dyads, your lack of desire to rear children, and the like. These are the fundamental premises that she criticises as the delimiting factor(s) of socio-sexual possibilities that, as one of the original scholars of queer theory, she sought to destabilise (1993: 5-9).

Gibson-Graham takes this premise to open up a queer theory potential for dislocating capitalism as an always already monolithic formation with hegemonic effects.

> More generally, Sedgwick's vision calls into question the project of representing societies and economies as hegemonic formations. What if we were to depict social existence *at loose ends with itself,* in Sedgwick's terms, rather than producing social representations in which everything is part of the same complex and, therefore, ultimately 'means the same thing' (e.g. capitalist hegemony)? *What might be the advantages of representing a rich and prolific disarray?* (1999: 81, my italics).

Working through Gibson-Graham's use of the 'queer' defines a mission for queer theory that looks past – while not forgetting – sex, sexuality and gender to become a methodological tool for excavating the possibility of alternative social worlds. 'For queer theorists *unwilling to accept that it is a 'heterosexual' world* in which queers may gain a toehold but will still be ultimately marginal or minoritised, various forms of queerness are everywhere to be found. The domain of the 'normal' retreats to the social and theoretical horizon' (Gibson-Graham 1999: 84, my italics). By positioning queer theory as a means to plot out a 'rich and prolific disarray', methodological potentials for research grow out of the destabilisation of liberal assumptions about modernity, seeking to find and cultivate queer practices both within and on the fringes of mainstream culture and politics.

The 'various forms of queerness' that exist between the tenuous connections of dominant discourses is the potential to radically redirect the trajectories of social and environmental justice and re-craft the ways in which we relate as social scientists to our human subjects. The intimacies in researcher/researched relations are an inevitable condition of studying human subjects that I am arguing can be deployed methodologically to queer the ethical strategies of social science research. These intimacies act to embed and animate the relationship of the researcher/researched into the knowledge, politics and alternative social worlds produced. A 'politics of intimacy' as an outcome and progenitor of research becomes a queer project in its disruption of normative considerations for research relationships, while challenging the conventional regimes of oversight for research methods. Critically destabilising the bureaucratic regimes that oversee and uphold an impossible set of interpersonal cleavages between the researcher and the researched allows for an ethical understanding of the dynamics that occur in human relations to potentially leverage a significant influence, if not driving force, on our methodologies.

If by queer, we mean to disrupt, parse out, critically analyze and fold together new and overlapping intersections on which difference and social justice can occur, we have met the threshold of a new kind of ethics in research. If we can reframe the fundamental set of relations that bind the researcher to the researched – cultivate its intimacies – a potential politics arises that brings new kinds of awareness and contingencies for social science research into view. And if, as I have stated in the introductory passages of this chapter, that ethics can be thought of as method, and if that queer ethics as method breaks apart the shell of a certain set of research taboos that limits the researcher's ability to relate, co-produce knowledge and indeed embed themselves within the intricate sets of intimacies that human relations produce, then there is indeed a moment toward plotting out a 'rich and prolific disarray'.

Relating to our Participants: Intimacy, Ethical Censorship and Action

In August of 2007 I was at the Royal Geographical Society with the Institute of British Geographers' Annual International Conference in London. While I was there I attended a session simply titled 'Open mike discussion' which became the initial inspiration for this chapter. It was sponsored by the Participatory Geographies Research Group and was designed to establish an open ended discussion on the ethics of research methods and methodologies. I raised the problem of the bureaucratisation of research ethics in the American context where IRBs place a particular set of restrictions on research with what are considered 'vulnerable populations' that distinctly limits research possibilities. By foregrounding the what/who/how of research, especially through the excessive attention to the nature of the relationship between the researcher and the researched, our ability to engage with the ethical formations of our participants, and establish bonds of trust, are hindered. In this way, human subjects review boards encumber academic progress and freedom (Lincoln and Tierney 2004), and potentially the social justice possibilities that these forms of knowledge and political alliances could promote.

Rachel Pain, whose work on participatory research I have used heavily in designing my own research methods, was also at the session. She rearticulated the problem that has become the phantom obstacle for promoting a politics of intimacy as a practice of social science research: What happens when the ethical standards of bureaucracy do not fall in line with the ethical formations, norms and values of the human subjects we study? Because the central tenet of my argument is drawn around the ethical constructions that result from researcher/researched relations deployed as a method for the production of particular types of empirical, activist, and intimate knowledges, the bureaucratic infrastructure that impedes such methodological approaches must be interrogated for the limitations they place on social science research. Namely, how can we gain the trust to engage our participants if we cannot engage them on their terms? What kinds of knowledges become hidden or lost when we are inhibited from these kinds of engagements? What might the relationship between the researcher and the researched produce without the hindrances of human subjects review boards?

These questions became distinctly important during our conversation in the open mike methods and ethics session when my friend and colleague Gavin Brown reflected upon his dissertation research in which he looked at a range of socio-sexual geographies and public sex environments of gay males in London (2008, 2004). In this 'observant participation' research,[6] he engaged with aspects of gay and queer men's lives that sought to examine the complexity of queer life beyond mainstream commercial gay 'scenes', including the nature of public sexual encounters. While not the primary method for conducting this research, his reflections upon being a participant in public sex spaces delve deeply into the intimacies of the population with whom he had pre-existing social and sexual interactions and relations.[7] What benefits about social realities do we get when the positionality and performance of the researcher is reflected upon through these intimacies? How do we better understand ourselves, our desire, our sexualities through research when the researcher is also recognised as a sexual and social actor within the borders of the researcher/researched relation?

Gavin, nevertheless, made it clear that with the recent installation of University Research Ethics Committees (URECs) in the United Kingdom that monitor the 'proper ethics' of research relationships, his research would not have been able to be done. This knowledge would not exist. Human subjects review boards pose a myriad of problems for queer and social science research that define, limit, and/ or delegitimise research relationships, not the least of which is the politicisation

---

6   In an email Gavin wrote to me on 10 September 2008 to clarify his point on 'observant participation', he said: 'I was researching ... sites (within the area where I lived) where I was already recognised as a participant. This was observant participation not participant observation, in many ways. The ethical perspective I adopted was primarily concerned with acknowledging and respecting the ethical norms of those sites and their users, rather than imposing more established "research ethics" that might have been disruptive to those sites and more threatening and potentially harmful to the other participants in them. This approach highlights the entanglement of those spaces (and my participation in them) with the rest of my life in the neighbourhood at that time – my choice to prioritise a reflective attention to the quotidian ethics of my relationships with friends, colleagues, neighbours and lovers, over conventional research ethics (in those circumstances, where the two potentially clash or jarred with each other).'

7   For another discussion on the complexities of sexual intimacies in researcher/ researched relations, specifically where the researcher does not have a pre-existing relationship with the researched and the limitations and ethical questions that poses, see Bain and Nash 2006.

of research around funding.[8] A full examination of these bureaucracies is neither possible nor warranted. For the purposes of this discussion, the problems IRBs and human subjects review boards cause for social science research shall remain limited to the problem that most relates to how ethics are deployed in research.

The conspicuous villain that most contributes to limiting the ethical constructions of research relationships through narrow definitions and untenable cleavages is that which orbits liberal notions of 'consent'. Consent is a seemingly innocuous conceit of post-Enlightenment liberalism. The idea that there is some discreet autonomous individuality, what David Butz has called 'an individuated liberal humanist research subject' (2008), independent of the structures that delineate who has the ability to consent and who does not animates this conception. Indeed, consent is itself a social process by which social technologies predetermine the moral/ethical compass on which consent is allowed to function (Schaffner 2002, 2005). To say that I consent only means that I have accepted my place within a dominant social structure that will lead me toward the directions I am meant to follow. If I fall outside the category of 'he who is able to consent', or my consent is somehow crippled because of my position in society (this often regards children in many situations, marginalised and underrepresented populations, the elderly and infirm, animals, and so on) my consent no longer matters because my consent is either not mine to give or invariably incapacitated.

Working through Hester Parr's critique of consent in relation to 'overt' and 'covert' ethnography, Alison Bain and Catherine Nash note, 'how the simplistic distinction between covert ethnography as 'bad' because it is non-consensual and overt ethnography as 'good' because it is open and consensual is problematic because it positions these research practices in opposition, when they should be understood as inherently intertwined' (2006: 103). This critique of consent enters IRBs exactly at the intersection of what is consent and how do we give it? What does it mean when we give it? What do we lose when we give it? (Butz 2008). And how are these politics of consent, which attempt to manage 'harm', disingenuous when attempting to co-produce knowledge in a way that is mutually beneficial to and across the researcher and the researched?

The obsessive pursuit of informed consent mapped onto IRBs in the United States, through inappropriate biomedical models (Mueller 2007, Bledsoe et al. 2007), is actually more about legal liability than the protection of human subjects (Bledsoe et al. 2007: 636) – all of which place intractable limitations on research. First, many cultures are sceptical of a governmental panopticon surveilling their movements (Foucault 1977) – which consent forms suggest – and in many cases consent forms are not congruent with their cultural values (Zamudio 2005). Second, the 'insistence on anonymity [as a function of informed consent] can muffle the voices of participants while authorising that of the researcher'

---

8   For discussions on the politicisation of research and/or the politics of funding, see Edgar and Rothman 1995, Lincoln and Cannella 2004a, 2004b, Mueller 2007, Rambo 2007.

(Bradley 2007: 346) straining researchers' ability to develop trust. Third, consent forms are legal documents that can dissuade many potential participants because of the limitations set on legal recourse and how they can be subpoenaed for legal purposes (Bledsoe et al 2007: 636–37). From here, we can see that informed consent often works to shut down and alienate the researcher from the researched rather than 'protect' human subjects.

IRBs have broadened their scope over the past 30 years, and this broadening scope has occurred in such small, seemingly unnoticeable increments that it has rarely been challenged – it is what John Mueller has described as 'mission creep' (2007). Yet it is this broadening scope that has severely cut into what can be considered research and as Mueller adds, 'today, particularly in the field of non-medical research, the institutional review process is more accurately described as censorship than safety screening' (2007: 810). The irony in all of this is that there is no empirical evidence to support the claim that the benefits argued to result from these procedural expansions have any basis in reality. However, there is substantial evidence to suggest that these procedural expansions have a negative impact on research (see Mueller 2007).

The presence of these obstacles is not mentioned to dissuade us from the task at hand in our attempt to queer(y) the ethics and methods of social science research. Rather, it lays bare a broader set of political implications that a politics of intimacy implies. As we attempt to negotiate and challenge a world embedded in liberal assumptions about modernity, forms of intimacy that fall outside these liberal assumptions are seen as unruly and dangerous (Povinelli 2006). Bracketing a set of antagonisms that exist around intimate approaches to social science research reveals how the political project of that research is already encumbered. While a politics of intimacy, as I have begun to describe, can be seen to advocate alternative social worlds, the dominant political resistance to this manoeuvre is already present in the institutionalisation of research. Therefore, the politics of intimacy is not merely a conceptual device for the conduct of research, but a political device that must combat ethical censorship from the outset of designing research[9].

The closest to a sustained precedent for a methodological/ethical intervention into these obstacles falls in line with the work of participatory methodologies. Scholars such as Rachel Pain (2006, 2004, 2003, 2001) with Peter Francis (2003), and Paul Cloke (2002) have in their research developed new kinds of political economies where mutual desires, affects, aspirations, and investment have begun to blur the boundaries between the researcher and the researched. What a queer ethics as method potentially gains from and contributes to participatory research (PR) and participatory action research (PAR) rests in the nature of blurring the lines between the researcher and the researched – possibly past recognition. Participatory

---

9 There is unfortunately no space to develop this argument here, but as we continue to attempt to queer social science research and its methodologies, we will have to continuously attend to this political problem – not just the material politics and advocacy of research on the ground, but also the politics of making that possible.

research and more recently participatory action research implicate the relationship between the researcher and the researched by deconstructing observatory understandings of research and explicitly deploying an understanding that the research produced is both between and through the researcher and the researched. This means that knowledge produced through research is reflexively dependent on the researcher/researched relationship that fundamentally deterritorialises any aspect that witnesses research as hierarchical (Pain 2003, 2004, Pain and Francis 2003, Blake 2007, Bradley 2007, Cahill et al. 2007, Elwood 2007).

If we stand by the argument that the knowledge resulting from research is a production rather than an observation, then we do not have far to stretch to imagine the political in research. If we ruminate on the classical feminist slogan from the 1960s and 70s that the 'personal is political' and its 1980s reframing as the 'political is personal' (Mohanty 1989-90: 204), the augmentation toward a politics of intimacy that moves past the site of the individual and toward the constitution of an ethically entangled network of dynamic and negotiated relations does not trail far behind. However, the kinds of radical/grassroots politics that I am aspiring to here should not be thought of as reducible to a politics of intimacy, ethics as method, or queer research. Research is still done for the sake of research, and activism still holds a discreet purpose, even if they operate in concert. Yet, this strategy to queer(y) the researcher/researched relationship through its intimacies and ethical constructions, that I have been working toward, can be an avenue for re-imagining political activism.

Toward a Queer Ethics for Research

It is in this radical notion of a queer attachment to the bonds created through research that I am advocating as a queer ethics as method. This is a formation contingent in its make-up, negotiated in its deployment, and destabilising in its constitution of researcher/researched relations as it forms new trajectories of social and environmental justice. It resembles what Norman Denzin (2003) calls an 'indigenous research ethic' which constitutes part of a methodology that he defines as 'performative ethics'. 'Because it expresses and embodies moral ties to the community, *the performative view of meaning serves to legitimate indigenous worldviews*. Meaning and resistance are embodied in the act of performance itself' (2003: 245, my italics). The negotiation, or 'performance', of co-producing knowledge is traced horizontally between and through the researcher and researched. Liberal fantasies of 'emancipating' or 'redeeming' 'subjugated voices' evaporate and are replaced with a more nuanced assemblage of voices working from their own authority (243). In this way, the ethical imperative that tethers us to our participants through the intimacies produced in research stretches past binomial interpretations and obliterates the fundamental definition of researcher/researched. The result is something unnameable and uniquely special that has the tendency to resemble something that looks much more like kinship.

It is not so easy, however, to just say that as researchers we can merely submit or 'play along' with our research participants as if our own ethical formations, social anxieties and personal reservations have no say in what we do and how we do it. Alison Bain and Catherine Nash (2006) have contemplated on this complexity in relating to their research subjects at a 'queer bathhouse event' in Toronto, Canada. The 'Pussy Palace' was designed as a women's only space to allow for 'uninhibited' sexual exploration. In their essay on the embodiment of the researcher as a 'contested site of knowledge production', they note:

> Several informants asked us directly whether we had participated in any of the sexual activities that had been planned by the organizers ... The authoritative queer gaze of several of the organizers whom we had interviewed identified us as researchers, observers and outsiders ... Did the organizers interpret our bodies as researchers as unruly and disruptive bodies because of all of our apparent inhibitions and reservations? (2006: 104)

In this instance of the complexity of the relationship between the researcher and researched, the production of knowledge is encumbered by a sense of reservation on the one side and scepticism on the other. While there is no truly unencumbered research relationship, it must be noted that these negotiations cannot operate outside the realm of the personal and are in a multifaceted state of slippages, evolutions and levels of comfort.

The impacts of research on the researcher are rarely talked about (Bondi 2005: 231). There is no denying that when research is done, the researcher enters into a particular relationship with the researched and that relationship evokes emotional responses. There is a long history – or perhaps mythology – as Liz Bondi (2005) points out, of 'partitioning emotion and research' that is increasingly coming under scrutiny. The emotive bonds and affective ties that research produces can no longer be overlooked. We are affected by our research and the participants we research are affected by us (Bondi 2005). This bourgeoning discussion of a dynamic and entangled researcher/researched relationship must come to bear on how we constitute ethics to understand the deeply embedded nuances and complexities that are produced as a result of research and what those mean. Obligation to our participants mapped onto a certain set of attachments that result from engaging in human subjects research – different forms of intimacy with them – serve to produce a kind of kinship (Povinelli 2006) that cannot be ignored.

In her recent work *The Empire of Love* (2006), Elizabeth Povinelli wages a critique against Western notions of the immutability of 'love' in contradistinction to other forms of intimacy. In this critique, she sketches out a notion of kinship that applies to how she is entangled with her research of an aboriginal tribe in Belyuen, Australia over 20 years and her more recent affiliation with the queer kinship making of radical faeries in the United States.[10] Exemplifying how these exsanguinated forms of kinship produce particular kinds of obligations for these two very different groups to whom she is affiliated results in a particular set of obligatory attachments, intimacies and ethical imperatives for inclusion to kinship ties. Speaking on how Elizabeth Wilson elaborates on Freud and 'obligation', she notes:

> What Wilson suggests, and what is conceptually useful here, is that Freud is attempting to sketch a system of governance in which the mutual constitution of soma and psyche, flesh and discourse, are no longer captured by the usual mechanics of 'cause and effect, origin and derivation.' They are instead the literal material of each other, different from each other but mutually obliged rather than caused or affected, *vulnerable to* rather than *subject of* (2006: 9, italics in original).

While this passage speaks primarily to the site of the body as constituted through an irreducible entanglement of flesh and discourse, we can read this to suggest that as the researcher/researched relationship develops through discourses that constitute the flesh, the dynamics of that constitution simultaneously materialise discourse into a mutually entangled vulnerability of bodies engaged in intimate interactions. It is in this mutually entangled vulnerability that the emergence of intimacies craft new ethical constructions that transform and shape alternative social worlds.

The move toward a politics of intimacy through a queer ethics as method lies in how the mutual entanglements of these new ethical constructions and intimacies are embodied in their own materialities, or carnalities to use Povinelli's term, where 'carnality [is] the socially built space between flesh and environment' (2006: 7). Carnality arises as an evolving set of questions for Povinelli who attempts to attend to the contradictions that occur at the intersections of liberal governance and the problems of different kinds of social worlds and intimacies. The goal of Povinelli's work on carnality is not to write redemptive tales for social difference (25), but to criticise and reframe liberal fantasies of autonomous individuality through the optic of a political calibration that analyzes the insufficiency and culpability of liberal subjecthood, while tracing the embeddedness of the flesh in the intimacies that tether her to her research kin.

Povinelli's critique of liberal governance over the flesh and intimacy does at least two things for us, as we develop a queer ethics as method through a politics of intimacy. First, by explicating the complexities of bodily intimacies

---

10   In the spirit of queer ethics as method and the intimacies produced therein, I should note that I am also affiliated with the community and kinship bonds to the radical faeries in Tennessee where diverging and diverse forms of sexual citizenship are practiced and celebrated. The radical faerie movement, as Povinelli notes, is not a movement *per se,* but rather, 'a set of allegiances to a moving and contested set of qualities and stances toward normative masculinity and sociality' (2006: 23).

and interactions through the material/rhetorical reality of the flesh, conventional mythologies of discretion for research relationships are cracked open to be filled with a new kind of research relationship – one reliant upon the intimacies and ethical constructions that converge at the intersection of the researcher and the researched. Second, through a critique of liberal exceptionalism that privileges particular intimate formations as legitimate through the Western fantasy of 'true love', while excluding others (2006: 175–236), alternative forms of intimacy are given a space to emerge creating new kinds of political voices and interventions destabilising dominant discourses on intimacy.

The tethering of the researcher to their researched (and equally vice versa) through the bonds of intimacy creates a political space – or ethical terrain – that binds one to the other. It is in this binding that new kinds of alternative social worlds are formed and defended. The empathic sensibilities resulting from these political spaces render a new kind of ethical relationship. A queer ethics as method simultaneously constitutes and enervates these political intimacies. It is in the ability to take ones ethics and methodologically deploy them as a negotiated set of social and intimate interactions toward the constitution of these alternative social worlds that holds the potential for a politics of intimacy to emerge as a new form of social advocacy.

Conclusion

I was in a methodologies class aimed at producing methods for researching marginalised and underrepresented people during my tenure at the University of Kentucky. It was a fruitful class and during the course of the semester, I was able to draft the methods and theoretical framework that became critical to writing my dissertation research proposal. Yet, what became evidently clear as our discussions in the seminar went on was that there is an institutionalised expectation for some mythical, discreet separation between the researcher and the researched. I hold the professor who taught the seminar in highest regard; however, I could not help but think that the ethical problems we discussed were embedded in the conflict between biomedical models of consent and a progressive ethics of intimacy. Not being able to speak with research participants outside of a study; not even being able to say 'hello' in casual social settings bemused me. I realised that this is the creep of institutional bureaucracy and that IRBs wield enormous power in curtailing the nature of the relationships that researchers engage in with their participants.

In this chapter, I have deliberately left more questions than answers. Defining a queer ethics as method is a fluid construction negotiated across a difficult terrain of contingencies and complexities that this short chapter can only attempt to address. If we as researchers cannot negotiate and engage the ethical terrains that we are inevitably faced with when dealing with social science research, if we cannot craft methodologies that investigate the contingencies and possibilities of such ethical constructions, if all we are left with is the zero sum of an ethical vacuum that does not have the capacity to contemplate complexity, what kinds of research are left undone or avoided entirely? Western notions of 'professionalism' that are extremely uncomfortable with the intimacy that is developed in these relationships have to be rethought. If we are to de/construct contemporary political economies, create new kinds of knowledge, and advocate a progressive politics that is inclusive – as inclusive can be, realising there is no inclusion without exclusion – our task is clearly laid out in rethinking the nature of research; who it is supposed to benefit, what its ethics are, and how in queer(y)ing them they can be deployed as methodology. If anything, I hope this chapter contributes to a new kind of receptiveness for ethics and ethical constructions in their relationship to methods and methodologies even while certain omissions are unavoidable.

The most blatant omission in this chapter stems from an unfortunate concentration on the position of the researcher in the role of this production even while feigning a mutual if not automatic reciprocity of the researched with the researcher. We cannot ignore how the privilege of the researcher functions in these relations. How do those being researched bring their ethical formations, intimacies, aspirations and knowledges to the conduct of research? What are their anxieties, scepticisms, criticisms, short-comings, and so on and how do they impact the development of these methods? What levels of coercion are placed on the bodies of the researched at the behest of the researcher and how are those negotiated? By exacting new ethical insertions into the lives of research participants as a methodological imperative, how do resentments, feelings of exploitation, as well as hopes and desires resolve themselves into what I have called here a politics of intimacy? Indeed, how do we account for our privilege(s) as researchers if intimacy is our goal?

These are not easy questions, but they are ethical questions that must be continuously attended to by the disciplines of the social sciences. The argument of this chapter for a more available terrain of ethical interaction with research participants is not a call for a slippery, relativist set of ethics that opportunistically engages research by any means necessary. Rather, it is a call for a more unyieldingly rigorous engagement with ethics and the ethical that, while challenging the aseptic ethical standards of a short-sighted and misinformed bureaucracy, takes the responsibility of ethical interactions with sober perseverance. It is exactly in the sober perseverance of queer(y)ing and reframing ethics as an inevitable part of research, that ethics become not merely a management tool for methodology, but a methodological tool for the constitution of methods itself.

Chapter 11

Method Matters:
Ethnography and Materiality

Mark Graham

Most readers of this chapter probably live in consumer societies that are awash with a profusion of artefacts unparalleled in human history. These are the things with which we live and which play such an important part in constituting us as sexed and gendered subjects. Indeed, the very notion of a 'subject' in Western capitalism arose in contrast to 'objects' that are considered to be external to it (Baudrillard 1973). It seems reasonable to assume that queer theory would have a lot to say about such artefacts, whether they be washing machines, ballpoint pens, toothbrushes, iPods, coffee beans, or socks. Yet thus far queer theory has had very little to say on the subject of things. One reason may be the cautious relationship to materiality it has inherited from feminism.

On the subject of materiality, Stacey Alaimo and Susan Hekman (2008: 1) conclude that 'the guiding rule of procedure for most contemporary feminisms requires that one distance oneself as much as possible from the tainted realm of materiality by taking refuge within culture, discourse, and language'. Such is the opprobrium that greets material (read natural/biological) theories of gender difference that materiality qualifies as queer, in the sense of an unintelligible, logically impossible, even monstrous phenomenon in relation to feminist orthodoxies. The denigration of matter in feminism was part of a necessary political project aimed at undermining the biological essentialisms deployed to justify women's subordination. It was an extremely fruitful scholarly and political move, but it left the field of biology/nature to the natural sciences and provided no bulwark against continued and persistent patriarchal and conservative claims about the 'naturalness' of what are culturally and socially produced gender differences. In anthropology, a similar demotion of materiality to a passive role took place a century ago as attention increasingly turned to social relations rather than artefacts. Material culture was relegated to museums.

In recent years, however, thanks to the work of feminist scholars, another picture of materiality has emerged, one in which matter is performative, active, unpredictable, even literate (Kirby 1997, 2008, Barad 2007, Alaimo and Hekman 2008). In the light of this research, we can no longer claim that matter can only be approached as a sign (e.g. Butler 1993a: 49) because the distinction between materiality and culture is untenable. Anthropological research today has begun to take things more seriously, attending to aspects of materiality including the power of fetishes (Pels 1998), the agency of artefacts (Gell 1998), and how things can act as windows onto other ontologies (Henare et al. 2007). In this growing literature, as in the feminist studies, things emerge as inscrutable. They lead lives of their own and are not always *what* they appear to be, *where* they appear to be, nor even *when* they appear to be (cf. Pinney 2005).

What these studies all point to is the queerness of matter and things. By this I mean that matter and things are performative, provisional, indeterminate (despite their apparent material obduracy), and, in the case of artefacts, continually gesturing beyond themselves to their, often disavowed, constitutive outsides. Thinking about materiality in this way is surely attractive to those of a queer theoretical bent who are suspicious of essences, stable objects, and the fixed and self-contained subject positions of sexological truths. This is a materiality that is hospitable to feminist and queer projects. If regimes of the (hetero)normative expect and enforce an alignment of qualities (most usually identified in queer theoretical writings as sex-gender-sexuality) and localise them to bodies understood to occupy a specific place (like objects), then on closer inspection matter in general and things in particular regularly fail to live up to normative expectations. The closer we look at them the less aligned they appear to be and the less localisable to a particular place.

This is all well and good, but when we confront things on a daily basis, they do tend to present themselves as solid, straightforward appearances with little or no hint of their queer dimensions. The inherent dynamism of things (to which I return later) is reified and occluded when they become stable objects. Their heterogeneity, or thingness, is eclipsed. In some respects this is fortunate. If we were to be aware of and forced to consider everything that went into the production of a laptop computer, we would never have the time to write on it. There is an intrinsic and necessary forgetting in our relationships to things, but this is also a forgetting with political dimensions, sometimes backed by the interests of powerful actors, and one upon which invidious exclusions are parasitic. Moreover, such exclusions obscure the violence and injustice congealed and hidden in many an artefact. The method best suited to revealing the hidden sides of objects is, I argue, ethnography, but there are several other reasons for advocating an ethnographic approach to materiality.

To begin with, things constitute and are constituted in *social* relationships, and are fundamental to their reproduction and change. Things are also *personal*. We often put them to our own, sometimes very idiosyncratic, uses, such as when owners, collectors and artists queer the heteronormative femininity of Barbie dolls by dressing them variously as battered women, Aids patients, colonised subjects and butch dykes (Rand 1995). Engaging with things is also a *sensory* matter. Our synæsthetic (multisensory) involvement with materiality goes well beyond treating things as signs and language; we touch, taste, see, hear, and smell things. Things also shape our *bodies* through the acquisition of practical skills, like playing an instrument, handling tools and wearing (gendered) clothing. They are also *emotional*, and as such contribute to forming the kind of relationship we have with them and whether they appear to us as taken-for-granted objects we scarcely notice, or as irritating or offensive things that demand our attention (Heidegger 1962: 105).

To study our social, sensory, emotional and embodied relationships to things and acquiring an appreciation and understanding of the part materiality plays in people's lives demands an ethnographic method, one that includes long-term fieldwork involving detailed observations, interviews, life-histories, visual and other forms of documentation, listening to people's interpretations of the material dimensions of their lives, inventories of possessions, and the learning of sensory involvement and the practical uses and skills associated with things. Moreover, precisely because many of our relationships to things are of a practical nature rather than discursive, prolonged observation of and participation in what people actually *do* with material culture is indispensable in the absence of verbal statements and explicit knowledge.

Many things in consumer societies are produced and exchanged within widely dispersed assemblages of manufacturing, markets and governance that organise and consolidate social, economic, cultural and political relations in multiple and far-flung settings. In response to this, ethnography nowadays is increasingly multi-sited in form and designed to access these 'global assemblages' (Ong and Collier 2005).

All of the dimensions of things listed above demonstrate the indispensability of social science and in particular, I would argue, ethnography to the study of materiality. Without the perspective ethnography affords us the multifaceted nature of our relationships to materiality and, importantly, many of the exclusions that lie behind objects and which give them their queer dimensions are likely to be lost. Queer methods, at least when addressing materiality, ought, then, to place themselves in the critical tradition that can trace its roots back to Marx on commodity fetishism and forward through the dereifying ambitions of the Frankfurt School. Not surprisingly, perhaps, this affinity is often ignored in genealogies of queer theory that routinely neglect materiality in favour of textual and linguistic attention to objects of study.

Although I am making a strong claim for an ethnographic method, I want to make it clear that I do not believe that any method is inherently queer. All methods can be put to queer political ends that disrupt normative alignments. However, not all methods are equally useful for a queer analysis of things and materiality. A naive empiricism is unlikely to take us much beyond appearances, which is essential when dereifying objects and restoring to them their complexity and heterogeneity. This is of particular importance when tackling heteronormative phenomena. A major bulwark of heteronormative privilege is the exclusion of competitors from public representation to ensure that the heteronormative appears as an unquestionable and natural truth. Moreover, all methods are partial, regardless of whether they are put to queer political ends or not, and for reasons that will become clear shortly, we must be aware of what a method constitutes as well as what it excludes and fails to materialise, for methods are not only revelatory, they are also *productive* devices.

My attention to the study of materiality starts at the level of matter itself, focusing on the relationship between the material and the discursive and how objects are cut from the materiality of the world. I go on to illustrate this relationship with a social example, the gift. Drawing on recent anthropological work, I then advocate a 'naive' approach to things, one that does not reproduce what we already know but encourages us to discover new material worlds by thinking through things. This naive approach is followed by a 'worldly' method that reveals how things are created within the macro processes of global capitalism. But before reaching the global level we must first look more closely at matter, indeed at the nature of the universe, as it is materialised in quantum physics and explicated in the work of Karen Barad.

Cuts

Barad's (2007) work is a remarkable fusion of ideas from feminism, quantum mechanics (most especially the philosophical writings of Niels Bohr), queer theory, post-structuralism and philosophies of science. Barad takes issue with a modernist realism which regards matter as an unchanging truth that is represented variously in different epistemologies but which retains an essential character that pre-exists the conceptual apparatuses we use to comprehend it. In its place she espouses an 'agential realism' in which 'matter is given agency by a particular theory' (Hekman 2008: 103). Our concepts and practices allow us to comprehend but do not produce matter, which is only ever partially disclosed, or constituted, by our concepts even though it is inseparable from them. In short, Barad's work combines the discursive and the material in a way that does not privilege either.

Following Bohr, Barad argues that the world is not made up of individual objects awaiting our description. As Barad puts it: 'Neither the subjects nor the objects of knowledge practices can be taken for granted…one must inquire into the material specificities of the apparatuses that help *constitute* objects and subjects' (2007: 28, emphasis added). Scientific knowledge is not, as in realist accounts, simply a matter of representation in which words and other forms of expression re-present already existing objects. Scientific practice helps to *constitute* those objects. In classical Newtonian physics, the observer does not significantly affect the character of the observed, whereas in quantum physics the interaction between the experimental apparatus and an object is an *inseparable* part of scientific practice and the very nature of the physical world as it reveals itself to us in these experiments. This inseparability is what Bohr calls 'quantum wholeness' (Barad 2007: 118–9). The starting point for physics ought therefore not to be independently existing objects but *phenomena*.

Phenomena, not objects, are the primary ontological units of physics (Barad 2007: 141) and the basic building blocks from which knowledge is constructed. Physics describes phenomena which are comprised of 'the observations obtained under specified circumstances, including an account of the whole experimental arrangement' (Bohr quoted in Barad 2007: 119). This arrangement includes not only experimental apparatuses but also wider discursive-material practices of knowledge production. Concepts, too, are inextricably part of *material* arrangements: 'Discursive practices are not speech acts' (Barad 2007: 335). Concepts are part of material arrangements – the apparatuses – that manifest them. The meaning of the concept electron, for example, is inseparable from the particular experimental arrangement that manifests an electron (see below). It thus follows that 'method, measurement, description, interpretation, epistemology, and ontology are not separable considerations' (Barad 2007: 121).

Different measuring apparatuses will produce different objects from within the phenomena. Barad calls the process one of '*intra*-action', rather than '*inter*-action', because the latter suggests objects that precede the experimental situation and then inter-act with each other (2007: 128). This is not what phenomena are about. They produce the objects from *within* – intra – themselves. Phrased slightly differently: 'A phenomenon is a specific *intra*-action of an "object" and the "measuring agencies", the "object" and the "measuring agencies" *emerge* from, rather than precede, the intra-action that produces them' (2007: 128, emphasis added). The process enacts what Barad calls an 'agential cut' that separates 'subject' and 'object' *within* the phenomena. Prior to the cut matter is certainly present, but it is all ontological and semantic indeterminacy. The point to appreciate here is that the objects and the subjects that are part of an experiment crystallise out and are made 'determinate' in the moment of measurement itself, they do not precede that moment.

A classic example is the electron. Depending on the experimental apparatus used, an electron can appear as a particle with a location or like a wave. It cannot be observed as both at the same time because the apparatus needed to make a particle appear excludes the appearance of the wave, and vice versa. It is not possible to subtract the effect of the apparatuses to access the truth of the electron beyond wave or particle, or even to achieve a synthesis of both, because the two forms belong to mutually exclusive phenomena, and phenomena, remember, not things, are the primary ontological units. There is only the possibility of freezing 'the electron' into a particle or a wave when its position is measured within a specific phenomenon, up until that moment it remains indeterminate. Indeed, indeterminacy is the very nature of matter.[1]

One immediate consequence of looking at phenomena is that the observer is not located outside them in some neutral space. In a very real sense the human agent,

---

1   Werner Heisenberg believed that the effect of the apparatus could be compensated for in calculations. Bohr objected that this leaves us with pre-existing objects, electrons, whereas the electron is, he argues, in fact created in the agential cut that materialises it as either particle or wave. Bohr writes of *indeterminacy* that is integral to the nature of matter, an ontological indeterminacy, whereas Heisenberg's *uncertainty* is epistemological. Importantly, Heisenberg eventually agreed with Bohr and wrote a postscript to his famous paper on uncertainty to that effect (Barad 2007: 115–16).

with determinate corporeal boundaries, is also part of the 'whole experimental situation' and is constituted by the agential cut in the phenomenon along with the 'natural' objects (Barad 2007: 148, 160). On this point Barad criticises Bohr because he assumed that an experimental apparatus has clear boundaries outside of which the observer is located. But, argues Barad, an apparatus has no inherent outer boundary (2008: 134). Apparatuses are open-ended practices. Hence Bohr's conventional piece of laboratory equipment is too narrow a definition of an apparatus. Where then should we draw the line when determining the boundary of an apparatus? Is it an instrument display, infrared interfaces, the laboratory scientists, printers, the paper in the printer, the journal in which experimental results are published, the readers of the article, universities, funding bodies, or government policies? Ought all to be included? There is no simple answer to this question that does not imply a degree of arbitrariness. Agential cuts are unavoidably selective; not everything can be made determinate and materialise at once, because 'there is no outside to the universe, there is no way to describe the entire system, so that the description always occurs from within: *only part of the world can be made intelligible to itself at a time, because the other part of the world has to be the part that it makes a difference to*' (Barad 2007: 351, emphasis in original).

From this several important points follow. The enactment of boundaries around things, including human subjects, concepts, and apparatuses entails exclusions for which we can be held accountable: Who/what did not materialise/matter and why? But this partiality also leaves the universe open. There is no final completion, no things-in-themselves locked up with their essences. Matter is a ceaseless intra-active becoming continually refiguring local structures, boundaries and properties (Barad 2008: 135). Matter, we might say, is always an open matter, not a simple matter of fact. Moreover, if matter is indeed a continual *becoming* and not a fixed state, then it would seem to be a poor candidate for a stable and invariant substrate capable of determining the essential nature of its own temporary configuration in the form of sexed, gendered and racialised bodies. This kind of materiality is far less attractive a stomping ground for misogynists, homophobes and racists who believe in eternal – that is, purely 'natural' – 'truths' about the people they despise because said truths supposedly derive their indisputable character from the stable foundation of matter itself. This is a materiality that is useful and important for queer theorists as well as having clear implications for methodologies.

Gifts

Before going on to look at things in more detail, I want to apply Barad's ideas outside the laboratories of quantum physics. This is not easy, but Barad herself argues that it can be done. The classic anthropological topic of the gift (Mauss 1990) will serve as a vehicle for the attempt.

Gifts are usually given as though they have no strings attached and no demand for a return gift, so called 'pure' gifts (Malinowski 1922). Yet anyone who has ever given a gift but never received one in return knows that at some point if the return gift never materialises the relationship will suffer as a consequence. Yet that expectation cannot be acknowledged openly, even by the donor to herself, without jeopardising the relationship. The secret of pure gifts is that they are not pure. A gift harbours within itself something that demands to be reciprocated; a thing that creates relationships of indebtedness that can be manipulated. For a gift to be a gift, its inherent indeterminacy must be maintained. There is something rather queer about gifts. Their character resembles the epistemology of the closet (Sedgwick 1990), a form of open secret about what they really are – 'don't ask, don't tell'. Like the disavowed homosexuality at the heart of heterosexuality, calculation haunts the altruistic heart of the gift. Within it, a constant duel between altruism and interest plays itself out each one usurping the other depending on how we look at the gift. Like the wave and the particle, they cannot appear together.

What are the methodological implications? How do you study a thing that is inherently indeterminate without making it determinate through analytical cuts? Or, how do you keep it queer? Some scholars, such as Pierre Bourdieu (1977), reduce the gift's ambiguity to economic calculation and manipulation. Some, like Iris Marion Young (1997: 54–5), side with the angels and see only altruism. Others embrace the ambiguity but as a consequence lose a firm analytical grip on the gift – although in doing so arguably provide a more satisfactory picture of it (see Osteen 2002).

What happens if we treat a gift exchange like a quantum phenomenon? What occurs if we recalibrate our measuring apparatuses and bring unmentionable self-interests into focus? Imagine that an insensitive ethnographer casually remarks on the manipulative character of gifts while observing the giving of one. His words risk enacting an agential cut that transforms donor and recipient into exploiter and exploited. They introduce a temporal frame and make manifest the expectation of a pay back at some point in the future. They lay bare human interests and calculations. They render determinate that which ought to remain indeterminate, the fine balance between altruism and interest. The words do not only radically alter the present moment, they also imply that the relationship under study is probably based on a lie of some duration, and have serious consequences for its future, assuming it has one.

Moreover, the cut not only alters the meaning of the exchange, it is not only conceptual, it also has somatic consequences; it affects bodies. If I expose your 'gift' as nothing more than calculation, a question of profit for you rather than an expression of your kindness towards me, you may well blush at having been exposed and lower your head in shame, or break into an uncomfortable sweat. Or you might feel hurt and burst into tears. Alternatively, you become outraged, tremble with indignation and clench your fists. The ethnographer who witnesses the scene, or whose ill-considered comments may even have caused it, will also experience a series of physical and emotional states, as will any onlookers who witness the situation. The words penetrate the materiality of their bodies. They do not merely inscribe a surface; they cut to the quick, reconfiguring heartbeat, respiration, and exocrine and endocrine systems.

Studying as ambiguous a thing as a gift demands attention to the passage of time that reveals (part of) the gift's character, the inevitable return gift. It also demands understanding the social relationships that constitute the gift and how gifts constitute those relationships. In order to access these aspects in their full complexity, ethnographic fieldwork is necessary. Not least, it demands tact in how an ethnographer discusses gifts with the people, with whom she must spend time, and sensitivity to how different theoretical optics can radically alter the nature of the gift. Finally, the theoretical urge to disambiguate ambiguous phenomena in pursuit of scientific exactitude is out of place when examining such a queer thing. As Wittgenstein once remarked, a good picture of a fuzzy object is a fuzzy picture.

Naivety

From the phenomenon of gifts we now move to things, the everyday artefacts that fill our lives. The word 'thing' derives from the Germanic *thingan* and is related to the Gothic *theihs*, time. The thing was the appointed time for deliberation, accusation, judicial process, and decisions. It came to stand for the place where these proceedings occurred, such as the Icelandic parliament, the *Althing*, or an electioneering speech from a husting. In English, the phrase 'the thing is' still refers to the subject of discussion. The word finally came to refer to a physical object. Embedded in the word's etymology is a very different kind of thing than the stable material object we often refer to by the word.[2] It is this reified version of things that allowed anthropology to assimilate them to a Durkheimian sociology in which they were compliant surfaces onto which social meanings were projected. For this school of thought things represented some-thing else, society or culture. They were not especially interesting in themselves.

For Amira Henare and colleagues (Henare et al. 2007), however, things are not merely material representations of something more basic. They reject the cultural-material divide implied in this approach to things, arguing that material things are also semantic. An understanding of foreign things (or of familiar things in a 'foreign' or novel way) furnishes us with another conceptual handle on the world. By the same logic, when the concepts are radically foreign they refer to foreign material worlds, not only different conceptual worlds. Things point us towards different ontologies, not epistemologies. Henare and colleagues argue that 'alterity can quite properly be thought of as a property of things – things, that is, which *are concepts* as much as they appear to us as "material" or "physical" entities' (2007: 27). They conclude that 'there may be as many ontologies (and therefore novel analytical frames) as there are things to think through – provided we start

---

2   On how this 'sexes' things, see Graham (2004).

by heeding the injunction that meanings and artefacts are of an essence' (ibid).[3] Their claim resonates with the onto-epistemology of Barad and her emphasis on the inseparability of the material and the discursive, although they arrive at their conclusion by a different route.

Things, then, can act as portals into different worlds if we think through them. In order to do so, we need under-determined concepts with which to grasp them. That is, concepts that act as heuristics and do not block alternative ontologies, rather than exact analytical tools. The authors give the example of the concept of the person as developed by Marilyn Strathern (1988). Strathern employed an under-determined concept of person in her work on Melanesian exchange. In Melanesia, gifts are not exchanged between pre-existing persons, the exchanges themselves *constitute* persons as 'dividuals', literally divisible persons who are distributed throughout their exchange networks in the form of transacted substances that include material gifts, foodstuffs, mother's milk, semen, and blood. Because these substances are differentially gendered, they make the ascription of one unambiguous gender to the persons they constitute difficult. The new concept of 'dividual' does justice to the Melanesian context but was possible only because Strathern did not hold fast to a Western concept of the individual that assumes a fixed, closed entity, but instead attended to the network of constitutive relations between persons and things. We can call this a naive methodology because the 'gullibility' of the concepts leaves them susceptible in a very productive way to new suggestions.

The Melanesian dividual person can be reapplied back home to disturb western relationships to things. It is not only in the Melanesian context that the person-thing (or subject-object) distinction is unstable. Once we acknowledge the hold things have on us, the fetishistic dimension of things that take (perhaps more accurately capture) our fancy (see Pels 1998), our own status as self-contained, gendered subjects starts to look flimsy. We move towards a different ontology of the subject, one that provides us with a different perspective on ourselves. If things constitute gender and do not only reflect it, then the gendered subject is not closed, but opens onto things. What then if these things themselves are better understood in more dynamic, open terms?

Worldliness

If the above is what I have called a naive methodology, what does a worldly methodology look like? I use worldly here both in the sense of being in the world and of a knowing attitude born out of that experience, which can be described as a sceptical, perhaps even cynical, knowing. One axiom for a queer worldly method

---

3   It behoves those who baulk at the suggestion that there are multiple ontologies and not one true nature (accessible only to western science) to identify the one, true, ontology/ nature that is independent of our conceptual/experimental grasp of it. This is no easy matter in the light of what Bohr and Barad argue about phenomena.

for studying things might be to abandon the object and follow its lines of flight into the world to see where they take us.

One obvious contender for such a method is the study of commodity chains (Hopkins and Wallerstein 1986, Haugerud et al. 2000). Commodity chain studies focus on the networks of production and labour processes, marketing, and retail that go into the manufacture of artefacts. Clothing makes an attractive object of study, not only because the links in the clothing industry are relatively transparent from producers to consumers (Collins 2003: 19), but also because clothing is usually strongly gendered. As a rule, garments ought to display a (hetero)normative alignment of sex, gender and sexuality. Yet once we take into account more than a garment's immediate facticity, and look to the relations and materials condensed in it, all of which have their own genderings (rather like Melanesian 'dividuals'), there is no simple sex, sexuality or gender. How we attribute sex-sexuality-gender, and any other quality to a garment, depends on how we cut it. And every cut, as Barad makes clear, excludes in order that objects may emerge and mean something. It is only relatively easy to sex and gender objects if we sever them from the materials and processes that constitute them, and by the same logic only relatively easy to sex and gender persons in accordance with heteronormative ontologies of the subject if they are divorced from the objects that make them subjects. Once we readmit these materials and processes, objects and subjects become increasingly indeterminate but also available for alternative cuttings.

Following commodity chains has much to recommend it but like all methods it has its limitations. The chain metaphor ought not to be taken too literally, otherwise we risk substituting one reified thing, the commodity, for another, the chain. Attention to chains must not displace concrete social actors. The processes of which commodity chains are part may be global (or at least encompassing several sites that are not specific to a nation or even continent), but at each 'level' these processes happen because social actors act. The global is manifested in local interactions (Latour 1993: 120–21) which we can study in situ, for example through multi-sited ethnographies (Marcus 1995).

The lines of flight that lead away from an object and admit ever more context can never arrive at a definitive contextualisation. They do not lead to a final truth about things. In fact, they can increase doubts and uncertainties as the different ways of understanding the thing multiply along with the different avenues that lead to and from it. Indeed, the contestability of the original 'thing' may be restored.

Tracing commodity chains is mainly a retrospective method that examines a past to explain the presence of the object in the present. It has relatively little to say about its future and the uses social actors make of it. If we ignore how people use artefacts, we risk reducing them to props or reflections of class cultures, or legitimating ideologies. Once again things can be read as simply saying something about something else while their materiality, and the part they play in social relationships, is neglected. If we want to look at what people actually do with their stuff, then the best method is long-term fieldwork.

Finally, we must not forget the intellectual apparatus that stabilises things as commodities and the production process as a chain thereby turning them into objects of study. Research is no less a material process than manufacturing, and no less capable of constituting a reifying process. It too is part of the phenomenon under consideration.

Final Thoughts

At first glance, materiality may seem like an inhospitable area for queer approaches because of its seemingly obdurate nature. Perhaps even more than identity categories, the sheer stubbornness of objects seems to lend weight – literally – to the cultural norms they encode and nowhere more so than in the myriad ways things are mobilised to maintain gender. Yet, as feminist philosophies of science make clear, this obduracy is not the whole story. Matter at its most basic level is strangely queer, while everyday artefacts, if only we were more literate about them and more attentive to what they say, can tell us some very queer tales that undermine the heteronormative gendering of persons.

Taking my initial cues from the new ontology revealed in the work of feminist philosophies of materiality and the challenges this ontology throws out to essentialisms I have intentionally moved from the smallest scales of matter to global processes of commodity production via the artefacts that fill our lives, and have tried to draw out some of the methodological implications at each level.

The queerness of matter and things, their inherent dis-location rests on exclusions found at all levels of materiality, from the basic components of matter to global manufacturing. These exclusions are not solely a matter of Derridean supplements; they are concrete social processes that demand sociological methods of study. Disclosing them not only shows how things are created but also how they could be created differently, by, for example, putting pressure on companies to change homophobic policies by boycotting their products. Our methods cannot therefore be local, whether confined to texts or individual things. We have to enter the world beyond the object to find out how the object was put there. Queer theories that focus on signification and resignification as strategies of resistance risk dealing only with the final object and, without a stronger sociological approach, float atop, or are at least unable to grasp fully the inequalities that lie behind appearances; indeed they may even be complicit in them.

Yet, in our methods we must also be local if we want to discover the, sometimes very personal, relationships between social actors and things and furnish ourselves with the material needed to improve our theories. As Henare and colleagues (2007) argue, it is through greater attention to the material that we can renew ossified concepts and create new ones. Such a methodology employs a radical empiricism as the locus of theoretical innovation. Rather than the abstract (theory) being realised in the concrete (the empirical object), the abstract must itself be explained. Moreover, it is the new that is the goal, not empirical demonstrations of universals. Gilles Deleuze (drawing on A.N. Whitehead) writes that this kind of radical empiricism analyses 'the state of things, in such a way that non-pre-existent concepts can be extracted from them' (Deleuze and Parnet 1987: vii-viii). One of the advantages of ethnographic fieldwork is precisely its ability to generate material that does not fit into pre-existing theoretical schema. It combines a shifting inductive and deductive approach to empirical material.

I have stressed the importance of attending to how objects are created through the enactment of cuts and of undoing these cuts to restore their dynamism or thingness to them. I have also argued for the importance, indeed indispensability, of an ethnographically based empiricism that is both naive and worldly, one that reveals the queerness of materiality. An important lesson that emerges at every level of scale and with every method used is the need for humility. All methods have their limitations and all play a part in producing the very objects they study. Methodology is performative to the core and as such never able to claim closure. A queer rendering of materiality is itself only ever partial, something is inevitably excluded. Furthermore, although materiality seems to be user friendly, there is no guarantee that the users will be friendly to queer ambitions. This much is already abundantly clear in the way materiality is mobilised in the pursuit of normative regimes, not least in appeals to assumed natural, because material, truths and in the way categories of objects induce categories of persons by the policing of social meanings, and the significations they engender. We would do well to remember that the indeterminacy of matter and things may indeed make them available for resistant queer strategies, but sometimes it may also make them resistant to resistance.

Chapter 12

Autoethnography is a Queer Method

Stacy Holman Jones and Tony E. Adams

Knowing Artistry

The drive-thru line at the new Starbucks – the latest corporate fixture to take up residence in my increasingly gentrified neighbourhood – is ten cars deep. I am in my pyjamas, returning from driving my girlfriend to work. The now impossible anonymity of participating in the capitalist caffeinated takeover of the neighbourhood is not enough to overcome my need for a $3.49 iced coffee. Not even close. So I go in and order my coffee and wait, reading over the tastefully displayed propaganda proclaiming Starbuck's environmental sensitivity and staring too long at the cover of a Sheryl Crow CD until I hear the barista call my name. When I reach for my drink she says,

> 'Hey, you go to Blockbuster.'
> 'Um, yeah.'
> She lifts the bill of her Starbucks cap so that I can see her eyes.
> 'I used to work there.'
> I steal a glance at her nametag. Sarah. Still, nothing.
> 'Yeah,' I say, unsure. I'm not sure *why* we're having this conversation, either, but it fills the space between her calling my name and me claiming my coffee, so I don't linger on questions of relevance.
> 'My wife works there.'
> 'Oh, *yeah.* She always has to call me because I forget to put the movies back in the cases before I return them.'
> 'You know her?' She smiles. 'You know who she is?'
> 'Yeah. Sure.'
> She hands me a straw. 'Enjoy your coffee.'
> 'I will. Nice to see you again.'

Now, this exchange was brief, unremarkable. And that, of course, is what was so remarkable about it. In a matter of moments, in a matter of sentences, I understood that I – that we *recognized* each other. I understood that Sarah – and her wife – knew about me. And that I knew about them. I suppose that's pretty easy when you work at Blockbuster. After all, it's not hard to remember which customers rent entire seasons of *The L Word.* And it isn't hard for me to notice which Blockbuster employees comment on what happens in Season 2 between Dana and Alice. Still, what was remarkable about this encounter was the unremarkable ease with which we slipped into another conversation – the conversation about who we were, there in the Starbucks and everywhere else. Known and unknown, hidden and present, all at once.

It was a conversation about Foucault's (1980) subjugated knowledge, about what Gingrich-Philbrook (2005: 311) calls 'lost arts, hidden experiences'. Such knowledges – now multiple – are present but disguised in theory and method, criticism and scholarship, experience and disciplinary (and disciplining) conversations. Gingrich-Philbrook contrasts *subjugated knowledges* with *knowledge of subjugation* – stories of struggle, oppression and humiliation. The importance of telling these stories notwithstanding, he wonders if our hunger for and valuing of stories of loss, failure, and resistance don't often work as 'advertisement for power' (2005: 312). And furthermore, if autoethnography privileges stories of oppression over and against the stories of affirmation we might like – and need – to tell and hear (312). Do such stories ask us to embrace an overly formalist view of what not only constitutes autoethnography but what makes for successful, viable and remarkable personal storytelling in the *name* of autoethnography or any other academic pursuit? Does our interest in realism, in evocation, in proving – once and for all – that what autoethnographers are doing *is scholarship* – trades in and betrays literary ambiguity, author vulnerability, institutional bravery, difference and artistry? Gingrich-Philbrook suggests that telling stories of subjugated knowledges – stories of pleasure, gratification and intimacy – offers one possibility for writing against and out of the bind of sacrificing a multitudinous *artistry* for clear, unequivocal *knowledge.*

As I leave the Starbucks, this is what is remarkable to me: the ease with which Sarah and I acknowledged each other and the pleasure involved in this. And the way in which we became present and accountable to one another in this public space. Of course, no one else noticed, no one else knew. So maybe it doesn't count.

I wonder if this moment deserves my words, warrants the hour or more I spend writing it. Perhaps I'm just procrastinating, putting off more important, more rigorous, more consequential work. It is most definitely my experience – particular to *me.* I'm not sure it has any cultural significance or insight, even though I want to believe, as I write it, that something larger than me and Sarah, that something socially and culturally and politically significant – something *queer* – happened at Starbucks. I'll never know that. Sure, I could return and ask her. Though even if Sarah shared my interpretation, even if she confirmed my telling of our story, I'm not sure that makes my efforts to write it into significance any more or less successful, any more or less significant in the big scheme of things.

But then, what is the big scheme of things? What are the possibilities of particular, ambiguous, mundane, queer stories of encounter? Of intimacy? What are the promises and possibilities of this artistry (a word I substituted, just now, for *work*) for qualitative research and queer methodologies? Will such stories help generate some type of agreement about the value, seriousness and commitment of autoethnographic work, our approach in engaging such work and our recognition of those who are doing it and doing it well? Will such stories provide a counterpoint to the balancing act of telling of loss and pleasure, despair and hope? Will such stories help us decide who gets invited to speak, who gets an audience, who gets tenure, who gets acknowledged? Will such stories help us build communities, maintain borders, live somewhere in between? I'm not sure they will and I'm not sure I want them to. What I am sure about is: linking queer theory with autoethnography offers some of the promise and the possibility for navigating and fulfilling these questions.

Autoethnography and Queer Theory

Autoethnography and queer theory share conceptual and purposeful affinities: Both refuse received notions of orthodox methodologies and focus instead on fluidity, intersubjectivity and responsiveness to particularities (Plummer 2005, Ronai 1995, Slattery 2001, Spry 2001). Both refuse to close down inventiveness, refuse static legitimacy (Foucault 1981, Gingrich-Philbrook 2005). Both embrace an opportunistic stance toward existing and normalizing techniques in qualitative inquiry, choosing to 'borrow,' 'refashion,' and 'retell' methods and theory in inventive ways (Hilfrich 2006: 218–19, Koro-Ljungberg 2004, Plummer 2005). Both take up selves, beings, or 'I's, even as both work against a stable sense of self-subjects or experience. Both work to map how self-subjects are accomplished in interaction and how these subjects act upon the world (Adams 2005, Berry 2007, Butler 1990, 1993, Jackson 2004, Spry 2006). And both are thoroughly *political*, displaying a clear commitment to refiguring and refashioning; questioning normative discourses, and acts, and undermining and refiguring how lives (and lives worth living) come into being (Denzin 2006, Warner 1993, Yep, Lovaas and Elia 2003).

Autoethnography and queer theory are both also often criticized for being too much and too little – too much personal mess, too much theoretical jargon, too elitist, too sentimental, too removed, too difficult, too easy, too white, too Western, too colonialist, too indigenous. Yet at the same time, too little artistry, too little theorizing, too little connection between the personal and political, too impractical, too little fieldwork, too few real-world applications (e.g. Alexander 2003, Anderson 2006, Atkinson 1997, Atkinson and Delamont 2006, Barnard 2004, Buzard 2003, Gans 1999, Gingrich-Philbrook 2005, Halberstam 2005, Johnson 2001, Kong, Mahoney and Plummer 2002, Lee 2003, Madison 2006, Owen 2003, Perez 2005, Watson 2005, Yep and Elia 2007).

In this chapter, we position autoethnography as a queer research method, one that not only works against canonical methodological traditions and 'disciplining, normalizing, social forces' (Seidman 1993: 133) but also one that satisfies the call and need to provide a pragmatic, accessible way of representing research, a way that devotes itself with 'grounded, everyday life' (Plummer 2003: 522).

While autoethnography and queer theory have clear connections, as written and practiced, they have been held apart – by focus, by context and by discipline. Here, we hinge the affinities and commitments of queer theory to the purposes and practices of autoethnography. We hinge experience and analysis, distance and closeness, equality and prioritizing oppression, conversation/dialogue and irony/ rebellious debate, accessibility and academic activism, subjugated knowledges with canonical doctrine. We strive to be 'inclusive without delimiting' and try to 'remap the terrain' of autoethnography and queer theory without 'removing the fences that make good neighbors' (Alexander 2003: 352, Gingrich-Philbrook 2003). We put into practice and illustrate what autoethnography and queer theory do and should do, as well as what they do to, for and in research methodology and scholarship.

Throughout this chapter, we also use 'I' to tell our stories to combine us, as authors and readers, into a shared experience. My experience – our experience – could be your experience. My experience – our experience – could reframe your experience. My experience – our experience – could politicize your experience and could motivate, mobilize you, and us, to action. Our 'I' is fashioned after Pollock's (2007: 246) 'performative "I"', a subjectivity both productive and self-productive, a processual and perpetually 'becoming "I" on the verge of a becoming "we"'. A performative 'I' moves out of the first-person narrator traditionally constructed in scholarly discourse, often self-referential and unavailable to criticism or for revision. By contrast, a performative 'I'

> enjoys neither the presumption of a foundational ontology nor the convenience of conventional claims to authenticity. It is (only) possibly real. It is made real through the performance of writing. Accordingly, its reality is never fixed or stable. To the very extent that it is written, it is always already about to fly off the page into being and becoming. (Pollock 2007: 247)

Our 'I' hinges us – Stacy and Tony – to 'us' and to 'we', a community of scholars ready to write ourselves into new ways of being and becoming.

Hinge

Autoethnography, whether a practice, a writing form, or a particular perspective on knowledge and scholarship, hinges on the push and pull between and among analysis and evocation, personal experience and larger social, cultural and political concerns. Our attempts to locate, to tie up, to *define* autoethnography are as diverse as our perspectives on what autoethnography is and what we want it to do. Attempts at such pinning down and hemming in – the stuff of methods books – delineate the relationship of a self or selves (informant, narrator, I) and others/ communities/cultures (they, we, society, nation, state).

And so, autoethnography looks to 'extract meaning from experience rather than to depict experience exactly as it was lived' (Bochner 2000: 270). It puts the 'autobiographical and personal' in conversation with the 'cultural and social' (Ellis 2004: xix). Autoethnography locates 'the particular experiences of individuals in tension with dominant expressions of discursive power' (Neumann 1996: 189, see also Denzin 1997, Ellis and Bochner 2000, Reed-Danahay 1997). Autoethnography is analytically reflexive; it presents a 'visible narrative presence' while 'engaging in dialogue with informants beyond the self' in order to improve our 'theoretical understandings of broader social phenomena' (Anderson 2006: 375).

Autoethnography is also painted as an evocatively rendered, aesthetically compelling and revelatory encounter. In this view, autoethnography is 'the kind [of art] that takes you deeper inside yourself and ultimately out again' (Friedwald 1996: 126). It works to exhibit aesthetic merit, reflexivity, emotional and intellectual force and a *clear* sense of a cultural, social, individual or communal reality. It is an effort to set a scene, tell a story and create a text that demands attention and participation, makes witnessing and testifying possible and puts pleasure, difference and movement into productive conversation (Holman Jones 2005a: 765).

Another way of looking at things, of approaching autoethnography, is to open up definitional boundaries. Here, autoethnography is a 'broad orientation toward scholarship' and not a method, a specific set of procedures, or a mode of representation (Gingrich-Philbrook 2005: 298). Such opening up does not abandon intersections or interests but instead makes the politics of knowledge and experience central to what autoethnography is and does, as well as what it wants to be and become. And, with particular attention to performance and embodiment, autoethnography enacts 'a way of seeing and being [that] challenges, contests or endorses the official, hegemonic ways of seeing and representing the other' (Denzin 2006: 422). In other words, autoethnographers believe that the 'point of creating autoethnographic texts is to change the world' (Holman Jones 2005a: 765).

The actions and meanings we invoke and engage when we utter and inscribe the word *autoethnography* conjure a variety of methodological approaches and techniques, writing practices and scholarly and disciplinary traditions. Those interested in autoethnography have eschewed and, in some cases, warned against settling on a single definition or set of practices (Charmaz 2006, Ellis and Bochner, 2000, Richardson and St. Pierre 2005). In this view, an abstract, an open and flexible space of movement is necessary to let the doing of autoethnography begin, happen and grow. However, this considered, differential positioning has caused worry about whose or what traditions we're working in, which methods of analysis and aesthetic practice we're using (or ignoring) and whether we can coexist peacefully while at the same time generating positive movement (and change) in our multiplicity.

Within and beyond the crises of legitimation, representation and praxis (see Denzin 1997, Holman Jones 2005a), questions persist about the relationship between analysis and evocation, personal experience and larger concerns and the reason we do this work at all. Is it to advance theory and scholarship? Is it to engage in an artistic and necessarily circuitous practice? Is it to render clean lines of inquiry and mark sure meanings and thus knowledge? Is it to change the world? Are we talking, as Denzin (2006: 420) wonders, about different things; apples and oranges? If so, we can agree, 'reluctantly and respectfully', to part ways by acknowledging our differences and claiming versions of autoethnography as our own (Denzin 2006: 422). To each his, her, their, *own.*

We could also return to the oppositions and to the *hinge* that work these oppositions. And, returning there, we could ask what the hinge holds and pieces together, here solidly, there weakening, in many places coming undone: analysis and evocation, experience and world, apples and oranges, the need to do the work we love and the need for approval of the work we do (Gingrich-Philbrook 2005). We could also ask what our hinges *do,* what versions of lives, embodiments and power these hinges put in motion, what histories they make *go* (Pollock 1998a).

These questions go beyond contextualization, historicization and reflexivity to intervene in the very construction of such constructions (Scott 1991: 779). These questions are about 'discourse, difference, and subjectivity as well as about what counts as experience [as analysis, as autoethnography] and who gets to make that determination' (1991: 790). These questions are about what counts – as experience, as knowledge, as scholarship, as opening up possibilities for doing things and being in the world differently. More, these are questions about who is recognized – as visible, worthy, right, and, ultimately, human (Butler 2004). Asking these questions suggests that we dismantle the hinge – that we become 'unhinged' – from 'linear narrative deployment,' creating work and texts that turn 'language and bodies in upon themselves reflecting and redirecting subaltern knowledges,' and in which 'fragments of lived experience collide and realign with one another, breaking and remaking histories' (Spry 2006: 342). These questions also remind us of the necessity of the hinge, of the link that it makes, however tenuously, to others. This necessity speaks to the threat of 'becoming undone altogether,' creating selves, texts and worlds that no longer incorporate the 'norm' (of sociality, of discourses, of knowledges, of intelligibility) in ways that make these selves, texts, and worlds recognizable as such (Butler 2004: 4). Of the movements of hinges, of their doings and undoings, Butler writes,

> There is a certain departure from the human that takes place in order to start the process of remaking the human. I may feel that without some recognizibility I cannot live. But I may also feel that the terms by which I am recognized make life unlivable. This is the juncture from which critique emerges, where critique is understood as an interrogation of the terms by which life is constrained in order to open up the possibility of different modes of living. (2004: 3–4)

The juncture, the critique, the hinge. The *claiming* of experience, of a personal story, of humanity in the struggle over self-representation, interpretation and recognition

(L.T. Smith 1999). The accounting for oneself as constituted relationally, socially, in terms not entirely (or in any way) one's own (Butler 2005). The movement between two 'traps, the purely experiential and the theoretical oversight of personal and collective histories' (Mohanty 2003: 104). The performative space both within and outside of subjects, structures and differences where the activist (the writer, the performer, the scholar) becomes in the moment of acting (the moment of writing, performing, doing scholarship). Where we are made in the same way the judge, 'promiser' or oath taker is made in the act of judging, promising, or swearing an oath (Sandoval 2000). The hinge is an instrument of transitivity, a moral movement that is inspired and linked, acting and acted upon. The hinge asks us to align what may seem divided perspectives – without forgetting their differences or their purposeful movements – in order to 'puncture through the everyday narratives that tie us to social time and space, to the descriptions, recitals, and plots that dull and order our senses' (2000: 140–141). Rather than agree to disagree or to decide the form, subject, purpose and value of autoethnography once and for all, this chapter takes up Sandoval's call for a 'differential' methodology that aims at tactically, and we might add tectonically, shifting ways of being, knowing and acting (2000: 184).

As one point, or tactic for departure, we explore the hinge that links autoethnography and queer theory. We wonder if, in the binding and alliance of autoethnography and queer theory – if in recognizing their tensions and troubles and the ways these 'broad orientations' complement and fail each other – we might emerge with something else, something new. We are not after a homogenizing blend *or* a nihilistic prioritizing of concerns, as such attempts leave us, marking and marked, 'yearning for more'. Instead, we want a transformation of the identities and categories, commitments and possibilities that autoethnography conjures and writes, as well as the identities and categories, commitments and possibilities of autoethnography itself. We wonder what happens when we think, say, do and write: *autoethnography is a queer method.*

Undone

I arrive early. I don't want to be late for the plenary session for which I am an invited speaker. Plenary: plentiful, absolute and unqualified. A session for all members of the collective. I arrive early and discover that I am not ready, that I am unprepared. Before the conference, I had begun by writing a paper, then stopped when I learned the session was to be devoted to discussion of truth and evidence, knowledge and spirit. I turned my attention to a response rather than a call, a conversation rather than a representation. When I arrive for the session, I am asked to present – to make evident, to provide, full and absolute – my paper. I am asked for my prose, my discourse, my words inscribed in unequivocal terms. I do not have words to give. I have, instead, fragments, lists and a poetic reading of poetry prepared for yet another panel.

We begin and when I am called upon to do something – to *say* something – I decide on the poetry, on the poetics. I decide that poetry is the most 'economical' of arts, the one that requires the 'least physical labor, the least material, and the one which can be done between' other paper presentations, right there in the conference room 'on scraps of surplus paper' (Lorde 1984: 116). I decide, with Lorde, it is no mistake that poetry is made into a 'less "rigorous" or "serious" art form' (116) by the command of economic, gender, sexual, racial and ethnic – not to mention academic, institutional and socio-cultural – *superiority*. And yet, poetry is a place for voicing experience, for recognizing and challenging difference and indifference, for doing the 'political work of witnessing' (Hartnett and Engles 2005: 1045, Lorde 1984). And so I begin.

I begin with Minnie Bruce Pratt's (1990) poem, 'All the Women Caught in Flaring Light,' part of her poetry collection *Crime Against Nature.* The back cover of the collection declares Pratt a 'lesbian poet, essayist, and teacher'. The inside cover – the scrap of paper folded over and holding in Pratt's words – tells me that her poems take their title from the 'statute under which the author would have been prosecuted as a lesbian if she had sought legal custody of her children' after she came out. After she became queer. Was queered. After that, there are poems, a place to 'write what happened' (1990: 17). In 'All the Women', Pratt writes,

> I often think of a poem as a door that opens into a room where I want to go. But to go in here is to enter where my own suffering exists as an almost unheard low note in the music, amplified, almost unbearable, by the presence of us all, reverberant pain, circular, endless, which we speak of hardly at all, unless a woman in the dim privacy tells me a story ... (1990: 31)

I write,

> All the women caught
> in the flaring light, incandescent
> movement of loss, separation, and denial
> banishment from the ranks of the entitled
> still offering hope. Poetry for
> something else, something other
> for pleasure and for *freedom.*
>
> A few words, some gesture of our hands, some
> bit of story
> cryptic as the mark gleaming on our hands,
> the ink
> tattoo, the sign that admits us to the this room,
> iridescent
> in certain kinds of light, then vanishing,
> invisible. (Pratt 1990: 32)

Shimmering reflection of not only what *was* possible, but what *is* possible.

Saying this, I begin. I begin with poetry, with words of my own and words I make my own. I look up and I am signalled to continue. I say that I am reading and writing Pratt's poetry and my own (in her voice, in my voice, in ours) because the stories these poems tell are *queer* – they invoke and defy alliances, categories and desires. I say,

> This story is a 'door that opens
> into a room where I want to go' (Pratt 1990: 31)
> I want to go. To go in and to go on

> I enter this room, not pausing at the threshold,
> but moving over the gap into the texts
> where I recognise my own experience
> Not *my* experience, evidential,
> foundation for an argument
> My experience as always
> inseparable from language
> from self-subject, from others, from discourse
> from difference
> This is what and all I know in the world
> the starting and ending points of a life.

I pause, then begin, again. I want to say that this poetry does not stop or end with queer. That our poetry does not stop or end with radical historization, with questioning categories or normalization, with turning cutting language inside out or making manifest violent and colonizing hierarchies, though these are things that must be done. I want to say that such poetry, such a poetics, is *also* a chance for movement, a means to transform the static of a noun – *queer* – into the action of a verb – *queering*. I want to speak about moving theory into methodological activism. I want to say, *autoethnography is queer.* I want to make autoethnography into performative speech that creates a freedom from having to be 'careful about what we say' (Pratt 1990: 30).

> A queering talk
> a 'commotion of voices' (Pratt 1990: 33)
> that doesn't undo the things
> that have been done to us
> the things we have done
> the ways we have become
> things and beings unbecoming
> becoming undone

I want to say this, but I do not. I cannot. Before I can get the word out, I am stopped. I am asked, then told, that I am finished. Thank you. Next. I leave the podium, the place of plenty and absolute attendance, and reclaim my seat. The words, full and ripe in my mouth, will wait. Unfinished, but not undone.

Queer Theory

Queer theory is best conceived of as a shifting sensibility rather than a static theoretical paradigm. Queer theory developed in response to a normalizing of (hetero)sexuality as well as from a desire to disrupt insidious, social conventions. Fluidity and dynamism characterize queer thought, motivating queer researchers to work against disciplinary legitimation and rigid categorization. In this section, we discern three characteristics of queer theory, and illustrate how and why autoethnography functions as a queer research method.

Queer theory primarily developed from the work of three scholars: Judith Butler (1990, 1993, 1997a, 1997b, 1999, 2004, 2005), Teresa de Lauretis (1991) and Eve Sedgwick (1985, 1990, 1993, 2000, 2003). Queer theory has roots in feminism (e.g. Frye 1983, Lorde 1984, Moraga and Anzuldúa 1984), lesbian and gay studies (e.g. Chesebro 1981, Katz 1978, McIntosh 1968) and identity politics (e.g. Alcoff 1991, Foucault 1978, Keller 1995, Phelan 1993). 'Queer' can function as an identity category that avoids the medical baggage of 'homosexual', disrupts the masculine bias and domination of 'gay', and avoids the 'ideological liabilities' of the 'lesbian' and 'gay' binary (de Lauretis 1991: v, Anzaldúa 1991). As Sedgwick (1993: 8) argues, queer can also refer to 'the open mesh of possibilities, gaps, overlaps, dissonances and resonances, lapses and excesses of meaning when the constituent elements of anyone's gender, of anyone's sexuality aren't made (or *can't be* made) to signify monolithically' (see also Corey and Nakayama 1997, Khayatt 2002, Nakayama and Corey 2003).

Queer can also serve as a temporary and contingent linguistic home for individuals living outside norms of sex and gender (e.g. intersex, trans) and, as such, must not be limited to transgressions of sexuality (Berlant and Warner 1995, Gamson 2003, Henderson 2001); a person can claim a queer signifier if she or he works against oppressive, normalizing discourses of identity (Butler 1993a, Sedgwick 2000, Thomas 2000). As a critical sensibility, queer theory tries to steer clear of categorical hang-ups and linguistic baggage, conceive of identity as a relational achievement (thus removing identity from essentialist and constructionist debates) and commit itself to a politics of change – all of which are characteristics autoethnography, as method, desires or strives to do.

Navigating (In)Visibility

I own a hat, a shirt and a cheque-book, all of which possess the Human Rights Campaign (HRC) logo, a logo that consists of a yellow equal sign housed within a blue square and that belongs to one of the largest organizations based in the United States that addresses lesbian, gay, bisexual, transgender and queer (LGBTQ) concerns.

I use my hat, shirt and cheques to mark my everyday, mundane body, to show others that I am, at the very least, LGBTQ friendly, to potentially get recognized by others as possessing an LGBT and/or Q identity, to breed connection and make meaningful relationship building possible. But not everyone knows the HRC logo; its LGBTQ connotations are only known by those who seek to align with, who are aware of, or who advocate against LGBTQ rights.

***

A trip to Starbucks. I'm wearing my shirt with the HRC logo.

> 'Tall half-caf Americano, please,' I say to the barista. 'And a bottle of water.'
> '$1.82', he responds.
> Based on mathematical estimation, my bill should be around $4.00. 'Did you charge me for my water?' I ask.
> 'Yeah, but I didn't charge you for the Americano. I like your shirt.'

'Thanks', I say, happy to achieve recognition and a free drink, ambivalent about the special treatment I receive for marking myself in a particular way, pleased that I have an experience based on my making nonheterosexuality visible or at least an experience with what can happen when nonheterosexual support becomes marked.

***

My boyfriend and I take a roundtrip trip from Tampa, Florida, to Chicago, Illinois. We arrive to the Chicago airport to return to Tampa. I'm wearing my hat with the HRC logo. 'All four of your bags weigh more than 60 pounds,' the male attendant says. 'The weight limit is 50 pounds for each bag.'

I'm upset that I/we bought so many used books. I/we forgot that the books would add a significant amount of weight. We'll now have to pay extra money to board the plane, money that will counteract the savings we received by buying used books.

'But I like your hat', the attendant says, disrupting my used-book, additional-weight thought processing. 'Don't worry about compensating for the extra weight.' Making a non-visible sexuality visible: the benefits, experiences, recognition.

***

A trip to Chipotle, a restaurant. I'm wearing my HRC shirt. I place my order, a vegetarian burrito, and arrive at the register.

'What is that logo?' the employee asks, pointing toward my shirt. I know he knows what the logo is and thus I know that he wants to make conversation.

'It's the logo for the Human Rights Campaign, an organization that advocates for lesbian, gay, bisexual, transgender and queer issues,' I say. 'Oh,' he replies and says nothing else. When I arrive to my table, I see that he has written his name and phone number on the back of my receipt: '714–874–9824. Kevin. Call me.'

***

A checkout line at Publix, a grocery store. A male customer ahead of me pays, grabs his bags and walks away from the grocery bagger and the cashier. Upon his departure but out of hearing range, I hear the cashier tell the bagger that the former customer 'was a flaming faggot'. Both begin to laugh as I move forward in the line.

The cashier begins to scan my groceries while the bagger bags. Both still laugh about the cashier's flaming faggot remark and neither pay much attention to me. The casher soon says what I owe. While I usually pay for my groceries with a credit card, I decide, this time, to use a cheque, a cheque that has 'Working for Lesbian, Gay, Bisexual and Transgender Equal Rights' printed above the signature line. My move to pay by cheque will, I hope, force the cashier to ask for my ID in order to verify the cheque's signature and therefore possibly see the printed text.

'May I see your ID?' he asks. 'Sure', I respond as I innocently retrieve my wallet. I give him the ID. He looks at its signature and then compares it to the check. It is here where he pauses. I know that he's reading the print above the signature line, and I know that he begins to know that I know he laughed at the flaming faggot that passed through the checkout line before me.

'Uh … thank you', he says, followed by 'I'm sorry for what I said about that man.' 'No problem', I respond. 'Thanks for your help.' Recognition: It can subvert. Violent, colloquial philosophy: Kill them with kindness. And even if I may have been cast as a second flaming faggot after I left the checkout line – a casting which I would have once avoided but now very much embrace – I know that I received an apology from a person who called someone else a flaming faggot, an apology from a person to a person – a faggot – who likes to make flames as well.

Categorical Hang-Ups and Linguistic Baggage

Queer theory values 'definitional indeterminacy' and 'conceptual elasticity' (Yep et al. 2003: 9, see also Haraway 2004, Henderson 2001, Thomas 2000, Wilchins 2004). Many queer theorists simultaneously reject 'labeling philosophies' and reclaim marginal linguistic identifiers (Butler 1993a, Muscio 1998, Nicholas 2006, Watson 2005), work to disrupt binaries of personhood and remain inclusive of identities not subsumed under canonical descriptors (Bornstein 1994, Gamson 2003, Hird 2004, Khayatt 2002, Sedgwick, 1990, C. Smith 2000). Queer theory revels in language's failure, assuming that words can never definitively represent phenomena or stand in for things themselves.

For instance, how might we definitively define *woman* (Butler, 1996, 1999, Fryer 2003)? Do essential qualities exist for this category? We might say, 'All women can have babies', but this would position persons unable to have babies as nonwomen or unable to claim women status. We might say, 'All women are terrible at math and science', but would thus position persons who excel at these subjects as non-women or unable to claim women status. We might say, 'All women have vaginas', but this would position persons lacking vaginas as non-women or as persons unable to claim women status (e.g. a male-to-female transgendered person who does not desire sex reassignment surgery). The more we interrogate identity categories, the more we fall into linguistic illusion, the more we recognize language's fallibility. Such an illusory, fallible condition, however, creates a 'greater openness in the way we think through our categories', which is a queer research aim (Plummer 2005: 365). With identity, this linguistic failure becomes important: While we interact with others via socially established categories, these labels crumble upon interrogation, thus making a perpetual journey of self-understanding possible.

Autoethnography, as method, allows a person to document perpetual journeys of self-understanding, allows her or him to produce queer texts. A queer autoethnography also encourages us to think through and out of our categories for interaction and to take advantage of language's failure to capture or contain 'selves', ways of relating and subjugated knowledges (see Berry 2007, Carver 2007, Corey 2006, Holman Jones 2005b, Jago 2002, Jones 2002, Meyer 2005, Pelias 2006, Pineau 2000, Spry 2006).

Identity-as-Achievement

Queer theory conceives of identity as a relational 'achievement' (Garfinkel 1967). An achievement metaphor situates identities *in* interaction, in processes where we are held accountable for being persons of particular kinds – kinds that we sometimes know or try to present ourselves *as,* but also kinds about which we have no definitive control (Hacking 1990, 1999). A queer, identity-as-achievement logic implies that we are held accountable for identities that often take the form of linguistic categories but implies we can never know what categories others may demand of us or what kinds of people others will consider us as; we can try to pass as kinds of persons, but we may not succeed or know if we succeed (Adams 2005). A queer identity-as-achievement logic implies that selves emerge from, and remain contingent upon, situated embodied practices; acts that rely on compulsory, citational, stereotypical performances about being kinds of people (Butler 1990a, 1993a, 1999, 2004, Sedgwick 1993, West and Fenstermaker 1995, West and Zimmerman 1987). Furthermore, a queer identity-as-achievement logic implies that identities fluctuate across time and space, thus requiring constant attention and negotiation; identities may come across as 'singular, fixed, or normal' *in* an interaction but may not be singular, fixed or normal across *all* interactions (Watson 2005: 74, see also Butler 1990a, Freeman 2001, Gamson 2003).

Viewing identity as an achievement also distances identity from essentialist *and* constructionist debates of selfhood. Essentialists view identity as something innate, biological and fixed. Constructionists view identities as socially established and maintained through interaction. A queer identity-as-achievement logic, however, works outside of essentialist and constructionist perspectives: It embraces the contextual achievement of being, and passing as, certain *kinds* of people. In one context, a person may be perceived as heterosexual whereas in another context, the person may be perceived as bisexual or homosexual. In one context, a person may pass as White and in another context, may pass as Black, and in another context, may pass as multiracial (Greenberg 2002). In one context, a person may pass as Catholic, and in another context pass as Baptist, and in another context pass as Jewish. An identity-as-achievement perspective does not imply that biology has nothing to do with interaction, nor does it foreground environmental influences on selfhood; the essence of selves and the processes through which selves are made are not the foci of queer theory. Queer theory not only recognizes that identities are conditioned and constrained by operations of power, but also works, simultaneously and perpetually, to transgress, alter or call attention to these formative conditions and constraints (Sedgwick 1993).

However, the permanency of print, the representational livelihood upon which many autoethnographers rely, can make a queer sensibility come across as 'singular, fixed, or normal' for both writers and readers (Watson 2005: 74, see also Sontag 1964). With the exception of a virtual text like blogging, a written text can function as a permanent representation, an uncompromising snapshot of culture. Finished texts solidify human trajectories in time and space, making it possible for life, for experience, for movement to become textually fixed. Such permanency fixes identity regardless of an autoethnographer's intentions, qualifiers and desires to present a 'partial, partisan, and problematic' account (Goodall 2001: 55). When we turn autoethnographic research into print – when we present it at a conference or publish it as a journal article or book chapter – we solidify an identity in text and harden a community, never allowing us or it to change unless we produce a second, solidifying account to accompany the first. We could provide two textual stories rather than just one, two accounts of a self to try to emphasize, display, the trajectories of a self-in-process, but we now have fixed two immobile versions of a self and suggest, by way of the print medium, a lack of movement.

By considering autoethnography queer, we recognize that identities may not be singular, fixed or normal across *all* interactions (see Ellis 1986, 1995, 2007, Johnson 2001, Pelias 2000, 2004, Rambo 2005, Ronai 1995, Wyatt 2005, 2006).

Identities constructed through a queering of autoethnography are relational; they shift and change. We are held accountable for being particular kinds of people by numerous seen and unseen forces, but our/these kinds are in constant need of attention, negotiation and care.

A Politics of Change

Queer theory values 'political commitment' (Yep et al. 2003: 9), deconstructs what passes as 'natural' and 'normal' (Garfinkel 1967, see Berlant and Warner 1995, Dilley 1999, Kong et al. 2002, Plummer 2003, Seidman 1993, R. Smith 2003, Warner 1993), focuses on how bodies both constitute and are constituted by systems of power as well as how bodies might serve as sites of social change (Althusser 1971, Berlant 1997, Bornstein 1994, Butler 1990a, 1993a, 1999, 2004, Foucault 1978, Yep and Elia 2007) and embraces a 'politics of transgression' (Watson 2005: 68, Hird 2004). Queer theorists revel in 'symbolic disorder' (Baudrillard 2001: 125), pollute established social conventions (Crawley 2002, Haraway 2004) and diffuse hegemonic categories and classifications. As Henderson (2001: 475) suggests, normalcy 'needs perversion to know itself' (see also Bell 1999). Queer projects function as this denormalizing perversion often by re/appropriating marginal discourse. While it could be argued that all re/appropriations are political, queer projects intentionally re/appropriate phenomena to pollute canonical discourse, to question what may pass as normal. Queer re/appropriation tries to 'twist' social order (Betsky 1999: 18), counter canonical stories (Bochner 2001, 2002) and make discursive 'trouble' (Butler 1990a).

The use of 'queer' in 'queer theory' is an example of a queer act. As Butler writes, something becomes 'queered' when it is 'redeployed' and 'twisted' from a 'prior usage' in 'the direction of urgent and expanding political purposes' (1993a: 228, see also Kong et al. 2002). Watson (2005: 73) suggests that 'reclaiming the word, "queer" empties the category of its effects'. Queer theory re/appropriates the once-taboo word and tries to reclaim abject power. Prior to this re/appropriation, *queer* possessed negative connotations deeming phenomena as out of the norm and 'slightly off kilter' (Walker, cited in Johnson 2001: 1). By using 'queer' in an affirmative sense – by incorporating it into mainstream discourse and associating the term with academically valued 'theory' – queer endcavours can emerge as desirable and esteemed. A queer re/appropriation is similar to how individuals try to reclaim other words for political purposes (e.g. 'nigger' (cf. Kennedy 2003), 'cunt' (cf. Muscio 1998) and 'vagina' (cf. Ensler 2001)).

Queer projects work to disrupt insidious, normalizing ideologies by way of re/appropriating parts of discursive systems and explicitly advocating for change. For instance, Cvetkovich (2003) shows how Dorothy Allison's work disrupts common storylines of abuse in that Allison shows how she both was a victim and survivor, expanding notions of how child abuse can function. Alexander (2008) demonstrates how the film *Brokeback Mountain* (2005) can function as a conservative story that perpetuates heteronormativity and subordinates raced 'Others' (e.g. Mexican male prostitutes) to white desire; Alexander's reading thus disrupts the text's assumed liberal status. And another intentional queering of canonical discourse involves the television program *Noah's Arc,* a scripted show that features experiences of five, assumed-gay Black men, individuals whose sexuality is implicitly perceived to rub against canonical religious doctrine and the rampant homophobia found in predominantly Black communities (see Yep and Elia 2007). Naming the show *Noah's Arc* is also a queer act in that it mixes the religious baggage of Noah and the Arc with nonheterosexual storylines, thus potentially disrupting and reframing common understandings of religion *and* sexuality.

A politics of change, as deployed in queer projects, constitutes much of current autoethnographic work as many autoethnographers intentionally, politically try to make ideological and discursive *trouble* (Butler 1990a, see Corey and Nakayama 1997, Foster 2008, Jeffries 2002, Johnson 2001, Lee 2003, Nakayama and Corey 2003, Owen 2003, Pelias 1999, 2006, Rambo 2007, Taylor 2000).

Manoeuvring

I have a female friend who had two male friends, both of whom called me a 'homo-phoney'. According to her friends, a homo-phoney described a man who identified as gay but did not have any 'gay qualities' and a man who would be identified as gay solely to establish intimate, sexual relations with women. According to her friends, I was straight. My gendered performances conflicted with a sexuality I claimed.

A colleague once asked why I was attending the National Communication Association convention. I told him I was participating on a gay-themed research panel. 'Are you gay enough to be on that panel?' he asked. Gender and sexuality conflict, again.

In graduate school, a professor frequently informed me that there was a 'woman out there for me' since I did not 'act gay', even though she knew of my intimate relationships with men. I regularly asked her why she thought this, but because of her authoritative role of 'professor' and mine of 'student', I felt I could press the fake-gay issue only so far.

Each of these situations makes conditions for queering possible, conditions that I now embrace and intentionally challenge in my everyday, embodied affairs. For instance, after disclosing my sexuality to a class I taught, a student told me that he thought I was a 'geek' rather than gay. 'You wear black-rimmed glasses', he said. 'But you're masculine. It wasn't until you said you couldn't operate a laptop computer where I began to think you might be gay.' At the end of the semester when students completed course feedback, one student later told me about two debates that occurred during the feedback process: Some students believed that I was lying about my gayness; others felt that I was transgendered, a man with a vagina who wanted to undergo sex reassignment surgery. Even though I still may perpetuate scripts of masculinity by intentionally working against an effeminate gay male stereotype, such comments also suggest that my intentional queering of the categories and normative conceptualizations of sex, gender and sexuality; I use my (perceived) sexed, gendered and sexualized body – and stereotypes about this body – to generate confusion, blur categories and motivate questioning.

Queering Autoethnography

Queer autoethnography embraces fluidity, resists definitional and conceptual fixity, looks to self and structures as relational accomplishments and takes seriously the need to create more livable, equitable and just ways of living. The hinge that links queer theory and autoethnography is, like Sandoval's (2000: 184) resistive semiology, a differential and oppositional form of consciousness. It is performative in the transitive sense of a hinge, a middle position, a form 'that intervenes in social reality through deploying an action that re-creates the agent even as the agent is creating the action . . . the only predictable final outcome is transformation itself' (2000: 157).

A differential, oppositional, performative and above all transformative, queer approach to autoethnography is one which recognizes that bodies are immersed in, and fixed by, texts, but also recognizes these bodies as doing, speaking and understanding beings, forthrightly incomplete, unknown, fragmented and conflicting. Failing to recognize these contingencies, ellipses and contradictions, autoethnographers textually paint themselves into a corner where boundaries are policed, disciplinary and scholarly turf is defined and fought over and systems for what and who 'counts' and doesn't count undermine the liberatory impulses we imagine for our work. In the place of relationality, performativity and transitivity, we create singularity, clarity and certainty. In short, we create *good stories:* stories that report on recognizable experiences, that translate simply and specifically to an 'actionable result' – an emotional response, a change in thinking or behaviour, a shift in policy or perception, publication, tenure (Eisenberg et. al. 2005: 394).

For instance, as scholars have responded to a perceived need for good autoethnographic stories, we have:

- Favoured *clarity and transparency* of knowledge via criteria or 'rules of art' over *ambiguity* and room for interpretation, misunderstanding, not knowing, leaving things unfinished, unanswered (Gingrich-Philbrook 2005, Madison 2006, Pollock 2006);
- foregrounded *knowledge* claims and publication in sanctioned or legitimate outlets (journals, academic books) and glossing over *aesthetic* (literary) concerns (Gingrich-Philbrook 2005, Richardson and St.Pierre 2005);
- sought proof of *worth* and *legitimacy* by creating typologies for good stories to enact (Bochner 1997, 2000, 2001, Clough 2000, Ellis 2000, Holman Jones 2005a, Pollock 1998b), even as we resisted doing so;

- engaged in recursive debates about how to define autoethnography, what constitutes authentic or legitimate autoethnographic research, and the purposes and meanings of autoethnographic work for research, for academic careers, for ourselves, and the wider public (Alcoff 1991, Anderson 2006, Atkinson and Delamont 2006, Bochner 2000, Buzard 2003, Corey 2006, Denzin 2006, Gans 1999, Madison 2006, Pelias 2004, Rambo 2007, Ronai 1995, Spry 2006).

The necessity and helpfulness of methodological primers and criteria for the evaluation of our work notwithstanding, a queering of autoethnography asks us to find ways of living together, 'without agreement, without confirmation, without clarity' (Gingrich-Philbrook 2005: 298). As we noted earlier, Gingrich-Philbrook (2005) recommends writing subjugated knowledges, stories that are present but disguised (see Conquergood 2002), stories of pleasure, of gratification, of the mundane, as they intersect, criss-crossing rhizomatically with stories of subjugation, abuse and oppression. One of the most ready forms for such tellings is found in the stories of our lives.

And so, autoethnography is a queer method. Saying so means taking a stand on a poetics of change. Saying so treats identities and communities as performative and relational achievements. Butler reminds us that whatever stories we choose to tell and however provisionally *or* transparently we work to tell them, we are always doing so in order to make ourselves 'recognizable and understandable' (2005a: 37). This is recognition of a need to unfasten the hinge that separates experience and analysis and the personal and the political, even as we need it to create an intelligible humanity, a life both livable and worth living. It is a recognition of humanity that doesn't end or stop in the move from the space of illegitimacy, all breath and speech, dark and hollow, to the place of legitimacy, resplendent and lucid in word and text (see Delany 2004). In another work, however, Butler ends with the pleasure and ethics of being *undone* in a radical relationality:

> We must recognise that ethics requires us to risk ourselves precisely at moments of unknowingness, when what forms us diverges from what lies before us, when our willingness to become undone in relation to others constitutes our chance of becoming human. To be undone by another is a primary necessity, an anguish, to be sure, but also a chance – to be addressed, claimed, bound to what is not me, but also to be moved, to be prompted to act, to address myself elsewhere, and so to vacate the self-sufficient 'I' as a kind of possession. (2005a: 136)

We wonder if the ethics of undoing that Butler describes enacts both the pleasures and the oppressions of autoethnography and, furthermore, if it anticipates the juncture, the stitching together – the hinging – of autoethnography and queer theory. Consider, for example:

- Making work that *becomes,* like a perpetual horizon, rather than an artifact of experience; making work that acts *as if* rather than says *it is.* Such work understands and emphasizes, the importance of being tentative, playful, and incomplete in equal measure with radical historicization, persistent questioning, and perpetual revision.
- Making work that simultaneously imagines fluid, temporary, and radically connected identities *and* that creates and occupies *recognizable* identities. Such work views identities as relational achievements: manifestations of selves that shift and change, that must be negotiated and cared for and for which we are held personally, institutionally and ethically responsible.
- Making work that advocates for trouble, that takes a stand in and on the otherwise. Such work disrupts taken-for-granted, normalizing stories and posits more open, more free and more just ways of being in the world.

Making autoethnography a queer method offers a way to trade in the debates around legitimacy, value and worth and for conversations about practicality, necessity and movement. It is a move autoethnographers are ready to take and are taking. We encourage you to claim and reclaim the word *queer* in the name of autoethnography, in the name of challenging categories and achieving identities and communities that are fluid yet complex, multiple yet cognizant of the attention, negotiation and care that impinge on any scholarly project. We encourage you to twist autoethnography from its prior usages, whether diminishing or valorizing, and put it to use for altogether new and other political purposes.

Recognition

Making coffee at home – a home I share with my girlfriend and my son – I thought about a conversation I had with my mother a few months after I left my other home, my other life. For months, I could not summon the courage to tell my mother the details of the split, of my reversal, my betrayal. And then, in an unremarkable moment, I told that story in a sentence. When my mother asked if I was interested in having another relationship some day, if I would date someone and maybe be married again, I simply said, 'No'.

> 'Oh ... why?'
> 'Mom, I'm not interested in dating.'
> 'What if you meet someone nice? A good man?'
> 'Mom, I'm not interested in dating men.'
> 'Oh ... *oh.* Okay. As long as you're happy.'

And that was the story. Unremarkable except for the remarkable way she chose to accept and, yes, *believe* my story – a queer story with no immediate recognition, no diagnosis or translation, no ready or apparent ending – as true. Or at least good enough. Later, we would talk about this story in more detail and still, my mother did not waver in her acknowledgment of what she could not know. She did not read or tell this story as extraordinary or rare, mournful or wasted. She did, however, share one concern: She was worried I'd be alone. That I wouldn't have someone to share my life with, to grow old with. All I could say was, 'There's no guarantee of that – of having someone – for anyone. I don't think it's any different for women. Maybe we just don't see women growing old together. Or maybe we do, but we don't recognize it.' – I don't know whether this satisfied her or put her or my worries about what is surely the inevitability of loneliness in life at bay, but that was the end of our conversation, at least for now.

Making coffee at home, I thought about my mother's gift to me: an unblinking, unmoving acceptance of the 'lost arts' and 'hidden experiences' that had become my life. In her recognition of me, in her acknowledgment and claiming of my story, she taught me what I could not teach myself in those long months: the importance of risking ourselves in moments of unknowingness, the necessity of resisting offers of certainty or stability and the flattery of legitimacy. The importance of taking a chance motivated not out of a misplaced or, worse, righteous self-sufficiency, but a willingness to become undone *and* moved to act. Why not write over, on and through the boundaries of what constitutes and contributes to autoethnography – to qualitative and critical research – by creating a few queer stories, a few queer autoethnographies? Why not embrace a critical stance that values opacity, particularity, indeterminateness for what they bring and allow us to know and forget, rather than dismissing these qualities as slick deconstructive tricks, as frustrating, as unmoving and unrecognizable? Why *not* write (Gingrich-Philbrook 2005: 311)? *Why not?*

Chapter 13

Queer Techne: Two Theses on Methodology and Queer Studies[1]

Tom Boellstorff

Introduction: Queer Studying

What does it mean to say that a *method* is queer? This question has profound implications, because it destabilizes the often implicit definition of 'queer studies' as either the study of 'queer persons', or as the study of texts and other cultural artefacts produced by and about 'queer persons'. There is nothing remiss in such definitions, which animate most work in queer studies and which I employ in much of my own research. However, they define queer studies in terms of object: 'studies' acts as a noun, and the outcome of queer studies is understood as knowledge about these queer objects and the dominant discourses with which they are imbricated. Questions of *epistemology* have thus loomed large in queer studies – most famously, in Eve Kosofsky Sedgwick's *Epistemology of the Closet*, which worked to show how 'many of the major nodes of thought and knowledge in twentieth century Western culture as a whole are structured – indeed, fractured – by a chronic, and endemic crisis of homo/heterosexual definition' (1991: 1). Questions of *ontology* have also been salient in queer studies, as can be seen in longstanding essentialist/constructionist debates over the 'causes' of sexual orientation, debates that have incorporated everything from Freudian theory to claims about gay genes (Hamer and Copeland 1994, Stein 1992).

Turning attention to *methodology* complicates these understandings of queer studies. How might a shift to method, 'a word [queer studies] rarely uses' (Plummer 2005: 366), open conceptual space for interpreting queer studies as a modality of inquiry potentially applied to any topic? How might the 'studies' of 'queer studies' thereby act less like a noun and more like a verb, a 'queer studying' even of things not self-evidently queer? How might such a reframing help contribute to, for instance, debates over the constitutive and intersectional relationships between queer studies,

    1   Acknowledgments: I thank Kath Browne and Catherine J. Nash for their support and helpful feedback. I thank, as always, my interlocutors in Indonesia and Second Life for their patience, insight, and good cheer. I also thank the Department of Anthropology at the University of California, Irvine for fostering a wonderful intellectual environment, as well as the many organizations that have supported my research (see Boellstorff 2005, 2007a, b, c, 2008 for lists of these organizations).

women's studies, critical race theory, and the critique of neoliberal capitalisms (e.g. Butler 1997, R.A. Ferguson 2004, Joseph 2002, Wiegman 2002)?

In service of exploring this potential reframing, in this chapter I set forth two emphatically heuristic theses regarding what a queer method might look like. My two theses are concerned with the relationship between theory and data as a *methodological* problem. This reflects what I term the 'data-theory-method triangle' – the way in which data, method, and theory cannot be understood or even defined in isolation from each other. What counts as 'data' depends upon the methods used to gather it and the theories used to explicate it; what counts as 'theory' depends on the data used to substantiate it and the methods used to support it; what counts as 'method' depends on the data it is to obtain and the theories it is to inform.

While the intentionally provisional character of these theses means they could be germane to a range of approaches, in this chapter I focus on the ethnographic methods I know best, particularly participant observation. However, the focus on ethnographic methods is part of a broader trend, since 'often, queer methodology means little more than literature theory rather belatedly coming to social science tools such as ethnography and reflexivity ... Queer theory does not seem to me to constitute any fundamental advance over recent ideas in qualitative inquiry – it borrows, refashions, and retells' (Plummer 2005: 369).

With Plummer's well-taken scepticism toward methodological novelty in mind, my goal in this chapter is to set forth two theses that could nonetheless be seen as 'queer' in a methodological sense. I do not make the normative claim that only methods seen to conform to these theses are 'queer', but see them as points of departure; working concepts in service of emergent paradigms. I could have easily illustrated these theses with reference to the work of other scholars, and have elsewhere discussed the breadth of outstanding queer ethnographic scholarship (Boellstorff 2006, 2007a, 2007b: Chapter 6). In this chapter, however, I discuss my own anthropological research in Indonesia and also in the virtual world Second Life, as best represented by my monographs *The Gay Archipelago*, *A Coincidence of Desires*, and *Coming of Age in Second Life* (Boellstorff 2005, 2007b, 2008). This offers me the opportunity to forge a comparative discussion, exploring the queer valence of my methods across two very different fieldsites that are themselves highly variegated and complex. In particular, by the end of this chapter I will ask how voicing the question of queer methodology in terms of technology – more precisely, 'techne', human action that alters the world through crafting – might suggest modalities of queer studying that will be of relevance to a broad range of questions and debates.

Thesis 1: Emic Theory

A queer method might work through emic theory. At the outset of modern ethnographic research, Bronisław Malinowski distinguished between *what people do* and *what people say they do* as culturally consequential, emphasizing that the former could not simply be extrapolated from the latter (see Kuper 1996: 14). Malinowski thus noted that 'the Ethnographer has in the field ... the duty before him of drawing up all the rules and regularities. ... But these things, though crystallized and set, are nowhere explicitly *formulated*' (Malinowski 1922: 11, emphasis in original). This insight had monumental methodological implications. If the goal is understanding culture as lived experience and sociopolitical dynamic, a researcher cannot rely solely upon methods predicated on elicitation like interviews, surveys and focus groups. Nor can researchers rely solely on methods predicated on analysing cultural products like texts, art or law. Malinowski and others did not construe these methods as useless by any stretch of the imagination, for people's words and opinions have consequences and cultural artefacts can reveal taken-for-granted conceptual frameworks. However, researchers cannot assume that such words and opinions are isomorphic with social action or cultural logic.

Theoretical justification for such a view was not difficult to find in the early twentieth century. Marxist and Freudian thought questioned any assumption of a transparently self-aware subject (albeit in distinct ways), a line of argument developed in a different but linked manner by critics of racism and colonialism (Du Bois 1903, Fanon 1952), by feminist thinkers (de Beauvoir 1949), as well as in other fields of inquiry. Within anthropology itself another key theoretical intervention was structuralism. This intervention spread throughout the social sciences and humanities before its displacement by poststructuralist theory – a displacement, however, that remains partial insofar as structuralist thought remains influential, if often only implicitly (it is now acknowledged as a productive paradigm almost exclusively in linguistics). In anthropology the greatest impact of structuralism came through Claude Lévi-Strauss (1963), who drew upon the canonical linguistic structuralism of de Saussure and Jakobson to craft a theory of culture that powerfully decentered the speaking self as the essence of the human (de Saussure 1959, Jakobson 1980).

I illustrate the crucial methodological implications of the classic structuralist paradigm to my students by showing them some aspect of English phonology – say, how the 'n' of 'inconceivable' appears as 'm' in 'impossible' because of phonological assimilation. 'P' is an unvoiced bilabial plosive (with the lips as place of articulation), and the nasal sound 'n' assimilates to this bilabial place of articulation in a word like 'impossible', becoming the nasal bilabial plosive 'm'. I emphasize to my students that they have 'known' this phonological rule all their lives, or if not native speakers of English, learned this rule without explicit instruction during later language acquisition. Yet despite this 'knowledge', English speakers cannot typically provide the rule to a researcher if asked via an elicitation method like a survey or interview. To discover this rule and others like it, the researcher would have to spend time in everyday interaction with speakers – that is, conduct participant observation. Furthermore, to even describe the rule – much less analyse it, critique it, or discuss its broader implications – the researcher would need to present it in the researcher's own theoretical language, using terms like 'bilabial' that are in all likelihood not part of the explicit conceptual repertoire of those being studied. All English speakers use bilabial plosives ('b', 'p', and 'm') in nearly every utterance, but save that small subset of speakers with training in linguistics, none of these speakers 'know' what a bilabial plosive is or that there are three of them in English: there is no everyday-language synonym for 'bilabial plosive'. This is significant. Too often contemporary queer studies scholarship (and much scholarship more generally, including ethnographic scholarship) presumes a kind of robustly self-aware, intentional subject – consonant with dominant notions of identity politics as well as neoliberal ideologies of the choosing, consumerist self – wherein the minimalist methodological goal of the researcher is to present the ostensibly authentic, unmediated voices of those studied.

By 'emic theory', I refer to a methodological procedure that steers clear of either the structuralist disinterest in self-understanding, or the intentionalist contention that the revoicing of an ostensibly transparent self-understanding is the endpoint of analysis. The terms 'emic' (insider's point of view) and 'etic' (outsider's point of view) were coined by the philosopher Kenneth Pike, who developed the terms from the linguistic distinction between phonemic and phonetic sounds, recalling my example from language above (Pike 1967). The terms fit so well with anthropological understandings of culture-internal versus observer perspectives that anthropologists from Ward Goodenough to Clifford Geertz drew upon them (Geertz 1983, Goodenough 1970). Many research methods distinguish between data, assumed to be emic, and theory, assumed to be etic. Researchers get their data by studying 'others' – even when researchers are, as is often the case, members in some fashion of the communities they study. They then theorize in a context of 'writing up' (Gupta and Ferguson 1997) presumed to be separate from the fieldsite.

One element of queer methodology might thus be to trouble this distinction via a notion of 'emic theory'. This notion of emic theory has longstanding analogues in the social sciences – for instance, in the notion of a 'grounded theory' that is based upon 'the discovery of theory from data' (Glaser and Strauss 1967: 1). Unlike the idea of 'grounded theory', however, which in its classic formulation assumed that 'an effective strategy is, at first, literally to ignore the literature of theory and fact on the area under study' (Glaser and Strauss 1967: 37), I mean the notion of emic theory to frame theory as emerging from both 'within' and 'without', recalling Malinowski's observation that:

> Good training in theory ... is not identical with being burdened with 'preconceived ideas'. If a man sets out on an expedition, determined to prove certain hypotheses ... needless to say his work will be worthless. But the more problems he brings with him into the field, the more he is in the habit of moulding his theories according to facts ... the better he is equipped for the work. Preconceived ideas are pernicious in any scientific work, but foreshadowed problems are the main endowment of a scientific thinker, and these problems are first revealed to the observer by his theoretical studies. (Malinowski 1922: 8–9)

'The Gay Archipelago' as Emic Theory

I can illustrate this notion of emic theory with reference to my research in Indonesia, though the phrase 'emic theory' is one I have never used prior to this chapter. In my Indonesia work, I developed the notion of the '*gay* archipelago' to refer to how Indonesians using the Indonesian terms *gay* or *lesbi* to describe or understand themselves in at least some contexts of their lives saw their communities as 'islands' in a national archipelago of *gay* and *lesbi* communities – and, at another spatial scale, saw Indonesia writ large as an 'island' in a global archipelago constituted through relations of similitude and difference, including sameness and difference between forms of *gay* male and *lesbi* female experience.[2] At the level of subjectivity, I have explored how *gay* and *lesbi* Indonesians often evince what I termed 'archipelagic subjectivities' wherein, for instance, a sense of being *gay* or *lesbi* and a life as part of a heterosexual couple are two 'islands' of selfhood (see Boellstorff 2005).

In other words, one form of archipelagic subjectivity can be seen in the large number of *gay* men who are married heterosexually to women at the same time (and *lesbi* women married heterosexually to men at the same time). These persons typically see their *gay* of *lesbi* subjectivity as additive, not supplanting what they often term their '*normal*' heterosexual subjectivities. Another form of archipelagic subjectivity can be seen in the ways that *lesbi* women usually see Indonesian *lesbi* subjectivity as one island in a global archipelago of 'lesbian' identities and communities (and *gay* men usually see Indonesian *gay* subjectivity as one island in a global archipelago of 'gay' identities and communities). In my research, it was clear that *lesbi* women and *gay* men always knew that *lesbi* and *gay* were not 'traditional' Indonesian categories of selfhood, but relatively novel terms in the Indonesian context, terms with analogues beyond Indonesia. There was always a sense among my *gay* and *lesbi* interlocutors that there were 'gay' and 'lesbian' people elsewhere in the world, to which they were related in a grid of similitude and difference. The theoretical framework of the *gay* archipelago is one key way by which I have worked to better understand these complex cultural logics of sexuality and selfhood, and relate them to dynamics of globalization and national belonging.

Now, where does this theoretical framework of the *gay* archipelago originate? In Indonesia, the nation-state has, since independence in 1945, promulgated what it terms the archipelago concept (*wawasan nusantara*) as a key metaphor for national unity and diversity. Additionally, one of the first and most influential *gay* organizations in Indonesia calls itself *GAYa Nusantara*, where *gaya* means

---

2   I use the phrase '*gay* archipelago' rather than '*gay* and *lesbi* archipelago' in my work to reflect how I have more data on *gay* men than *lesbi* women, but nevertheless do not wish to erase my fieldwork with *lesbi* Indonesians and thus speak of '*gay* and *lesbi* Indonesians' when discussing either fieldwork data gathered with both *gay* men and *lesbi* women, or when speaking of social formations that transcend a single gender (see Boellstorff 2005: 12).

style in Indonesian but with the first three letters capitalized invokes *gay* as well, and where *nusantara* is Indonesian for 'archipelago'. The most salient possible meaning for the phrase is 'archipelago style'. As I discuss extensively in *The Gay Archipelago*, archipelagic ways of thinking and acting crop up in the lives of *gay* men and *lesbi* women in all kinds of ways, from the notions of a '*gay* world', '*lesbi* world', and 'normal world' that have island-like distinctiveness, to a sense of discontinuous but powerful linkage between *gay* and *lesbi* communities across Indonesia. Yet my *gay* and *lesbi* Indonesian interlocutors did not walk around saying things like 'I feel like an archipelago today' or 'our communities are like an archipelago'. The notion of a *gay* archipelago was not as foreign to everyday understanding as 'bilabial plosive' is to an English speaker who nonetheless uses four bilabial plosives to say 'my plants should be pruned today'. Yet neither was it as present to consciousness as, say, the concept 'hungry', or 'sister'.

The notion of the '*gay* archipelago' is thus neither wholly emic nor wholly etic. It is a theoretical term for which I am clearly responsible, yet it also clearly arises from an engagement with *gay* and *lesbi* Indonesians as sources of theoretical insight, not just 'data' narrowly defined. This is what I mean by 'emic theory' as a methodological procedure, one that in my own work is intimately linked to participant observation. In particular, it means that I treat the data I gain from my Indonesian interlocutors as theorizations of social worlds, not just as documentation of those social worlds. It is also a procedure that can be used with methods other than participant observation: for instance, I employ it when exploring how the informal magazines produced by *gay* Indonesian men shape 'zones' of desire for national belonging (Boellstorff 2007b, chapter 1). Researchers who develop emic theories need not be queer or engaging in work they identify as queer studies scholarship, but 'emic theory' can nonetheless be seen as a queer method in that it is predicated on reworking and transforming, rather than transcending, the concepts with which it engages – as queer studies has consistently done, beginning with the term 'queer' itself.

'Techne' as Emic Theory

That emic theory as method is not limited to subjects more obviously 'queer' can be seen from my Second Life research. For instance, one key theoretical claim in *Coming of Age in Second Life* involves the crucial role of techne, roughly 'craft', in virtual-world sociality. During my ethnographic research in Second Life, I saw how residents emphasized notions of creativity and making things in a range of contexts, including not just virtual objects but their virtual embodiment as avatars, their online friendships and relationships, and so on. Yet the Greek term 'techne' never appeared explicitly during my participant observation work. I took this term from a range of thinkers, including Martin Heidegger and Bernard Stiegler, but particularly Michael Foucault, who discusses techne in volumes 2 and 3 of *The History of Sexuality* (1985, 1986). Foucault is arguably the quintessential figure of queer studies. Yet this is not a case of pasting academic theory onto a fieldsite context where that theory is utterly alien. As in the case of the 'gay archipelago' concept, the notion of 'techne' is an instance of emic theory.

I do not claim that in speaking of techne or the *gay* archipelago, I am presenting the unmediated, authentic voices of my interlocutors. But I also do not claim that the concepts originate solely at the table of the researcher-as-theorist, the same table that is the thing 'nearest to hand for the sedentary philosopher' (Banfield 2000: 66 cited in Ahmed 2006: 3). To insist that researchers can only discuss that which their interlocutors explicitly state would be like a linguist waiting for speakers of the English language to provide the term 'bilabial plosive'. Yet there is also understandable concern with methodologies where a theoretical paradigm is applied to a fieldsite context for no apparent reason other than the fact that the 'travelling theory' in question is au courant in the academy (Clifford 1989, Said 1983). Why use Derrida to discuss labour disputes in Paraguay? The answer I seek to offer with the notion of emic theory is that there is an alternative to responding either 'go ahead, it doesn't matter if Derrida is irrelevant to the lives of the persons in Paraguay of whom you speak' or 'you are limited to theories that the persons in Paraguay, of whom you speak, themselves employ'. A queer method might thus involve a commitment to developing theory as well as data from a vulnerable engagement with one's interlocutors in a fieldsite (Behar 1996), making it possible to speak not just of situated knowledge (Haraway 1988), but situated methodology.

Of course, the idea of situated methodology is in a sense self-evident to ethnographers, for whom a flexible, emergent toolkit is central to effective research. This is a key distinction between the paradigms of 'fieldwork' and 'experiment'. An experimental approach is based upon the idea of controlling an environment and modifying most often a single variable so as to gain knowledge that can predict some future state of affairs: the rock dropped will fall again with the same rate of acceleration. In the classic formulation of Clifford Geertz, ethnographic methods work instead through a form of 'clinical inference':

> Rather than beginning with a set of observations and attempting to subsume them under a governing law, such inference begins with a set of (presumptive) signifiers and attempts to place them within an intelligible frame... it is not, at least in the strict meaning of the term, predictive. The diagnostician doesn't predict measles; he decides that someone has them, or at the very most anticipates that someone is rather likely shortly to get them. (Geertz 1973: 26)

That is, it is a situated knowledge produced through a situated methodology. With the notions of emic theory and surfing binarisms (to which I turn below), I gesture toward ways in which queer studies might contribute to the ongoing development of situated methodologies to respond in a synergistic rather than confrontational manner to the continuing salience of science and technology in human affairs. We can argue for the *increasing* relevance of humanistic and social 'scientific' approaches not by trying to make them look like experimental science, but by demonstrating through our research the long-known yet oft-forgotten fact that not all science works by experiment and not all robust, valuable scholarly inquiry terms itself 'science'. To cite Geertz once again, 'There is no reason why the conceptual structure of a cultural interpretation should be any less formulable, and thus less susceptible to explicit canons of appraisal, than that of, say, a biological observation or a physical experiment' (Geertz 1973: 24).

Thesis 2: Surfing Binarisms

A Queer Method Might Surf Binarisms

My intellectual growth was shaped by a fascination with how binarisms might influence thought, an interest dating to my high school years in Nebraska and largely determining my decision to major in linguistics in college. I later found my fascination with binarisms shared by much queer studies scholarship, which is one reason why my second thesis on queer method concerns them. Sedgwick can serve again as exemplar, since she emphasized how the homosexual/heterosexual binarism has informed a 'metonymic chain of binaries' shaping twentieth-century Western culture (Sedgwick 1991: 73). Pivotal to Sedgwick's argument was the insight that with regard to these binarisms, from nature/culture to behaviour/ identity, at issue was 'not the correctness or prevalence of one or the other side... but, rather, the persistence of the deadlock itself' (Sedgwick 1991: 91). It is the construal of the social field in terms of binarisms in the first place that creates the 'self-evident' idea that insight is generated by deconstructing them, for instance by adding a third term or by consolidating a binarism into a single category or spectrum (as in the case of the Kinsey scale).

How, then, to advance an argument when it no longer seems possible to locate the moment of intellectual insight and critical intervention in the mere identification of a binarism, but when the moment of deconstructing binarisms seems equally shopworn? The key move can be methodological and can build upon the emic/etic discussion above. Since I referenced my youth in Nebraska, it seems fitting that I now reference California – where I have lived most of my adult life – to forge a notion of 'surfing' binarisms (with reference to waves as much as webpages). I base this notion on the observation that binarisms are ubiquitous in all languages; no human analytic can avoid them. For instance, when I noted above that merely identifying binarisms no longer constitutes a critical intervention, but deconstructing them seems equally shopworn, I advanced my argument via an implicit binarism of identification/deconstruction. The emic/etic distinction is, of course, a binarism as well.

The ubiquity – indeed, the necessity – of binarisms means that claims of transcending them typically turn out to be exercises in obfuscation. This insight was, for instance, central to Akhil Gupta's conclusion that postcolonial nationalism 'depends on the reversal, not the disavowal, of many binaries that are central to colonialism' (Gupta 1998: 169). Gupta's use of 'reversal' recalls how Foucault developed the notion of reverse discourse to identify how in the Western tradition, 'homosexuality began to speak on its own behalf, to demand that its legitimacy or "naturality" be acknowledged, often in the same vocabulary, using the same categories by which it was medically disqualified' (Foucault 1978: 101). This notion of reverse discourse, and also Foucault's conceptual preference for 'resistance' rather than 'liberation' (to invoke yet another binarism), all reflect a specific approach to binarisms that is central to the histories and current practices of queer studies.

Given this context, we might ask: is it necessarily the case that our only two options are to transcend binarisms – to impossibly levitate above the stormy seas, so to speak – or to remain submerged within them, like the water that fish, as the adage goes, never apprehend because it surrounds them as their condition of existence? Might there be a way to 'surf' binarisms? To surf is to move freely upon a wave that constrains choice (you cannot make it move in the opposite direction), but does not wholly determine one's destination. A wave in a sense does not exist, for it is but a temporary disturbance in the ocean, yet waves are consequential: they not only move surfers but can destroy buildings in tsunamis, or erode coastlines of the hardest rock. While any analogy is imperfect, what I mean to underscore with this notion of surfing binarisms is that a queer method could recognize the emic social efficacy and heuristic power of binarisms without thereby ontologizing them into ahistoric, omnipresent Prime Movers of the social.

Surfing the Sameness/Difference Binarism in Indonesia

I can illustrate the methodological implications of this notion of surfing binarisms with reference to my own research. I discovered early on during fieldwork in Indonesia that notions of sameness and difference were central to how *gay* and *lesbi* persons understood their relationship to the global, and to each other across lines of gender, class, religion and place. Never did I encounter *gay* or *lesbi* Indonesians who did not know that in some sense the terms '*gay*' and '*lesbi*' originated 'outside' Indonesia (as is the case for the term 'Indonesia' itself); yet never did I encounter *gay* or *lesbi* Indonesians who confused themselves with gay Australians, lesbian Japanese, and the like. They did not think of themselves in any simple sense as either 'the same' or 'different' from persons outside Indonesia terming themselves lesbian or gay, but this was not because the sameness/difference binarism had been surpassed or dissolved. Sameness and difference were constantly evoked as lived elements of everyday experience, from a *gay* man's desire for another man to a sense of difference a *lesbi* woman might feel from schoolmates looking forward to marrying a future husband. The binarism persisted, but not as something ontologized into an unchanging first principle.

Thus it was that one of the greatest moments of insight during my research occurred when I realized that the key question was not 'how are *gay* and *lesbi* Indonesians similar to and different from gay and lesbian Westerners?' That question remained submerged, so to speak, within the binarism of sameness/difference. Yet ignoring rubrics of sameness and difference altogether was impossible, not least because of my interest in homosexuality, a desire understood in a powerful sense as a 'desire for the same' (*suka sama*), distinguished as such from the desire for difference, known as heterosexuality (*heterosexualitas*, but in everyday Indonesian parlance often simply the telling loanword *normal*). Since the sameness/difference binarism was a lived element of everyday experience, an ethnographic approach predicated on participant observation was necessary to understanding it. As a result, the key question needed to be 'how is the binarism of sameness/difference itself caught up in globalizing processes?' This freed me to 'surf' the binarism and thus to treat sameness/difference as an ethnographic object. Posing the question in a methodological register also allowed me to place culturally specific understandings of the sameness/difference binarism among *lesbi* and *gay* Indonesians in conversation with culturally specific understandings of the sameness/difference binarism among anthropologists, about whom I had noted that 'difference is seen to be our contribution to social theory. It is expected … Similitude, however, awakens disturbing contradictions … there is a sense that contamination has occurred and authenticity compromised' (Boellstorff 2005: 93).

This reframed relation to the sameness/difference binarism transformed my anthropological understanding of participant observation. I was openly gay throughout my research, yet I was also obviously not Indonesian. In anthropology, an earlier near-consensus that anthropologists could only be objective if they were not members of the communities they studied gave way to critiques from many quarters, not least 'native' anthropologists (cf. Abu-Lughod 1991), leading to a broadly shared (if not unanimous) conclusion that the quality of ethnographic work varies independently from the ways in which the researcher is seen (by herself or himself, and by others) to be a member of the communities studied. Researchers 'from' the communities studied can produce excellent or substandard ethnographic research, as is the case for researchers 'not from' the communities studied, and indeed with reference to all the complex shadings within that binarism of belonging/not belonging.

In my own research, a new understanding of the belonging/not belonging binarism (made possible by my reconceptualization of the sameness/difference binarism) was crucial to my methodological approach. When *gay* men in Java, Bali, or elsewhere would sometimes say that I was 'the same' as them, I treated this not as an existential assertion to be refuted (say, by noting that I was white, or American, as if they were not already aware of such things) or accepted (say, by concluding that I could take my own feelings, thoughts, and actions as ethnographic data, since we were 'the same'). Instead, this became a moment to ask my Indonesian interlocutors 'in what way am I the same?' Such a question led to more than one impromptu debate in a park late some Saturday night, producing invaluable insights regarding how *gay* Indonesians understood homosexual desire, national belonging, and transnational connection. *Lesbi* women for the most part did not spend time in parks, but I was able to socialize with them in the places where they found community: shopping malls and clubs, but above all within each other's homes or rented rooms. In such spaces we would talk about differences and similarities regarding women's same-gender desires in Indonesia versus outside Indonesia, and also about differences and similarities between *lesbi* women and *gay* men. This topic would sometimes come up because of my own presence as a man in an otherwise woman-only space, but it was not uncommon for *lesbi* women to socialize with *gay* men – for instance, in a salon after working hours, or at the home of a friend, and these co-gendered spaces stimulated reflection on the genderings of Indonesian homosexualities.

One unforgettable illustration of how *gay* and *lesbi* Indonesians surf the sameness/difference binarism with regard to the belonging/not belonging divide occurred early in my fieldwork, when in the mid-1990s I travelled to a Southeast Asian regional conference on HIV/AIDS with several *gay* men who were members of activist organizations. There were several simultaneous sessions and we were rushing around to take in as much as we could. A meeting was scheduled one afternoon about networking for gay organizations in Southeast Asia. One of the Indonesian activists came up to me about thirty minutes before this meeting was to start and said: 'the rest of us need to be at other meetings. Could you please attend this meeting to represent Indonesia?'

I was taken aback. At both a theoretical and a political level (though it is probably more accurate to say a 'politically correct' level), the idea of having a white American speak for Indonesians was abhorrent, a reinscription of colonial discourse in the context of new regimes of governmentality within domains of health and sexuality. But my Indonesian colleague had no time for such qualms; he was off to his meeting, leaving me holding a pad of paper with the networking meeting about to start down the hall. Then the pieces fell into place. I was not being asked to speak 'for' *gay* Indonesians but to speak 'about' them. The Indonesian *gay* activists were perfectly aware of my non-Indonesian status, but felt my knowledge about the Indonesian situation and ability to speak English meant I could function effectively in this context. I was not being asked to lead a *gay* Indonesian organization, or speak some timeless truth about homosexuality in the archipelago; I was being asked to sit in on a single meeting and report back to the *gay* Indonesians so they could further their work. My Indonesian interlocutors had a better grasp than I on what the methodology of 'participant observation' entailed, theoretically and politically.

Surfing the Virtual/Actual Binarism in Second Life

The concept of 'surfing binarisms' that I developed in the context of my Indonesia fieldwork turned out to be unexpectedly crucial to my fieldwork in Second Life. In that seemingly radically different fieldsite I also encountered a prevalent binarism, typically glossed by terms like 'real life' (often abbreviated 'rl' or 'irl' for 'in real life') versus 'Second Life' (often abbreviated 'sl' or 'inworld'). A few previously unpublished excerpts from my Second Life fieldnotes will illustrate this binarism, often phrased in terms of 'offline' versus 'online'. On 29 April 2006, I was in Second Life at an event with about 30 persons present in avatar form. The location was a café set in a beautiful village square, and we were all listening to Trudy, a friend of mine in Second Life, make an insightful presentation about differing ways to make money in Second Life.[3] After she finished, I turned to her and said:

> Tom: Your presentation on the different kinds of jobs in Second Life is simply superb
> Trudy: hehe well
> Tom: The best I've seen, with all the pros and cons and all that [...]
> Tom: Well, I will let you keep greeting [the other persons present in avatar form], sorry to bother you, but I'll catch you soon.
> Trudy: Sure, lol [laugh out loud]
> Trudy: And I'll have to forbid you to flatter me in public ;) ['winking' emoticon]
> Trudy: I'm blushing irl, I'm glad it doesn't show!!

In this exchange, Trudy responds to my compliment by joking she will have to 'forbid me to flatter her in public', but the 'public' in question is a virtual public, a public in Second Life itself. She then states 'I'm blushing irl, I'm glad it doesn't show!!' The reason Trudy's blushing 'doesn't show' is because it is a physical-world blush that 'shows' only offline. As in the Indonesian case, we see invocations of a binarism, in this case between online and offline. Trudy moves back and forth across the binarisms – surfs it, in fact – but these crossings of the binarism do not dissolve it; the binarism itself is never in doubt. Trudy and I are clearly having a discussion online about a presentation in Second Life about jobs in Second Life, but her blushing is clearly taking place offline. Joking surfings of the online/offline binarism also appear in the following fieldwork excerpt, which took place on 10 January 2006. I was playing the game Tringo at a well-known club in Second Life with several other people, including Marlen, Sue, and Bob, who was the host for that evening. Bob was getting the next game prepared when Marlen said:

> Marlen: One more for me and then back to rl for a while.
> Bob shouts: Everyone ready [to play a new game of Tringo]?
> Marlen: Ready.
> Sue: This isn't rl? hmmm
> Marlen: Yeah, you're right. sl is part of rl.

Here, Marlen and Sue joke about the relationship between online and offline. Marlen first demarcates Second Life and 'real life' from each other, speaking of going 'back to rl', but following Sue's question revises his assessment, stating that 'sl is part of rl' – even while he is clearly aware that once offline, he will not be

---

3   As in all my writings, screen names and other details have been altered to preserve the anonymity of Second Life residents.

able to play Tringo with Sue, Bob, and myself. Banter of this kind, pleasurably surfing the online/offline binarism, was quite common during my fieldwork. But those words and actions of Second Life residents that surfed the online/offline binarism did not deconstruct the binarism; online sociality remained distinct and in many cases the source of deep meaning, such that residents would go to great lengths to access their online friends and intimates. For instance, on 2 December 2005, I had the following exchange with Becca, a Second Life acquaintance:

> Tom: In rl I'm away from home for a week, at a conference, but sneaking away for a bit to log in from my hotel room lol
> Becca: I know how that is. The family is going on a cruise for Christmas.
> Becca: I am definitely going to get internet access on the ship. I want to be with my sl family on Christmas.
> Becca: We will be at sea Christmas day, everyone pretty much does their own thing.
> I just put [the Second Life program] on my laptop. It runs pretty good. But my friend said satellite access is slower than dialup. Guess I will have to see how it works when I get there.

Twenty-three days later, I was playing a quick game of Tringo with some friends when Becca 'instant messaged' ('IM-ed') me from another part of Second Life:

> IM: Becca: Hi Tom, Merry Christmas.
> IM: Becca: I just came on for a few. I am using satellite access from the cruise ship.
> IM: Becca: I was hoping to see [two members of my Second Life family]. But they're not on[line].
> IM: Becca: I am having bad withdrawal
> IM: Becca: This is worse than quitting smoking.

Here, Becca was 'surfing' the online/offline binarism while literally aboard a ship on the ocean. She felt that she had family on both sides of the binarism, and that her online family in Second Life was real to her, a source of support and meaning significant enough that separation from them could be understood as withdrawal (drawing upon a commonly encountered and contested notion of online 'addiction'). But while notions of family existed on both sides of the online/offline binarism, this did not result in 'blurring' the line between the two categories; Becca did not explore the cruise ship hoping to find members of her Second Life family there (nor did she seek members of her physical-world family within Second Life). Becca and others like her were quite aware of the distinction between their offline and online families. Both might include persons who were biologically related, as well as persons anthropologists sometimes term 'fictive kin'. However, even when (in some cases) some individuals might be part of both one's offline family and online family, the notions of 'online family' and 'offline family' did not blur or stand in for each other. Becca's social interactions with her family on the cruise ship did not substitute for social interactions with her online family; they did not lessen the sense of longing she felt for the family she had helped create within Second Life.

After only a few months of fieldwork in Second Life, it was clear to me that the binarism of online/offline was as important to Second Life socialities as the sameness/difference binarism was to *gay* and *lesbi* Indonesian socialities. It was also clear that as in the Indonesian case, the punchline had to be one of 'surfing', rather than dissolution or deconstruction, if my goal was to craft a framework that was in any substantial way an 'emic theory' reflecting the lived experience of my interlocutors. I eventually settled on the terms 'virtual' versus 'actual' as an analytical framework, noting the risk that:

> I will be seen to be creating or reifying a rigid binarism. I set them forth in an ethnographic sense, not an ontological one. The binarism of virtual/actual is an experientially salient aspect of online culture … Like all binarisms, it persists in spite of attempts to deconstruct it by adding a third term or conflating the two into one. (Boellstorff 2008: 19)

In other words, I soon learned that while some scholars claimed that the virtual and actual were being blurred, such claims of conflation were incorrect. The binarism was not being dissolved; it was being surfed. People who participated in Second Life clearly knew if they were online or offline at any particular time. Cultural assumptions forged in the actual-world lives of Second Life residents influenced their virtual-world lives (everything from gravity to the idea that you face someone with whom you are talking). In the other direction, experiences in Second Life could influence actual-world life (say, learning that one enjoyed designing clothing, or had a knack for organizing music events, or because one became good friends with someone living 3,000 miles away). But these indexicalities, influences, and references had cultural force precisely because they were emically understood to move back and forth across the virtual/actual binarism. Characterizing this movement in terms of 'blurring' is thus misleading, because it is through the perduring presence of the binarism that the 'movement' can have cultural consequences.

The virtual/actual binarism I encountered during fieldwork in Second Life was just as real as the sameness/difference binarism I encountered during fieldwork in Indonesia. It was not a theoretical nicety I could sweep aside in the face of the complexities of everyday experience, because it played a powerful role in shaping that experience. Yet the binarisms were not generative principles: they were in both cases ontologically subsequent to the cultural context. This is in line with the poststructuralist critiques that have played such an important role in queer theory, but as in the case of my Indonesia research, the realization that one must surf binarisms had pivotal *methodological* implications. With regard to my research in Second Life, the insight that the virtual/actual binarism was experientially real allowed me to see that one legitimate strategy for research in virtual worlds is to conduct that research wholly 'within' the virtual world in question. A methodologically fatal implication of any attempt to dissolve the virtual/actual binarism is to contend that no method for studying a virtual world is valid unless it involves meeting one's interlocutors in the actual world as well. What this methodological presumption obscures is that residents in a virtual world typically meet only a handful, if any, fellow virtual-world residents in the actual world (where they are, after all, typically scattered around the globe). As a result, for certain kinds of research, including my research on cultural logics as they formed and were lived within Second Life, it was imperative to treat Second Life 'in its own terms' and not assume, for instance, that an interview with a Second Life resident inside Second Life was only valid if coupled with an interview of that selfsame resident in the actual world. Yet on the other hand, it proved productive to remain attuned as a researcher for ways in which the actual world showed up *inside the virtual world itself*, and examine how such 'surfings' of the virtual and actual shaped Second Life culture.

Conclusion: Queer Techne

In this chapter, I have worked to set out two theses regarding queer method. By showing how these theses have shaped my research practice in two highly divergent fieldsites – only one of which is immediately legible as 'queer' – I hope to highlight the possibility of queer studying, of queer methods not bound to ethnographic objects deemed 'queer' at the outset. I do not wish to reduce method to 'technique' in the narrow sense of the term – that is, to research practices that disavow their theoretical investments. But regardless of this wish it is clear that, as noted in the introduction to this chapter, construing knowledge as the endpoint of queer studies limits conceptualizations of both queer method and the scope of that method.

In this regard, it bears noting that 'virtual/actual' was not the only salient binarism I encountered during my Second Life research. I discussed earlier how the notion of techne became a central element of the emic theory I developed to better understand Second Life. However, the theorization I eventually set forth framed techne as one term within a binarism of techne/episteme. This is, very roughly, a distinction between craft and knowledge.[4] The distinction is germane because queer studies is by definition a knowledge project – the outcome of 'study' is knowledge, episteme.

---

4 Some scholars define techne as a form of practical knowledge (e.g. Haney 1999), a definition compatible with my understanding of techne as craft, since craft presupposes this kind of knowledge.

What, however, might queer studies look like if it sought to produce not episteme, but techne?[5] How might queer studying, as a queer craft of engagement, shift debates over method in queer studies and beyond? How might it reconfigure the political and activist valences of queer studies, transposing them in new ways into the immanent research practices of queer studies itself? Plummer honed in on this issue when noting how 'what seems to be at stake, then, in any queering of qualitative research is not so much a methodological style as a political and substantive concern with gender, heteronormativity, and sexualities' (Plummer 2005: 369).

Plummer's observation here is correct, but a statement of practice to date – the future might differ. My goal in this chapter has therefore been to suggest how 'methodological style' *could* be not only 'at stake', but pivotal to the queering of research. Such interest in method need not depoliticize queer studies: indeed, I would assert it has the opposite effect and can place queer studies centrally into vital debates over scientific knowledge founded in situated methodologies. I thus intend my theses on emic theory and surfing binarisms to disrupt the exteriorization of the queerly political in conceptualizations of queer studies research, and gesture toward a reframing of intersectionality in terms of method as well as object of queer study.

---

5   I ask this question of anthropology as well (Boellstorff 2008: 59).

Chapter 14

Queer Quantification or Queer(y)ing Quantification: Creating Lesbian, Gay, Bisexual or Heterosexual Citizens through Governmental Social Research[1]

Kath Browne

Introduction

In the United States context sexual demographics have offered some measure of lesbian, gay and bisexual (LGB) populations and/or heterosexual people (Black et al. 2000, Gates and Ost 2004). Yet there can be no doubt that there has been an emphasis on qualitative data in studies of sexual lives – particularly the deconstruction of sexual subject positions within queer studies (Gamson 2003, Green 2002, Seidman 1995, Valocchi 2005), along with the assumptions of individualised deviancy that have historically pervaded scientific studies of sexualities (Gamson 2003, Reynolds 2001). There is a shortage of critical engagements with quantitative methods and methodologies by queer and sexualities researchers. Quantitative research poses interesting challenges to queer anti-normative and deconstructive tendencies, where the absence/questioning of sexual subject positions are key enquiries. This chapter examines the messy processes of creating a 'sexuality question' for governmental social research in England and Wales.

The chapter begins by addressing governmentality and the 'counting' of ethnic identities arguing that this is an act that is productive of, and legitimates, certain identities and lives. It then moves on to briefly consider the limitations of anti-normative queer theorisations and the possibilities of a more messy conception of 'queer' that refuses to be placed within particular definitional categories. The chapter then examines the complexities of creating a quantitative sexual identity question exploring the processes of creating and trialling of a sexual identity question in England and Wales. It reconsiders how queer can/cannot use quantitative methods, recognising that:

1   I would like to thank Catherine J. Nash, Michael Brown and Niels Spierings for their insightful comments on this chapter.

even the most sophisticated statistical analyses are shot through with interpretive junctures (even if their practitioners refuse to admit that). Conversely, all queer scholarship makes positivist gestures (even if its practitioners refuse to admit that).[2]

Including sexual identity/identities questions in government social research tools could be seen as 'queer' because it challenges heterosexual assumptions that currently pervade. Yet, queer's questioning of the sexual subject positions contests this, and can be located within the long recognised frictions between identity politics and deconstruction of marginalised subject positions (see for example Harstock 1996, Gamson 1995, 2003). The final section of this chapter will argue for the disruptive potentials of 'lesbian, gay, bisexual or heterosexual' categories in social government research, holding in tension deconstruction and identity politics.

Counting Populations:
'Knowledge does rather than simply is' (Sedgwick 2003: 124)

There can be little doubt that statistics not only measure and calculate, but also create, control and inform (Crampton and Elden 2006, Legg 2006). As Crampton and Elden contend:

> Diverse peoples too are understood as a population, a way of conceiving of bodies in plural, that can be conceptualised as a group with norms, either statistical or moral (Crampton and Elden 2006: 681).

Census data, as one of the key modes in which governments measure and 'know' their populations, are often treated as 'basic facts, as raw material for socio-economic analyses and for public policies' (Nobles 2002: 43). Although the Census and other government forms of knowledge are partial (Reynolds 2001), they powerfully create 'truths' often by presuming objectivity and calculation as a neutral act. State depictions can also be read as forms of governmentalities that are not imposed but operate through processes of biopower (M. Brown 2000, Brown and Knopp 2006, Foucault 1991, Legg 2005). Considering the productive potentials of counting and measuring using conceptualisations of governmentality, Brown and Knopp (2006: 224) note:

> when we see ourselves through state knowledges, this 'biopower' impels us to wilfully and unwittingly conform to particular ways of being. ... an obvious means by which individuals see – and govern – themselves ... [is] the Census.

---

2   Michael Brown, personal communication.

Not only do individuals see themselves in the representations that the Census provides, but as categories alter, this also alters self-perceptions (Krieger 2000). Such productive impulses are mutual and informed by dominant popular consciousness and government agendas. These categories can be used, deployed and discarded by those they supposed name depending on whether their terms are useful or not.

State quantitative data collection is more than a question of how many people live where (Prewitt 2003). As counting is always a qualitative decision of what and how to count, the creation and legitimisation of particular groups is a political as well as productive decision. Thus, Census gathering is 'as much a political act as an enumerative one' (Nobels 2000: 1). These politicised and powerful governmental research tools create identity categories that are then measured and measurable:

> the Census does much more than simply reflect social reality, rather it plays a
> key role in the construction of that reality. In no sector is this more importantly
> the case than the ways in which the Census is used to divide national populations
> into separate identity categories: racial, linguistic, or religious (Kertzer and Arel
> 2002: 2).

Consequently as Crampton and Elden (2006: 683) argue, the politics of space, as well as the production and management of resources, has been 'framed in terms of the calculable', what Legg (2005) calls the 'politics of numbers'. This type of framing needs critical interrogation. Discussions of race and ethnicity in the Census offer opportunities for critically considering the effects and possibilities of quantitative research design that not only identifies but (re)creates ethnic groupings (Ballard 1997, Bulmer 1986, Huag 2001, Kertzer and Arel 2002, Nobles 2000, McKenny and Bennett 1994, Sillitoe and White 1992). Such counting is fraught with controversy and this offers some beginnings for considering a sexualities question.[3]

Rather than perceiving racial categories on the Census as 'transparent and politically neutral', racial boundaries are set and legitimate particular identities through the processes of Census creation and collection (Gunaratnam 2003, Kertzer and Arel 2002, Kreiger 2000, Nagel 1994, Nobles 2000, 2002, McKenny and Bennett 1994, Prewitt 2005). Such creations of knowledge do particular things, 'bringing into being the racial reality that Census officials presume is already there, waiting to be counted' (Kertzer and Arel 2002: xi). Racial categorisations do not simply create racial identifications, but inform political debates regarding these

---

3   A more in depth discussion of race and ethnicity in the Census is beyond the scope of this chapter, yet it is important to recognise tendencies both to racialise sexuality categories and to sexualise ethnicity categories, often within specific concepts of white/non-white and Anglo-American concepts of gay, lesbian and LGBT (see Luibhéid and Cantú 2005, Morgan and Wieringa 2005). It should also be noted that queer theorists have worked to question these boundaries, borders and categorisations (see for example Ahmed 2004, Puar 2007).

identities (Kreiger 2000, Kretzer and Arel 2002, Nobles 2000).[4] Nobles (2000: 163) reasons that these are mutually (in)formative, 'political contestation over racial categorisation in Censuses persist – not in spite of larger racial politics but precisely because of them'.

The Census and statistics gathering are part of modernising and colonialising of nation states and 'counts of bodies' are crucial to modern state power/ knowledge relationships (M. Brown 2000, Crampton and Elden 2006, Krieger 2000, Kertzer and Arel 2002, Legg 2006). Where knowledge is productive of specific forms of power – social government research 'knows' the population and plans for them (see Purdam et al. 2008, Foucault 1991, Kertzer and Arel 2002). As tools for the control of populations, through making them understandable and governable (M. Brown 2000), these forms of research shape public discourses and policies rather than just reflecting them (Nobles 2000, 2002). The Census and government social research tools can thus be seen as 'the most visible, and arguably the most politically important means by which states depict collective identities' (Nobles 2002: 3).

Census data and government collection tools create rather than simply record, calculate or measure, thus moulding collective identities such that social power relations can be created and played out through the production of government data. Where identity groupings and collectives are not simply 'waiting to be counted', what government collection tools do is profound. In this conceptualisation the scientific work of quantitative research is read as social (Hegarty 2003) with numbers, charts and formulas understood as more than 'strategies of communication' (Porter 1995). The formulation of meaningful numbers is thus infused with Leggs's (2005) 'politics of numbers'. The critical engagements with ethnicity categories on the Census often explores how post-Census statistics create lives, discourses and allocate resources (Nobles 2000, Kertzer and Arel 2002). The creation of identity questions and the messiness and inconsistencies that arise from such a process can be presumed to exist solely in the realm of demographers and statisticians who focus on accuracy (Nobles 2002). Yet the pursuit of 'accuracy' is itself a social phenomenon. This chapter extends the call for more work to explore 'the workings of state agencies of various kinds – from legislators to Census takers' (Nobles 2000: 6) to include the creation of (state) questions, particularly as calculation has 'practical political effects' (Crampton and Elden 2006: 684).

Queer Quantification?

It has long been recognised that homosexual/heterosexual categories and binaries are historically and culturally specific, such that names, categories and collective identities are social and cultural productions (Weeks 1985, 2007). Such

---

4 Including allowing access to benefits and services when certain groupings are validated – this will be addressed below.

identities, embodiments, dichotomies and dualisms have been a rich area for queer theorists to deconstruct, render fluid, performative and contingent (Corber and Valocchi 2003, Gamson 2003, Puar 2007). Currently, it can be argued that queer theories are focused on anti-normativities and deconstructive tendencies (see Browne 2006, G. Brown, Browne and Lim 2007, Gamson 2003, Puar 2007, Stychin 2006). This has resulted in a questioning of lesbian and gay subject positions and the existence, or even possibilities, of such sexual subjectivities (Gamson 2003, Green 2007, Oswin 2008).

Queer can be usefully deployed to interrogate gay and lesbian lives, identities politics and practices as well as lesbian and gay research that invisiblises particular sexual/gendered lives (Brown 2000, Browne 2008). Valocchi (2005: 751) believes that queer insights are relevant to empirical work and that there is an imperative 'to make these insights amenable to empirical analysis'. Whilst textual and discourse analysis forms the majority of this area of inquiry, he contends that ethnography can examine 'incoherencies and ambivalences' central to queer understandings (2005: 763). 'Queer' social science research has focused on qualitative enquiries. Participant observation, interviews and qualitative questionnaires undertaken have drawn on and developed queer theorisations of the fluid construction of bodies and spaces (see for example G. Brown 2004, Browne 2004, 2007, Johnston 2005). This allows for the exploration of difference, contestation of rigid categories as well as addressing moments of disturbance, breaks and unfixity. In this way such research techniques enable the possibilities of queer readings to a larger extent than has been the case in certain strands of applied social research, which rely on categories, tick boxes and questionnaires.

Arguments regarding the power-laden creation of racial categories through the Census and quantitative data can open up queer investigations of quantitative social science methodologies (Browne 2008). This enables an examination of the construction of such data through the questions posed, how these are conceived, as well as the interpretations, identities and meanings that they are given after the data has been collected. The possibilities of queer interrogations of the formation of subject positions unfold questions of not only who is being counted, when and how, but also, in parallel with discussions above, reiterate how calculation can produce that which it measures. More than this, 'queer' can be used to interrogate gay and lesbian quantitative research (see Brown and Knopp 2006). Quantitative gay and lesbian research can produce celebratory and uncontested discourses such as 'the pink pound', the 'educated gay' and other classed, racialised and gendered assertions that are then spatialised into particular areas (Badgett 2003). As attentions turn to sexual lives that were once considered 'deviant' and are now privileged through state recognition – alongside class, gender, ethnicity – queer theorisations have explored forms of (homo-)normalisations that privilege certain lesbian and gay normativities (Duggan 2002). To deconstruct methods and methodology that count and create state sanctioned subjectivities could be read as a 'queer' pursuit, particularly when the objects in question are based on sexualities and, potentially, normalisations within sexual identity categories (Stychin 2006, Valocchi 2005).

A queer deconstruction of quantitative research tools could (and some would argue should) conclude in using queer tools to deconstruct normative categorisation impulses. However, this would be to exclude the excess to these critical insights, particularly the possibilities which a government sexualities question appears to offer. The anti-normativity and deconstructive approaches may for instance fail to address the potentials of (re)creating forms of normativities from that which was once deviant (see also Puar 2007). The reconstruction of the once heteronormative and invisibilising state research methods needs a nuanced consideration that enables queer to be fluid, mutable and locally contingent, and is working through normativities to unsettle and stabilise rather than solely pursuing the 'anti-normative' other. Thus, this chapter, following Sedgwick's (2003), challenges the presumed imperative to engage in critical critique and explores the possibilities of governmental data. It will argue for a consideration of the potentials of inclusion beyond discussions of 'new normativities' contending that whilst all will not gain, altering the status of those who were once (and continue in particular spatial and temporal contexts to be) deviant should not be dismissed. These complexities also build on Bell and Binnie's (2000) assertions that gay consumption cannot simply be viewed in terms of an 'unprincipled sell out'. In this way the chapter queers methodologies beyond some of the contemporary deployments of queer[5] and yet questions the common sense understandings of 'sexual identity' as it is deployed in the sexual identities project.

The Sexual Identities Project

In 2006 the United Kingdom Office for National Statistics (ONS) released a rationale for not recommending a sexuality question[6] for the 2011 Census. The ONS concluded that:

---

5   Although 'queer' is read here in part as the mode of inquiry and politics that contests normalisations (Browne 2006, Halberstam 2005), this chapter has an ambiguous relationship with this project and how it is manifested through texts, reviewing systems and the policing of the boundaries of queer in constricted and fixed ways. Seidman (1997: xi) argues that 'queering does not mean improving upon or substituting one set of foundational assumptions and narratives for another, but leaving permanently open and contestable the assumptions and narratives that guide social research'. An ambiguous relationship with queer deconstructive moves and the fluidities, messiness and deregulation that this implies will be clear throughout the remainder of the chapter.

6   In not addressing the scope of LGBT identities, the sexual identity project has caused some angst around trans identities. However, as trans is considered as an aspect of gender identities and dealt with under separate legislation as well as conceptually differentiated from sexualities, this project does not include it. At the time of writing, a project to identify a 'transgender' question was being developed.

> ONS has significant concerns surrounding the issues of privacy, acceptability, accuracy, conceptual definitions and the effect that such a question could have on the overall response to the Census. ... Despite the above concerns, the increasing requirement for the information is clear and must be addressed by the ONS and others. A programme of work will be established to meet this need (ONS 2006).

Recognising the importance of information, but also the incompatibility between privacy, acceptability, accuracy, definitions and the 'truth' objects that the Census presents,[7] the ONS commissioned a sexual identity project. This project was understood as unique in testing a sexual identity question that will be administered by government (Taylor 2008). The sexual identity project aims to develop, test and evaluate a question on sexual orientation to be used in government social surveys (Wilmot 2007, Taylor 2008a, b) adding to 'larger family of state categorising practices' that includes the Census (Nobles 2000: 5). Because the Office for National Statistics argued against the inclusion of a sexuality question on the 2011 Census, the sexual identity project created a question for other governmental surveys including the Integrated Household Survey, General Lifestyle Survey. Interestingly some of the 'mistakes' made on the ethnicity question in the 1991 Census, including its rushed inclusion and the lack of clarity around the concept being measured (for example those reported in Ballard 1997, McKenney and Claudette 1994) were key considerations for the ONS in designing a sexual identity question which had clear parallels in relation to subjective identifications.

Since its instigation, this project has released a number of publications. These have explored international and British based studies, undertaken investigations of the contemporary legislative context as well as reporting findings from question trials (Betts 2008, Betts, Wilmot and Taylor 2008, Hand and Betts 2008, Malagolda and Traynor 2008, Taylor 2008a, b, Taylor and Ralph 2008, Wilmot 2007, see also http://www.ons.gov.uk/about-statistics/measuring-equality/sexual-identity-project/index.html). The sexual identity project has a clear rationale and methodology for creating a sexual identity question and uses both a user group and an expert group to inform these

---

7 One of the key things to note is that the Census requires by law people to fill it out, but it does not require truth or accuracy from respondents. This has numerous possibilities for disruption, as checking the 'truth' of each response would not be possible. There is little that can be done beyond ensuring that questions are answered 'accurately' (as defined by those designing the question) during trials and omitting categories after the research has been undertaken, such as 'Jedi' despite the 390,000 people who identified their religion as such in the 2001 Census. This indicates the collective disruptive possibilities that could be used and points to the fallibility of Census data, reliant as it is on those who complete it.

discussions.[8] The methodology includes qualitative (focus group and one to one cognitive interviews) and quantitative trials (see Wilmot 2007 for a full breakdown). These are designed to form 'robust' categories. Robust in this context pertains to the understanding that people have of a sexual identity question, such that they can answer it 'accurately' (Betts, Wilmot and Taylor 2008). Yet the uncertainty and careful way in which the sexual identity project is engaged with creating a sexualities question, indicates a messiness that will not be apparent when the sexuality question is used on government surveys. Using the data from this project, this chapter will now reflect on the creations of lesbian, gay bisexual and heterosexual subject positions as these become measurable by exploring the processes of establishing the 'thing' to be measured and the search for 'accuracy'.

What Exactly are we Measuring?

Wilmot's (2007) ONS report states: 'In order to facilitate statistical analysis, the goal of any quantitative survey of people is to classify and categorise'. Supporting Nobles' (2000) view that 'rather than viewing social links as complex and social groupings as situational, the view promoted by the Census is one in which populations are divided into neat categories' (Nobles 2000: 6). Implicit from the outset of the sexual identity project, and indeed with the ONS's original statement, is an understanding that there is 'something' that can be measured, counted and quantified (which stands in contrast to queer deconstructions of such a 'thing', Gamson 2003). Nobles (2000: 1) asks: 'to count race is to presume there is "something" there to be counted, but what exactly is it?' In the UK, equality legislation has 'sexual orientation' as one of the seven strands of equality. The 'thing' to be counted then is 'sexual orientation'. This assumption becomes problematic in view of queer theorists' challenging of the necessary links between desire, bodies, identities, primary emotional attachments and other taken for granted normalisations (Butler 1990a, Corber and Valocchi 2003, Jagose 1996b). Similarly, in the sexual identity project sexual orientation was considered to be a dubious measurement. 'Orientation' towards a, or a set of, particular object/s and the psychological inferences, as well as issues of fantasy, lifestyles and multiple areas of engagement within rendered this concept problematic for quantification purposes (Betts 2008, Wilmot 2007). Sexual identity was considered to be a more measureable construct, the reasoning and processes through which this

---

8   In 2006 I was asked to join an 'expert committee' which was paralleled by a user group. It should be noted that my feelings of ambivalence and uncertainty regarding the development of a sexual identity question come from my involvement in the messy, complex and fluid process of creating such a question and my experiences of sitting on a committee that so obviously contests heteronormativity in diverse and incoherent ways.

was established, and a question stem created, offer insights into how sexual lives become measurable.

In the sexual identity project the use of 'user groups' and 'expert groups', as well as the focus groups, influenced the decisions and politics that underpin the drive for a sexuality question.[9] In the expert and user discussions of the 'thing' to be measured key areas of complexity were discussed, including: the plethora of identity categories used, the convoluted and sometimes absent links between sexual identity, desire and behaviour, the place of those who are celibate in categorisations and the place of 'other' as an option in tick box sexual identity questions. The political nature of sexual identities and the 'simple' ethnicity question that had 16 categories were also noted. Moreover the project acknowledged the temporality of a sexual identity question that would not provide 'accurate' data until such questions had become embedded in popular consciousness (see Betts, Wilmot and Taylor 2008). Despite these complexities, it was agreed that the focus on sexual identity would be most useful for 'user requirements':

> Users require data on those who self identify to a particular sexual identity (Gay, lesbian etc.) as opposed to measuring orientation, desire or behaviour (ONS 2006).

Such 'users' are considered to be, 'Central government departments, local government, public service providers, LGBT service providers, LGB population, Academia and other research organisations' (Wilmot 2007, Betts 2008). Perhaps it is to be expected that 'the goal of statistical analyses' (Wilmot 2007) will be of particular interest for such users. Yet such a decision clearly has implications in terms of the valorisation of particular forms of knowledge and ways of understanding sexual identity and marginalisation.

With a focus on statistical analysis, the project needed categories that are meaningful and could be 'tested'. Weinrich et al.'s (1993) concept of 'splitters and lumpers' was used to argue that there are two ways of measuring sexual identities. Splitters seek to show differences between groups making these 'difficult and/ or intricate' and lumpers who reduce sexual classification to the bare minimum number of categories (Weinrich et al. 1993: 157, see also Wilmot 2007). It is argued that much of the research in the areas of sexualities studies has 'failed to

---

9   It should be noted that in the expert group and the user groups the emphasis was on LGB groups, although those who may 'object' to the question were also noted. It was presumed that such an objection would come from Christian groups and those who have homophobic tendencies, rather than those who may wish to contest state knowledges regarding sexual practices, identities and/or lives. Thus, 'sexuality' was conflated with lesbian, gay and bi people presumed to be afraid to 'disclose', or unsure of their 'true' identity. Presumptions of queer contestations were not addressed. This is perhaps because most of those in the room were invited because of their 'expert knowledges' regarding the statistical measuring of sexual identities, such that the 'queering' of sexuality categories was not foregrounded.

define the term at all' (McManus 2003). The absence of defined and agreed upon concepts is problematic for those who seek to measure through classification, yet it is interesting to note how this is rationalised. The splitters are not denied or ignored, rather they are rendered less useful for this form of research. It was continually recognised that sexual identities are complex, subjective and fluid, changing over time and with respect to individuals (Wilmot 2007). However, considering (queer?) forms of enquiry that break down categories is problematic for 'the users' because this form of research cannot establish baseline data, cannot measure regional populations, or be used for central/local government models that dictate the allocation of resources.

Question titles are important given that studies have argued that using race/ ethnicity/origin in the title of such questions influences the response (Hirschman et al. 2000). Nobles (2000) contends that *what to ask* is a crucial political decision and not simply a representation of a reality. 'Sexual identity' as the thing to be measured is not included in the final draft of the question stem (that is the question itself). Embarrassment related to 'sex' and the relationship between this and sexual behaviour, rather than 'identity' was seen as having the potential to generate 'inaccuracies' in the data. The stem of the final question uses the phrase: 'best describes how you think of yourself' (Betts, Wilmot and Taylor 2008: 5). It is believed that this allows for qualification, fluidity and change over time, because 'best describes, doesn't ultimately describe' (quoted in Betts, Wilmot and Taylor 2008: 33). The 'common-sense' nature of this question was reinforced through the trials of the question. These trials showed that categories were understood without direct reference to (or at times reading) the question stem itself. Nevertheless, for the project the use of this stem suggests a question that is far from fixed, but instead captures an approximation of an identity that can change throughout the lifecourse. Whilst the state is legitimising particular categorisations, these are not fixed or stable (or even necessarily read as such), moreover they are being simultaneously used and reproduced in popular cultures.

The reasons given for using sexual identity were: identity was the 'most stable' dimension 'over time', attraction and behaviour were too intrusive, and user and expert groups were clear that identity was the most appropriate category. Further, Betts, Wilmot and Taylor (2008: 39) contend that scales refer to behaviour and attraction whereas identities are 'discrete categories'. Thus lesbian/gay, bisexual or heterosexual (the categories decided upon) are seen as mutually exclusive identities and therefore measurable. The move from discussions recorded at user and expert group meetings and the complexity of focus group insights to official positions and final questions is reductive, offering a consensus that was dubious at best. Yet to only read the reasoning outlined in the 'official' presentations (although interesting not in all publications, see Wilmot 2007) misses the broader and nuanced considerations that were part of, and excessive to, the decision to use 'sexual identity' as the category for analysis, 'lesbian/gay', 'bisexual' or 'heterosexual' as the categories to be ticked and 'best describe' for the stem. Tailoring for particular audiences is of course a factor here, but as sexual identity gains currency and the argument becomes briefer, the fluidities and complexities of 'sexual identity' may easily be forgotten. The discussions within user and expert groups, as well as the nuanced arguments presented by the sexual identities project (Wilmot 2007) illustrate some of the processes that informed what 'thing' is to be measured. Whilst linear narratives may be constructed at the conclusion of research, such linearity is rarely available in the process. In the legitimisation of sexual identity questions, state processes and social lives can be seen as mutually constituted.

Creating the 'Magic Number': Sexuality Question Trials

Creating an 'accurate' number, is dependent on the question being both understood and used 'correctly', according to the parameters set by question designers. The 'magic number' in this context was understood as complex due to issues of privacy, lifestages and fear of abuse. It was recognised that sexual identities could change within lifecourses and vary by context and consequently at the outset:

> Distinction was made between measuring the 'magic number' of the LGB proportion of the population (which was hypothetical since sexual orientation is a multi-faceted phenomenon) and identifying a subgroup about which differences from the majority are of interest (Minutes, 13 August 2007).

However, it is argued now that within 3 years an 'accurate' measure of local authorities who have larger populations and higher levels of lesbian, gay and bisexual populations (<5 %) would be possible with indicative estimates for other local authorities, although a single precise count is still 'unlikely' (Betts, Wilmot and Taylor, 2008). Michael Brown (2000) asserts that quantitative questions can be reinterpreted by those who are completing the Census. In testing questions for these surveys, it is this re/misinterpretation of questions that is being analysed, such that the concept being measured is understood and has shared meaning across different identity groups. The point of undertaking trials and focus groups is to explore 'the ways the enumerated interpret and understand what is asked of them' (M. Brown 2000: 96) or in the terms of the project: to understand 'how the questioning is conceptualised, the basis on which answers are given and whether or not an accurate answer is provided' (Betts, Wilmot and Taylor 2008: 4).[10] Due to 'the volume of literature available' and although unusual in the development of quantitative questions, the sexual identity project conducted quantitative trials on the questions early on in the project (Wilmot 2007). The key (discrete and common sense) categories were thus decided in advance, with advice from user groups

---

10   The potential for a sexuality question to result in a withdrawal from the survey was also a key consideration. This relates to the sensitivity of a sexual identity question and the need to balance between 'not offending any particular group and considering comprehension issues for all' (Betts, Wilmot and Taylor 2008: 4). The project did not find significant withdrawal following asking the sexual identity question to be an issue.

with the potential to open these up through qualitative enquiries in trial four. In testing questions to create the 'magic number' the project grappled with questions of 'other' categories, the complexity of identity categories and the location of the data collection within the household.

In trials one and two the questions posed were different. Trial one asked: 'which of the following best describes your sexual identity, heterosexual, gay or lesbian, bisexual, other, prefer not to say'. In trial two, when 'heterosexual' became 'heterosexual/straight', there was a reduction in the category prefer not to say from 4.6 % to 1.5 % (Taylor 2008a). It is perhaps unsurprising that heterosexuals failed to recognise themselves on classifications of sexual identities. Similarly, the 'prefer not to say' category offered insights into those who eventually defined themselves as heterosexual, rather than 'queer' objections/objectors (Betts, Wilmot and Taylor 2008). The 'prefer not to say' category arises from New Zealand Census where 'object to answer' is a common response possibility across different questions. The initial discussion in the sexual identity project revolved around the desire for 'religious groups' to have the ability to protest against questions on sexualities by ticking this box. However, when further enquiry was made as to why respondents had 'preferred not to say', three key categories emerged: those who objected to the question, those who were concerned about confidentiality or privacy and those with comprehension issues (Wilmot 2007). There was a relationship between those who preferred not to say and 'low educational achievement, low socio-economic classification and high deprivation' (Wilmot 2007). It was then asserted that this could be due to respondents being less well educated in relation to equalities monitoring as they were typically not experiencing this in workplaces, but also due to the ability to use laptops (Wilmot 2007), rather than any questioning of the question itself and the categories presented. Nevertheless when the 'prefer not to say' option was removed in trial four, the heterosexual/straight category increased and the non-responses decreased (Malagoda and Traynor 2008), indicating that those who would otherwise define as 'other'/'prefer not to say' then move into heterosexual categories. Reducing/removing the categories of 'other' and 'prefer not say' is interpreted as reducing the ambiguity of sexual identities, locating them within 'proper' categories. Yet in improving/creating a 'heterosexual/straight' category through reducing fringe options, labelling those who complete these as confused, unaware or miscomprehending also limits certain queer disruptions.

There was an assumption that LGB people who were nervous of 'coming out' would use the 'other' or 'prefer not to say' option to disguise their sexuality. In contrast to this, during the lesbian, gay and bisexual focus groups respondents said that if they were fearful about revealing their lesbian/gay identities they would define as straight/heterosexual in order to draw minimum attention to themselves (Betts, Wilmot and Taylor 2008). The 'other'/'prefer not say' categories would be insufficient in hiding their identities.[11] Thus closeting could be again used as

---

11   Yet it should be noted that although confidentiality and privacy issues were identified as reasons for filling out the 'prefer not to say' option, the respondents still moved

a strategy of protection (M. Brown 2000), but also produces an *over*count in the heterosexual category. In this light, there is ongoing discussion (Betts, Wilmot and Taylor 2008) regarding the inclusion of an 'other' category as this (from the quantitative trials) is seen to harbour mainly heterosexuals and little inferences can be made from this category, thus invisibilising 'sexual minorities' (Betts, Wilmot and Taylor 2008: 6) and limiting the ability to obtain the 'magic number'.

A sexual identity question was seen as relatively unique in the way answers can change due to the survey's location particularly within the home. Wilmot (2007) pointed to the spatialities of data collection as *where* the survey was undertaken could influence how respondents identified their sexual identities. Some household members could be put into (potentially very real) danger by answering a sexual identity question, or even having that question posed in ways that could be answered/seen by another member of the household (Betts, Wilmot and Taylor 2008, Taylor and Ralph 2008). Therefore it was decided that this question will not be answered by proxy, which although it undercounts and 'closets', shows an understanding of the power relations within the context of certain (heterosexual) homes (Betts, Wilmot and Taylor 2008, Johnston and Valentine 1995). Moreover, bisexual respondents indicated that they may not reveal this answer within a non-heterosexual homeplace where they were not out. This was reduced to a 'privacy' issue in Betts, Wilmot and Taylor (2008), where it was contended increased privacy and particular precautions would improve 'accuracy'. Such challenges to 'accuracy' place quantitative research within social contexts that cannot be predicted in advance, and reiterate Michael Brown's (2000) point that questions will be re-interpreted, in this case where they are posed. Ironically, it could be argued that the legitimisation of lesbian, gay and bisexual subject positions through their inclusion on government social surveys is in part designed to challenge such power relations.

Interestingly, trial four's report (Betts, Wilmot and Taylors 2008) offers complex and nuanced understandings of how heterosexuals, lesbians, gay men and bisexuals understood sexual identities. In the focus group aspect of the sexual identity project, lesbian/gay women, gay men, heterosexual and bisexual men and women's groups were conducted. Sexual identity was problematised by heterosexuals who did not have a 'ready-made' answer and bisexuals who were the least likely to identify (Betts, Wilmot and Taylor 2008). The bisexual group was classified as 'reluctant identifiers', 'political identifiers' and 'fluid identifiers' and these were not mutually exclusive categories. However, those in the focus groups argued that 'bisexual' was a term attributed to them, preferring terms such as 'open' or 'gender apathetic' (Betts, Wilmot and Taylor 2008). In questioning the term bisexual, one respondent said that he hated the term bisexual because of its 'pseudo medical' associations that 'you can sort of apply percentages to'! (quoted in Betts, Wilmot and Taylor 2008: 26).

The use of focus groups by identity categories was of course an interesting means of reiterating categories that were supposedly being 'tested'. Yet the

into the heterosexual category, indicating the potential overcounting of 'heterosexuals'.

nuances, contradictions and complexities are clear, such that in the conclusion of trial four it was asserted that 'measuring the proportion of the population defined as heterosexual, homosexual or bisexual is difficult since sexual orientation is a multi-dimensional phenomenon' (Betts, Wilmot and Taylor 2008: 30). This illustrates an understanding of the fluidities within categories, diverse behaviours and preferences for continuums, fluidities and openness, yet in all the focus groups participants were able to 'identify with a category in a way appropriate to the intended data requirement' (Betts, Wilmot and Taylor 2008: 30). If read through certain queer deconstructive lenses the categories that formed the basis of the trials would be rendered unusable. However, in this context, the emphasis was on sexual identities as quantitative categories and confirming the 'lumpers' suspicions, the report argued that all groups would tick the box that they felt most represented the identities that were assigned to in joining the groups. Such discussions reveal the contingencies (and contradictions) of quantitative research, as well as the vast range of identifications and differences that can be 'lumped' together in order to provide 'accurate' data, as judged by the ONS. The chapter will now consider the potentialities of measuring, counting and being counted in relation to lesbian, gay or bisexual identities, and the possibilities of identity politics within rhetorics of 'equalities', examining the paradoxes of queer thinking in relation to social movements (Gamson 1995).

Lesbian, Gay and Bisexual Citizens: Is Counting Necessarily Bad?

In Britain the impulse to count can be seen as part of the 'inclusion' of marginalised identities that seek to render 'other' lives knowable in terms of the equalities legislation. In establishing baseline data it is asserted that services and facilities can be improved through knowing how their clients (sic) compare to the breakdown of the population groups in their geographical area (Brown 2000, Huag 2001, Purdam et al. 2008, Sillitoe and White 1992):

> ... excluding sexual orientation data [from the 2011 English and Welsh Census] places LGBT groups at a disadvantage, as local authorities don't have an idea of numbers of LGBT people in their communities when they are allocating resources for services. (http://www.tuc.org.uk/equality/tuc-14307-f0.cfm [accessed 27 January 2009])

Such comparative identity measurements can provide valuable data regarding inequality and, in the context discussed here, perhaps institutional homophobia and biphobia (Kreiger 2000). In the creation of an ethnicity question the justification for why such a question is needed was related to resource allocation and the 'need to know the extent to which equalities opportunities programmes are succeeding in reducing the inequalities resulting from discriminatory practices' (Sillitoe and White 1992: 141). Prewitt (2005) contends that in order for public policies to make use of, and refer to, racial categories to provide racially differentiated services, there is an imperative to make use of Census categories. Moreover, such categories can 'monitor progress or setbacks in addressing racial/ethnic inequalities' including health differentiations and access (Kriger 2000: 688). Consequently where groups are rendered invisible by tools such as the Census their voices can also be silenced and their needs ignored (Purdam et al. 2008). My discussion here seeks to hold questions of queer deconstructions and the potentials of identity politics in tension, often finding them to be inter-dependant.

Reynolds (2001) contends that the heteronormative state does not statistically acknowledge those who exist outside of heterosexuality and by doing so can then also ignore claims to rights, equality and justice. The decision not to include a sexuality question on the 2011 Census was contested by some LGB groups and media. Their arguments contended that baseline data for LGB populations was necessary in order to ensure the 'proper' allocation of resources, to aid service provision and monitoring, to develop appropriate policies and to provide, in the words of the ONS, 'reliable and comprehensive information about the LGB community' (2006). Thus, numbers come with the promise of recognition and 'resources'. The rights, privileges and resources afforded within equalities legislation are monitored through providing information that allows:

> Central and local government, health authorities and many other organisations use the facts the Census provides to target their resources more effectively. Funding and planning for these housing, education, health and transport services rely on this accurate information on people's needs for years to come (ONS 2007).

Thus, measuring the numbers of 'lesbians', 'gay men' and 'bisexuals' is increasingly lobbied for as part of the tool that decides the allocation of resources in an 'equitable' way and challenges the heteronormative state to include once pathologised citizens (Reynolds 2001), making 'non-heterosexuality … unremarkable' (Betts, Wilmot and Taylor 2008: 43).

The reliance on 'robust evidence' to translate equalities legislation into social change (Purdam et al. 2008, Reynolds 2001) is a key element in the debate. On one hand, from the section above, it can be seen that the question formed will be related to 'user requirements', which could simplistically be read as homonormalising sexual identities through categorising these within quantitative research modes. However, on the other hand, how the question should be used was not limited to neutral government departments, rather it was argued that it can affect social change. If services, organisations and groups can be held accountable, by the absence or presence of the 'magic number' of lesbian, gay and/or bisexual 'clients', there is a hope for change that is not reliant on individual complaints to pass through judiciaries. The collective press for a question is one that hopes for 'a better' society in which LGB people have a basis to argue for provision of social services that cater for them.

This discourse is so powerful, and the assertion of potential equalities so great, that it becomes difficult to consider other logics, as well as closeting and exclusions. There needs to be a critical consideration of the 'normative effect' as the counting of sexual identities becomes 'acceptable'. Queer imperatives to deconstruct sexual subjectivities could partially enable this questioning of sexual categories that normalise lives, experiences and practices through the practices of knowing and creating sexual identities, legitimacies and positionings. The move to establish a sexuality question undeniably (re)constitutes lesbians, gay men and bisexuals as citizens in ways that enable particular forms of governmental surveillance, as well as invisibilising and excluding and rendering some subjects and subject positions unintelligible (see M. Brown 2000, Butler 2004).[12]

To solely locate the 'queering' of state data collection methods within the normalising tendencies (such as 'lumping') ignores the origins of such a question within heteronormative orders:

> In the last meeting I attended, I found myself in the unusual and rather unexpected position of justifying the need for a sexuality question and the difficulties in administering it to a rather suspicious budget holder. As she asked question after question regarding acceptability, visibility and norms that would influence the creation of such data and also the point of having the data itself, it became clear that the creation of such a question was a political move, one that questioned the heteronormativity of an institution that had thus far allocated resources, created citizenships and protected or advocated particular privileges on the assumption of heterosexuality. (Personal Research Diary)

There can be no denying that the privileges and resources that could be redistributed will be uneven, but in the contemporary moment, a proposition that measures lesbian/gay and bisexual citizens as such, questions and continues to challenge (hetero)normative contexts. Self-surveillance and questions on intelligibility will probably mean 'queer' lives are reduced to four categories, lesbian/gay, bisexual, straight/heterosexual, or other. Thus in assessing the quantification of sexual lives through the creation of governmental knowledges, such knowledges will not be 'queer' as in the deconstructive sense, or 'queer' as in the questioning of the normalisation of gay and lesbian privileges (Duggan 2002, Green 2007, Valocchi 2005). But queer histories, moments, potentials and possibilities will nevertheless remain amongst the presumed fixed 'homonormativity' that 'sells its soul' to the governmental surveillance.

Yet, the assertion that only some will become visible and then only through particular collectivities and categories is also important in politically questioning the value placed on unhelpful numbers. The measure of LGB populations is predicted

---

12   There is much more to be said about closeting and the creation of intelligible LGB identities that is beyond the scope of this chapter. Suffice to note that the creation of these cannot necessarily be read as apolitical.

to be between 1.5–3% of the population. If the argument is for services, facilities and monitoring on the basis of establishing baseline figures, data such as this has the potential to render arguments for LGB equality mute, or at least toned down, in comparison to assertions of LGB populations in the region of 5–7%, which was the figure used in the civil partnership debates. Key to the ongoing demand for inclusion and provision will be the assertion of an undercount. This may be based on the excesses of categories that cannot contain gender and sexual difference, or perhaps, as has already been argued by the research that informed the creation of the sexual identity question, lesbian, gay and bisexual subjects will put themselves into heterosexual categories for fear of being out. In other words, queer positions and deconstructions may become necessary to argue for the complexity of sexual identities that challenges the assertion of one knowable 'magic number'.

Conclusion

The Office for National Statistics' concern that there should be statistical knowledge regarding sexual identities in order to action particular governmental initiatives (in the main based in equalities and services provision), but its reluctance to collect statistical data due to the absence of a 'reliable question' and 'accurate' measurements (in their terms) offered an interesting moment in considering queering methodologies and methods. The reliance on counting, percentages, and the 'diversity of a client base' to create a sexual identity question, requires particular fixities that reconstruct sexual identities. These identities are (re)created within mutually exclusive categories that have implications for lives through resource allocation, the provision of services and other productions of 'British' society. The normalisation of lesbian, gay, and bisexual subject positions takes place through the awarding of such legitimacies. Yet, the fixing of sexual identities within governmentalised categories, continue to offer the possibilities of disruptions and complexities.

The example of the recent push to include a sexuality question on the English and Welsh Census, and the subsequent development of a sexual identity question for inclusion on government social research, illustrates how quantitative questions come to take shape in contemporary eras and within culturally specific conceptualisations of sexualities. Rather than contend state production will create sexual identities, as can be seen for some ethnicity categories and identities (Kertzer and Arel 2002, Nobles 2000), this chapter has seen the quantification of sexual identity as mutually constituted though the social and governmental. It is possible then to argue that the governmentalisation of sexualities through such processes could 'homonormalise' lesbians, gay men and bisexuals as populations that can be measured, counted and monitored. Yet such a 'queer' reading neglects another possible reading, one that uses queer deconstruction to reveal the nuances of the possibilities, slippages and contradictions inherent to constructing questionnaire data. In queering the method of constructing the sexuality question through offering glimpses of the messiness and complexities of this process, the chapter has revealed the contingency of what could become a specific object in the creation of governmental knowledge (see also Browne 2008). By deconstructing how categories come into being in the inclusion of sexual identity as a category for questioning, and the negotiated process of creating concepts and categories, it showed that anti-normative and disruptive moments are part of the creation of quantitative categories. It may be tempting to then contend that the objects of the research (in this case questionnaire data) are stable, fixed and permanent, merely waiting to be ticked and analysed, yet, as Brown and Knopp (2006) illustrate, such data is not fixed or permanent; it can be redefined, reused and reassert diverse views that take account of diverse social realities. Thus, as research regarding the use of ethnicity categories on Censuses show, such knowledges 'do' rather than simply 'are' (see Brown and Knopp 2006, Kertzer and Arel 2002, Nobles 2000, 2002, Sedgwick 2003).

Queer methodologies can be used to explore how government quantitative social research tools produce political regimes, creating identities and potentially shaping lives through the production of exclusive and legitimate sexuality categories (see M. Brown 2000, Brown and Knopp 2006, Butler 2004, Crampton and Elden 2006). However, to only focus on normalising impulses also denies the possibilities and positive effects of legitimisation for those once invisibilised. Recognising the continued privileging of 'heterosexual' is key to grasping how creating and ticking the lesbian/gay/bisexual box can be a political act queering what was once a, by default, heterosexual tool with associated citizenship status. It is important to question the privilege, and differential realisation, of who can become lesbian, gay or bisexual citizens, and the nuanced positioning of those who become intelligible and unintelligible within such discourses and regimes. Yet, the disruption to the heteronormative state in recognising lesbians, gay men and bisexuals as citizens that are legitimate should not be reduced to only the critical. Rather, conversations could open up the nuanced possibilities of understanding, if such categories do not merely reflect, but constitute social realities, these realities may be 'better than' others. Access to state legitimisation, services and provision is of course fraught with controversy, but can be embraced as progressive social change for some (Weeks 2007). The question remains if this 'some' should then be denied queer status hoisted into the subject position of the 'homonormative' in ways that refuse multiple forms of identifications, practices and economics (see G. Brown 2009). Such positioning potentially simplifies and reduces complex and often anti-normative and messy processes to simplistic readings of gay/queer.

Methodologically this chapter opens up questions of the use of quantitative methods by queer theorists. It is an ambivalent proposition. Quantitative methods require the use of categories and queer's deconstructive tendencies often eschews the use of labels and definitional fixities in favour of fluid discussions of practices, lives and relegating processes. One tentative conclusion could be that whilst governmental social research tools can be deconstructed using queer theories rendering them fluid, unstable and permanently re-definable, the normative categorisations required of quantitative tools that rely on social norms for their formation and the adherence to such norms for their 'reliable' and 'valid' completion leave such tools problematic for queer researchers. Yet this is a limitation (and contradiction) of queer, as much as it is a constraint of quantitative research. Where ticking the boxes, and the interpretation of data, contest objectionable and exclusionary social norms, they can also offer anti-normative (and thus in some ways queer) politics and potentials.

Bibliography

Abu-Lughod, L. 1991. Writing against culture, in *Recapturing Anthropology*, edited by R. Fox. Santa Fe: School of American Research Press, 137–62.

Adam, B.D. 1998. Theorizing homophobia. *Sexualities*, 1(4), 387–404.

Adams, T.E. 2005. Speaking for others: Finding the 'whos' of discourse. *Soundings*, 88(3–4), 331–45.

Adkins, L. 2000. Mobile desire: Aesthetics, sexuality and the 'Lesbian' at work. *Sexualities*, 3(2), 201–18.

———. 2002. *Revisions: Gender and Sexuality in Late Modernity*. Buckingham: Open University Press.

Age Concern. 2002. *Issues Facing Older Lesbians, Gay Men and Bisexuals*. [Online: Age Concern England] Available at: http://www.ageconcern.org.uk/AgeConcern/Documents/OLGMppp.pdf. [accessed: 4 February 2008].

Ahmed, S. 2004. *The Cultural Politics of Emotion*. Edinburgh: Edinburgh University Press.

———. 2006. *Queer Phenomenology: Orientations, Objects, Others*. Durham: Duke University Press.

Alaimo, S. and Hekman, S. 2008. Introduction: Emerging models of materiality in feminist theory, in *Material Feminisms*, edited by S. Alaimo and S. Hekman. Bloomington: Indiana University Press, 1–19.

Alcoff, L. 1991. The problem of speaking for others. *Cultural Critique*, (20), 5–32.

Alexander, B. 2003. Querying queer theory again (or queer theory as drag performance). *Journal of Homosexuality*, 45(2–4), 349–52.

Alexander, B.K. 2008. Queer(y)ing the postcolonial through the western, in *Handbook of Critical and Indigenous Methodologies*, edited by N.K. Denzin, Y.S. Lincoln and L.T. Smith. Thousand Oaks, CA: Sage, 101–33.

Alexander, M.J. 2005. *Pedagogies of Crossing: Meditations on Feminism, Sexual Politics, Memory, and the Sacred*. London: Duke University Press.

Almack, K. 2007. Out and about: Negotiating the layers of being out in the process of disclosure of lesbian parenthood. *Sociological Research Online* 12(1). Available at: http://www.socresonline.org.uk/12/1/almack.html doi:10.5153/sro.1442 [accessed: 2 June 2010]

Althusser, L. 1971. Ideology and ideological state apparatuses (notes towards an investigation), in *Lenin and Philosophy and Other Essays*. London: NLB.

Altman, D. 2001. *Global Sex*. London: University of Chicago Press.

Anderson, B. 2002. A Principle of Hope: Recorded Music, Listening Practices and the Immanence of Utopia. *Geografiska Annaler: Series B, Human Geography* 84, 211–27.

Anderson, L. 2006. Analytic autoethnography. *Journal of Contemporary Ethnography*, 35(4), 373–95.

Anzaldúa, G. 1991. To(o) queer the writer–Loca, escritora y chicana, in *InVersions: Writings by Dykes, Queers, and Lesbians*, edited by B. Warland. Vancouver: Press Gang, 249–63.

———. 1999. *Borderlands/La Frontera: The New Mestiza*. San Francisco: Aunt Lute Press.

Atkinson, P. 1997. Narrative turn or blind alley? *Qualitative Health Research*, 7(3), 325–44.

Atkinson, P. and Delamont, S. 2006. Rescuing narrative from qualitative research. *Narrative Inquiry*, 16(1), 164–72.

Atkinson, P. and Hammersley, M. 1989. *Ethnography: Principles in Practice*. London: Routledge.

Babcock, B. 1980. Reflexivity: Definitions and discriminations. *Semiotica*, 30(1–2), 1–14.

Badgett, M.V.L. 1997. Beyond biased samples: Challenging the myths on the economic status of lesbians and gay men, in *Homo Economics: Capitalism, Community and Lesbian and Gay Life*, edited by A. Gluckman and B. Reed. New York: Routledge, 65–71.

———. 2003. *Money, Myth and Change: The Economic Lives of Lesbians and Gay Men*. Chicago: University of Chicago Press.

Bailey, R. 1999. *Gay Politics, Urban Politics: Identity and Economics in an Urban Setting*. New York: University of Columbia Press.

Bain, A.L. and Nash, C.J. 2006. Undressing the researcher: Feminism, embodiment and sexuality at a queer bathhouse event. *Area*, 38(1), 99–106.

———. 2007. The Toronto women's bathhouse raid: Querying queer identities in the courtroom. *Antipode*, 39(1), 17–34.

Baker, C. 2000. Locating culture in action: Membership categorisation in texts and talk, in *Culture and Text: Discourse and Methodology in Social Research and Cultural Studies*, edited by A. Lee and C. Poynton. St Leonards, NSW: Allen & Unwin, 99–113.

Baldo, M. 2008. Queer in Italian-North American women writers. *Graduate Journal of Social Science*, 5(2), 35–62.

Ballard, R. 1997. Negotiating race and ethnicity: Exploring the implications of the 1991 census. *Patterns of Prejudice*, 30(3), 3–33.

Banfield, A. 2000. *The Phantom Table: Woolf, Fry, Russell, and the Epistemology of Modernism*. Cambridge: Cambridge University Press.

Bank-Munoz, C. 2008. *Transnational tortillas: Race, gender, and shop-floor politics in Mexico and the United States*. London: Cornell University Press.

Barad, K. 2003. Posthumanist performativity: Toward an understanding of how matter comes to matter. *Signs*, 28(3), 801–31.

———. 2007. *Meeting the Universe Halfway: Quantum Physics and the Entanglements of Matter and Meaning*. Durham: Duke University Press.

————. 2008. Posthumanist performativity: Toward an understanding of how matter comes to matter, in *Material Feminisms*, edited by S. Alaimo and S. Hekman. Bloomington: Indiana University Press, 120–54.

Barnard, I. 2004. *Queer Race: Cultural Interventions in the Racial Politics of Queer Theory*. New York: Peter Lang.

Baudrillard, J. 1973. *The Mirror of Production*. Translated by M. Poster. St Louis: Telos Press.

————. 1988. *Consumer Society: Myths and Structures*. London: Sage.

————. 2001. *Jean Baudrillard: Selected Writings*. Stanford: Stanford University Press.

Beck, U. 1992. *Risk Society*. London: Sage.

————. 2000. *What Is Globalization?* Translated by P. Camiller. Malden, MA: Polity Press.

Behar, R. 1996. *The Vulnerable Observer: Anthropology that Breaks Your Heart*. Boston: Beacon Press.

Behar, R. and Gordon, D. (eds) 1996. *Women Writing Culture*. Berkeley: University of California Press.

Bell, D. and Binnie, J. 2000. *The Sexual Citizen: Queer Politics and Beyond*. Cambridge: Polity Press.

————. 2004. Authenticating queer space: Citizenship, urbanism and governance. *Urban Studies*, 41(9), 1807–20.

Bell, D. and Valentine, G. (eds) 1995. *Mapping Desire: Geographies of Sexualities*. London: Routledge.

————. 1995. Queer country: Rural lesbian and gay lives. *Journal of Rural Studies*, 11(2), 113–22.

Bell, E. 1999. Weddings and pornography: The cultural performance of sex. *Text and Performance Quarterly*, 19(3), 173–95.

Benhabib, S. 1995. Feminism and postmodernism, in *Feminist Contentions*, edited by S. Benhabib, J. Butler, D. Cornell and N. Fraser. London: Routledge, 17–34.

Benko, G. and Strohmayer, U. (eds) 1997. *Space and Social Theory: Interpreting Modernity and Postmodernity*. Oxford: Blackwell

Bennett, K. 2002. Interviews and focus groups, in *Doing Cultural Geography*, edited by P. Shurmer-Smith. London: Sage, 151–62.

Benwell, B. and Stokoe, E. 2006. *Discourse and Identity*. Edinburgh: Edinburgh University Press.

Berger, J. 1991. *And Our Faces, My Heart, Brief as Photos*. New York: Vintage International.

Berlant, L. 1997. *The Queen of America goes to Washington City*. Durham: Duke University Press.

Berlant, L. and Warner, M. 1995. What does queer theory teach us about X. *PMLA*, 110(3), 343–49.

Bernstein, M. and Reimann, R. (eds) 2001. *Queer Families, Queer Politics: Challenging Culture and the State*. Columbia: Columbia University Press.

Berry, K. 2007. Embracing the catastrophe: Gay body seeks acceptance. *Qualitative Inquiry*, 13(2), 259–81.

Bersani, L. 1995. *Homos*. Cambridge: Harvard University Press.

———. 2000a. Sociality and sexuality. *Critical Inquiry*, 26(4), 641–56.

———. 2000b. *The Culture of Redemption*. Cambridge: Harvard University Press.

Betsky, A. 1997. *Queer Space: Architecture and Same-Sex Desire*. New York: William Morrow and Company.

Betts, P. 2008. *Developing Survey Questions on Sexual Identity: UK Experiences of Administering Survey Questions on Sexual Identity*. [Online: Orientation Office for national Statistics]. Available at: http://www.ons.gov.uk/about-statistics/measuring-equality/sexual-identity-project/quest-dev/uk-exper.pdf [accessed: 12 December 2008].

Betts, P., Wilmot, A. and Taylor, T. 2008. *Developing Survey Questions on Sexual Identity: Exploratory Focus Groups*. [Online: Office of National Statistics]. Available at: http://www.ons.gov.uk/about-statistics/measuring-equality/sexual-identity-project/sexual-identity-focus-group-report.pdf [accessed: 12 December 2008].

Billig, M. 1999. Whose terms? Whose ordinariness? Rhetoric and ideology in conversation analysis. *Discourse and Society*, 10(4), 543–58.

Binnie, J. 1997. Coming out of Geography: Towards a queer epistemology. *Environment and Planning D: Society and Space*, 15(2), 223–37.

———. 2007. Sexuality, the erotic and geography: Epistemology, methodology and pedagogy, in *Geographies of Sexualities: Theory, Practices and Politics*, edited by K. Browne, J. Lim and G. Brown. Aldershot: Ashgate, 29–38.

Bishop, R. 1998. Freeing ourselves from neo-colonial domination in research: A Mâori approach to creating knowledge. *Qualitative Studies in Education*, 11(2), 199–219.

Black, D.A., Gates, G.J., Saunders, S. and Taylor, L.J. 2000. Demographics of the gay and lesbian population in the United States: Evidence from available systematic data sources. *Demography*, 37(2), 139–54.

Black, D.A., Sanders, S.G. and Taylor, L.J. 2000. The economics of lesbian and gay families. *Journal of Economic Perspectives*, 21(2), 53–70.

Blackman, L. 2009. The re-making of sexual kinds: Queer subjects and the limits of representation. *Journal of Lesbian Studies*, 13(2), 122–36.

Blackwood, E. 1995. Falling in love with an-Other lesbian, in *Taboo: Sex, Identity, and Erotic Subjectivity in Anthropological Fieldwork*, edited by D. Kulick and M. Willson. London: Routledge, 51–75.

———. 1998 Tombois in West Sumatra: Constructing masculinity and erotic desire. *Cultural Anthropology*, 13(4), 491–521.

———. 2007. Transnational sexualities in one place: Indonesian readings, in *Women's Sexualities and Masculinities in a Globalizing Asia*, edited by S. Wieringa, E. Blackwood and A. Bhaiya. New York: Palgrave Macmillan, 181–99.

Blake, M. 2007. Formality and friendship: Research ethics and review and participatory action research. *ACME: An International E-Journal for Critical Geographies*, 6(3), 411–21.

Bledsoe, C.H. et al. 2007. Regulating creativity: Research and survival in the IRB iron cage. *Northwestern University Law Review*, 101(2), 593–642.

Blunt, A. 2005. *Domicile and Diaspora: Anglo-Indian Women and the Spatial Politics of Home*. Oxford: Blackwell.

Bochner, A.P. 1997. It's about time: Narrative and the divided self. *Qualitative Inquiry*, 3(4), 418–38.

———. 2000. Criteria against ourselves. *Qualitative Inquiry*, 6(2), 266–72.

———. 2001. Narrative's virtues. *Qualitative Inquiry*, 7(2), 131–57.

———. 2002. Perspectives on inquiry III: The moral of stories, in *Handbook of Interpersonal Communication*, edited by M.L. Knapp and J.A. Daly. Thousand Oaks, CA: Sage, 73–101.

Boellstorff, T. 2005. *The Gay Archipelago: Sexuality and Nation in Indonesia*. Princeton: Princeton University Press.

———. 2006. Queer studies under ethnography's sign. *GLQ: A Journal of Gay and Lesbian Studies*, 12(4), 627–39.

———. 2007a. Queer studies in the house of anthropology. *Annual Review of Anthropology*, (36), 1–19.

———. 2007b. *A Coincidence of Desires: Anthropology, Queer Studies, Indonesia*. Durham: Duke University Press.

———. 2007c. When marriage falls: Queer coincidences in straight time. *GLQ: A Journal of Gay and Lesbian Studies*, 13(2–3), 227–48.

———. 2008. *Coming of Age in Second Life: An Anthropologist Explores the Virtually Human*. Princeton: Princeton University Press.

Bondi, L. 1992. Gender and dichotomy. *Progress in Human Geography*, (16), 98–104.

———. 1993. Gender and geography: Crossing boundaries. *Progress in Human Geography*, 17(2), 241–46.

———. 2005. The place of emotion in research: From participating emotion and reason to the emotional dynamics of research relationships, in *Emotional Geographies*, edited by J. Davidson, L. Bondi and M. Smith. Aldershot: Ashgate, 231–46.

Bookchin, M. 1995. *Social Anarchism or Lifestyle Anarchism: An Unbridgeable Chasm*. Edinburgh: AK Press.

Bornstein, K. 1994. *Gender Outlaw*. New York: Routledge.

Bourdieu, P. 1977. *Outline of a Theory of Practice*. Translated by R. Nice. Cambridge: Cambridge University Press.

———. 1999. Understanding, in *The Weight of the World: Social Suffering in Contemporary Society*. London: Polity Press.

———. (ed.) 1999. *The Weight of the World: Social Suffering in Contemporary Society*. London: Polity Press.

Bradley, M. 2007. Silenced for the own protection: How the IRB marginalizes those it feigns to protect. *ACME: An International E-Journal for Critical Geographies*, 6(3), 340–349.

Braidotti, R. 1994. *Nomadic Subjects: Embodiment and Sexual Difference in Contemporary Feminist Theory*. Princeton: Columbia University Press.

———. 2002. *Metamorphoses: Towards a Materialist Theory of Becoming*. London: Polity Press.

Bravmann, S. 1997. *Queer Fictions of the Past: History, Culture and Difference*. Cambridge: Cambridge University Press.

Brickell, C. 2008. *Mates and Lovers: A History of Gay New Zealand*. Auckland: Random House.

Brown, G. 2004. Sites of public (homo)sex and the carnivalesque spaces of reclaim the streets, in *The Emancipatory City: Paradoxes and Possibilities*, edited by L. Lees. London: Sage, 91–107.

———. 2008. Ceramics, clothing and other bodies: Affective geographies of homoerotic cruising encounters. *Social and Cultural Geography*, 9(8), 915–32.

———. 2009. Thinking beyond homonormativity: Performative explorations of diverse gay economies. *Environment and Planning A*, forthcoming.

Brown, G., Browne, K. and Lim, J. 2007. Introduction, or Why have a book on Geographies of Sexualities, in *Geographies of Sexualities: Theory, Practices and Politics*, edited by K. Browne, G. Brown and J. Lim. Aldershot: Ashgate, 1–20.

Brown, M. 2000. *Closet Space: Geographies of Metaphors from the Body to the Globe*. London: Routledge.

Brown, M. 2007. Counting on queer geography, in *Geographies of Sexualities: Theory, Practices and Politics*, edited by K. Browne, J. Lim and G. Brown. Aldershot: Ashgate, 207–14.

Brown, M. and Knopp, L. 2003. Queer cultural geographies – We're here! We're queer! We're over there, too!, in *Handbook of Cultural Geography*, edited by K. Anderson et al. London: Sage, 313–24.

———. 2006. Place or polygons? Governmentality, scale and the Census in The Gay and Lesbian Atlas. *Population, Space and Place*, 12(4), 223–42.

Browne, K. 2003. Negotiations and fieldworkings: Friendship and feminist research. *ACME: An International E-Journal for Critical Geographers*, 2(2), 132–46.

———. 2004. Genderism and the bathroom problem: (Re)materialising sexed sites, (re)creating sexed bodies. *Gender, Place and Culture*, 11(3), 331–46.

———. 2006. Challenging 'queer' geographies. *Antipode*, 38(5), 885–93.

———. 2007a. A party with politics?: (Re)making LGBTQ Pride spaces in Dublin and Brighton. *Social and Cultural Geography*, 8(1), 63–87.

———. 2007b. Drag queens and drab dykes: Deploying and deploring femininities, in *Geographies of Sexualities: Theory, Practices, and Politics*, edited by K. Browne, J. Lim and G. Brown. Aldershot: Ashgate, 113–24.

———. 2008. Selling my queer soul or Can queer research be quantitative? *Sociological Research Online*, 13(1). Available at: http://www.socresonline.org.uk/13/1/11.html.

Browne, K., Lim, J. and Brown, G. (eds) 2007. *Geographies of Sexualities: Theory, Practices, and Politics*. Aldershot: Ashgate.

Browne, K., Munt, S.R. and Yip, A. 2010. *Queer Spiritual Spaces: Sexuality and Sacred Places*. Aldershot: Ashgate.

Bryne, B. 2006. *White Lives: The Interplay of 'Race', Class and Gender in Everyday Life*. Routledge; New York.

Bulmer, M. 2008. A controversial census topic: Race and ethnicity in the British Census. *Journal of Official Statistics*, 4(2), 471–80.

Burke, J.C. (ed.) 2009. *Visible: A Femmethology*. Ypsilanti: Homofactus Press.

Burt, S. and Code, L. (eds) 1995. *Changing Methods: Feminists Transforming Practice*. Orchard Park, NY: Broadview Press.

Butler, J. 1990a. *Gender Trouble: Feminism and the Subversion of Identity*. London: Routledge.

———. 1990b. Performative acts and gender constitution: An essay in phenomenology and feminist theory, in *Performing Feminisms: Feminist Critical Theory and Theatre*, edited by S.E. Case. Baltimore: The John Hopkins University Press, 270–82.

———. 1991. Imitation and gender insubordination, in *Inside/Out: Lesbian Theories, Gay Theories*, edited by D. Fuss. London: Routledge.

———. 1993a. *Bodies that Matter: On the Discursive Limits of 'Sex'*. London: Routledge.

———. 1993b. Critically queer. *GLQ: Journal of Lesbian and Gay Studies*, 1(1), 17–32.

———. 1994. Against proper objects. *Differences*, 6(2–3), 2–26.

———. 1996. Gender as performance, in *A Critical Sense: Interviews with Intellectuals*, edited by P. Osborne. New York: Routledge, 109–25.

———. 1997a. *Excitable Speech: A Politics of the Performative*. New York: Routledge.

———. 1997b. *The Psychic Life of Power: Theories in Subjection*. Stanford: Stanford University Press.

———. 1997c. Merely cultural. *Social Text*, 15(3–4), 265–77.

———. 1999. Performativity's social magic, in *Bourdieu: A Critical Reader*, edited by R. Shusterman. Oxford: Blackwell, 113–28.

———. 2002. Explanation and exoneration, or what we can hear. *Social Text*, 20(3), 177–88.

———. 2004. *Undoing Gender*. London: Routledge.

———. 2005a. *Giving an Account of Oneself*. New York: Fordham University Press.

———. 2005b. *Precarious Life: The Powers of Mourning and Violence*. London: Verso.

———. 2009. *Untitled Interview with Leonor Silvestri in Buenos Aires, Argentina*. [Online]. Available at: http://www.megaupload.com/?d=M16XIW8Q [accessed: 7 July 2009].

Butz, D. 2008. Sidelined by the guidelines: Reflections of the limitations of standard informed consent procedures for the conduct of ethical research. *ACME: An International E-Journal for Critical Geographies*, 7(2), 239–59.

Buzard, J. 2003. On auto-ethnographic authority. *The Yale Journal of Criticism*, 16(1), 61–91.

Cahill, C., Sultana, F. and Pain, R. 2007. Participatory ethics: Politics, practices, institutions. *ACME: An International E-Journal for Critical Geographies*, 6(3), 304–18.

Call, L. 2002. *Postmodern Anarchism*. Oxford: Lexington Books.

Caputo, V. 2000. *Constructing the Field: Ethnographic Fieldwork in the Contemporary World*. New York and London: Routledge.

Carrington, C. 1999. *No Place Like Home: Relationships and Family Life among Lesbians and Gay Men*. Chicago: University of Chicago Press.

Carver, M.H. 2007. Methodology of the heart: A performative writing response. *Liminalities: A Journal of Performance Studies*, 3(1), 1–14.

Casey, M. 2004. De-dyking queer space(s), Heterosexual female visibility in gay and lesbian spaces. *Sexualities*, 7(4), 446–61.

Castaneda, C. 2002. *Figurations: Child, Bodies, Worlds*. Durham: Duke University Press.

Castells, M. 1983. *The City and the Grass Roots: A Cross Cultural Theory of Urban Social Movements*. London: Edward Arnold.

Charmaz, K. 2006. The power of names. *Journal of Contemporary Ethnography*, 35(4), 396–99.

Chesebro, J.W. 1981. *Gayspeak: Gay Male and Lesbian Communication*. New York: The Pilgrim Press.

Chisholm, D. 2004. *Queer Constellations: Subcultural Space in the Wake of the City*. Minneapolis: University of Minnesota Press.

Chödrön, P. 2002. *Comfortable with Uncertainty: 108 Teachings on Cultivating Fearlessness and Compassion*. Boston, MA: Shambhala.

Clarke, C. 1999. Right on sister, in *Inside Out: An Australian Collection of Coming Out Stories*, edited by E. Shale. Melbourne: Bookman, 175–79.

Clarke, V. 2001. The psychology and politics of lesbian and gay parenting: Having our cake and eating it? *Lesbian and Gay Psychology Review*, 2(2), 36–42.

Clifford, J. 1988. *The Predicament of Culture: Twentieth-Century Ethnography, Literature and Art*. Harvard: Harvard University Press.

———. 1989. Notes on theory and travel. *Inscriptions*, (5), 177–88.

———. 1997. *Routes: Travel and Translation in the Late Twentieth Century*. Cambridge, MA: Harvard University Press.

Clifford, J. and Marcus, G.E. (eds) 1986. *Writing Culture: The Poetics and Politics of Ethnography*. Berkeley: University of California Press.

Cloke, P. 2002. Deliver us from evil? Prospects for living ethically and acting politically in human geography. *Progress in Human Geography*, 2(5), 587–604.

Clough, P.T. 2000. Comments on setting criteria for experimental writing. *Qualitative Inquiry*, 6(2), 278–91.

Clune, J. 2003. My crime against the lesbian state. *The Guardian Weekend*, 14 June, 24–9.

Code, L. 1991. *What Can She Know? Feminist Theory and the Construction of Knowledge*. London: Cornell University Press.

———. 1993. Feminist epistemology. In *A Companion to Epistemology*, edited by J. Dancy and E. Sosa. Oxford Blackwell, 375–79.

Coffey, A. 1999. *The Ethnographic Self – Fieldwork and the Representation of Identity*. London: Sage.

Coffey, A., Holbrook, B. and Atkinson, P. 1996. Qualitative data analysis: Technologies and representations. *Sociological Research Online*, 1(1). Available at: http://www.socresonline.org.uk/socresonline/1/1/4.html.

Cohn, J. 2007. What is anarchist literary theory? *Anarchist Studies*, 15(2), 115–31.

Collins, J. 2003. *Threads: Gender, Labor and Power in the Global Apparel Industry*. Chicago: The University of Chicago Press.

Communities Scotland. 2005. *Precis #67: Housing and Support Needs of Older Lesbian, Gay, Bisexual and Transgender (LGBT) People in Scotland*. [Online: Communities Scotland]. Available at: www.communitiesscotland.gov.uk/ stellent/groups/public/documents/webpages/pubcs_008930.pdf. [accessed: 4 February 2008].

Conquergood, D. 2002. Performance studies: Interventions and radical research. *The Drama Review*, 46(2), 145–56.

Corber, R.J. and Valocchi, S. (eds) 2003. *Queer Studies: An Interdisciplinary Reader*. Oxford: Blackwell Publishing.

Corey, F.C. 2006. On possibility. *Text and Performance Quarterly*, 26(4), 330–32.

Corey, F.C. and Nakayama, T.K. 1997. Sextext. *Text and Performance Quarterly*, 17(1), 58–68.

Coser, L. 1975. Two methods in search of a substance: Presidential address. *American Sociological Review*, 40(6), 671–700.

Cosgrove, D.E. 1984. *Social Formation and Symbolic Landscapes*. Madison: University of Wisconsin Press.

Cram, F. 2001. Rangahau Maori: Tona tika, tona pono: The validity and integrity of Mâori research, in *Research Ethics in Aotearoa New Zealand*, edited by M. Tolich. Auckland: Longman, 33–52.

Crampton, J.W. and Elden, S. 2006. Space, politics, calculation: An introduction. *Social and Cultural Geography*, 7(5), 681–85.

Crawley, S.L. 2002. 'They still don't understand why I hate wearing dresses!' An autoethnographic rant on dresses, boats, and butchness. *Cultural Studies ↔ Critical Methodologies*, 2(1), 69–92.

Cromwell, J. 1999. *Transmen and Ftms: Identities, Bodies, Genders and Sexualities*. Urbana: University of Illinois Press.

Cronin, A. 2004. Sexuality in gerontology: A heteronormative presence, a queer absence, in *Ageing and Diversity: Multiple Pathways and Cultural Migrations*, edited by S.O. Daatland and S. Biggs. Bristol: Policy Press, 107–22.

Cruz-Malavé, A. and Manalansan IV, M.F. (eds) 2002. *Queer Globalizations: Citizenship and the Afterlife of Colonialism.* New York: New York University Press.

Cvetkovich, A. 2003. *An Archive of Feelings: Trauma, Sexuality, and Lesbian Public Cultures.* Durham: Duke University Press.

Cvetkovich, A. and Wahng, S. 2001. Don't stop the music. *GLQ: A Journal of Lesbian and Gay Studies*, 7(1), 131–51.

Dahl, U. 2003. Utklädningslådan, in *Såna Som Oss: Röster om Sexualitet, Identitet, och Annorlundaskap*, edited by S. Mobacker. Stockholm: Tidens Förlag, 64–74.

———. 2004a. *Progressive Women, Traditional Men: The Politics of 'Knowledge' and Gendered Stories of 'Development' in the Rural Northern Periphery of the European Union.* Ph.D. thesis, Department of Anthropology, University of California Santa Cruz, Santa Cruz.

———. 2004b. Femme-kamp. *Kom Ut*, 5.

———. 2006. Femme-inism. Bidrag till den Feministiska Sexualpolitiken. *Arena* [Online], August. Available at: http://www.tidskriftenarena.se/text/2006/08/femme-inism

———. 2007. Progressive women and traditional men: Gender equality as development discourse in the EU's northern periphery, in *The Gender of Globalization: Women Navigating Economic Marginality*, edited by A. Kingsolver and N. Guernevara. Santa Fe: SAR Press, 105–26.

———. 2008. Kopior utan original: Om femme drag. *Lambda Nordica*, (1–2), 89–105.

Davies, G. and Dwyer, C. 2007. Qualitative methods: Are you enchanted or are you alienated? *Progress in Human Geography*, 31(2), 257–66.

Davies, M. et al. 2006. *The Health, Social Care and Housing Needs of Lesbian, Gay, Bisexual and Transgender Older People: Literature Review.* Cardiff: Centre for Health Sciences Research, Cardiff University.

Dawn, A. and Kelly, T. (eds) 2005. *With a Rough Tongue: Femmes Write Porn.* Vancouver: Arsenal Pulp Press.

de Beauvoir, S. 1989 [1949]. *The Second Sex.* New York: Vintage.

de Lauretis, T. 1986. Feminist studies/critical studies: Issues, terms and contexts, in *Feminist Studies/Critical Studies*, edited by T. de Lauretis. London: Macmillan, 1–19.

———. 1987. *Technologies of Gender: Essays on Theory, Film and Fiction.* London: Macmillan.

———. 1990. Eccentric subjects: Feminist theory and historical consciousness. *Feminist Studies*, 16(1), 115–50.

———. 1991. Queer theory: Lesbian and gay sexualities. *Differences*, 3(2), iii–xvii.

de Saussure, F. 1959. *Course in General Linguistics.* New York: McGraw-Hill.

Delany, S. 2004 [1988]. *The Motion of Light in Water.* Minneapolis: University of Minnesota Press.

Deleuze, G. and Guattari, F. 1994. *What is Philosophy?* Translated by J. Tomlinson and G. Birchill. New York: Columbia University Press.

———. 1999. *A Thousand Plateaus: Capitalism and Schizophrenia*. Translated by B. Massumi. London: The Athlone Press.

———. 2000. *Anti-Oedipus: Capitalism and Schizophrenia*. Translated by R. Hurley, M. Seem and H. Lane. Minneapolis: University of Minnesota Press.

Deleuze, G. and Parnet, C. 1987. *Dialogues*. Translated by H. Tomlinson and B. Habberjam. London: Athlone.

Dempsey, J. and Rowe, J. 2004. Why poststructuralism is a live wire for the left, in *Radical Theory/Critical Praxis: Making a Difference beyond the Academy?*, edited by D. Fuller and R. Kitchin. Vernon, B.C.: Praxis(e)Press, 32–51.

Denzin, N.K. 1997. *Interpretive Ethnography: Ethnographic Practices for the 21st Century*. Thousand Oaks, CA: Sage.

———. 2003. *Performance Ethnography: Critical Pedagogy and the Politics of Culture*. London: Sage.

———. 2006. Analytic autoethnography, or déjà vu all over again. *Journal of Contemporary Ethnography*, 35(4), 419–28.

Devor, H. 1997. *FTM: Female to Male Transsexuals in Society*. Bloomington: Indiana University Press.

Diamond, M. 2004. *From the Inside Out: Radical Gender Transformation, FTM and Beyond*. San Francisco: Manic D Press.

Dilley, P. 1999. Queer theory: Under construction. *International Journal of Qualitative Studies in Education*, 12(5), 457–72.

Do or Die Collective. 2000. *Do or Die: Voices from the Ecological Resistance* (9).

Domosh, M. 1991. Towards a feminist historiography of geography. *Transactions Institute of British Geographers*, 16(1), 95–104.

———. 1997. Stout boots and a stout heart: Historical methodology and feminist geography, in *Thresholds in Feminist Geography: Difference, Methodology, Representation*, edited by H.L. Jones, J.P. Nast and S.M. Roberts. Oxford: Rowman and Littlefield, 225–40.

———. 1998. Geography and gender: Home again? *Progress in Human Geography*, 22(2), 276–82.

Dowling, R. 2005. Power, subjectivity, and ethics in qualitative research, in *Qualitative Research Methods in Human Geography*, edited by I. Hay. South Melbourne: Oxford University Press.

Du Bois, W.E.B. 2007 [1903]. *The Souls of Black Folk*. New York: Oxford University Press, 19–29.

Duggan, L. 2000. *Sapphic Slashers: Sex, Violence and American Modernity*. Durham: Duke University Press.

———. 2002. The new homonormativity: The sexual politics of neoliberalism, in *Materializing Democracy*, edited by R. Castronovo and D. Nelson. Durham: Duke University Press, 175–94.

Duggan, L. and McHugh, K. 2002. A femme-inist manifesto, in *Brazen Femme: Queering Femininity*, edited by C. Brushwood Rose and A. Camilleri. Vancouver: Arsenal Pulp Press, 165–70.

Duncan, N. (ed.) 1996. *BodySpace: Destabilizing Geographies of Gender and Sexuality*. London: Routledge.

Duncan, S. and Smith, D. 2006. Individualisation versus the geography of 'new' families. *Twenty-First Society*, 1(2), 167–89.

Dunn, K. 2005. Interviewing, in *Qualitative Research Methods in Human Geography*, edited by I. Hay. South Melbourne: Oxford University Press, 79–105.

Earthy, S. and Cronin, A. 2008. Narrative analysis, in *Researching Social Life*, edited by G.N. Gilbert. London: Sage, 420–39.

Edgar, H. and Rothman, D.J. 1995. The Institutional Review Board and beyond: Future challenges to the ethics of human experimentation. *The Milbank Quarterly*, 73(4), 489–506.

Eglin, P. and Hester, S. 2003. *The Montreal Massacre: A Story of Membership Categorization Analysis*. Waterloo, Ont.: Wilfrid Laurier University Press.

Eisenberg, E. et al. 2005. Communication in emergency medicine: Implications for patient safety. *Communication Monographs*, 72(4), 390–413.

Elder, G. 2002. Response to 'queer patriarchies, queer racisms, international'. *Antipode*, 34(5), 988–91.

Ellis, C. 1986. *Fisher Folk: Two Communities on Chesapeake Bay*. Lexington: University Press of Kentucky.

———. 1995. Emotional and ethical quagmires in returning to the field. *Journal of Contemporary Ethnography*, 24(1), 68–98.

———. 2000. Creating criteria: An ethnographic short story. *Qualitative Inquiry*, 6(2), 273–77.

———. 2004. *The Ethnographic I: A Methodological Novel about Autoethnography*. Walnut Creek, CA: AltaMira Press.

———. 2007. Telling secrets, revealing lives: Relational ethics in research with intimate others. *Qualitative Inquiry*, 13(1), 3–29.

Ellis, C. and Bochner, A.P. 2000. Autoethnography, personal narrative, reflexivity, in *Handbook of Qualitative Research*, edited by N.K. Denzin and Y.S. Lincoln. Thousand Oaks, CA: Sage, 733–68.

Elwood, S. 2007. Negotiating participatory ethics in the midst of institutional ethics. *ACME: An International E-Journal for Critical Geographies*, 6(3), 329–38.

Eng, D., Halberstam, J. and Muñoz, J.E. (eds) 2005. *What is Queer about Queer Studies Now? Social Text*. [Special double issue 23(3–4)]. Durham: Duke University Press.

Engebretsen, E.L. 2008. Queer ethnography in theory and practice: reflections on studying sexual globalization and women's queer activism in Beijing. *Graduate Journal in Social Science*, 5(2), 88–116.

England, K. 1994. Getting personal: reflexivity, positionality, and feminist research. *Professional Geographer*, 46(1), 80–89.

———. 1996. *Who Will mind the Baby? Geographies of Child-Care and Working Mothers*. London Routledge.

Ensler, E. 2001. *The Vagina Monologues*. London: Virago.

Fanon, F. 1967 [1952] *Black Skin, White Masks*. New York: Grove Press.

Fenstermaker, S. and West, C. 2002. *Doing Gender, Doing Difference: Inequality, Power and Institutional Change*. London: Routledge.

Ferguson, K. 2004. E.G.: Emma Goldman, for example, in *Feminism and the Final Foucault*, edited by D. Taylor and K. Vintges. Urbana: University of Illinois Press, 28–40.

Ferguson, R.A. 2004. *Aberrations in Black: Toward a Queer of Color Critique*. Minneapolis: University of Minnesota Press.

Filax, G. et al. 2005. Queer theory/lesbian and gay approaches, in *Research Methods in the Social Sciences*, edited by B. Somekh and C. Lewin. London: Sage, 81–9.

Fish, J. 2008. Navigating queer street: Researching intersections of lesbian, gay, bisexual and trans (LGBT) identities in health research. *Sociological Research Online*, 13(1). Available at: http://www.socresonline.org.uk/13/1/12.html

Floyd, K. 2009. *The Reification of Desire: Toward a Queer Marxism*. Minneapolis: University of Minnesota Press.

Forest, B. 1995. West Hollywood as symbol: The significance of place in the construction of gay identity. *Environment and Planning D: Society and Space*, 13(2), 133–57.

Foster, E. 2008. Commitment, communication, and contending with heteronormativity: An invitation to greater reflexivity in interpersonal research. *Southern Communication Journal*, 73(1), 84–101.

Foucault, M. 1977. *Discipline and Punish: The Birth of the Prison*. New York: Vintage Books.

———. 1978. *The History of Sexuality, Vol.1: An Introduction*. Translated by R. Hurley. New York: Vintage.

———. 1980. *Power/Knowledge: Selected Interviews and Other Writings 1972–1977*. Edited by C. Gordon. New York: Pantheon.

———. 1985. *The History of Sexuality, Vol. 2: The Use of Pleasure*. New York: Vintage Books.

———. 1986. *The History of Sexuality, Vol. 3: The Care of the Self*. New York: Vintage Books.

———. 1991. Governmentality, in *The Foucault Effect: Studies in Governmentality*, edited by G. Burchell, C. Gordon and P. Miller. Chicago: Chicago University Press, 87–104.

———. 2003. *'Society must be defended': Lectures at the Collège de France 1975–1976*. New York: Picador.

Franks, B. 2003. The direct action ethic: from 59 upwards. *Anarchist Studies*, 11(1), 13–41.

Fraser, M. 1999. Classing queer politics in competition theory. *Culture & Society*, 16(2), 107–31.

Freeman, M. 2001. From substance to story: Narrative, identity, and the reconstruction of self, in *Narrative and Identity: Studies in Autobiography, Self and Culture*, edited by J. Brockmeier and D. Carbaugh. Philadelphia: John Benjamins, 283–98.

Friedwald, W. 1996. *Jazz Singing: America's Great Voices from Bessie Smith to Bebop and Beyond.* New York: Da Capo.

Frye, M. 1983. *The Politics of Reality: Essays in Feminist Theory.* Trumansburg, NY: Crossing Press.

Fryer, D.R. 2003. Toward a phenomenology of gender: On Butler, positivism, and the question of experience. *Listening: Journal of Religion and Culture*, 37(2), 136–62.

Fuss, D. 1989. *Essentially Speaking: Feminism, Nature and Difference.* New York: Routledge.

———. 1991. Inside/out, in *Inside/Out: Lesbian Theories, Gay Theories*, edited by D. Fuss. London: Routledge, 1–10.

———. 1995. *Identification Papers.* New York: Routledge.

Gabb, J. 2001. Desirous subjects and parental identities: Toward a radical theory on (lesbian) family sexuality. *Sexualities*, 4(3), 333–52.

———. 2004. Critical differentials: Querying the incongruities within research on lesbian parent families. *Sexualities*, 7(2), 167–82.

———. 2005. Locating lesbian parent families: Everyday negotiations of lesbian motherhood in Britain. *Gender, Place and Culture*, 12(4), 419–32.

Gallie, W.B. 1956. Essentially contested concepts. *Proceedings of the Aristotelian Society*, 56, 167–98.

Game, A. and Metcalfe, A. 1996. *Passionate Sociology.* London: Sage.

Gamson, J. 1995. Must identity movements self-destruct?, in *Social Perspectives in Lesbian and Gay Studies*, edited by P.M. Nardi and B.E. Schneider. London: Routledge, 589–604.

———. 2003. Sexualities, queer theory, and qualitative research, in *The Landscape of Qualitative Research: Theories and Issues*, edited by N. Denzin and Y. Lincoln. London: Sage, 540–64.

Gans, H.J. 1999. Participant observation: In the era of 'ethnography' *Journal of Contemporary Ethnography*, 28(5), 540–48.

Garber, L. 2001. *Identity Poetics: Race, Class, and the Lesbian-feminist Roots of Queer Theory.* New York: Columbia University Press.

Garfinkel, H. 1967. *Studies in Ethnomethodology.* Englewood Cliffs, NJ: Prentice-Hall.

———. 1984. *Studies in Ethnomethodology.* Cambridge: Polity Press.

Gates, G.J. and Ost, J. 2004. *The Gay and Lesbian Atlas.* Washington D.C.: Urban Institute Press.

Gays and Lesbians Aboriginal Alliance. 1994. Peopling the empty mirror: Prospects for lesbian and gay Aboriginal history, in *Gay Perspectives II: More Essays in Australian Gay Culture*, edited by R. Aldrich. Sydney: Australian Centre for Gay and Lesbian Research, University of Sydney, 1–62.

Geertz, C. 1973. *The Interpretation of Culture.* New York: Basic Books.

———. 1983. 'From the native's point of view': On the nature of anthropological understanding, in *Local Knowledge: Further Essays in Interpretive Anthropology.* New York: Basic Books.

————. 1988. *Works and Lives: The Anthropologist as Author*. Stanford: Stanford University Press.

————. 1994. The uses of diversity, in *Assessing Cultural Anthropology*, edited by R. Borofsky. New York: McGraw Hill, 454–67.

————. 1995. *After the Fact: Two Countries, Four Decades, One Anthropologist*. Cambridge, MA: Harvard University Press.

Gell, A. 1998. *Art and Agency: An Anthropological Theory*. Oxford: Clarendon Press.

George, K. and Stratford, E. 2005. Oral history and human geography, in *Qualitative Research Methods in Human Geography*, edited by I. Hay. South Melbourne: Oxford University Press, 106–15.

Gibson-Graham, J.K. 1994. Stuffed if I know! Reflections on postmodern feminist social research. *Gender, Place and Culture*, 1(2), 205–24.

————. 1999. Queer(y)ing capitalism in and out of the classroom. *Journal of Geography in Higher Education*, 23(1), 80–85.

Giddens, A. 1987. *Social Theory and Modern Sociology*. Cambridge: Polity Press.

————. 1991. *Capitalism and Modern Social Theory: An Analysis of the writings of Marx, Durkhein and Max Weber*. Cambridge : University Press.

————. 1992. *The Transformation of Intimacy: Sexuality, Love and Eroticism in Modern Societies*. Cambridge: Polity.

Giffney, N. 2004. Denormatizing queer theory: More than (simply) lesbian and gay studies. *Feminist Theory*, 5(1), 73–8.

Giffney, N. and Hird, M. (eds) 2008. *Queering the Non/Human*. Aldershot: Ashgate.

Gilbert, M.R. 1994. The politics of location: Doing feminist research at 'home'. *The Professional Geographer*, 46(1), 90–96.

Gingrich-Philbrook, C. 2003. Queer theory and performance. *Journal of Homosexuality*, 45(2–4), 353–56.

————. 2005. Autoethnography's family values: Easy access to compulsory experiences. *Text and Performance Quarterly*, 25(4), 297–314.

Glaser, B.G. and Strauss, A.L. 1967. *The Discovery of Grounded Theory: Strategies for Qualitative Research*. New York: Aldine.

Gomez, J. 1988. Imagine a lesbian ... a black lesbian. *Trivia*, (12), 45–60.

Goodall, H.L. 2001. *Writing the New Ethnography*. Walnut Creek, CA: AltaMira.

Goodenough, W. 1970. *Description and Comparison in Cultural Anthropology*. Cambridge: Cambridge University Press.

Gopinath, G. 2005. *Impossible Desires: Queer Diasporas and South Asian Public Cultures*. Durham: Duke University Press.

Gordon, U. 2008. *Anarchy Alive! Anti-Authoritarian Politics from Practice to Theory*. London: Pluto.

Gorman-Murray, A. 2007a. Reconfiguring domestic values: Meanings of home for gay men and lesbians. *Housing, Theory and Society*, 24(3), 229–46.

————. 2007b. Sexy stories: Using autobiography in geographies of sexuality. *Qualitative Research Journal*, 7(1), 3–25.

————. 2008. Reconciling self: Gay men and lesbians using domestic materiality for identity management. *Social and Cultural Geography*, 9(3), 283–301.

Gorman-Murray, A., Waitt, G. and Gibson, C. 2008. A queer country? A case study of the politics of gay/lesbian belonging in an Australian country town. *Australian Geographer*, 39(2), 171–91.

Graeber, D. 2004. *Fragments of an Anarchist Anthropology*. Chicago: Prickly Paradigm Press.

Graham, M. 2004. Sexual things. *GLQ: Journal of Lesbian and Gay Studies*, 10(2), 299–303.

Green, A.I. 2002. Gay but not queer: Towards a post-queer study of sexuality. *Theory and Society*, 31(4), 521–45.

————. 2007. Queer Theory and Sociology: Locating the subject and the self in Sexuality Studies. *Sociological Theory*, 25(3), 26–45.

Greenberg, J.A. 2002. Definitional dilemmas: Male or female? Black or white? The law's failure to recognize intersexuals and multiracials, in *Gender Nonconformity, Race, and Sexuality*, edited by T. Lester. Madison: University of Wisconsin Press, 102–24.

Greenway, J. 2008. Desire, delight, regret: Discovering Elizabeth Gibson. *Qualitative Research*, 8(3), 317–24.

Griffin, G. 2009. *The Compromised Researcher: Issues in Feminist Research Methodologies*. Key note lecture at the Feminist Methodologies conference, Stockholm University, 4 February 2009.

Grosz, E. 1993. Bodies and knowledges: Feminism and the crisis of reason, in *Feminist Epistemologies*, edited by L. Alcoff and E. Potter. London: Routledge, 187–216.

Gunaratnam, Y. 2003. *Researching 'Race' and Ethnicity: Methods, Knowledge and Power*. London: Sage.

Gupta, A. 1998. *Postcolonial Developments: Agriculture in the Making of Modern India*. Durham: Duke University Press.

Gupta, A. and Ferguson, J. 1997. Discipline and practice: 'The field' as site, method, and location in anthropology, in *Anthropological Locations: Boundaries and Grounds of a Field Science*, edited by A. Gupta and J. Ferguson. Berkeley: University of California Press, 1–46.

————, (eds) 1997a. *Anthropological Locations: Boundaries and Grounds of a Field Science*. Berkeley: University of California Press.

————, (eds) 1997b. *Culture, Power, Place*. Durham: Duke University Press.

Hacking, I. 1990. Making up people, in *Forms of Desire: Sexual Orientation and the Social Constructionist Controversy*. New York: Garland.

————. 1999. *The Social Construction of What?* Cambridge, MA: Harvard University Press.

Haggerty, K.D. 2004. Ethics creep: Governing social science research in the name of ethics. *Qualitative Sociology*, 27(4), 391–414.

Halberstam, J. 1998. *Female Masculinity*. London: Duke University Press.

———. 2003. What's that smell?: Queer temporalities and subcultural lives. *International Journal of Cultural Studies*, 6(3), 313–34.

———. 2005a. *In A Queer Time and Place: Transgender Bodies, Subcultural Lives*. New York: New York University Press.

———. 2005b. Shame and white gay masculinity. *Social Text*, 23(3–4), 219–33.

———. 2008. Bees, bio-pirates and the queer art of cross-pollination, in *Inaugural Guest Lecture, Birkbeck Institute of Gender and Sexuality*. London.

Halperin, D.M. 1990. *One Hundred Years of Homosexuality: and Other Essays on Greek Love*. New York: Routledge.

———. 1995. *Saint Foucault: Towards a Gay Hagiography*. Oxford: Oxford University Press.

———. 2002. *How to Do the History of Homosexuality*. Chicago: University of Chicago Press.

———. 2003. The normalization of queer theory. *Journal of Homosexuality*, 45(2–4), 339–43.

———. 2007. *What Do Gay Men Want? An Essay on Sex, Risk, and Subjectivity*. Ann Arbor: The University of Michigan Press.

Hamer, D. and Copelan, P. 1994. *The Science of Desire*. New York: Simon & Schuster.

Hamilton, N. and Chinchilla, N.S. 2001. *Seeking Community in a Global City: Guatemalans and Salvadorans in Los Angeles*. Philadelphia: Temple University Press.

Haney, D.P. 1999. Aesthetics and ethics in Gadamer, Levinas, and romanticism: Problems of phronesis and techne. *PMLA*, 114(1), 32–45.

Hanson, S. and Pratt, G. 1995. *Gender, Work and Space*. London: Routledge.

Haraway, D. 1988. Situated knowledges: The science question in feminism and the privilege of partial perspective. *Feminist Studies*, 14(4), 575–99.

———. 1991. *Simians, Cyborgs and Women: The Reinvention of Nature*. London: FA.

———. 1996. *Modest_Witness@Second_Millennium. FemaleMan_Meets_ OncoMous: Feminism and Technoscience*. New York: Routledge.

———. 2004. *The Haraway Reader*. New York: Routledge.

Harding, S.G. 1986. *The Science Question in Feminism*. Ithaca: Cornell University Press.

———. (cd.) 1987. *Feminism and Methodology: Social Science Issues*. Milton Keynes: Open University Press.

———. 1991. *Who's Science, Whose Knowledge? Thinking From Women's Lives*. Milton Keynes: Open University Press.

Harding, S.G. and Hintikka, M. (eds) 1983. *Discovering Reality: Feminist Perspectives on Epistemology, Metaphysics, Methodology, and Philosophy of Science*. London: Reidel Publishing.

Hardy, T. 2000. Femme dyke slut, in *Sex and Single Girls: Straight and Queer Women on Sexuality*, edited by L. Damsky. Seattle: Seal Press, 175–82.

———. 2006. *Dis-Coarse*. Chapbook.

Haritaworn, J. 2007. Queer mixed race? Interrogating homonormativity through Thai interraciality, in *Geographies of Sexualities: Theory, Practices and Politics*, edited by K. Browne, J. Lim and G. Brown. Aldershot: Ashgate, 101–12.

———. 2008. Shifting positionalities: Empirical reflections on a queer/trans of colour methodology. *Sociological Research Online*, 13(1). Available at: http://www.socresonline.org.uk/13/1/13.html. [accessed: 11 November 2008].

Harris, L. and Crocker, L. (eds) 1997. *Femme: Feminists Lesbians and Bad Girls*. New York: Routledge.

Harrison, J. 2006. Coming out ready or not! Gay, lesbian, bisexual, transgender and intersex ageing and aged care in Australia: Reflections, contemporary developments and the road ahead. *Gay and Lesbian Issues and Psychology Interest Group of the Australian Psychological Society*, 2(2), 44–53.

Hartnett, S.J, and Engels, J.D. 2005. 'Aria in Time of War': Investigative poetry and the politics of witnessing, in *Handbook of Qualitative Research*, edited by N.K. Denzin and Y.S. Lincoln. Thousand Oaks, CA: Sage, 1043–67.

Hartsock, N. 1990. Foucault on power: A theory for women?, in *Feminism/Postmodernism*, edited by L. Nicholson. London: Routledge, 157–75.

Harvey, D. 1992. Social justice, postmodernism and the city. *International Journal of Urban and regional Research*, 16(4), 588–601.

Hastrup, K. 1992. Writing ethnography: The state of the art, in *Anthropology and Autobiography*, edited by J. Okely and H. Callaway. London: Routledge, 116–33.

Haug, W. 2001. Ethnic, religious and language groups: Towards a set of rules for data collection and statistical analysis. *International Statistical Review*, 69(2), 303–11.

Haugerud, A. Stone, P. and Little, P. (eds) 2000. *Commodities and Globalization: Anthropological Perspectives*. Boulder: Rowman & Littlewood.

Heaphy, B. 2007. Sexualities, gender and ageing: Resources and social change. *Current Sociology*, 55(2), 193–210.

———. 2008. The sociology of lesbian and gay reflexivity or reflexive sociology. *Sociological Research Online*, 13(1), 1–13.

Heaphy, B. and Yip, A.K.T. 2006. Policy implications of ageing sexualities. *Social Policy and Society*, 5(4), 443–51.

Heckert, J. 2005. *Resisting Orientation: On the Complexities of Desire and the Limits of Identity Politics*. Self-published Ph.D. thesis, University of Edinburgh, Edingburgh. [Online]. Available at: http://sexualorientation.info/thesis/ [accessed 7 July 2009].

———. 2010. Love without borders? Intimacy, identity and the state of compulsory monogamy, in *Understanding Non-Monogamies*, edited by M. Barker and D. Langdridge. London: Routledge, 255–66.

———. forthcoming. Fantasies of an anarchist sex educator, in *Anarchism & Sexuality: Ethics, Relationships & Power*, edited by J. Heckert and R. Cleminson. London: Routledge.

Hegarty, P. 2003. Pointing to a crisis? What finger-length ratios tell us about the construction of sexuality. *Radical Statistics*, (83), 16–30.

Heidegger, M. 1962. *Being and Time*. Oxford: Blackwell.

Hekman, S. 2008. Constructing the ballast: An ontology for feminism, in *Material Feminisms*, edited by S. Alaimo and S. Hekman. Bloomington: Indiana University Press, 85–119.

Henare, A., Holbraad, M. and Wastell, S. 2007. Thinking through things, in *Thinking Through Things: Theorizing Artefacts Ethnographically*, edited by A. Henare, M. Holbraad and S. Wastell. London: Routledge, 1–31.

Henderson, L. 2001. Queer communication studies, in *Communication Yearbook 24*, edited by W. B. Gudykundst. Thousand Oaks, CA: Sage, 465–84.

Hennessy, R. 1995. Queer theory, left politics. *Rethinking Marxism*, 7(1), 85–111.

———. 2000. *Profit and Pleasure: Sexual Identities in Late Capitalism*. London: Routledge.

Heritage, J. 1984. *Garfinkel and Ethnomethodology*. Cambridge: Polity Press.

Hesse-Biber, S.N. and Leavy, P. (eds) 2008. *Handbook of Emergent Methods*. New York: Guilford Press.

Hilbert, R.A. 1990. Ethnomethodology and the micro-macro order. *American Sociological Review*, 55(6), 794–808.

Hilfrich, C. 2006. 'The Self is a People': Autoethnographic poetics in Hélène Cixous's fictions. *New Literary History*, 37(1), 217–35.

Hines, S. 2006. What's the difference? Bringing particularity to queer studies of transgender. *Journal of Gender Studies*, 15(1), 49–66.

Hird, M.J. 2004. Naturally queer. *Feminist Theory*, 5(1), 85–9.

Hirschman, C., Alba, R. And Farley, R. 2000. The meaning and measurement of race in the U.S. census: glimpses into the future. *Demography*, 37(3), 381–93.

Hochschild, A.R. 1983. *The Managed Heart: Commercialisation of Human Feeling*. London: UCL Press.

Hodge, D. 1993. *Did You Meet Any Malagas? A Homosexual History of Australia's Tropical Capital*. Nightcliff, NT: Little Gem.

Hollibaugh, A. 2000. *My Dangerous Desires: A Queer Girl Dreaming Her Way Home*. Durham: Duke University Press

Holman Jones, S. 2005a. Autoethnography: Making the personal political, in *Handbook of Qualitative Research*, edited by N.K. Denzin and Y.S. Lincoln. Thousand Oaks, CA: Sage, 763–91.

———. 2005b. (M)othering loss: Telling adoption stories, telling performativity. *Text and Performance Quarterly*, 25(2), 113–35.

Hondagneu-Sotelo, P. 1994. *Gendered Transitions: Mexican Experiences of Immigration*. London: University of California Press.

———. 2001. *Domestica: Immigrant Workers Cleaning and Caring in the Shadows of Affluence*. London: University of California Press.

Hood-Williams, J. and Cealey-Harrison, W. 1998. Trouble with gender. *The Sociological Review*, 46(1), 73–94.

hooks, b. 1990. *Yearning: Race, Gender and Cultural Politics*. New York: South End Press.

———. 1994. *Teaching to Transgress: Education as the Practice of Freedom*. London: Routledge.

Hopkins, T. and Wallerstein, I. 1986. Commodity chains in the world economy prior to 1800. *Review*, 10(1), 157–70.

Horton-Salway, M. 2004. The local production of knowledge: Disease labels, identities and category entitlements in ME support group talk. *Health*, 8(3), 351–71.

Housley, W. and Fitzgerald, R. 2002. The reconsidered model of membership categorization analysis. *Qualitative Research*, 2(1), 59–83.

Howitt, R. and Stevens, S. 2005. Cross-cultural research: Ethics, methods, and relationships, in *Qualitative Research Methods in Human Geography*, edited by I. Hay. South Melbourne: Oxford University Press, 30–50.

Hubbard, P. 2007. Between transgression and complicity (or: can the straight guy have a queer eye?), in *Geographies of Sexualities: Theory, Practices and Politics*, edited by K. Browne, J. Lim and G. Brown. Aldershot: Ashgate, 151–58.

Hubbard, R. and Rossington, J. 1995. *As We Grow Older: A Study of the Housing and Support Needs of Older Lesbians and Gay Men*. [Online: Polari] Available at: http://www.casweb.org/polari/file-storage/download/As%20We%20Grow%20Older.pdf?version_id=66608 [accessed: 4 February 2008].

Hunt, R. and Minsky, A. 2005. *Reducing Health Inequalities for Lesbian Gay and Bisexual People: Evidence of Health Care Needs*. London: Stonewall.

Hutchings, J. and Aspin, C. 2007. *Sexuality and the Stories of Indigenous People*. Wellington: Huia Publishers.

Irigaray, L. 1985. *This Sex Which Is Not One*. Ithaca: Cornell University Press.

Jackson, A.Y. 2004. Performativity identified. *Qualitative Inquiry*, 10(5), 673–90.

Jackson, P. 1999. Postmodern urbanism and the ethnographic void. *Urban Geography*, 20, 400–402.

Jackson, P. and Sullivan, G. (eds) 1999. *Multicultural Queer: Australian Narratives*. New York: Haworth Press.

Jackson, S. 2001. Why a materialist feminism is (still) possible – and necessary. *Women's Studies International Forum*, 24(3–4), 283–93.

Jago, B.J. 2002. Chronicling an academic depression. *Journal of Contemporary Ethnography*, 31(6), 729–57.

Jagose, A. 1996a. Queer theory. *Australian Humanities Review* [Online], (4). Available at: http://www.lib.latrobe.edu.au/AHR/archive/Issue-Dec-1996/jagose.html [accessed: 10 April 2007].

———. 1996b. *Queer Theory: An introduction*. New York: New York University Press.

Jakobson, R. 1980. *The Framework of Language*. Ann Arbor: Michigan Studies in the Humanities.

Jeffreys, S. 1997. The queer disappearance of lesbians, in *Lesbians in Academia: Degrees of Freedom*, edited by B. Mintz and E. Rothblum. London: Routledge, 269–78.

———. 2003. *Unpacking Queer Politics: A Lesbian Feminist Perspective*. Oxford: Polity.

Jeffries, T. 2002. An autoethnographical exploration of racial 'I'dentity. *The Journal of Intergroup Relations*, 29(2), 39–56.

Johnson, E.P. 2001. 'Quare' studies, or (almost) everything I know about queer studies I learned from my grandmother. *Text and Performance Quarterly*, 21(1), 1–25.

Johnston, L. 2005. *Queering Tourism: Paradoxical Performances at Gay Pride Parades* London: Routledge.

———. 2005. *Queering Tourism: Paradoxical Performances at Gay Pride Parades*. London: Routledge.

———. 2007. Mobilizing pride/shame: Lesbians, tourism and parades. *Social and Cultural Geography*, 8(1), 29–45.

Johnston, L. and Longhurst, R. 2008. Queer(ing) geographies 'down under': some notes on sexuality and space in Australasia. *Australian Geographer*, 39(3), 247–57.

Jones, J.L. 2002. Performance ethnography: The role of embodiment in cultural authenticity. *Theatre Topics*, 12(1), 1–15.

Jordan, J. 1998. The art of necessity: The subversive imagination of anti-road protest and Reclaim the Streets, in *DIY Cultures: Parties and Protest in Nineties Britain*, edited by G. McKay. London: Verso, 129–51.

Joseph, M. 2002a. *Against the Romance of Community*. Minneapolis: University of Minnesota Press.

———. 2002b. Analogy and complicity: Women's studies, lesbian/gay studies, and capitalism, in *Women's Studies on Its Own: A Next Wave Reader in Institutional Change*, edited by R. Wiegman. Durham: Duke University Press, 267–92.

Katz, C. 1994. Playing the Field: Questions of Fieldwork in Geography. *Professional Geographer*, 46(1), 67–72.

Katz, J. 1978. *Gay American History: Lesbians and Gay Men in the USA*. New York: Avon.

Keith-Spiegel, P. and Koocher, G.P. 2005. The IRB paradox: Could the protectors also encourage deceit. *Ethics and Behavior*, 15(4), 339–49.

Keller, E.F. 1995 [1985]. *Reflections on Gender and Science*. New Haven, CT: Yale University Press.

Kellogg, S. and Pettigrew, S. 2008. *Toolbox for Sustainable City Living: A Do-It-Ourselves Guide*. Cambridge, MA: South End Press.

Kennedy, E.L. and Davis, M. 1993. *Boots of Leather, Slippers of Gold: The History of a Lesbian Community*. New York: Routledge.

Kennedy, E.L with M Davis. 1996. Constructing an ethnohistory of the Buffalo lesbian community: Reflexivity, dialogue, and politics, in *Out in the Field: Reflections of Lesbian and Gay Anthropologists*, edited by E. Lewin and W.L. Leap. Urbana: University of Illinois Press, 171–99.

Kennedy, R. 2003. *Nigger: The Strange Career of a Troublesome Word*. New York: Vintage.

Keogh, P. et al. 2004. *Doctoring Gay Men: Exploring the Contribution of General Practice*. [Online: SIGMA Research] Available at: http://www.sigmaresearch. org.uk/downloads/report04d.pdf. [accessed: 25 November 2008].

Kertzer, D. and Arel, D. 2002. *Census and Identity: The Politics of Race, Ethnicity and Language in the national Census*. Cambridge: Cambridge University Press.

Khayatt, D. 2002. Toward a queer identity. *Sexualities*, 5(4), 487–501.

Kindon, S., Pain, R. and Kesby, M. 2008. *Participatory Action Research Approaches and Methods: Connecting People, Participation and Place*. London: Routledge.

King, A. 2010. Membership matters: Applying membership categorisation analysis (MCA) to qualitative data using computer assisted qualitative data analysis (CAQDAS) software. *International Journal of Social Research Methodology*, 13(1), 1–16.

Kirby, V. 1997. *Telling Flesh: The Substance of the Corporeal*. London: Routledge.

———. 2008. Natural convers(at)ions: Or, what if culture was really nature all along?, in *Material Feminisms*, edited by S. Alaimo and S. Hekman. Bloomington: Indiana University Press.

Kirsch, M. 2000. *Queer Theory and Social Change*. London Routledge, 214–36.

Kitzinger, C. 2000. Doing feminist conversation analysis. *Feminism and Psychology*, 10(2), 163–93.

Klesse, C. 2006. Polyamory and its 'others': Contesting the terms of non-monogamy. *Sexualities*, 9(5), 565–83.

Knopp, L. 2007a. From lesbian and gay to queer geographies: Pasts, prospects and possibilities, in *Geographies of Sexualities: Theory, Practices, and Politics*, edited by K. Browne, J. Lim and G. Brown. Aldershot: Ashgate, 21–8.

———. 2007b. On the relationship between queer and feminist geographies. *Professional Geographer*, 51(1), 47–55.

Knopp, L. and Brown, M. 2003. Queer diffusions. *Environment and Planning D: Society and Space*, 21, 409–24.

Kobayashi, A. 1994. Colouring the field: Gender, 'race' and the politics of fieldwork. *The Professional Geographer*, 46 (1), 73–80.

———. 2003. GPC Ten years on: Is self-reflexivity enough? *Gender, Place and Culture*, 10(4), 345–49.

———. 2004. Anti-racist feminism in geography: An agenda for social action, in *The Companion to Feminist Geography*, edited by L. Nelson and J. Seager. London: Routledge, 32–40.

Kobayashi, A. and Peake, L. 2000. Racism out of place: Thoughts on whiteness and anti-racist geography in the new millennium. *Annals of the Association of American Geographers*, 90(2), 392–403.

Kong, T.S.K., Mahoney, D. and Plummer, K. 2002. Queering the interview, in *Handbook of Interview Research*, edited by J. F. Gubrium and J. A. Holstein. Thousand Oaks, CA: Sage, 239–58.

Koro-Ljungberg, M. 2004. Impossibilities of reconciliation: Validity in mixed theory projects. *Qualitative Inquiry*, (4), 601–21.

Kramer, J.L. 1995. Bachelor farmers and spinsters: Gay and lesbian identities and communities in rural North Dakota, in *Mapping Desire*, edited by D. Bell and G. Valentine. New York: Routledge, 200–219.

Kreiger, N. 2000. Counting accountably: Implications of the new approaches to classifying race/ethnicity in the 2000 census. *American Journal of Public Health*, 90(11), 1687–89.

Kulick, D. 1995. The sexual life of anthropologists: Erotic subjectivity and ethnographic work, in *Taboo: Sex, Identity, and Erotic Subjectivity in Anthropological Fieldwork*, edited by D. Kulick and M. Willson. London: Routledge, 1–28.

Kulick, D, and Willson, M. (eds) 1995. *Taboo: Sex, Identity, and Erotic Subjectivity in Anthropological Fieldwork*. London: Routledge.

Kulpa, R. and Liinason, M. 2009. Queer studies: Methodological approaches: Follow-up. *Graduate Journal of Social Science*, 6(1), 1–2.

Kumashiro, K. 2002. *Troubling Education: Queer Activism and Anti-oppressive Pedagogy*. New York: Routledge.

Kuper, A. 1996. *Anthropology and Anthropologists*. 3rd Edition. London: Routledge.

Kurdek, L. 2005. What do we know about lesbian and gay couples. *Current Directions in Psychological Science*, 14(5), 251–54.

Kwan, M. 2002. Is GIS for women? Reflections on the critical discourse in the 1990s. *Gender, Place and Culture*, 9(3), 271–79.

Lao Tzu. 1997. *Tao Te Ching: A Book about the Way and the Power of the Way*. Translated by U. LeGuin with J.P. Seaton. Boston, MA: Shambhala.

Latour, B. 1993. *We Have Never Been Modern*. Cambridge, Mass.: Harvard University Press.

———. 2005. *Reassembling the Social: An Introduction to Actor-Network-Theory*. Oxford: Oxford University Press.

Lauria, M. and Knopp, L. 1985. Towards an analysis of the role of gay communities in the urban renaissance. *Urban Geography*, 6(2), 152–69.

Law, J. 2004. *After Method: Mess in Social Science Research*. London: Routledge.

Law, J. and Hassard, J. 1999. *Actor Network Theory and After*. Oxford: Blackwell.

Lawson, V. 1995. The politics of difference: Examining the quantitative/ qualitative dualism in poststructuralist feminist research. *Professional Geographer*, 47(4), 449–57.

Leap, W.L. and Boellstorff, T. (eds) 2004. *Speaking in Queer Tongues: Globalization and Gay Language*. Urbana: University of Illinois Press.

Lee, W. 2003. Kuaering queer theory: My autocritography and a race-conscious, womanist, transnational turn. *Journal of Homosexuality*, 45(2–4), 147–70.

Legg, S. 2003. Gendered politics and nationalised homes: Women and the anti-colonial struggle in Delhi, 1930–47. *Gender, Place and Culture*, 10(1), 7–27.

————. 2005. Foucault's population geographies: classifications, biopolitics and governmental spaces. *Population, Space and Place*, 11(3), 137–56.

Le Guin, U.K. 1999. *The Dispossessed*. London: Orion.

————. 2001. *The Telling*. London: Gollancz.

————. 2004. *The Wave in the Mind: Talks and Essays on the Writer, the Reader, and the Imagination*. Boston, MA: Shambhala.

————. 2006. A message about messages', in *Cheek by Jowl: Talks & Essays on How & Why Fantasy Matters*. Seattle: Aqueduct Press. [Online]. Available at: http://dystopictimes.blogspot.com/2006/08/message-about-messages.html [accessed: 16 February 2009].

Lévi-Strauss, C. 1963. *Structural Anthropology*. New York: Basic Books.

Lewin, E. 1991. Writing lesbian and gay culture: What the natives have to say for themselves. *American Ethnologist*, 18(4), 786–92.

Lewin, E. and Leap, W.L. 1996. Introduction, in *Out in the Field: Reflections of Lesbian and Gay Anthropologists*, edited by E. Lewin and W.L. Leap. Urbana: University of Illinois Press, 1–28.

————. (eds) 1996. *Out in the Field: Reflections of Lesbian and Gay Anthropologists*. Urbana: University of Illinois Press.

————. (eds) 2002. *Out in Theory: The Emergence of Lesbian and Gay Anthropology*. Urbana: University of Illinois Press.

Liinason, M. and Kulpa, R. 2008. Queer studies: Methodological approaches. *Graduate Journal of Social Science*, 5(2), 1–4.

Limb, M. and Dwyer, C. (eds) 2001. *Qualitative Methodologies for Geographers*. New York: Oxford University Press.

Lincoln, Y.S. and Canella, G.S. 2004a. Dangerous discourses: Methodological conservatism and governmental regimes of truth. *Qualitative Inquiry*, 10(1), 5–14.

————. 2004b. Qualitative research and the radical right. *Qualitative Inquiry*, 10(2), 175–201.

Lincoln, Y.S. and W.G Tierney. 2004. Qualitative research and institutional review boards. *Qualitative Inquiry*, 10(2), 219–34.

Lindsay, J., Perlesz, A., Brown, R., McNair, R., de Vaus, D. and Pitts, M. 2006. Stigma or respect: Lesbian-parented families negotiating school settings. *Sociology*, 40(6), 1059–77.

Llewellyn, N. 2004. In search of modernization: The negotiation of social identity in organizational reform. *Organization Studies*, 25(6), 947–68.

Longhurst, R. 2008. Afterword. *Australian Geographer*, 39(3), 381–87.

Lorde, A. 1984. *Sister Outsider*. Berkeley, CA: The Crossing Press.

Lugosi, R. 2000. *Coming Out at Night. Performance Poetry*. Manchester: Purpleprose Press.

Luibhéid, E, and Cantú, L. 2005. *Queer Migrations: Sexuality, U.S. Citizenship and Border Crossings*. London: University of Minneapolis.

Lykke, N. 2008. *Kønsforskning: En Guide til Feministisk Teori, Metodologi og Skrift*. Fredriksberg: Samfundslitteratur.

MacDonald, E. 1998. Critical identities: Rethinking feminism through transgender politics. *Atlantis*, 23(1), 3–12.

Macpherson, H. 2009. Articulating blind touch: Thinking through the feet. *The Senses and Society*, (4), 179–93.

Madison, D.S. 2005. *Critical Ethnography: Method, Ethics, and Performance.* Thousand Oaks, CA: Sage

———. 2006. The dialogic performative in critical ethnography. *Text and Performance Quarterly*, 26(4), 320–24.

Maguire, L. 2001. Making sexual voices. *Marie Claire*, November, 90–96.

Malagoda, M. and Traynor, J. 2008. *Developing Survey Questions on Sexual Identity: Report on National Statistics Omnibus Trial 4.* [Online: Office for National Statistics]. Available at: http://www.ons.gov.uk/about-statistics/measuring-equality/sexual-identity-project/quest-test-and-implem/sexual-identity-project-report-on-national-statistics-omnibus-survey-trial-4.pdf [accessed: 12 December 2008].

Malinowski, B. 1922. *Argonauts of the Western Pacific.* London: Routledge.

———. 1929. *The Sexual Life of Savages in North-West Melanesia: An Ethnographic Account of Courtship, Marriage and Family Life among the Natives of the Trobriand Highlands, British New Guinea.* Boston: Beacon Press.

Manalansan IV, M.F. 2003. *Global Divas: Filipino Gay Men in the Diaspora.* Durham: Duke University Press.

Māori Sexuality Project. 2008. [Online]. Available at: http://www.arts.auckland.ac.nz/research/index.cfm?P=6254. [accessed:18 July 2008].

Marcus, G.E. 1986. Contemporary problems of ethnography in the modern world system, in *Writing Culture: The Politics and Poetics of Ethnography*, edited by J. Clifford and G.E. Marcus. Berkeley: University of California Press, 165–93.

———. 1994. After the critique of ethnography: Faith, hope and charity, but the greatest of these is charity, in *Assessing Cultural Anthropology*, edited by R. Borofsky. New York: McGraw Hill Inc, 40–52.

———. 1995. Ethnography in/of the world system: The emergence of multi-sited ethnography. *Annual Review of Anthropology*, 24, 95–117.

Marcus, G. E. and Cushman, D. 1982. Ethnographies as Texts. *Annual Review of Anthropology*, 11, 25–69.

Marcus, G.E. and Fischer, M. 1986. *Anthropology as Cultural Critique: An Experimental Moment in the Social Sciences.* Chicago: University of Chicago Press.

Marshall, J. 2002. Borderlands and feminist ethnography, in *Feminist Geography in Practice: Research and Method*, edited by P. Moss. Oxford: Blackwell, 174–86.

Martin, B. 1994. Sexualities without genders and other queer utopias. *Diacritics*, 24(2–3), 104–21.

———. 1996. *Femininity Played Straight: The Significance of Being Lesbian.* New York: Routledge.

Martin, B. and Mohanty, C.T. 1986. Feminist politics: What's home got to do with it?, in *Feminist/Textual Politics*, edited by T. de Lauretis. Bloomington: Indiana University Press, 191–212.

Martin, D.G. 2007. Bureaucratizing ethics: Institutional review boards and participatory research. *ACME: An International E-Journal for Critical Geographies*, 6(3), 319–28.

Massey, D. 1994. *Space, Place and Gender*. Minneapolis: University of Minnesota Press.

Massumi, B. 1999. Translator's foreword: Pleasures of philosophy, in Deleuze, G. and Guattari, F. *A Thousand Plateaus: Capitalism and Schizophrenia*, London: The Athlone Press.

Mattingly, D.J. and Falconer Al-Hindi, K. 1995. Should women count? A context for the debate. *Professional Geographer*, 47(4), 427.

Mattlida aka Matt Bernstein Sycamore. 2004. *That's Revolting: Queer Strategies for Resisting Assimilation*. Brooklyn: Soft Skull Press.

Mauss, M. 1990. *The Gift: The Form and Reasons for Exchange in Archaic Societies*. Translated by W.H. Hall. London: Routledge.

May, T. 1994. *The Political Philosophy of Poststructuralist Anarchism*. University Park: Pennsylvania State University Press.

———. 2001. *Our Practices, Our Selves: Or, What It Means to Be Human*. University Park: Penn State University Press.

Maynard, M. 1994. Methods, practice and epistemology: The debate about feminism and research, in *Researching Women's Lives From a Feminist Perspective*, edited by M. Maynard and J. Purvis. London: Taylor & Francis, 10–26.

McCall, L. 2005. The complexity of intersectionality. *Signs*, 30(3), 1771–1800.

McCormack, T. 1987. Feminism and the new crisis in methodology, in *The Effects of Feminist Approaches on Research Methodologies*, edited by W. Tomm. Calgary: Winfrid Laurier University Press, 13–30.

McDermott, E. 2004. Telling lesbian stories: Interviewing and the class dynamics of 'talk'. *Women's Studies International Forum*, 27(3), 177–87.

McIlvenny, P. 2002a. Critical reflections on performativity and the 'un/doing' of gender and sexuality in talk, in *Talking Gender and Sexuality*, edited by P. McIlvenny. Philadelphia: John Benjamins, 111–49.

———. 2002b. Introduction: Researching talk, gender and sexuality, in *Talking Gender and Sexuality*, edited by P. McIlvenny. Philadelphia: John Benjamins, 1–47.

McIntosh, M. 1968. The homosexual role. *Social Problems*, 16(2), 182–92.

McKenney, N. and Bennett, C. 1994. Issues regarding data on race and ethnicity: The Census Bureau experience. *Public Health Reports*, 109(1), 16–25.

McKinlay, A. and Dunnett, A. 1998. How gun-owners accomplish being deadly average, in *Identities in Talk*, edited by C. Antaki and S. Widdicombe. London: Sage, 34–51.

McLafferty, S.L. 1995. Counting for women. *Professional Geographer*, 47(4), 436.

McManus, S. 2000. *Sexual Orientation Research Phase 1: A Review of Methodological Approaches on behalf of the Scottish Executive.* [Online]. Available at: http://www.scotland.gov.uk/Publications/2003/03/16650/19351.

McNay, L. 2004. Agency and Experience: Gender as a Lived Relation, in *Feminism after Bourdieu*, edited by L. Adkins and B. Skeggs. Oxford: Blackwell, 175–90.

McRobbie, A. 1997. The Es and the anti-Es: New questions for feminism and cultural studies, in *Cultural Studies in Question*, edited by M. Ferguson and P. Golding. London: Sage, 170–87.

———. 2002. A mixed bag of misfortunes. *Theory Culture and Society*, 19(3), 129–38.

Menjivar, C. 2000. *Fragmented Ties: Salvadoran Immigrants Networks in America*. London: University of California Press.

Mertz, L. 2008. 'I am what I am?': Towards a sexual politics of contingent foundations. *Graduate Journal of Social Science*, 5(2), 19–34.

MetLife. 2006. *Out and Aging The MetLife Study of Lesbian and Gay Baby Boomers*. [Online: MetLife Mature Market Institute]. Available at: http://www. asaging.org/networks/lgain/OutandAging.pdf. [accessed: 4 February 2008].

Meyer, M.D.E. 2005. Drawing the sexuality card: Teaching, researching, and living bisexuality. *Sexuality and Culture*, 9(1), 3–13.

Mills, C. 1959. *The Sociological Imagination*. London: Oxford University Press.

Minh-ha, Trinh T. 1990. Not you/like you: Post-colonial women and the interlocking questions of identity and difference?, in *Making Face, Making Soul (Haciendo Caras): Creative and Critical Perspectives by Feminists of Color* edited by A. Gloria. San Francisco: Aunt Lute Books, 371–5.

Mintz, B. and Rothblum, E. (eds) 2003. *Lesbians in Academia: Degrees of Freedom*. London: Routledge.

Mohanty, C.T. 1989–90. On race and voice: Challenges for liberal education in the 1990s. *Cultural Critique*, special issue, 'Gender and Modes of Social Division II' 14: 179–208.

———. 2003. *Feminism without Borders: Decolonizing Theory, Practicing Solidarity*. Durham: Duke University Press.

Moloney, M. and Fenstermaker, S. 2002. Performance and accomplishment: Reconciling feminist conceptions of gender, in *Doing Gender, Doing Difference: Inequality, Power and Institutional Change*, edited by S. Fenstermaker and C. West. New York: Routledge, 189–204.

Moraga, C. 1983. *Loving in the War Years*. Boston: South End Press.

Moraga, C. and Anzaldúa, G. 1981. *This Bridge Called My Back: Writings by Radical Women of Color*. Watertown, MA: Persephone Press.

Moran, L. 2000. Homophobic violence: The hidden injuries of class, in *Cultural Studies and the Working Class: Subject to Change*, edited by S.R. Munt. London: Cassell, 206–18.

Moreno, E. 1995. Rape in the field, reflections for a survivor, in *Taboo: Sex, Identity and Erotic Subjectivity in Anthropological Fieldwork*, edited by D. Kulick and M. Willson. London: Routledge, 219–50.

Morgan, R. and Wieringa, S. (eds) 2005. *Tommy Boys, Lesbian Men and Ancestral Lives: Female Same-sex Practices in Africa*. Johannesburg: Jacana.

Morris, B.J. 2005. Valuing women-only spaces. *Feminist Studies*, 31(3), 618–30.

Moss, P. 1995a. Embeddedness in practice, numbers in context: The politics of knowing and doing. *Professional Geographer*, 47(4), 442.

Moss, P. 1995b. Reflection on the 'gap' as part of the politics of research design. *Antipode*, 27(1), 82–90.

———. 2001. *Placing Autobiography in Geography*. New York: Syracuse University Press.

———. (ed.) 2002. *Feminist Geography in Practice: Research and Methods*. Oxford: Blackwell.

———. 2006. Emergent methods in feminist research, in *Handbook of Feminist Research*, edited by S. Biber-Hesse. Thousand Oaks: Sage, 371–90.

Moss, P. and Falconer Al-Hindi, K. (eds) 2007. *Feminisms in Geography: Rethinking Space, Place and Knowledges*. Lanham: Rowman & Littlefield.

Mueller, J.H. 2007. Ignorance is neither bliss nor ethical. *Northwestern University Law Review*, 101(2), 809–36.

Muñoz, J.E. 1996. Ephemera as evidence: Introductory notes to queer acts. *Women and Performance*, (16), 5–16.

———. 1999. *Disidentifications: Queers of Color and the Performance of Politics*. Minneapolis: University of Minnesota Press.

Muñoz, L. 2008. *Tamales, Elotes, Champurrado: The Production of Latino Vending Street-Scapes in Los Angeles*. Ph.D. thesis, Department of Geography, University of Southern California, Los Angeles.

Murdoch, J. 1997. Inhuman/nonhuman/human: Actor-network theory and the prospects for a non-dualistic and symmetrical perspective on nature and society. *Environment and Planning D-Society and Space*, 15(6), 731–56.

Muscio, I. 1998. *Cunt: A Declaration of Independence*. Seattle: Seal Press.

Nader, L. 1982. Up the anthropologist – perspectives from studying up, in *Anthropology for the Eighties*, edited by J.B. Cole. New York: The Free Press, 456–70.

Nagel, J. 1994. Constructing ethnicity: Creating and recreating ethnic identity and culture. *Social Problems*, 41(1), 152–76.

Nakayama, T.K. and Corey, F.C. 2003. Nextext. *Journal of Homosexuality*, 45(2–4), 319–34.

Namaste, V.K. 2000. *Invisible Lives: The Erasure of Transsexual and Transgendered People*. Chicago: University of Chicago Press.

Narayan, K. 1993. How native is the native anthropologist? *American Anthropologist*, 93(5), 671–86.

Nash, C.J. 2001. Siting lesbians: Sexuality, space and social organization, in *Queer Country: Gay and Lesbian Studies in the Canadian Context*, edited by T Goldie. Vancouver: Arsenal Press, 235–56.

———. 2006. Toronto's gay village (1969 to 1982) plotting the politics of gay identity. *Canadian Geographer*, 50(1), 1–16.

————. forthcoming. Transecting the traditional gay ghetto: Trans experiences in lesbian and queer space. *Canadian Geographer*.

Nash, C.J. and Bain, A.L. 2007a. 'Reclaiming raunch'? Spatializing queer identities at Toronto Women's Bathhouse events. *Social and Cultural Geography*, 8(1), 47–62.

————. 2007b. Pussies declawed: Unpacking the politics of a queer women's bathhouse raid, in *Geographies of Sexualities: Theory, Practices and Politics*, edited by K. Browne, J. Lim and G. Brown. Aldershot: Ashgate, 159–68.

Nast, H.J. 1994. Opening remarks on 'Women in the Field'. *The Professional Geographer*, 46(11), 54–66.

————. 2002. Queer patriarchies, queer racisms, international. *Antipode*, 34(5), 874–909.

Nestle, J. 1983. My mother liked to fuck, in *Powers of Desire: The Politics of Sexuality*, edited by A. Snitow and C. Stansell. New York: Monthly Review Press, 468–70.

————. 1987. *A Restricted Country*. New York: Firebrand.

————. (ed.) 1992. *The Persistent Desire: A Femme-Butch Reader*. Boston: Alyson Books.

Neumann, M. 1996. Collecting ourselves at the end of the century, in *Composing Ethnography: Alternative Forms of Qualitative Writing*, edited by C. Ellis and A.P. Bochner. Walnut Creek, CA: AltaMira, 172–98.

New, C. 2001. Oppressed and oppressors? The systematic mistreatment of men. *Sociology*, 35(3), 729–48.

Newman, L. (ed.) 1995. *The Femme Mystique*. San Francisco: Alyson Books.

Newman, S. 2007. *Unstable Universalities: Postmodernity and Radical Politics*. Manchester: Manchester University Press.

Newton, E. 1979. *Mother Camp: Female Impersonators in America*. Chicago: University of Chicago Press.

————. 1995. *Cherry Grove, Fire Island: Sixty Years in America's First Gay Town*. New York: Beacon.

————. 2000. *Margaret Mead Made Me Gay: Personal Essays, Public Ideas*. Durham: Duke University Press.

Nicholas, C.L. 2006. Disciplinary-interdisciplinary GLBTQ (identity) studies and Hecht's layering perspective. *Communication Quarterly*, 54(3), 305–30.

Nikander, P. 2000. 'Old' vs 'little girl': A discursive approach to age categorization and morality. *Journal of Aging Studies*, 14(4), 335–58.

Noble, B. 2004. *Masculinities Without Men: Female Masculinity in Twentieth-century Fiction*. Vancouver: UBC Press.

————. 2006. *Sons of the Movement: FtMs Risking Incoherence on a Postqueer Cultural Landscape*. Toronto: Women's Press.

Nobles, M. 2002. Racial categorisation and censuses, in *Census and Identity: The Politics of Race, Ethnicity and Language in National Censuses*, edited by D. Kertzer and D. Arel. Cambridge: Cambridge University Press, 43–70.

———. 2008. *Shades of Citizenship: Race and the Census in Modern Politics.* Stanford: Stanford University Press.

Oakes, J.M. 2002. Risks and wrongs in social science research: An evaluator's guide to the IRB. *Evaluation Review*, 26(5), 443–79.

O'Brien, J. 2008. Afterword: Complicating Homophobia. *Sexualities*, 11(4), 496–512.

Office for National Statistics. 2006. *The 2011 Census: Assessment of Initial User Requirements on Content for England and Wales: Sexual Orientation.* [Online: Information Paper]. Available at: http://www.ons.gov.uk/about-statistics/measuring-equality/sexual-identity-project/sex-iden-consultation. pdf [accessed: 12 December 2008].

———. 2007. *All about the Census: Fact Sheet Four Census Text 2007.* [Online]. Available at: http://www.ons.gov.uk/census/2011-census/2011-census-project/2007-test/2007-fact-sheets/all-about-the-census---english.pdf [accessed: 12 December 2008].

Okely, J. 1992. Anthropology and autobiography: Participatory experience and embodied knowledge, in *Anthropology and Autobiography*, edited by J. Okely and H. Callaway. London: Routledge, 1–28.

Ong, A. and Collier, S.J. (eds) 2005. *Global Assemblages: Technology, Politics, and Ethics as Anthropological Problems.* Oxford: Blackwell.

O'Rourke, M. 2006. The becoming-deleuzoguattarian of queer studies. *Rhizomes*, [Online] (11/12). Available at: http://www.rhizomes.net/issue11.

Osteen, M. 2002. Introduction: Questions of the gift, in *The Question of the Gift: Essays across Disciplines*, edited by M. Osteen. London: Routledge, 1–41.

Oswin, N. 2005. Towards radical geographies of complicit queer futures. *ACME: An International E-Journal for Critical Geographers*, 3(2), 79–86.

———. 2008. Critical geographies and the uses of sexuality: Deconstructing queer space. *Progress in Human Geography*, 32(1), 89–103.

Owen, A.S. 2003. Disciplining 'sextext': Queers, fears, and communication studies. *Journal of Homosexuality*, 45(2–4), 297–317.

Pain, R. 2001. Gender, race, age and fear in the city. *Urban Studies*, 38(5–6), 899–913.

———. 2003. Social geography: On action-oriented research. *Progress in Human Geography*, 27(5), 649–57.

———. 2004. Social geography: Participatory research. *Progress in Human Geography*, 28(5), 652–63.

———. 2006. Social geography: Seven deadly myths in policy research. *Progress in Human Geography*, 30(2), 250–259.

Pain, R. and Francis, P. 2003. Reflections on participatory research. *Area*, 35(1), 46–54.

Pallotta-Chiarolli, M. 1999. 'Multicultural does not mean multisexual': Social justice and the interweaving of ethnicity and sexuality in Australian schooling, in *A Dangerous Knowing: Sexuality, Pedagogy and Popular Culture*, edited by D. Epstein and J.T. Sears. London: Cassell, 283–302.

Panetta, A. 2005. Harper: Same sex debate not over. *Halifax Chronicle-Herald*, 29 June, A1.

Pelias, R.J. 1999. *Writing Performance: Poeticizing the Researcher's Body.* Carbondale: Southern Illinois University Press.

———. 2000. The critical life. *Communication Education,* 49(3), 220–28.

———. 2004. *A Methodology of the Heart: Evoking Academic and Daily Life.* Walnut Creek, CA: AltaMira.

———. 2007. Jarheads, girly men, and the pleasures of violence. *Qualitative Inquiry,* 13(7), 945–59.

Pels, P. 1998. The Spirit of Matter: On Fetish, Rarity, Fact, and Fancy, in *Border Fetishisms: Material Objects in Unstable Places,* edited by P. Speyer. New York: Routledge, 91–121.

Penn, D. 1995. Queer: Theorizing politics and history. *Radical History Review,* (62), 24–42.

Perez, H. 2005. You can have my brown body and eat it, too! *Social Text,* 23(3–4), 171–91.

Phelan, P. 1993. *Unmarked: The Politics of Performance.* New York: Routledge.

Phelan, S. 1989. *Identity Politics: Lesbian Feminism and the Limits of Community.* Philadelphia: Temple University Press.

Phillips, R. and Watt, D. 2000. Introduction, in *De-Centering Sexualities: Politics and Representations beyond the Metropolis,* edited by R. Phillips, D. Watt and D. Shuttleton. New York: Routledge, 1–17.

Pichardo, G.J.I. 2003. Migraciones y opcion sexual, in *Sexualidades: Diversidad y Control Social,* edited by O. Guasch and O. Vinuales. Barcelona: Ediciones Bellaterra, 278–97.

Piercy, M. 1991. *Body of Glass.* London: Penguin.

———. 2000. *Woman on the Edge of Time.* London: The Women's Press.

Pike, K.L. 1967. *Language in Relation to a Unified Theory of Structure of Human Behavior.* 2nd Edition. The Hague: Mouton.

Pineau, E. 2000. Nursing Mother and articulating absence. *Text and Performance Quarterly,* 20(1), 1–19.

Pinney, C. 2005. Things happen: Or, from which moment does that object come?, in *Materiality,* edited by D. Miller. Durham NC: Duke University Press, 256- 72.

Plummer, K. 1998. Afterward: The past, present and futures of the sociology of same sex relations, in *Social Perspectives in Lesbian and Gay Studies: A Reader,* edited by P. Nardi and B. Scheider. London: Routledge, 605–14.

———. 2003. Queers, bodies and postmodern sexualities: A note on revisiting the 'sexual' in symbolic interactionism. *Qualitative Sociology,* 26(4), 515–30.

———. 2005. Critical humanism and queer theory: Living with the tensions, in *The Landscape of Qualitative Research: Theories and Issues,* edited by N. Denzin and Y. Lincoln. London: Sage, 357–73.

Podmore, J. 2001. Lesbians in the crowd: Gender, sexuality, and visibility along Montréal's Boulevard St.-Laurent. *Gender, Place, and Culture,* (24), 191–217.

———. 2006. Gone 'underground'? Lesbian visibility and the consolidation of queer space in Montreal. *Social and Cultural Geography,* 7(4), 595–625.

Pollner, M. 1991. Left of ethnomethodology: The rise and decline of radical reflexivity. *American Sociological Review*, 56(3), 370–380.

Pollock, D. 1998a. Introduction: Making history go, in *Exceptional Spaces: Essays in Performance and History*, edited by D. Pollock. Chapel Hill: University of North Carolina Press, 1–45.

———. 1998b. Performative writing, in *The Ends of Performance*, edited by P. Phelan and J. Lane. New York: New York University Press, 73–101.

———. 2006. Marking new directions in performance ethnography. *Text and Performance Quarterly*, 26(4), 325–29.

———. 2007. The performative 'I'. *Cultural Studies ↔ Critical Methodologies*, (7), 239–55.

Porter, T.M. 1995. *Trust in Numbers: The Pursuit of Objectivity in Science and Public Life*. Princeton: Princeton University Press.

Povinelli, E.A. 2002. *The Cunning of Recognition: Indigenous Alterities and the Making of Australian Multiculturalism*. Durham: Duke University Press.

———. 2006. *Empire of Love: Toward a Theory of Intimacy, Genealogy, and Carnality*. Durham: Duke University Press.

Povinelli, E.A. and Chauncey, G. 1999. Thinking sexuality transnationally. *GLQ: A Journal of Gay and Lesbian Studies*, 5(4), 439–50.

Power, T. 2009. For queer eyes only?: Creating queer performance art at university. *Graduate Journal of Social Science*, 6(1), 24–41.

Pratt, M.B. 1990. *Crime against Nature*. Ithaca, NY: Firebrand.

———. 1995. *S/he*. New York: Firebrand books.

Preston, J. 1993. *My Life as a Pornographer and Other Indecent Acts*. New York: Richard Kasak.

Prewitt, K. 2003. *Politics and Science in Census Taking*. New York: Russell Sage Foundation and the Population Reference Bureau.

———. 2005. Racial classification in America: Where do we go from here? *Daedalus*, 134(1), 5–17.

Prichard, A. Morgan, N.J. and Sedgely, D. 2002. In search of lesbian space? The experience of Manchester's gay village. *Leisure Studies*, 21(2), 105–23.

Probyn, E. 1993. *Sexing the Self: Gendered Positions in Cultural Studies*. London: Routledge.

———. 2003. The spatial imperative of subjectivity, in *Handbook of Cultural Geography*, edited by K. Anderson et al. London: Sage, 290–99.

Prosser, J. 1998. *Second Skin: The Body Narrative of Transsexuality*. New York: Columbia University.

Puar, J.K. 2001. Global circuits: Transnational sexualities and Trinidad. *Signs*, 26(4), 1039–65.

———. 2002. A transnational feminist critique of queer tourism. *Antipode*, 34(5), 935–46.

———. 2005. Queer times, queer assemblages. *Social Text*, 23(3–4), 121–39.

———. 2007. *Terrorist Assemblages: Homonationalism in Queer Times*. Durham: Duke University Press.

Puar, J.K., Rushbrook, D. and Schein, L. 2003. Sexuality and space: Queering geographies of globalization. *Environment and Planning D: Society and Space*, (21), 383–87.

Purdam, K. et al. 2008. Surveying sexual orientation: Asking difficult questions and providing useful answers. *Culture, Health and Sexuality*, 10(2), 127–41.

Quam, J.K. and Whitford, G.S. 1992. Adaptation and age-related expectations of older gay and lesbian adults. *The Gerontologist*, 32(3), 367–74.

Ramazanoðlu, C with J. Holland. 2002 *Feminist Methodology: Challenges and Choices*. London: Sage.

Rambo, C. 2005. Impressions of grandmother: An autoethnographic portrait. *Journal of Contemporary Ethnography*, 34(5), 560–85.

———. 2007. Handing IRB an unloaded gun. *Qualitative Inquiry*, 13(3), 353–67.

Rand, E. 1995. *Barbie's Queer Accessories*. Durham: Duke University Press.

Raymond, Janice. 1979 [1994]. *The Transsexual Empire: The Making of the She-Male* (with a new introduction on transgender). New York: Teachers College.

Rednour, S. 2000. *The Femme's Guide to the Universe*. San Francisco: Alyson Books.

Reed, C. 1996. Imminent domain: Queer space in the built environment. *Art Journal*, 55(4), 64–70.

Reed-Danahay, D.E. 1997. *Auto/ethnography: Rewriting the Self and the Social*. Oxford: Berg.

Reynolds, P. 2001. Accounting for sexuality: The scope and limitations of Census data on sexual identity and difference. *Radical Statistics*, (78), 63–76.

Richardson, D., McLaughlin, J. and Casey, M.E. (eds) 2006. *Intersections between Feminist and Queer Theory*. New York: Palgrave Macmillan.

Richardson, L. and St. Pierre, E.A. 2005. Writing: A method of inquiry, in *Handbook of Qualitative Research*, edited by N.K. Denzin and Y.S. Lincoln. Thousand Oaks, CA: Sage, 959–78.

Riessman, C.K. 2008. *Narrative Methods for the Human Sciences*. London: Sage.

Riggs, D. 2006. *Priscilla, (White) Queen of the Desert: Queer Rights/Race Privilege*. New York: Peter Lang.

———. 2007. Possessive investments at the intersection of race, gender and sexuality: lesbian and gay rights in a 'post-colonising' nation, in *Intersections: Gender, Race and Ethnicity in Australasian Studies*, edited by M. Allen and R. Dhawan. New Delhi: Prestige, 111–25.

Robina, M. 2001. 'Insiders' and/or 'outsiders': positionality, theory and praxis , in *Qualitative Methodologies for Geographers*, edited by M. Limb and C. Dwyer. New York: Oxford University Press, 101–14.

Rodríguez, J.M. 2003. *Queer Latinidad: Identity Practices, Discursive Spaces*. New York: New York University Press.

Ronai, C.R. 1995. Multiple reflections of child sex abuse. *Journal of Contemporary Ethnography*, 23(4), 395–426.

Rooke, A. 2007. Navigating embodied lesbian space: Towards a lesbian habitus. *Space and Culture*, 10(2), 231–52.

Rosaldo, R. 1989. *Culture and Truth: The Remaking of Social Analysis*. Boston: Beacon.

Roscoe, W. 1996. Writing queer cultures: an impossible possibility?, in *Out in the Field: Reflections of Lesbian and Gay Anthropologists*, edited by E. Lewin and W.L. Leap. Urbana: University of Illinois Press, 200–211.

Rose, C. Brushwood and Camilleri, A. (eds) 2002. *Brazen Femme: Queering Femininity*. Vancouver: Arsenal Pulp Press.

Rose, G. 1993. *Feminism and Geography: The Limits of Geographical Knowledge*. Minneapolis: University of Minnesota Press.

———. 1997. Situating knowledges: Positionality, reflexivities and other tactics. *Progress in Human Geography*, 21(3), 305–20.

Rosenberg, M.B. 2003. *Nonviolent Communication: A Language of Life*. Encinitas, CA: PuddleDancer Press.

Rosenberg, T. 2000. *Byxbegär*. Stockholm: Atlas.

———. 2002. *Queerfeministisk Agenda*. Stockholm: Atlas.

———. 2008. Locally queer. A note on the feminist genealogy of queer theory. *Graduate Journal in Social Science*, 5(2), 5–18.

Roseneil, S. 2000. *Common Women, Uncommon Practices: The Queer Feminisms of Greenham*. London: Cassell.

———. 2002. The heterosexual/homosexual binary: Past, present and future, in *Handbook of Lesbian and Gay Studies*, edited by D. Richardson and S. Seidman. London: Sage, 27–43.

Rosenfeld, D. 2002. Identity careers of older gay men and lesbians, in *Ways of Aging*, edited by F. Gubrium and J.A. Holstein. Oxford: Blackwell, 160–81.

Ross, B. 1995. *The House That Jill Built: A Lesbian Nation in Formation*. Toronto: University of Toronto Press.

Rothenberg, T. 1995. 'And she told two friends': Lesbians creating urban social space, in *Mapping Desire: Geographies of Sexuality*, edited by D. Bell and G. Valentine. London: Routledge, 166–81.

Rousselle, D. and Evren, S. (eds) 2010. *Anarchy at the Brink! The Post-Anarchism Anthology*. London: Pluto Press.

Rua'ine, G. 2007. Takatâpui and HIV – A personal journey, in *Sexuality and Stories of Indigenous People*, edited by J. Hutchings and C. Aspin. Wellington: Huia Publishers, 149–58.

Rubin, G. 1993. Thinking sex: Notes for a radical theory of the politics of sexuality, in *The Lesbian and Gay Studies Reader*, edited by H. Abelove, M.A. Barale and D.M. Halperin. New York: Routledge, 3–44.

Rushbrook, D. 2002. Cities, queer space, and the cosmopolitan tourist. *GLQ: A Journal of Lesbian and Gay Studies*, 8(1–2), 183–206.

Ryan-Flood, R. 2005. Contested heteronormativities: Discourses of fatherhood among lesbian parents in Sweden and Ireland. *Sexualities*, 8(2), 239–54.

Sacks, H. 1995. *Lectures on Conversation: Volumes 1 and 2*. Oxford: Blackwell.

Said, E.W. 1983. *The World, the Text, and the Critic*. Cambridge, MA: Harvard University Press.

Sandoval, C. 2000. *Methodology of the Oppressed*. Minneapolis: University of Minnesota Press.

Sanger, T. 2010. *Trans People's Partnerships: Towards an Ethics of Intimacy*. Basingstoke: Palgrave Macmillan.

Sawyer, L. 2008. Grama, Einstein and me. *Slut*, (2), 8–17.

Schaffner, L. 2002. An age of reason: Paradoxes in the U.S. legal construction of adulthood. *The International Journal of Children's Rights*, (10), 201–32.

———. 2005. Capacity, consent, and the construction of adulthood, in *Regulating Sex: The Politics of Intimacy and Identity*, edited by E. Bernstein and L. Schaffner. New York: Routledge, 189–208.

Schegloff, E.A. 2007. A tutorial on membership categorization. *Journal of Pragmatics*, (39), 462–82.

Scott, J.W. 1991. The evidence of experience. *Critical Inquiry*, 17(4), 773–97.

Sedgwick, E.K. 1985. *Between Men: English Literature and Male Homosocial Desire*. New York: Columbia University Press.

———. 1990. *Epistemology of the Closet*. Berkeley: University of California Press.

———. 1993. *Tendencies*. Durham: Duke University Press.

———. 2000. *A Dialogue on Love*. Boston: Beacon Press.

———. 2003. *Touching Feeling: Affect, Pedagogy, Performativity*. Durham: Duke University Press.

Seidman, S. 1993. Identity and politics in a 'postmodern' gay culture: Some historical and conceptual notes, in *Fear of a Queer Planet: Queer Politics and Social Theory*, edited by M. Warner. Minneapolis: University of Minnesota Press, 105–42.

———. 1995. Deconstructing queer theory or the under-theorization of the social and the ethical, in *Social Postmodernism*, edited by L. Nicholson and S. Seidman. Cambridge: Cambridge University Press, 116–41.

———. (ed.) 1996. *Queer Theory / Sociology*. Oxford: Blackwell.

———. 1997. *Difference Troubles: Queering Social Theory and Sexual Politics*. Cambridge: Cambridge University Press.

———. 2002. *Beyond the Closet: The Transformation of Gay and Lesbian Life*. London: Routledge.

Sillitoe, K. and White, P. 1992. Ethnic group and the British Census: The search for a question. *Journal of the Royal Statistical Society*, 155(1), 141–63.

Silverman, D. 1998. *Harvey Sacks: Social Science and Conversation Analysis*. Oxford: Polity Press.

Silvey, R. 2003. Gender and mobility: Critical ethnographies of migration in Indonesia, in *Cultural Geography in Practice*, edited by A. Blunt, et al. London: Arnold, 91–102.

Skeggs, B. 1994. Situating the production of feminist ethnography, in *Researching Women's Lives*, edited by M. Maynard and J. Purvis. Basingstoke: Taylor and Francis, 72–93.

———. 1997. *Formations of Class and Gender – Becoming Respectable*. London: Sage.

————. 2001. The toilet paper: Femininity, class and mis-recognition. *Women's Studies International Forum*, 24(3–4), 295–307.

————. 2002. Techniques for telling the reflexive self in *Qualitative Methods in Action* edited by Tim May, London: Sage, 349–74.

————. 2003. *Class, Self, Culture*. London: Routledge.

Slattery, P. 2001. The educational researcher as artist working within. *Qualitative Inquiry*, 7(3), 370–98.

Smith, C. 2000. How I became a queer heterosexual, in *Straight with a Twist: Queer Theory and the Subject of Heterosexuality*, edited by C. Thomas. Urbana: University of Illinois Press, 60–67.

Sontag, S. 1964. Notes on 'camp'. *Partisan Review*, 31(4), 515–30.

————. 1966. The anthropologist as hero, in *Against Interpretation and Other Essays*. New York: Picador.

Speer, S.A. 2002. What can conversation analysis contribute to feminist methodology? Putting reflexivity into practice. *Discourse and Society*, 13(6), 783–803.

————. 2005. *Gender Talk: Feminism, Discourse and Conversation Analysis*. London: Routledge.

Speer, S.A. and Potter, J. 2002. From performatives to practices: Judith Butler, discursive psychology and the management of heterosexist talk, in *Talking Gender and Sexuality*, edited by P. McIlvenny. Philadelphia: John Benjamins, 151–80.

Spry, T. 2001. Performing autoethnography: An embodied methodological praxis. *Qualitative Inquiry*, 7(6), 706–32.

————. 2006. A 'Performative-I' copresence: Embodying the ethnographic turn in performance and the performative turn in ethnography. *Text and Performance Quarterly*, 26(4), 339–46.

Stacey, J. 1988. Can there be a feminist ethnography? *Women's Studies International Forum*, 11(1), 21–7.

Stacey, J. and Biblarz, T.J. 2001. (How) does the sexual orientation of parents matter? *American Sociological Review*, 66(2), 159–83.

Staeheli, L. 1996. Publicity, privacy, and women's political action. *Environment and Planning D: Society and Space*, 14(5), 601–19.

Staeheli, L. and Lawson, V. 1994. A discussion of 'women in the field': The politics of feminist fieldwork. *Professional Geographer*, 46(1), 96–102.

Stainton Rogers, W. and Stainton Rogers, R. 1997. Does critical social psychology mean the end of the world?, in *Critical Social Psychology*, edited by T. Ibáñez and L. Íñigues. London: Sage, 67–82.

Stanley, L. 1990. Feminist praxis and the academic mode of production: An editorial introduction, in *Feminist Praxis: Research Theory and Epistemology and Feminist Sociology*, edited by L. Stanley. London: Routledge, 3–19.

————. 1997. Methodology matters!, in *Introducing Women's Studies*, edited by V. Robinson and D. Richardson. London: Macmillian, 198–219.

Stanley, L. and Wise, S. 1983a. *Breaking Out*. London: Routledge.

————. 1983b. 'Back into the personal' or: Our attempt to construct 'feminist research', in *Theories of Women's Studies*, edited by G. Bowles and R.D. Klein. London: Routledge, 192–209.

————. 1990. Method, methodology and epistemology in feminist research processes, in *Feminist Praxis: Research, Theory and Epistemology in Feminist Sociology*, edited by L. Stanley. London: Routledge, 20–60.

————. 1993. *Breaking Out ... Again*. London: Routledge.

————. 2000. But the Empress has no clothes! *Feminist Theory*, 1(3), 261–88.

Starhawk. 1993. *The Fifth Sacred Thing*. New York: Bantam.

Stein, E. (ed.) 1992. *Forms of Desire: Sexual Orientation and the Social Constructionist Controversy*. New York: Routledge.

Stokes, E. 1985. *Māori Research and Development*. A discussion paper prepared for the Social Sciences Committee of the National Research Advisory Council, National Research Advisory Council, Wellington.

Stokoe, E.H. 2003a. Doing gender, doing categorisation: Recent developments in language and gender research. *International Sociolinguistics*, 2(1), 1–12.

————. 2003b. Mothers, single women and sluts: Gender, morality and membership categorization in neighbour disputes. *Feminism and Psychology*, 13(3), 317–44.

————. 2004. Gender and discourse, gender and categorization: Current developments in language and gender research. *Qualitative Research in Psychology*, (1), 107–29.

Stonewall Cymru and Triangle Wales. 2006. *The Housing Needs of Lesbian, Gay and Bisexual (LGB) People in Wales*. [Online: Welsh Assembly] Available at: www.stonewallcymru.org.uk/documents/triangle_wale__report_engli.pdf [accessed: 4 February 2008].

Storr, M, and Nigianni C. (eds) 2009. *Deleuze and Queer Theory*. Edinburgh: Edinburgh University Press.

Strathern, M. 1988. *The Gender of the Gift: Problems with Women and Problems with Society in Melanesia*. Berkeley: University of California Press.

Stryker, S. 2006. (De)subjugated knowledges: An introduction to transgender studies, in *The Transgender Studies Reader*, edited by S. Stryker and S. Whittle. London: Routledge, 1–17.

Stryker, S. and Whittle, S. (eds) 2006. *The Transgender Studies Reader*. London: Routledge.

Stychin, C. 2006. Las Vegas is not where we are: Queer readings of the Civil Partnership Act. *Political Geography*, 25(8), 899–920.

Sullivan, M. 2001. Alma-mater: Family 'outings' and the making of the modern other mother (MOM), in *Queer Families, Queer Politics: Challenging Culture and the State*, edited by M. Bernstein and R. Reimann. New York: Columbia University Press, 231–53.

Sullivan, N. 2003. *A Critical Introduction to Queer Theory*. Edinburgh: Edinburgh University Press.

Sullivan, S. 2005. An other world is possible? On representation, rationalism and romanticism in social forums. *Ephemera*, 5(2), 370-92. Available at: http://www.ephemeraweb.org/journal/5-2/5-2ssullivan.pdf [accessed: 3 May 2008].

———. 2008. Conceptualising glocal organisation: From rhizomes to E=mc2 in becoming post-human, in *Metaphors of Globalisation: Mirrors, Magicians and Mutinies*, edited by M. Kornprobst et al. Basingstoke: Palgrave Macmillan, 149–66.

Sycamore, M.B. 2004. *That's Revolting! Queer Strategies for Resisting Assimilation*. New York: Soft Skull Press.

Taussig, M. 1987 *Shamanism, Colonialism, and the Wild Man: A Study in Terror and Healing*. Chicago: University of Chicago Press.

Taylor, J. 2000. On being an exemplary lesbian: My life as a role model. *Text and Performance Quarterly*, 20(1), 58–73.

Taylor, T. 2008a. *Developing Survey Questions on Sexual Identity: Report on National Statistics Omnibus Survey Trials 1 and 2*. [Online: Office for National Statistics] Available at: http://www.ons.gov.uk/about-statistics/measuring-equality/sexual-identity-project/quest-test-and-implem/omnibus-trials-1-and-2.pdf [accessed: 12 December 2008].

———. 2008b. *Developing Survey Questions on Sexual Identity: Review of International Organisations' Experiences of Administering Questions on Sexual Identity/Orientation*. [Online: Office for National Statistics] Available at: http://www.ons.gov.uk/about-statistics/measuring-equality/sexual-identity-project/quest-dev/inter-exper.pdf [accessed: 12 December 2008].

Taylor, T. and Ralph, K. 2008. *Developing Survey Questions on Sexual Identity: Report on National Statistics Omnibus Survey Trial 3*. [Online: Office for National Statistics] Available at: http://www.ons.gov.uk/about-statistics/measuring-equality/sexual-identity-project/quest-test-and-implem/omnibus-trial-3.pdf [accessed: 12 December 2008].

Taylor, Y. 2005. The gap and how to mind it: Intersections of class and sexuality. *Sociological Research Online*, 10(3). Available at: http://www.socresonline.org.uk/10/3/taylor.html.

———. 2007. *Working-class lesbian life: Classed Outsiders*. Basingstoke: Palgrave Macmillan.

———. 2009a. Interesting intersections? Researching class, gender and sexuality, in *The Intersectional Approach: Transforming Women's and Gender Studies through Race, Class and Gender*, edited by M. Berger and K. Guidroz, 193–209.

———. 2009b. *Lesbian and Gay Parenting: Securing Social and Educational Capital*. Basingstoke: Palgrave Macmillan.

Thomas, C. (ed.) 2000. *Straight with a Twist: Queer Theory and the Subject of Heterosexuality*. Urbana: University of Illinois Press.

———. 2000. Introduction: Identification, appropriation, proliferation, in *Straight with a Twist: Queer Theory and the Subject of Heterosexuality*, edited by C. Thomas. Urbana: University of Illinois Press, 1–7.

Tolley, C. and Ranzijn, R. 2006. Heteronormativity amongst staff of residential care facilities. *Gay and Lesbian Issues and Psychology Review*, 2(2), 78–86.

Tucker, A. 2008. *Queer Visibilities: Space, Identity and Interaction in Cape Town*. Oxford: Wiley-Blackwells.

Tuhiwai Smith, L. 1999. *Decolonizing Methodologies: Research and Indigenous Peoples*. London: Zed.

Tuhkanen, M. 2009. Queer hybridity, in *Deleuze and Queer Theory*, edited by M. Storr and C. Nigianni. Edinburgh: Edinburgh University Press, 92–114.

Turner, W. 2000. *Genealogy of Queer Theory*. Philadelphia: Temple University Press.

Tyler, C. 2003. *Female Impersonation*. New York: Routledge.

Valentine, G. 1993. (Hetero)sexing space: Lesbians perceptions and experiences of everyday places. *Environment and Planning D: Space and Society*, 11(4), 395–413.

———. 2002. People like us: Negotiating sameness and difference in the research process, in *Feminist Geography in Practice: Research and Methods*, edited by P. Moss. Oxford: Blackwell, 116–26.

———. 2007. Theorizing and researching intersectionality: A challenge for feminist geography. *Professional Geographer*, 51(1), 10–21.

Valentine, G. and Skelton, T. 2003. Finding oneself, losing oneself: The lesbian and gay 'scene' as a paradoxical space. *International Journal of Urban and Regional Research*, 27(4), 849–66.

Valocchi, S. 2005. Not yet queer enough: The lessons of queer theory for the sociology of gender and sexuality. *Gender and Society*, 19(6), 750–70.

Visweswaran, K. 1994. *Fictions of Feminist Ethnography*. Minneapolis: University of Minnesota Press.

Viteri, M.A. 2008. 'Latino' and 'queer' as sites of translation: Intersections of 'race', ethnicity and sexuality. *Graduate Journal of Social Science*, 5(2), 63–87.

Volcano, D.L.G. 1991. *Love Bites*. London: Gay Men's Press.

———. 2000. *Sublime Mutations*. Berlin: Konkurbuchverlag.

———. 2007. *Sex Works*. Berlin: Konkursbuchverlag.

Volcano, D.L.G. and Dahl, U. 2008. *Femmes of Power: Exploding Queer Femininities*. London: Sepent's Tail.

Volcano, D.L.G. and Halberstam, J. 1999. *The Drag King Book*. London: Serpent's Tail.

Waitt, G. and Gorman-Murray, A. 2007. Homemaking and mature-age gay men 'down under': Paradox, intimacy, subjectivities, spatialities, and scale. *Gender, Place and Culture*, 14(5), 569–84.

Waitt, G. and Markwell, K. 2006. *Gay Tourism: Culture and Context*. Binghamton: Haworth.

Waitt, G, et al. 2000. *Introducing Human Geography: Globalisation, Difference and Inequality*. Sydney: Longman.

Walker, L.M. 1993. How to recognize a lesbian: The cultural politics of looking like what you are. *Signs*, 18(4), 866–90.

————. 2001. *Looking Like What You Are: Sexual Style, Race, and Lesbian Identity*. New York: New York University Press.

Warner, M. (ed.) 1993. *Fear of a Queer Planet: Queer Politics and Social Theory*. Minneapolis: University of Minnesota Press.

————. 1993. Introduction, in *Fear of a Queer Planet: Queer Politics and Social Theory*, edited by M. Warner. Minneapolis: University of Minnesota Press, vii–xxxi.

————. 1999. *The Trouble with Normal: Sex, Politics, and the Ethics of Queer Life*. New York: The Free Press.

————. 2002. *Publics and Counterpublics*. New York: Zone Books.

Warner, T. 2002. *Never Going Back: A History of Queer Activism in Canada*. Toronto: University of Toronto Press.

Watson, K. 2005. Queer theory. *Group Analysis*, 38(1), 67–81.

Watson, R. 1997. Some general reflections on 'categorization' and 'sequence' in the analysis of conversation, in *Culture in Action: Studies in Membership Categorization Analysis*, edited by S. Hester and P. Eglin. London: International Institute for Ethnomethodology and Conversation Analysis/University Press of America Inc, 49–76.

Weed, E. and Schor, N. (eds) 1997. *Feminism Meets Queer Theory*. Bloomington: Indiana University Press.

Weeks, J. 1987. Questions of identity, in *The Cultural Construction of Sexuality*, edited by P. Caplan. London: Routledge, 31–51.

————. 1989. *Sex, Politics and Society: The Regulation of Sexuality Since 1800*. 2nd Edition. London: Longman.

————. 2003. *Sexuality*. London: Routledge.

————. 2007. *The World We Have Won*. London: Routledge.

Weeks, J. Heaphy, B. and Donovan, C. 2001. *Same Sex Intimacies: Families of Choice and Other Life Experiments*. London: Routledge.

Weinrich, J.D. et al. 1993. A factor analysis of the Klein sexual orientation grid in two disparate samples. *Archives of Sexual Behaviour*, 22, 157–68.

West, C. and Fenstermaker, S. 1995. Doing difference. *Gender and Society*, 9(1), 8–37.

West, C. and Zimmerman, D.H. 1987. Doing gender. *Gender and Society*, 1(2), 125–51.

Westbrook, D. 2008. *Navigators of the Contemporary. Why Ethnography Matters*. Chicago: University of Chicago Press.

Westerling, K. 2006. *La Dolce Vita: Trettio År med Drag*. Stockholm: Normal Förlag.

Weston, K. 1991. *Families We Choose: Lesbians, Gays, Kinship*. New York: Columbia University Press.

————. 1997. The virtual anthropologist, in *Anthropological Locations: Boundaries and Grounds of a Field Science*, edited by A. Gupta and J. Ferguson. Berkeley: University of California Press, 163–84.

————. 1998. *Long Slow Burn: Sexuality and Social Science*. London: Routledge.

Whittle, S. 2000. *The Transgender Debate: The Crisis Surrounding Gender Identities*. Reading: South Street.

Wiegman, R. 2002. Difference and disciplinarity, in *Aesthetics in a Multicultural Age*, edited by E. Elliott, L.F. Caton and J. Rhyne. Oxford: Oxford University Press, 135–56.

Wilchins, R. 2004. *Queer Theory, Gender Theory*. Los Angeles: Alyson.

Wilcox, M.M. 2006. Outlaws or in-laws? Queer theory, LGBT studies, and religious studies. *Journal of Homosexuality*, 52(1–2), 73–100.

Wilkinson, S. 1998. Focus groups in feminist research: Power, interaction, and the co-construction of meaning. *Women's Studies International Forum*, 21(1), 111–25.

Willis, P. and Trondman, M. 2000. Manifesto for Ethnography. *Ethnography*, 1(1), 5–16.

Willson, M. 1995. Perspective and difference: Sexualisation, the field and the ethnographer, in *Taboo: Sex, Identity, and Erotic Subjectivity in Anthropological Fieldwork*, edited by D. Kulick and M. Willson. London: Routledge, 251–76.

Wilmot, A. 2007. In Search of a Question on Sexual Identity, in *62nd Annual Conference for the American Association of Public Opinion Research*.

Winddance Twine, F. 1999. Transracial mothering and antiracism: The case of white birth mothers of 'Black' children in Britain. *Feminist Studies*, 25(3), 729–46.

Winnubst, S. 2006. *Queering Freedom*. Indianapolis: Indiana University Press.

Wolf, D.L. (ed.) 1996. *Feminist Dilemmas in Fieldwork*. Boulder: Westview Press.

Wyatt, J. 2005. A gentle going? An autoethnographic short story. *Qualitative Inquiry*, 11(5), 724–32.

————. 2006. Psychic distance, consent, and other ethical issues. *Qualitative Inquiry*, 12(4), 813–18.

Yep, G.A. and Elia, J.P. 2007. Queering/Quaring blackness in Noah's Arc, in *Queer Popular Culture: Literature, Media, Film, and Television*, edited by T. Peele. New York: Palgrave Macmillan, 27–40.

Yep, G.A., Lovaas, K.E. and Elia, J.P. 2003. Introduction: Queering communication: Starting the conversation. *Journal of Homosexuality*, 45(2–4), 1–10.

Young, I. 1990. *Justice and the Politics of Difference*. Princeton: Princeton University Press.

Young, I.M. 1997. *Intersecting Voices*. Princeton: Princeton University Press.

————. 2005. *On Female Body Experience: 'Throwing Like A Girl' and Other Essays*. Princeton: Princeton University Press.

Young, R.M. and Meyer, I. 2005. The trouble with 'MSM' and 'WSW': Erasure of the sexual-minority person in public health discourse. *American Journal of Public Health*, 95(7), 1144–49.

Zamudio, S. 2005. Institutional review boards: The structural and cultural obstacles encountered in human biological research, in *Biological Anthropology and*

Ethics: from Repatriation to Genetic Identity, edited by T.R. Turner. New York: State University of New York Press, 149–64.

Zimmerman, D.H. and Pollner, M. 1990 [1970]. The everyday world as a phenomenon, in *Ethnomethodological Sociology*, edited by J. Coulter. Aldershot: Edward Elgar, 96–137.

Index